Norms of Rhetorical Culture

DISCARD

DISCARD

Norms of Rhetorical Culture

Thomas B. Farrell

Yale University Press
New Haven and London

Copyright © 1993 by Yale University.
All rights reserved.
This book may not be reproduced, in whole or in part, including illustrations, in any form (beyond that copying permitted by Sections 107 and 108 of the U.S. Copyright Law and except by reviewers for the public press), without written permission from the publishers.

Designed by Jill Breitbarth and set in Trump Medieval type by Tseng Information Systems, Durham, North Carolina.

Printed in the United States of America by Vail-Ballou Press, Binghamton, New York.

Library of Congress Cataloging-in-Publication Data
Farrell, Thomas B., 1947–
Norms of rhetorical culture / Thomas B. Farrell.
p. cm.
Includes bibliographical references and index.
ISBN 0-300-05385-1 (cloth)
    0-300-06502-7 (pbk.)
1. Rhetoric. 2. Reason. I. Title.
P301.F37 1993
808—dc20   93-16229
     CIP

A catalogue record for this book is available from the British Library.

The paper in this book meets the guidelines for permanence and durability of the Committee on Production Guidelines for Book Longevity of the Council on Library Resources.

10 9 8 7 6 5 4 3 2

Dedicated to
Thomas Bernard Farrell
and Mary Catherine Farrell
on the occasion of my father's
eightieth birthday.

Contents

Acknowledgments

Writing this book has taught me that I am a small part of its title: a "rhetorical culture," however imperfect the concept and my part in its realization. Many people have suggested, contested, and provoked these ideas: more than I can recognize, let alone acknowledge. The seed was planted at a marvelous conference on philosophy and rhetoric at Northwestern University, organized by Michael Hyde. The stimulation of controversy and interdisciplinary intrigue got my juices flowing. Special thanks to Michael for this and many other things. A year essential to this work's conceptual invention (in 1986–87) was made available to me through the good auspices of Northwestern's Van Zelst Chair and the generosity of Ted and Louann Van Zelst, for which I remain grateful. To my former dean, Roy Wood, who termed my ambition for the project "outrageous," thereby forcing my hand, thanks. Friends and colleagues— Tom Frentz, Gerard Hauser, David Zarefsky, Walt Fisher, Tamar Katriel, Mike Leff, Jim Klumpp, Anne Laffoon, Jan Rushing, and Meg Zulick— each read hefty portions of earlier versions of the manuscript and made suggestions for improvement. Elizabeth Anscombe, for no good reason, gave me her only copy of a brilliant keynote lecture and changed my life.

I want to extend special appreciation to my friend and colleague Tom Goodnight, who has an uncanny gift for imagining what I should be thinking and writing two or three years before I get there. More than once I have picked up notes and suggestions of his made to me years earlier and have marveled that I have finally arrived at the same conclusion all by myself! It is a strange form of quality control; but I trust it implicitly.

Colleagues and friends near and far sensed that I was up to something and tried their best to keep me honest. Here I think of Bob Scott, Gale

Auletta (who also sent me Jarrett's program), Mac Parks, Jim Jasinski, Bob Craig, Mike MacFarland, Dilip Gaonkar, Bren Murphy, Mark Pollock, Mara Adelman, and many more. They have all enriched this more than they know. Special thanks to my editor friend in Chicago, Doug Mitchell, whose rhetorician's gift for timely hyperbole and overall encouragement helped me find whatever coherence of vision is expressed here, and to Jonathan Brent, whose counsel and support were there when they were most needed. Special thanks to Jean van Altena for translating me into proper English.

Finally, to Vera and Thomas, who nagged, cajoled, hassled, loved, and sustained Pappa to keep working, whatever humanism has found its way into these words is due to you.

Introduction

———————————————————

———————————————————

———————————————————

Ad bellum purificandum.

—Kenneth Burke

A rhetorical culture is an institutional formation in which motives of competing parties are intelligible, audiences available, expressions reciprocal, norms translatable, and silences noticeable. It may seem odd, even confounding, to introduce certain norms or "goods" where the notoriously crafty business of rhetoric is concerned. Today we have spin doctors and image consultants, audience-manipulators of every ideological stripe—hence the much discussed flight of audiences from the public arena. But this is not really so surprising. Rhetoric has always been a practiced imperfection, the worst fear of idealized reason and the best hope for whatever remains of civic life. This is another way of saying that, regardless of circumstance, a rhetorical culture is first and foremost an idea.

This book is about that idea. Formally speaking, rhetoric is the collaborative art of addressing and guiding decision and judgment—usually public judgment about matters that cannot be decided by force or expertise. Rhetorical inquiry, more commonly known as the study of public communication, is one of the few areas of research that is still actively informed by its own traditions—for its overall definition, its objects of study, and perhaps even its objectives for analysis. The rhetorical tradition is archaic. Nevertheless, rhetoric is also a critical area of contemporary research. For philosophers, rhetoric is becoming unavoidable and even enticing, since the quest for ultimate principles and absolutes has stalled in a kind of intellectual dead heat of agreeable agnosticism. For literary theorists, rhetoric is what is studied—now that it has become apparent that the text is non-finalizable, and a product of the latest, most convincing interpretation. For anthropologists, rhetoric is taking on a naive allure as one of the few commonplaces of virtually all cultures—in one form or another. But what I want to argue is that rhetoric is more than a last-resort fallback position for disciplines that are in flux, but rather is a worthy subject of investigation and research in its own right.

Today rhetoric is as indispensable to practice as it is problematic to theory. In contemporary culture it is approached by two rather extreme, antithetical routes. As a practice, this once magical art is depreciated as content-free fluff, sound-bites, and buzzwords. As a theory, if this term is even applicable, it is seen as either an archaic longing for an original, lost ideal or reason's evil twin, the carnivalesque sideshow of figurative relativism. This latter view has justifiably provoked suspicion from what remains of philosophy. But neither of these views does us much good when it comes to empowering, engaging, and trying to ameliorate the collaborative practices of civic life.

What "us" am I referring to here? To direct an old rhetorical question to myself, who is my audience? I intend, first and foremost, those who would educate. No matter how we teach whatever we teach in the humanities, rhetoric has implications for our own and our students' life practices. During its richest and most influential periods of existence, rhetoric was part of a pedagogical philosophy. This, I will argue, is as it should be, since any practice worthy of the name should be capable of being performed by some others. This, in turn, implies some mode of "habituation," through teaching and training. At a time when there is great confusion both within and outside the university, we could do worse than reflect on the prospects for a renewed sense of mission in pedagogy.

But I also want to include in my audience those reform-minded individuals and groups who still hope for more responsive and participatory civic institutions. All too often, we assume that the goods we might cultivate for ourselves and others are only to be found in the world of the private. But rhetoric is not comfortable on the sidelines. For all that has been relegated to the barracuda tacticians of modern politics, much of our civic life is still absorbed with projects, rituals of affiliation, and speech performances that ultimately turn on the mysteries of trust and fellow feeling. From questions of war and peace to caring for the needs of strangers, such accents of the familiar tend to immerse us in the ambiguities of equally ordinary intuitions and judgment. In every such matter of public choice, we must grapple with issues at once ethical and aesthetic. Whether choosing a political candidate, challenging a school redistricting, or dangling a yellow ribbon from our front window, we are—as advocates—implicated in regions of practical consciousness that are crucial to our collective conduct. Yet, almost by definition, the very things that determine our participation in "public appearances" seem least accessible to systematic reflection. It often proves easier for the academy, therefore, to leave the incorrigible business of rhetoric to the interstices of the hoi polloi "where it belongs."

In this study, I want to recapture the theory of rhetoric in a way that will inform the practice of contemporary advocacy, while at the same time holding out some hope of improving it. To do this, I must come up with a working vocabulary of critical norms, or standards, for interpreting and appraising advocacy as it emerges in the public forum. Within an ethical and aesthetic rendering of one rhetorical tradition, that of Aristotle, I see some exciting but neglected possibilities for revivifying the practice of rhetoric. This requires some initial discussion of terminology. In the process of introducing three families of concepts especially pertinent to rhetoric, those pertaining to theory, practice, and criticism, I will also be offering a preview of the argument guiding this study.

Theory, Practice, and Criticism

Theory in the area of study called *rhetoric* can be divorced from practice only at great cost to both. For the very aim of rhetorical theory has always been to define and articulate a vision of what the highest potential of rhetorical practice might be. In part, this is because the integrity of rhetorical practice has always been under suspicion. However, it is also because the competencies crafted by the arts of practical reason—reading situations creatively, setting out positions clearly, appraising alternatives with prudence and practical judgment—are not simply impersonal, neutral capacities. They admit—indeed require—some qualitative differentiation. And so, just as a theorist of chess would not be interested in giving us a compendium of bad openings, so theorists of rhetoric are absorbed in an enterprise that is unmistakably of ethical, aesthetic, and normative significance. They are concerned with modes of realizing the highest possibilities of the practice known as rhetoric. This may be one reason why the aims of all the touchstone rhetorical theories, whether ethical (to reform the corrupt quality of rhetorical conduct and style—Aristotle), political (to train the best sort of orator-statesman—Cicero and Quintilian), religious (to bring the message of God to man—Augustine), or even philosophical (to bring the theory and practice of rhetoric into line with the most important advances in the science of human nature—George Campbell), are unmistakably prescriptive.

The corollary to this conception of theory is that practice—as we are using the term here—is not a neutral concept either. In his important study of classical moral theory, *After Virtue*, Alasdair MacIntyre defines the concept of a practice, as a coordinated form of activity whose standards of accomplishment, when mastered and implemented, lead to the development of praiseworthy human qualities as well. In other words, whether one wishes it or not, to excel at certain sorts of practice requires that we cultivate certain characteristic virtues along the way. To paraphrase Plato's Socrates, scratching an itch is not a practice. Is rhetoric a practice? At the risk of undue guardedness, I would say that this is the overall issue for discussion.

Whether rhetoric is a practice depends on what theory is able to identify, qualify, and stipulate as defensible norms and qualities worthy of emulation, given the tradition and the state of the art of contemporary rhetorical conduct. But theory, at least as it is elaborated here, cannot content itself with generalized, abstract pronouncements. In the humanities tradition of rhetoric, theory does not propose to find and explain what is already present; rather, it is about discerning what is implicit in the uncertainties and frailties of human affairs.

Theory and practice in rhetoric cannot be integrated without a third form of discourse, which I will call *criticism*. In the fields of discursive practice, criticism must attend systematically to qualitative differences among human artifacts. To what end? Better artifacts. Richer human experience. Enlightened civic participation. The explicit goals may differ, but usually they have something to do with the advancement of civic discourse. But if it is to be more than glandular reaction, criticism must be informed by method, so that others can see why we reason about quality the way we do. Moreover, the norms for criticism can come only from the history of systematic reflection about principles and techniques that guide practice—in other words, theory. And so we have come full circle, albeit with a codicil or two to protect us from the tyranny of one, singular type of discourse.

Where theories of rhetoric are concerned, we are obliged to leave room for reflection on the variable quality of artifacts. This too is a realm of criticism. Theory that posits as settled the disappearance of texts, authors, subjects, and audiences may be right or wrong; but we will never really know. For such theory has insulated itself from the only genuine heuristic test of its own postulates: the reflective test of discursive appraisal. Something similar might be said of certain literary theories of rhetoric that find one dark secret at the core of every text, whether it be death, the phallus, the other, the hegemony of the "gaze," or some ghoulish synthesis.

I would not want to trust the secrets of my republic to the heroism and loyalty of any rhetorical text. Tortured by enough painstaking critique, the average everyday discourse will betray both friend and country, confessing to anything, including crimes it never committed. The problem with totalizing pronouncements is that no test is sufficiently encompassing and impartial to disconfirm their more esoteric assumptions. With scholars such as Baudrillard and recent Kristeva, there seems to be no way of even questioning whether there is always *one* secret concealed in every text or whether it is always the same secret or some other. To question in this way is to become party to the aforementioned dark conspiracy of repression. So perhaps it is time for some kind of Miranda rule where discourse is concerned. At the very least, it could be useful to imagine possible conditions contrary to fact that might open the door to better, as opposed to ever more degenerate, cases of rhetorical practice.

Criticism that has no use for theory usually reads as merely contemptuous; it says nothing to those who are not already interested in the same artifact. Further, the frequently illuminating criticism that assumes that texts are *themselves* condensed theories, forming communities with us, instructing us as to how to read them, and so forth, still begs the whole question of how a text becomes interesting and rich enough to form a community in the first place. Where do we find such texts? James Boyd White's own work is quite instructive. He cites Thucydides, Homer, Plato, Jane Austen, Jefferson, and Madison. Minor figures need not apply. With the proponents of "close reading," the very questions of how we are addressed and how we attend to the fact of address seem buried in an ineffable domain, a domain that has a lot in common with theory.

All this is simply to urge a healthy dialogue between theory and criticism over the normative dimensions of rhetorical practice: what is worthy of attention and emulation, what is not. When theory takes over and lays claim to the whole terrain, it becomes radical critique and leaves no room for practice. When criticism follows only its own intuitions, on the other hand, we are usually left with not much else to reflect upon.

My aim here is to bring about an enriched understanding of modern rhetorical practice, based on critical readings that are informed by the traditions of rhetorical theory. If my argument is successful, then we will at least know what to look for in our three families of concepts as we attempt to reconstitute a contemporary rhetorical culture. But to do this, I must articulate a coherent position on several related and troubling issues. First, I must pinpoint and appropriate those aspects of the classical rhetorical tradition that are meaningful for today's world, distinguishing them from those that are not. Secondly, I must come to terms with the prevailing alternative senses of rhetoric which have reemerged in late modernity, by which I mean the aforementioned free-floating signification, as well as Kantian vestiges of pre-modern idealism. While neither is what I would call a "user-friendly" approach, both have something important to contribute to my perspective. Finally, and most important, I need to introduce and elaborate my own rendition of rhetorical art, as well as demonstrate its utility in several interrelated respects as a theory of practical discourse, as a *dynamis* and *technē* of rhetorical invention, and as a meaningful vocabulary for rhetorical criticism. This is the conceptual agenda. But let us now return to the state of the argument.

So far, the discourses of theory and practice have been drawn together through their intricate concern and connection with normative matters. But in an age such as ours, skeptics are entitled to ask how any normative concern may be defended. Surely not by recourse to any of the grand, transcultural teleologies of the past. Even contemporary vestiges of Kant, whether in Habermas's discourse ethics or Gadamer's aesthetics of hermeneutic interpretation, seem to allow little room for the more humble, earthbound verities of rhetorical practice. A major challenge for my project is to show how the norms of rhetorical culture and the modern presumptions of emancipatory discourse may be reconciled with each other. In the meantime, it is worth asking where the ameliorative tendencies of rhetorical practice might be found.

I will argue for three interrelated senses of place, or *topoi*, for the location and reconstitution of rhetorical norms. First, norms are invoked, implied, abused, or set aside by the "sermonic" character of rhetorical practice. As James Boyd White has shown, a culture of mutual justification has always entailed the preservation of self-interest. Read unsympathetically, such traditional "culture" is merely the cunning of reason in disguise. But White finds in some of Athens's worst historical episodes the basis for a different view. Using the ancient Corcyrean debate as an example, White writes:

> Even if neither Athens nor the other two cities feel much interest in doing the just thing because it is just, all of them have a very real interest in refraining from behavior that is "unjust" in the special sense that it cannot be justified in terms of the discourse spoken here. That is, as Thucydides implicitly presents it, it is not particularly important to Athens that what she does actually be right, but it is important that she be able to claim that it is right by saying, for example, that it is the proper act of an ally or a colony, or is authorized by the treaty, or is motivated by gratitude.[1]

With this sense of justice as justification, we are at least able to engage in public relationships with others in some improvised framework of language community. Without it—in either ancient or modern forms of life—we have only force. And this is precisely White's point: there is no guarantee that we shall always be the stronger party. This is also the place in White's analysis where we acquire a fundamental insight, one that—I believe—only a sense of audience can teach: that values are always in conflict with one another if they are worth defending in practice.

Second, norms may be articulated through the principles, conventions, genres, and procedures of the rhetorical tradition—a tradition that is necessary to the recognition and advancement of rhetorical practice. Now tradition, by itself, does not validate much of anything. It needs to be received and revised if its normative content is to speak to subsequent generations of rhetorical actors.

Third, norms are made available to practice through the still developing conditions and conventions of what I will call *rhetorical culture.*

In that most harmonious of settings, a writer's study, my threefold placement of norms implies as well a fragile agenda for the reunion of theory and practice. As I set forth the position here, the normative impetus and power of the values invoked by rhetorical practice are best recognized through an acquaintance with the rhetorical tradition; for this is, quite literally, how we are able to see what is involved, risked, and interwoven in the fabric of practice. But the norms of the tradition are far more likely to exert real-life influence on rhetorical conduct through their manifestation in contemporary settings that encourage or mandate the sophistication of rhetorical practice. Here it becomes a kind of mission for the theorist/critic to *cultivate* rhetoric. Thus we all participate, however indirectly, in the invention (or *prevention*) of a rhetorical culture.

The argument offered in the first three chapters suggests that there are valuable heuristic qualities intrinsic to the rhetorical tradition itself, or at least to a certain reading of that tradition. To focus on just one such normative tendency, it is difficult to see how the traditions of rhetorical theory could maintain themselves for long without some affiliation with practical reason, practical wisdom, *phronēsis*, or prudence (all these terms mean approximately the same thing). Judgment, for instance, is obviously problematic, because it calls for more than the formal properties of reason alone. It is, to paraphrase Charles Maier, an activity of mind and conscience, and even of reflective vision. It is never entirely liberated from subjectivity; yet it is crucial for aesthetics, ethics, politics, and all that is unfinished about history.[2] Reason can never be sufficient for all that judgment implies and involves; yet the idea of judgment as something divorced from reason would make both terms virtually nonsensical.

To retrieve a judgment-centered conception of rhetoric is nevertheless to embark on a quest that many postmodernist sages would regard as quixotic, to say the least. Rhetoric may be the only area of inquiry in which the most foundational tradition of meaning takes root in the ongoing question of whether it has any right to exist at all. Aristotle temporarily resolved the problem of rhetoric's place in the pantheon of methods in the humanities by attaching it to other more distinguished methods and faculties: namely, dialectic and *logos*. Yet it is precisely this placement of rhetoric that today seems most controversial. If theory and practice have come together in our day, it has been an ironic reunion in which rhetoric itself is questioned.

Reading the Aristotelian Rhetorical Tradition

In the best moments of its distinguished history, rhetoric provided the public language for a flourishing culture. For the Greeks and the Romans, as well as for early Christian apologists, rhetoric afforded the primary arts of forming public convictions and doctrines and presenting them. During the medieval period, as well as in the definitive accomplishments of the Renaissance and Enlightenment projects, rhetoric expressed for the prevailing culture the most important connections between memory, meaning, and action. But, these pivotal periods which constitute the landmarks of Western cultural history aside, it is becoming apparent that no culture or public life project can survive for long without some form of rhetorical practice, some coherent, symbolic manner of securing collaborative public action. Whether or not there are translatable universals that apply to every culture, there is at least this covering law of particularity: that every culture requires some avenue for addressing and thereby explicating its identities, accomplishments, and needs—and hence some form of rhetorical practice.

But, as the modern experience well demonstrates, requirements and enactments are two different things. Our Western cultural temperament, which projects its worst indulgences on the popular idiom, considers rhetoric to be—as if by definition—a discourse not to be trusted. And rhetorical performers, who have often earned the distrust of their constituencies, themselves include within their verbal artillery the denigration of their opponents' discourse as "mere rhetoric." Typically, the pronouncements of our political animals abound in disavowals such as: "What we need on problem X [the environment, the poor, the "deficit"] is less rhetoric and more action from our elected officials." At this point, the discourse usually trails off, until it comes to land on some equally agreeable truism. What is lost in such verbal contrivance is the irony whereby public oratory participates in its own diminishment: first, by alluding to some vaguely privileged position that is juxtaposed to the whole tawdry world of rhetoric, and second, by doing so through what is unmistakably a pallid form of rhetoric itself.

Despite this, I will attempt to illuminate the nature and function of rhetorical practice in our time. It is understandable that the quality of our public discourse is more frequently disparaged than appreciated. A legion of deservedly anonymous public relations apparatchiks have earned this depreciation.

Nonetheless, I will be proposing a corollary possibility: namely, that the quality of a practice, diminished or not, also speaks to some capacity for correction and refinement. The classical ideal, embodying both thought and action, both individuation and participation, *in the same activities,* may appear far from ideal in our world and time. But closer appraisal reveals that the art most responsible for realizing this practical ideal has been under the most radical of indictments from its very beginnings. It is an art that, if it is to exist at all, does so as a suspicious, contested enterprise. It is an art for the rest of us.

And if this practical possibility of rhetoric is granted, then it is, I believe, the definitive vocabulary of Aristotle's *Rhetoric* that allows us to glimpse and grasp the normative openings for rhetoric as ethically significant conduct within *any* culture. This is a bold claim, of course, one that I will make from two rather different perspectives.

Initially, I will examine the *Rhetoric* from the combined perspectives on ethical character found in the *Nicomachean Ethics*, the *Eudemian Ethics*, and the *Politics*. My intent, like that of some classical commentators, is revisionistic; but I believe it to be faithful in spirit to Aristotle's original project for practical reason. Rhetoric is the only art which evokes the capacity for practical reason from a situated audience. Therefore, alone among the arts, it presents a public audience with the possibility of becoming, for a time, an accountable moral agent. The process of elaborating the qualities of a developed rhetorical ethic also allows us to underscore certain norms for rhetorical competence: chiefly those aspects of *ēthos*, agency, practical reason, and civic friendship which help to foster reciprocal measures of responsibility and belonging in the advocates and audiences of civic life.

But there is another rendering of Aristotle's text, one that is highly pertinent to the variable quality of rhetorical practice; and that is as the treatment of an art. Reading the *Rhetoric* as an aesthetic treatise, I see its relationship to the *Poetics* as establishing several of rhetoric's more durable discursive features: for instance, its comic orientation with respect to contingency, moral luck, and the future, the uncertain mimetic status of its discourse, and its peculiar inversion of tragic recognition as public judgment and action. I believe that an aesthetic rendering of rhetorical practice, together with its ethical Aristotelian heritage, helps to capture an internal tension that is essential to rhetoric's modern narrative project, even as it helps to free the traditional vision of rhetorical practice from its problematic teleological foundation. Rhetoric is thus defended by Aristotle on both ethical and aesthetic grounds. And the relational "goods" of civic friendship; phronēsis, or practical wisdom; ethos, or public virtue, are joined to an overarching sense of propriety in public *form*. Although Aristotle takes the partialist position on ethical matters (to the chagrin of Kantian philosophers), he directs the theorist and practitioner of rhetoric to the exposure of partisanship in all its forms, so that more reliably prudent judgments become possible.

Reading Aristotle's *Rhetoric* from these two conflicting stances, one ethical, the other aesthetic, allows for a larger comprehension of logos, a comprehension which may be more in keeping with its original, expansive vision. So understood, rhetoric might uncover and engender new sources of *creative reason*.

Recovering the Rhetorical Tradition

The test of any tradition, of course, is the power and traction of its legacy. More than simply attempting to capture this Aristotelian sense of rhetoric, I hope in this book to offer theorists, critics, and practitioners alike something to look for in the activities of contemporary civic life. Here, in outline, is the overall course and direction of my argument.

First, I will claim that there is, among our myriad methods and perspectives, a place for an identifiable mode of inquiry that is rhetorical. This sort of inquiry emerges as a characteristic way of engaging particular features of assembled phenomena called *appearances*. Aristotle's *Rhetoric* emerges as a prototype, for both the inquiry and the practice of rhetoric. Following an overview of the central perspective of the project, I will then present a defense of the Greek rhetorical tradition as a repository of norms for the practice of rhetoric and for what a culture that fosters an appreciative understanding of that practice might be like. This latter, more speculative notion points to my overall concept of a rhetorical culture. Thus, the movement of rhetoric is from a practical capacity to a technē with ethical significance to a theoretically comprehended practice capable of producing collaborative "goods" for a responsible civic life.

Secondly, I hope to craft from the vocabulary of the rhetorical tradition a normative mission for rhetorical culture. The classical Greek tradition remains defensible, I believe, so long as we can defend and demonstrate the power and resilience of practical reason in human affairs. In later chapters I will argue that we can recover from it norms of competence, performance, coherence, and distance applicable to our own era. As this essay is written, the failures of reason and the onslaught of "dark times" seem all but palpable. The old, ringing verities now usher us forth on behalf of ever more destructive courses of conduct. And the "sins" of rhetoric, as the propaganda, regimentation, and scapegoating of yet other war cultures, become increasingly difficult to ignore and impossible to absolve.

I cannot absolve them here. Instead, I will embark on what is perhaps a more constructive course: to show potential grounds of compatibility between Aristotelian rhetoric and emancipatory reason. A painstaking appraisal of two rather striking attempts to do away with reason, those of Tertullian and Max Horkheimer, may be sufficient to show the futility of reflection in the dark and what I believe to be the only plausible alternative approaches to a responsible practice of civic life. Contemporary debates about the decline of reason and the onslaught of dark times really amount to the old argument over whether virtue can be taught. While there may be reason to doubt the wisdom of our teachers, we ultimately have no option but to hope that it can. To the extent that rhetoric, together with pedagogy, religion, and other forms of socialization, provide a form of habituation for the denizens of modernity, then even our tragic mistakes may eventually yield to recognition, reflection, and perhaps renewal.

In the final section of the book I attempt to bring together the work of Jürgen Habermas on universal pragmatics and the more collaborative languages of performance in rhetorical argument. Rhetoric is reintroduced as a particularistic language in which meaning is redeemed not through the analytic justification of validity claims, but through their collaborative performance. The enthymeme is shown to be a form of meaning and reflection that runs counter to universal pragmatics but also admits the invocation of generalizable conventions as possibilities to ground collaborative civic conduct. The norms of rhetorical culture, founded in and recovered from the Aristotelian rhetorical tradition, are shown not only to be applicable to the eloquent exceptions discussed throughout this volume, but also to be in evidence in the more homespun examples of our own time: Benjamin Linder's mother before the House Western Hemisphere Subcommittee, Philipp Jenninger before the German people on the fiftieth anniversary of Kristallnacht, even struggles over the future of our own local communities.

A critical issue of popular empowerment is implied by these suggestions. Regardless of the actual state of discourse, we do not have to wait for some new Lincoln or Roosevelt to lead us out of the rhetorical wilderness. Through our own habituated capacity as audience to reflect on, engage in, or resist the call of discourse, we can help to decide whether ours is a culture of wrath and destruction or a rhetorical culture of *communitas*.

In the discovery, and perhaps rejection or correction, of distortions and deformations occasioned by rhetoric, we are constantly reinvigorating our own ad hoc norms of justification, just as Protagoras once promised. And in debating and disputing the proper parameters and ground for authority, integrity, and accountability in our own volatile time, we are also constituting and reconstituting our sense of perspective, issue, and conscience from stances of competence, performance, coherence, and distance—the norms of rhetorical culture.

Rhetoric and Dialectic as Modes of Inquiry

> To ask a question means to bring into the open. The openness of what is in question consists in the fact that the answer is not settled. It must still be undetermined, in order that a decisive answer can be given. The revelation of the questionability of what is questioned constitutes the sense of the question. The object has to be brought into this state of indeterminacy, so that there is an equilibrium between pro and contra. The sense of every question is realized in passing through this sense of indeterminacy, in which it becomes an open question. Every true question achieves this openness.
>
> —Gadamer, *Truth and Method*

> In the same way the rhetorical figure of question and answer beguiles the audience into thinking that each deliberately considered point has been struck out and put into words on the spur of the moment.
>
> —Longinus, *On the Sublime*

> The inequality between one who gives orders and one who must obey is not as radical as that between one who has a right to demand an answer and one who has the duty to answer . . . a changing of the guard; a new power had appeared, the only one capable of toppling the former professional power brokers, until then the politicians. Toppling them from their throne not by means of arms or intrigues, but by the mere force of questioning.
>
> —Kundera, *Immortality*

> But what guarantees the inner connection of the constituent elements of a person? Only the unity of answerability. I have to answer with my own life for what I have experienced and understood in art, so that everything I have experienced and understood would not remain ineffectual in my life. . . . Art and life are not one, but they must become united in myself—in the unity of my answerability.
>
> —Bakhtin, *Art and Answerability*

Asking questions is a curious business. The larger the question, the less likely the questioners are to be satisfied with the answer. And *rhetorical* questions seem the most elusive of all. They are questions in name only, introduced for effect; questions for which we already have answers. Still, they continue to provoke us.[1] Earlier this century, two fascinating public figures struggled with that strange amalgam of power, suspicion, and curiosity that is implied by the thoughtful question. The figures were as different from one another as the questions that engaged them. One was a formidable intellectual, a political revolutionary, a jailed dissident, and perhaps the finest literary critic of this century. The other was a simple country lawyer who came to Washington in order, as he put it, "to ask some questions, and—if I didn't like the answers—to ask some more."[2] The questions were different too. One of the questioners wished to uncover the meaning of events, of history itself, now veiled by the enigma of appearances. His questions were dialectical. The other wished to reassert the integrity of the ordinary in a climate of suspicion. His questions were rhetorical.

Now that the triumphant murmuring of postmodernism has subsided, it may be time to survey the wreckage, which has been substantial. In randomizing the notion of significance in messages, while definitively pronouncing that their own humanities project is dead, our weary antirationalists gave up the ghost for the machine. Meanwhile the technologies of our culture have had their own quite serious—even lethal—messages to share. The serious study of rhetoric is thus caught between two horrific alliances: the cunning of technical reason and the airy disregard of the new academic sophistic. In presenting rhetoric as a genuine method of thought and action, rather than the residue of failed philosophy, I hope to show that alternative historical outcomes are still available to us and that the triumph of the logic of disintegration is not yet assured. This is nothing less than an expression of good faith. But in a less precarious way, all serious work in the humanities must be based on some such presupposition.

What are we doing when we engage in a rhetorical inquiry? What presuppositions do we bring to the enterprise? What traditions are invoked, evoked, or left behind? What terms are contested, what taken for granted? In a milieu in which rhetoric is frequently appraised so discordantly, one would not expect to find a foundational set of commonalities, or "correct" meanings, across schools. But we can at least survey the possibilities.

THE PARADOX OF METHOD

Rhetoric may mean anything from figuration generally to unrestricted intentionality to free-floating signification to power to the *pathē* of manipulation and seduction. As we reach out to learn and master any craft or activity, we usually begin with what is most easily and immediately grasped. A deeper understanding and appreciation of the activity's complexity emerge only developmentally, over time. Any serious attempt to teach must take this longer view, even as it must assume some further development of rhetorical understanding for teaching to occur. For instance, no serious teacher considers praise to be *only* a form of flattery. Before it is anything else, rhetoric is a way of looking at things. Yet this way of looking, this method, does not dawn on us all at once. It too emerges only after considerable time and effort. This may be one reason why the teachers and those gifted in rhetoric have often been resentful of one another.

I want to probe for the interrelations among rhetoric and other methods of inquiry for *one* legacy of rhetorical meanings: namely, the original Aristotelian tradition.

In their original meanings, analytic and dialectic do not exhaust the modes of logos as inquiry; in fact, they are inherently incomplete so far as social materials for inquiry are concerned. Further, rhetoric's unique approach to inquiry lies in its concern with the specificity of appearances as these impinge on human thought and action. Thus dialectic and rhetoric raise and address questions within the world of appearances quite differently.

Rhetoric is an acquired competency, a manner of thinking that invents possibilities for persuasion, conviction, action, and judgment; it may be developed and sophisticated and, above all, critiqued and improved. It may be used against the past, and often is so used. But one can acquire it only *from* the past, for that is where its traditions, and finally its meanings, reside. Rhetoric helps us to invent public thought. Moreover, whatever we may think of our own thought, the task seems to be ongoing and in need of improvement, which is where Aristotle's contribution comes in.

We can now speculate as to the reason for the return to Aristotle. On almost all intellectual fronts in the late twentieth century we witness a collapse of grand systems. Among the victims we can surely include the proclamations of Enlightenment reason and their unintelligible residues in linguistic philosophy and ordinary language analysis and the grand dialectical programs of politics and cultural emancipation. It is my view that Aristotle offers us the possibility of a constructive reconciliation with the fragments of this century's failed systems and projects. In one of his more apocalyptic moments, Hans-Georg Gadamer characterized reason as reconciliation with ruination.[3] While it is not clear whether he intended this as a compliment, today, it comes close to something we might willingly accept. Reason involves facing up to what we have done, picking up the pieces, and moving on. As a non-Utopian thinker, Aristotle may have something to say to our times. He also raises the somewhat neglected question of what it means to live a good and decent life in non-Utopian times. He may not have the best answer to this question, but it is a good and worthy question to raise. Prior to this question, however, is a more basic one. For if Aristotle were to engage Gadamer's proclamation, he would want to know precisely *how* reason reconciles us with ruination and how the logos might discover that the world of particulars came to be ruined in the first place. But, characteristically, he would be suspicious of any univocal answer to this question.

Since the whole basis for differentiation among methods (analytic, dialectic, and rhetoric) turns on the way each method frames, addresses, poses, and interprets questions, we begin by tracing Aristotle's original treatment of inquiry in the *organon*. It may be helpful if I first offer my own understanding of the following statement from the first book of the *Analytica Priora* (30): "The way is the same in all cases, in any art or study."[4] Aristotle goes on to say: "We must look for the attributes and subjects of both our terms, and we must supply ourselves with as many of these as possible, and consider them by means of the three terms, refuting statements in one way, confirming them in another, in the pursuit of truth starting with premises in which the arrangement of the terms is in accordance with truth, *while if we look for dialectical syllogisms we must start from probable premisses*" (*Analytica Priora* 46a7–10; emphasis added). What seems to be intended here is that the methods are in every case determined by the degree of clarity, precision, and reliability allowed by the subject matter under investigation. With this in mind, we proceed similarly: advancing propositions, confirming them, and integrating them within defensible generalizations appropriate to our subject matter. This is what is systematic about Aristotle's "way" of inquiry.

But can we know what method a given subject matter calls for? Indeed, can any subject matter be characterized in advance of scrupulous application of a method? And if not, do we not encounter either a problem of false hierarchy (mathematics and physics as models of "First Philosophy" and on down the scale until we reach the barnyard scramble of rhetoric) or—what may be worse—an infinite regress of subject matter and method?

So far as the hierarchy of methods is concerned, it is probably best to leave the desirability of closure and the outcomes to fall out where they may. Aristotle's overarching contribution to the infinite regress problem, however, is his realization that we cannot relativize subject matters and methods simultaneously. Whatever we intend to *do* with a subject matter, the very attempt to do it requires a way of doing it that is comprehensible to others. At least for a time, we must hold our manner of thinking and direction of approach constant. This does not mean that we should have no answer to the quite legitimate question "Where do your methods come from?" My answer, developed in this chapter, has a hermeneutic base: namely, that for what we might call *rhetorical inquiry*, the architectonics of method come from the linguisticality of the rhetorical tradition.

Once we acknowledge this point and consider its implications seriously, we can appreciate the sort of textual community that Aristotle had in mind. We can spell out the different ways in which the modes of analytic, dialectic, and rhetoric approach and engage questions, thereby obtaining differing notions of what a subject matter might be, how it might best be studied, how we might evaluate our findings, and so forth. I hope to explore the nature of these differences by way of practical illustration and example.

Rhetoric and dialectic are held by Aristotle to be universal arts, whereas analytic is viewed as a way of exploring the interrelations and interdependencies of all scientific knowledge. Their respective material domains, therefore, can hardly be said to be proprietary or exclusive. Rather, the differences we seek are to be found in the manner in which object domains are constituted and treated by analytic, dialectic, and rhetoric and the manner in which questions are raised and problems defined. It is not argued that these original distinctions are definitive for possible relationships among questions and the arts of the "probable." But, as McKeon has demonstrated, dialectic and rhetoric have shifted their contents far more often than their forms throughout history.[5] Hence the contemporary dismantling of the forms of both rhetoric and dialectic must be judged to be something of an anomaly.

ANALYTIC AND DIALECTIC AS METHODS

In book 2 of the *Analytica Posteriora* Aristotle is concerned with finding and structuring the principles of the sciences. The provocative first statement of the book indicates clearly the importance of questions for this project: "The kinds of questions we ask are as many as the kinds of things we know. They are in fact four: (1) whether the connection of an attribute with a thing is a fact; (2) what is the reason of this connection; (3) whether a thing exists; (4) what is the nature of the thing" (89b20–25). These questions are taken, at this early point, to exhaust the possible avenues to scientific knowledge. We begin with what we can be said to know (deriving from the *Categories*) and proceed from there to ask after what we do not know. It now becomes necessary to determine what would count as a satisfying answer to each of the questions.

Aristotle's observation here might puzzle those who consider analytic to imply an empty linguistic structure: "Now when we ask whether a connection is a fact, or whether a thing without qualification *is*, we are really asking whether the connection of the thing has a 'middle'; and when we have ascertained either that the connection is a fact or that the thing *is*—i.e. ascertained either the partial or unqualified being of the thing—and are proceeding to ask the reason of the connection or the nature of the thing, then we are asking what the 'middle' is" (89b35–90a1–5). Aristotle's allowance that the being of a thing may be partial or unqualified suggests that the modalities of truth apply not only to propositions, but also to manners of existence, agency, and change. Yet the questions require some sort of reasoned connection as a knowledge-constituting answer. Though based on what is and can be known, they are themselves devoid of preexisting truth content.

Of course, some reasoned connections provide better answers than others. From Aristotle's (frequently misunderstood) point of view, it is the answers which come closest to the reason, or "cause," of a thing that provide the best answer to questions of inquiry. This also turns out to be identical to what the nature of a thing is. As Aristotle put it in his famous example of an eclipse of the moon: "It is clear that the nature of the thing and the reason of the fact are identical: the question 'What is eclipse?' and its answer 'The privation of the moon's light by the interposition of the earth' are identical with the question 'What is the reason of eclipse?' " (90a8–15).[6] Aristotle's treatment of the four analytic questions presents inquiry as a search for answers which come closer and closer to essential nature, the reasons for things themselves.

But how are we to establish the relationship between analytic questions as a logic of inquiry and demonstration as a mode of proof? This is one of the key problems of the organon. The limits to analytic solution are revealed in Aristotle's important treatment of *definitional* questions. During the course of a complex and intricately developed argument, Aristotle observes, first, that demonstration, while it proves a connection, does not prove the essential nature of an object; and second, that definition, while it may reveal essential nature, does not prove it. So reason cannot be adduced without the apprehension of existence; analogously, definable form may not be offered without an existential presupposition. As for this presupposition, Aristotle seems to be suggesting that it depends on the manner in which we participate in the appearances (*phainomena*) of our inquiry. As he puts it: "If we were on the moon, we should not be inquiring either as to the fact or the reason, but both fact and reason would be obvious simultaneously" (90a25–30).

But what is equally obvious is our inability to demonstrate existence. Aristotle has had to move outside the form of demonstration proper to connect the knowledge of essential nature as cause with demonstration. This could well have become the occasion for cutting reflection short and introducing mythic *archai* of primordial being.[7] Instead, Aristotle adopts the more reliable method of inviting and testing multiple definitions of reason and cause as a way of arriving at the best available approximations of essential nature. As he indicates later, "Different things require different demonstrations" (91a1–5). The remainder of book 2 of the *Analytica Posteriora* is concerned with methods for attaining the "definable form" of things. Aristotle answers the four analytic questions in the most concrete of ways: by looking to the world of existing particulars and constructing from their commonalities and distinguishing characteristics their respective essential natures. Interestingly, the most elusive of all the features of existence, the *substance* of phenomena, is captured by Aristotle in a curiously indirect manner. It is at best a nature that can be reduced no further, he says. But even this is qualified by his noting that the most definitive answers to analytic questions admissible are composed of pluralities.

In summary, our examination of the four analytic questions in book 2 of the *Analytica Posteriora* as revealed that:

(1) The four questions are seen as exhausting the possibilities for scientific inquiry, and answers to them are thought to constitute reliable scientific knowledge.

(2) The questions, although they start with what is known, do not

put forth generalizable causal connections, but rather ask after the cause in each specific instance.

(3) Neither demonstration nor definition actually proves essential nature, but demonstration may exhibit essential nature by setting forth a conclusion which is a definition.

(4) Aristotle (in the course of his proof of the third point) links the "knowing of essential nature" to the sense in which we know that the fact, of which it is the cause, exists. These senses are variable and depend on our situated observation of, or participation in, the phainomena themselves.

(5) There are four causes (which are, in turn, answers to the four kinds of analytic questions), and all four are arrived at by finding the proper definable form within existing particulars.

(6) Substance, allegedly the ultimate form of answer to the analytic questions, is in fact a synthesis of attributes that are each (in their individual character) generalizable beyond the thing itself. Thus, substance is composed of particulars.

The most immediate implication of this preliminary treatment is the structuralist idea that signs—either in combination or as a structural system—are somehow definitive or exhaustive of meaning. Such theories, prominent in Continental thought, are, in part at least, the result of not having read far enough into the organon (that is, past the *Categories*). For once assembled, phainomena are qualified through the human, participatory act of definition. But where definitions may be offered, they may also be contested. Thus their very composition is open to the mediation of perspective. In assuming that signification is always a mediation among localized points of reference, semiotic theory misses the more fundamental point that, ultimately, reference cannot be localized. Throughout the book, I will be taking issue with the doctrine that rhetoric is simply part of an ideological code, criticism a kind of signet decoding ring, and Utopia (or postmodernist bliss) a jumble of free-floating signifiers fanning out over the Western skies. But at this early juncture, I cannot improve on Eugene Rochberg-Halton's excellent critique:

> In rigidly separating language [as meaning system] from speech [as mere instance], the semiological tradition appropriates meaning from living human action and speech, denying what for the Greeks was the essence of human nature itself, the capability to engage in

living communicative dialogue, to cultivate and criticize purposive community. Meaning, as the medium of human social life, not only is robbed of its critical dimension as human instrument but vanishes from the concrete world itself to that nether region of "the deep structure." Symbolic signs may be constituted by conventional "codes," but codes themselves operate within a broader sign-web of purpose.[8]

Even a cursory sketch of Aristotle's analytic of inquiry suggests that the semiotic signification position is an unwarranted intrusion of analytic theory into the realms of dialectic and rhetoric. In addition, there is the undeniable gap between categories and contentious thinking generally. Whereas categories may be fixed, characterizations, once generalized, may always be disputed. Hence we find in the inevitable limitations of analytic a space for dialectical method.

In the opening lines of book 1 of the *Topica,* Aristotle suggests an alternative way of looking at the methods of human inquiry: "Our treatise proposes to find a line of inquiry whereby we shall be able to reason from opinions that are generally accepted about every problem propounded to us, and also shall ourselves, when standing up to an argument, avoid saying anything that will obstruct us. First, then, we must say what reasoning is, and what its varieties are, in order to grasp dialectical reasoning: for this is the object of our search in the treatise before us" (100a18–25). It is significant that Aristotle should begin with the tacit acknowledgment that there are differences among modes of inquiry, and that the situated stance of the "arguer" is relevant. Here, in clear language, is a projected treatment of arguments in a problematic context, the materials for which are constructed out of generally accepted opinions. On the face of it, this seems a rather different order of business from the aims of analytic (where presumably unproblematic principles and materials are found and ordered). This, in short, is the business of dialectic. Yet it is clear that dialectic's universe of application is not exclusive of analytic inquiry. The difference turns, rather, on what is done within this universe. As Aristotle states the matter:

Reasoning, on the other hand, is dialectical if it reasons from opinions that are generally accepted. Things are true and primary which are believed on the strength not of anything else but of themselves: for in regard to the first principles of science it is improper to ask any further for the why and wherefore of them; each of the first principles should command belief in and by itself. On the other hand, these opinions are "generally accepted" which are accepted by everyone or by the majority, or by the philosophers; i.e. by all, or by the majority, or by the most notable and illustrious of these. (100a30–100b25)

We have here a subtle shift in position regarding the status of first principles in the sciences. In book 2 of the *Analytica Posteriora* Aristotle conceded that the existence of essential nature could not in itself be demonstrated. Capturing essential nature was the task of definable form, an enterprise which admitted of varying degrees of success. But here, where Aristotle has shifted his focus to the realm of the probable (that is, to belief and generally accepted opinion), first principles of demonstration are themselves defined in terms of belief. Indeed, they are seen to compel or command belief, in and of themselves. So viewed, there is no need to go outside the realm of demonstration (at least, as long as belief continues to be so compelled). There appears also to be a contrasting suggestion in the above statement, although it has not yet been elaborated: namely, that dialectical premises command belief not intrinsically, but for reasons outside the statements. This is in apparent opposition to successful demonstration in the *Analytica Posteriora* which may be presumed consistently valid only so long as its presuppositions go unquestioned:

Further, just as in syllogizing we do not premise that syllogistic inference is (since the premises from which we conclude must be related as whole and part), so the definable form must not fall within the syllogism but remain outside the premises posited. *It is only against a doubt as to its having been a syllogistic inference at all* that we have to defend our argument as conforming to the definition of syllogism. It is only when someone doubts whether the conclusion proved is the definable form that we have to defend it as conforming to the definition of definable form which we assumed. (92a10–20; emphasis added)[9]

Dialectic enters the fray as a kind of second-order reflective method, to be used only when an otherwise reliable method of demonstration has been called into question. It also seems to be the case, based on the above passage, that there are two more general occasions for dialectic: when the questions raised are already general and probable, as in the case of less technical discussions of philosophy (though Aristotle is careful to point out that the philosopher still uses dialectic "with an eye to truth"), and when otherwise reliable and compelling principles come to be doubted, thereby becoming material for dialectic. Note the following discussion: "It [dialectic] has a further use in relation to the ultimate principles used in the several sciences. For it is impossible to discuss them at all from the principles proper to the particular science in hand, seeing that the principles are the *prius* of everything else; it is through the opinions generally held on the particular points that these have to be discussed, and this task belongs properly, or most appropriately, to dialectic: for dialectic is a process of criticism wherein lies the path to the principles of all inquiries" (*Topica* 101a35–101b5). We are left, then, with the less than satisfying result that dialectical reasoning must go *outside* its own premises for foundational support and that demonstrative reasoning must go *outside* its grammatical and formal relationships for the principles (or starting points) of the various sciences. Thus it is that, in dialectic, questions present us with an exclusive as well as an inclusive dimension. Aristotle's method of collection and division, derived from Plato, excludes the more open-ended questions and indeterminate materials of analytic; indeed, some prior discrimination must be made in the form of the question itself in order for it to be affirmed or denied. But this very capacity for affirmation and denial is what brings forth the inclusivity of dialectical questions. Unlike analytic, where premises are laid down and participation is entirely outside the realm of demonstration, dialectical questions invite participatory answers. Some "other" is required conversationally, in order to affirm or deny the general claims implied by the question's very meaning.

This leaves us with something of a paradox. As the interlocutor of dialectic moves into a more direct participatory relationship with the logos of a dialectical partner, he or she tends to move further away from the particularity, the individuated facticity, of phenomena. Yet these, after all, are the materials from which collections and divisions are made. Put another way, the dialectician participates more directly in what "men in general, or the most notable of men, believe" and less directly in the worlds *of which* they believe. We will pursue this paradox at greater length when we explore the countervailing tendencies of rhetoric.

RHETORIC AND APPEARANCES

In order to show how the *Rhetoric* poses and addresses questions, we must reacquaint ourselves with its characteristic approach to materials. For Aristotle, appearances constitute the logical beginning of all inquiry; nonetheless, there are multiple sorts of "truths" and relationships in the world of phainomena. But if so, then it follows that there must be multiple ways, or methods, of getting at them. Among these multiple ways, the following are important. First, there is the systematic form of inquiry known as *analytic*, which is concerned with the grammatical relations among subjects and predicates; for example, "An eclipse is the privation of the moon's light by the interposition of the earth." But analytic is not the only game in town. Second, there is *dialectic*, which has to do with dichotomous relationships among general propositions linked by question and answer; for example: "Isn't justice the interest of whoever is stronger, noble Socrates?" "Oh, no, it isn't, dear Polus," and so forth. Although it is Plato's favorite, it was Aristotle who systematized this method as a form of inquiry taking us beyond collection and division. But in the process of doing this, dialectic too leaves us with a gap in the world of appearances.

However, there is a third cognitive path, a way of making ongoing sense of appearances by expressing them as proposed themes and arguments, inviting decision, action, and judgment—in short, as rhetorical propositions. Much of the world comes to us as already assembled culturally meaningful configurations of phainomena. In addition to presenting curiosities for analysis or anomalies for synthesis, these already ordered cultural "givens" raise practical questions for choice or avoidance. This third method engages the modalities of appearance insofar as they admit open-ended themes involving emotion, conviction, and judgment; and the method is rhetorical.

If we review our earlier treatment of analytic and dialectic, we will now uncover a further, rather startling inventional transformation that necessarily implicates the questions of rhetoric in inquiry generally. Working through the sometimes confusing arrangement of the *Topica*, we now find Aristotle's original ten categories at work as types of topical predication (101b10–15). The four questions have emerged as points of contention: as agreement or disagreement over genus, definition, property, and accident. But Aristotle now seems to concede that there is movement along the continuum representing his four primary and universal *topoi:* subject and predicate, problem and proposition, universal and particular, accident and definition (or essence). We begin with only potential connections among subjects, problems, particulars, and accidents (104a8–12). But as we make increasingly convincing actual unities and distinctions among essence, quantity, quality, relation, place, time, position, state, activity, and passivity, the objects (or subjects) of our discussion may also move or change their status: from accident to definition, particular to universal, and so forth (158a30–40).

Something else has happened too. For as questions have moved from open-ended inquiries into subject matter to general objects of contention, they have introduced four sorts of predicables to three different audiences: those of the philosopher or specialist, the most notable of men or statesman, and the generality of men or citizens. Rhetoric is viewed as the counterpart (*antistrophos*) of dialectic, primarily because Aristotle realized that not all problematics dissolve differences into reliable univocal categories. Some may climb the locus of uncertainty to rest reliably on the steady course of common opinion. But many others will not. Why?

To answer this question about questions, we need to realize that some matters find their very locus of meaning and definition within their particularity. Either not enough information or fact is available, or the case involves circumstance, interest, and value in a way that cannot be subsumed by higher, purer categories. In any case, the very actuation of five Aristotelian categories (quality, place, time, activity, and position) is practically implicated in the decision and judgment of some *other*. Thus it is, reasoning backwards, that Aristotle employed his questions first as tools of inquiry, then as spaces of general contention, and eventually as particular points of disturbance, with three sorts of audience giving rise to three different forms of rhetoric. Later, these would be called demonstration, deliberation, and judgment.[10] The objectives of showing, thinking, and deciding seem virtually to exhaust the possibilities of dealing with an unfinished, plural world in a practical, responsible way. These too are means of raising and answering questions.

It needs to be remembered, however, that this opening for rhetoric as inquiry rests not only on Aristotle's repositioning of categories, however dazzling, but also on his deeper sense that objects of inquiry are themselves multiple and exhibit different orders of composition, levels of complexity, degrees of tractability, and prospects for refinement. Although it may seem an unlikely source, a statement that Merleau-

Ponty once made about Cézanne offers an apt characterization of the founder of our Western traditions:

> He did not want to separate the stable things which we see and the shifting way in which they appear; he wanted to depict matter as it takes on form, the birth of order through spontaneous organization. He makes a basic distinction not between the "senses" and "the understanding" but rather between the spontaneous order of the things we perceive and the human organization of ideas and sciences. We see things; we agree about them; we are anchored in them; and it is with "nature" as our base that we construct our sciences.[11]

Aristotle has long been considered the great systematizer; and I have done little to dispel this view with my reading to this point. It is true that Aristotle wished to inquire into the relationships among worldly and human phainomena in things, thoughts, and terms. This is surely the major aim of the organon. The special contribution of the *Rhetoric* to inquiry, however, is its sense that appearances admit to a tension between their stability and "the shifting way in which they appear."

Appearances come to us as configurations, as ensembles of objects, habitats, paths, tools, tasks, icons, and more or less recognizable characters that engage and reassure us with their own emergent familiarity. For the most part, most of the time, most of us are at home in the world of appearances. The stability of the familiar and the persistence of the recognizable lend a solidity to one another. Yet it is in their very particularity that appearances can begin to seem ambiguous or even equivocal and incomplete. When we have some stake, or interest, in the array of things around us, for instance, we are not likely to be concerned with an underlying cause or a larger, more inclusive general opinion. For the particularity of things has become a provocation. We cannot leave well enough alone. We also disagree about things. We may try to ignore them. We may take issue as regards what they mean. Eventually—perhaps sooner than we wish—we may have to own up to them, make judgments about them, and act on them. This is the tension that Aristotle captures with his rhetorical mood of *contingency*. Here we suddenly have the unsettledness of appearances, wherein differences are crystallized in opposed directions which may be resolved one way or the other. Our readings of the ethical and aesthetic norms of rhetorical culture depend strongly on the critical importance of contingency for propitious conduct and judgment. But what is already clear is that the very meaning of rhetoric's materials—

the probable or contingent, what may be one way or another—derives from rhetoric's characteristic approach to appearances.

Rhetorical questions thus offer a provisional, but engaged, sense of meaning in particular to a changing complex of appearances. Usually such questions are contentious as well and will move and change as the issues in a controversy develop or recede in importance. Rhetorical questions attempt to provide an appropriate caption for our ongoing experience with appearances. For, as Martha Nussbaum has noted, "The *phainomena* present us with a confused array, often with direct contradiction. They reflect our disagreements and ambivalences. The first step must, therefore, be to bring conflicting opinions to the surface and set them out clearly."[12] Here, of course, Nussbaum is addressing Aristotle's procedure *qua* philosopher; and this philosopher's aim, as we have seen, is to discover and explain the nature of things in a manner consistent with their appearances. But now consider, by contrast, this rather typical passage on honour from the beginning of Aristotle's *Rhetoric:*

> Honour is the token of a man's being famous for doing good. It is chiefly and most properly paid to those who have already done good; but also to the man who can do good in the future. Doing good refers either to the preservation of life and the means of life, or to wealth, or to some other of the good things which it is hard to get either always or at that particular place or time—for many gain honour for things which seem small, but the place and occasion account for it. The constituents of honour are: sacrifices; commemoration, in verse or prose; privileges; grants of land; front seats at civic celebrations; state burial; statues; public maintenance; among foreigners, obeisances and giving place; and such presents as are among various bodies of men regarded as marks of honour. (1361a25–40)

For those who are less than sympathetic to classical rhetoric, this sort of passage may confirm their worst stereotypes. It reads as little more than a list. But of what? This is surely an unusual way of approaching the virtue of honour. Here we have tokens and marks of honour, accounted for by place and occasion, hence presents and even seating position, what is taken as signifying honour. The very mundaneness of the items is revealing; for this is an overview of the *appearances* of honour presented as materials for rhetoric—how honour may be recognized, presented, framed, and depicted.

Interestingly, Aristotle moves directly from this overview in book 1 to an examination of the various public "excellences." When he arrives at "the good," he confounds Platonists and Sophists alike by beginning with good luck and citing the good in itself as only one of over forty differing and often contradictory senses of goodness (1362a–b). What is going on here? Again, Aristotle is giving us an overview of the appearances of value construed rhetorically.

How, then, does rhetoric form and frame appearances? We have begun to answer this question through our initial distinctions among analytical, dialectical, and rhetorical questions. But now it is important to ask how dialectic and rhetoric engage the pluralities of life in our day. I will begin my consideration of this question from a perspective which strays from the classical Aristotelian corpus while making deliberate use of Aristotle's categories (quality, place, time, activity, and position). My aim is to discriminate generally among traits which depict appearances primarily in an *ethically* significant manner and those which emphasize their *aesthetic* "transmission," figuration, and distortion.[13] Later, the interdependence of ethical and aesthetic norms in rhetoric will provide a larger context for this preliminary overview.

Looked at rhetorically, appearances have undeniable aesthetic properties. But as we noted in our earlier discussion of method, these properties are likely to be overlooked to the extent that we break them down into a "grammar" of component parts. This is another way of saying that even the identifiable features of appearances shade into one another and that appearances come to us as "configurations," with both coherence and form. At first glance, this figurative coherence might seem to be at odds with the developing sense of "plurality" in Aristotle's *Rhetoric*. But this is so only if we forget that all configurations of appearance are also *partial*. As John Berger has noted, "Appearances both distinguish *and* join events."[14] So we may select a restaurant, at least in part, for its view, for the configuration of appearances it affords us. But at the same time, perhaps even in the same proximate vicinity, other viewers encounter other configurations (perhaps drug deals, graffiti, or wharf rats) that are totally at odds with our own tranquil scene. The particularity of any configuration of appearances is available to us rhetorically only because each configuration is decidedly *not* the whole picture.

We should also remind ourselves that coherence of form in any configuration does not negate the tension, disturbance, struggles, and conflict that may lie at the core of what appears. In the great Russian film version of *War and Peace*, there is a remarkable scene where Pierre wanders through the fiercely chaotic, seemingly random pathologies of battle. It is the most visceral depiction of entropy imaginable. But then the camera recedes and seems to move ever upward, away from the battle-fields. Gradually the separate scenes of irrational carnage and bloodshed seem to distance themselves, until they become mere striations, minia-turized marks within a larger panorama of intelligibility. This scene has remained with me for twenty years; it is that powerful.[15] But its power is at odds with its intention, I suspect. Many configurations are composed of otherwise random, partisan, unintelligible bits of disturbance. This is not to cancel or transcend all that is local and immediate, however. The cinematic vision (like all sweeping historical re-visionings) is also a par-tial configuration. Its coherence is presented to us as something larger than it really is; for what we really have here is an ensemble of images and props, made for a positioned lens, a director, and a particular film.

I am now in a position to identify and explore some properties of appearance that are of great interest for rhetoric. Synchronically, appear-ances present us with a scene in which we in some sense participate. And although we cannot freeze the scene, as in a photograph, we do know that the more compelling features of appearances do tend to arrest the unfolding tendencies of events and hold our attention. Among the synchronic features of appearance which are of particular importance, consider the following:

(1) *Aspect.* This refers to primary visual features of appearance that stand out and seem to impose themselves on us. We wait for hos-tages to descend from a plane. *There* they are! A lone civilian tries to stop a tank, or a parched farmland is shown directly adjacent to a lush, freshly irrigated field. Through contrast, found irony, or other dramatic tension, particular features of appearances will stand out, causing others to recede in immediate significance.

(2) *Aura.* First emphasized in the work of Walter Benjamin, *aura* refers to the boundedness of appearances, our sense of their spe-cific locale, within a situated horizon of surroundings.[16] The Eiffel Tower, for instance, usually includes an urban Parisian landscape as part of its aura. Figures of the American West, cowboys and cattle ranchers, tend to have some iconography of the Western frontier as their aura: a campfire, sagebrush, cacti, fenceposts, and so forth. One of Benjamin's critical insights is that this stable originary context for recognition has been undermined by the

mass media. The Eiffel Tower may be imposed on a perfume bottle, the old West behind a package of cigarettes. But whether an aura is weak or strong, there seems to be a situated horizon of some sort that adds presence and immediacy to any configuration of appearances.

(3) *Tone.* Usually an aural reference to sound quality, the emphasis here derives from Bakhtin.[17] In considering tone, we ask how stable, and how intensely focused the emotional resonances of appearances are. Are they subdued, muted, disguised, or overwhelming? As I am using the term, *tone* refers to the degree of ambiguity, clarity, and intensity of pathos within appearances. When these intersect with a participatory interest, there is obviously a call for rhetoric.

(4) *Texture.* This is a closely related term that is also used metaphorically. Texture refers to the accessibility or remoteness of appearances and all the variations in between. How refined or rough is the delineation of appearances? What is there in any configuration for us to take hold of? What traction is offered for our own participatory conduct? Do these appearances deserve careful scrutiny? Are they too remote from our view or too much in flux to allow any direct intervention? Do they require further interpretation before anything else is possible? In short, when we inquire about texture, we are asking what contours for participation are presented to us by any configuration of appearances.

The vocabulary offered here is intended as no more than a sketch of overlapping synchronic qualities available to a rhetorical reading of phainomena. Without stretching the meaning of *definition* too much, it may also be said that, as in the methods of analytic and dialectic, the definitional question remains uppermost for rhetoric. Here we think of aspect, aura, tone, and texture as collaborative qualities yielding a recognizable shape or outline to appearances. This will be their definition. And although definitional properties are frequently disputed in rhetoric, it is the function of rhetorical questions to identify signs, probabilities, and examples on either side of an issue so that the topography of appearances may be represented with sufficient clarity to yield prudent decision and conduct.

It is also the case that, once a configuration of appearances has been engaged by rhetorical definition, it takes on more than a synchronic dimension. Implicated in decisions and prospective outcomes, appearances take on an unfolding, sequential quality that gives them a cumulative meaning over time. They acquire, in short, a diachronic dimension. The art of rhetoric is what makes this transfiguration possible. In this connection John Berger has observed that appearances comprise something of a partial, or "half," language.[18] But if so, rhetoric must surely be the other half.

Whereas the world of appearances seems to draw forth a teleological manner of thinking (typified by this very sentence), it is rhetoric which elicits this provisional teleology. By attending to certain configurations of appearance in the first place, as if to say, "Look! A massacre!" or "See? A heroic achievement!" rhetorical utterances lend to appearances a sense of *duration*, an existence that is likely to persist beyond our current attention span. Rhetoric also helps to make appearances accessible and intelligible to us by articulating their mood. Loosely analogous to the "moods" of propositions discussed in *De Interpretatione* (19a5–24) are the "manners" of engaging unfinished configurations of appearance through rhetoric. We have the imperative and compulsion of necessity (as in "We must act!") and the Utopian beckoning of possibility ("Imagine").[19] Most of the time, we have a configuration of appearances construed as a *contingency*, a unique particularity about which one or more things should or should not be done. This is also how our sense of provisional teleology is made available to appearances. For rhetoric, alone among the arts, approaches appearances through the interpretative lens of interested common opinions (*endoxa*); reconsidered as signs, probabilities, and examples, appearances become the material of public argument. As such, they take on the emergent sense of impetus and unfolding direction that is characteristic of action generally. Of course we know that appearances do not act all on their own. But such statements as "The people will ultimately win!" or "God is on our side" or "In the end good triumphs over evil" present us with themes that tell an equally interesting, albeit tragic, story. Configurations of appearance therefore take on an impetus and direction that sometimes succeed in convincing their own creators; that is, they develop a "life of their own." By means of rhetoric, appearances shared by assembled human beings are *re*-presented in the guise of a practical consciousness which guides and legitimates collective human conduct. Rhetoric regards appearances as the primary aesthetic material for the continual reinvention of human *agency*, which, in turn, offers some preliminary construal of their ethical possibility.

DIALECTICAL VERSUS RHETORICAL
RESPONSES TO APPEARANCES

Captivated by the spell of modern dialectic, the tendency of inquiry has been to treat appearances as somehow juxtaposed to the deeper, polar term *reality* or even to regard appearances themselves as a structure of domination, a kind of inescapable regime. Of course, the very interests we have in phainomena and their multiple construals invite recurring contests over meaning and understanding. As regards judgment and conduct, however, a classical understanding of rhetoric usually assumes that some judgments and courses of action are more serviceable and better founded than others. Further, as the still widespread practice of censorship illustrates, some configurations of appearance, once they have been disclosed to others, make their own powerful, albeit unfinished, statement. If the Platonic philosopher-king banished purveyors of appearance as liars, modern agencies of martial law do much the same thing because they have something to hide. Censorship is the negative tribute paid by modernity to the power of appearances.[20]

We are now in a position to clarify and briefly illustrate the differing ways in which dialectic and rhetoric address a world of particulars. Although both were introduced originally as universal arts of the probable constrained by no fixed subject matter, there are striking differences in their presuppositions and tendencies. As we have seen, dialectic tends to presuppose an already identifiable problematic. Working with imposed commonplaces and predicable relationships, its aim is to generate propositions which may be affirmed or denied. It tends to move from the alleged facts of particularity to more general truths. It encourages the participation of generalized "forces" in a logocentric language of conflict, even as it tends to discourage participation from the world of phenomena. Rhetoric, by contrast, contests the realm of the problematic, even as it aims to facilitate judgment based on persuasion. While language continues to value logos, the very grounds of disputation are found in the particularities of appearances. As Grimaldi encapsulates it, "This is the *logos* of the material, what the subject matter does or can say of itself."[21]

These differences are thrown into even sharper relief with the expanded scope of the probable and the intervention of modernity in the form of history and cultural development.[22] In virtually all its variations, dialectic continues to presuppose the law of contradiction, the assumption that truth inheres in the generality and is tested by the opposition of equally general claims, and the idea that truth must ultimately join the process of inquiry as method with its own emergent product.[23] I have tried to present these presuppositions in a value-neutral way. But even the most neutral observer will be aware of their characteristic approach to the treatment of pluralities. An advance notice of what we might expect comes from the way dialectic typically deals with itself: that is, with its own method in other variations. Consider Marx's critique of Feuerbach, Feuerbach's of Hegel, and Lukács' of any of the above.[24] Once dialectic has been converted from a free-flowing give and take among interlocutors in conversation to a univocal style of writing, it must improvise the role, place, and voice of its various subjects. This is why in the entire modern history of written dialectic there is no recorded case of a dissenting voice which, like one of Dostoevsky's characters, refuses to be subjugated. This absence of a genuine "double-voicedness" is somewhat ironic, given the origins and etymological roots of the word *dialectic*; but however dogged and relentless it is as a method of critical reflection, the absence of a real participatory audience is inherent in its procedures. Only very rarely, as in the early work of Habermas,[25] does it take on the position and voice of the "losing side." This is not to say that the dialectician always knows his or her own destination in advance and is always guilty of bad faith. It is just that dialectic, despite its pretense to suspenseful opposition, usually has a predisposition toward protagonists and antagonists. And even if it cannot tell the outcome in advance, the plot and the author are never far removed from one another.

All this is by way of suggesting that dialectic tends to be more powerful as a retrospective critical system than as a prospective guide to action. In the interpretation and judgment of past events and actions, it may find the larger tension at work in smaller oppositions. It may also employ its still pertinent topoi of accident and definition, problem and proposition, universal and particular, subject and predicate, to characterize messy, recalcitrant details within a larger picture. To the dialectician, appearances from the past are primary evidence of work still to be done; but appearances in the present are less easily dealt with.

We have already noted that the dialectician tends to see appearances as either the duplicitous surface of a deeper, albeit hidden, reality or as the unfalsifiable ideology of false consciousness. These two positions, removed from each other historically, are closely related conceptually and could be dubbed the Platonic and the Marxist positions. Despite his or her general aversion to the particularity of phainomena, however, the dialectician inevitably comes face to face with appearances when confronted with serious problems of choice and action. Now it is not a lethal indictment of either dialectic or rhetoric to claim that those employing them occasionally make the *wrong* decision.[26] Every method of inquiry yields outcomes that are off the mark; and in the sciences, at least, the discovery and recognition of error are usually viewed as some measure of progress. The point, rather, is to determine how the methods of dialectic and rhetoric characteristically approach pluralities of appearance when these present problems.

Georg Lukács and Dialectic

To illustrate and characterize the dialectical approach, I have chosen someone who was arguably the most gifted dialectician and literary theorist of the twentieth century, Georg Lukács. During the course of a turbulent life, Lukács was a political reformer, a party propagandist, a loyal Bolshevik, a prisoner, and a revolutionary hero of conscience. It is also relevant that, whether in his masterful *Theory of the Novel*, his early study *Soul and Form*, his political books *Tactics and Ethics* and *History and Class Consciousness*, Lukács was obsessed with the problem of validating "correct" action.[27]

As he makes clear in his important essay "What is Orthodox Marxism?" he never wavered in his acceptance of Marxism as an orthodoxy. He shows that the core, or practical essence, of this orthodoxy consists in scrupulous adherence to the Marxist dialectic. In one particularly revealing passage, he writes: "This dialectical conception of the totality seems to have put a great distance between itself and reality, it appears to construct reality very 'unscientifically.' But it is the only method capable of understanding and reproducing reality. Concrete totality is, therefore, the category that governs reality."[28]

At work in the formidable apparatus of this dialectic are the traditional dialectical topoi of part and whole (here envisioned as the totality), the accidents of history versus their (defined) necessity, and the problematic of indefinitely deferred revolution versus the party as an obviously partisan entity. For Lukács, as many have noted, there is a need to capture the true consciousness of totality within the still partisan vehicle of a social class. Hence the party functions as a kind of double synecdoche: for class consciousness (not yet mature enough to grasp the whole picture) and then for the totality itself.[29] Lukács also reintroduces an ancient dualistic trope in modern guise: that of appearance and essence. This takes us to the core difficulty of his dialectic as method.

Lukács, despite—or perhaps because of—his subservience to a higher worldly good, was a profoundly ethical thinker. His dialectical sensibilities allowed him to anticipate sweeping transformations before any of his contemporaries. Thus, before anyone else, he anticipated that the Bolshevik Revolution would occur not in an advanced industrial state, but in Czarist Russia.[30] It was also Lukács who, before his beloved party, was forced to renounce his "premature anti-Fascist" position. Yet it was the nagging particularity of circumstance and appearance that plagued Lukács at every turn.[31] He sought always to capture, and even transform, the essential truths conveyed in each succession of appearances. In "What is Orthodox Marxism?" he writes poignantly:

> It then becomes impossible to impose the subjective will, wish or decision upon the facts or to discover in them any directive for action. A situation in which "the facts" speak out unmistakably for or against a definite course of action has never existed, and neither can or will exist. The more conscientiously the facts are explored— in their isolation; i.e. in their unmediated relations—the less compellingly will they point in any one direction. It is self-evident that a merely subjective decision will be shattered by the pressure of uncomprehended facts acting automatically—"according to laws." Thus dialectical materialism is seen to offer the only approach to reality which can give action a direction.[32]

In this passage we have the essence of the quandary. As a materialist, Lukács could not disavow the appearances confronting humankind in each "succession." But as a dialectician, he found the very partiality of these appearances a nagging insufficiency; again and again, he violated his own prescription and conscientiously explored facts with an eye to the emerging total picture.

As Lukács introduces criteria for the validation of action, the imposing horizon of totality is everywhere to be found. Four steps or criteria are required for the validation of "correct" action.[33] First, action must interrupt and disrupt the "reified structure of existence." This can happen only if "the immanent contradictions of the process are made conscious." Yet, as is well known, this requires Lukács's highly idealized proletarian consciousness to "point out the road along which the dialectics of history is objectively impelled." How do we determine this road? Lukács acknowledges that we cannot know it in advance; hence the second criterion: "Inseparable from this is the fact that the relation to totality does not need to become explicit, the plenitude of the totality does not need to be consciously integrated into the motives and objects of action." This is reassuring insofar as such integration might seem a Utopian aspiration at best. But there is this codicil: "What is crucial is that there should be an aspiration towards totality, that action should serve the purpose, described above, in the totality of the process." Does this mean that purity of motive vindicates action? Not exactly; for this is where the third criterion comes in: "When judging whether an action is right or wrong it is essential to relate it to its function in the total process. Proletarian thought is practical thought and as such is strongly pragmatic." But in light of this pragmatism, what is to determine the proper relationship to the whole process? Here we have another codicil: "Whether an action is functionally right or wrong is decided ultimately by the evolution of proletarian class consciousness." This leads to the fourth criterion, which seems to complete the circle: "The eminently practical nature of this consciousness is to be seen . . . in that an adequate, correct consciousness means a change in its own objects, and in the first instance, in itself."

More is going on in these passages than a tortured, evasive wordplay. Lukács is aware that he cannot use proletarian consciousness as a criterion to evaluate action when the very object of action is to refine and articulate true proletarian class consciousness. He attempts, teleologically, to baptise action with an aura of totality in advance of its full accomplishment. Whether by accident or design, there is a fascinating, albeit oblique, parallelism between these questions and the earlier analytic of inquiry. We begin with a disruption of the existence question, work through the problem of defining the part in light of the totality, redistribute the problem of determining quality, and finally discover—in an ironic reversal of the analytic search for cause—that the "why" question returns procedurally to rest in the stasis of subject as self.

What is finally so arresting and poignant about this great thinker is that throughout his many recantations and self-criticisms, he never abandoned his faith in the significance of collective thought and action. Hannah Arendt once noted that action is inherently ironic, because its consequences spin out potentially to infinity, and at any point along the way, consequence might reverse the best of original intentions.[34] Lukács lived long enough to see many such reversals; yet we find him in his eighties still conversing about the historic prospects for revolution.[35] He was deeply sensitive to the problem of action's reversibility and the irony of its origins; yet even in the midst of all this, he was impelled toward the dialectical closure of recurring rhetorical problems.

Regarding the junctures of choice and avoidance, Lukács's agnosticism was that of an unhappy consciousness; for the plurality of phainomena with their multiple well-intended understandings must be considered a serious dilemma. Here is a particularly revealing passage from near the end of his classic essay "Reification and the Consciousness of the Proletariat":

> Becoming is also the mediation between past and future. But it is the mediation between the concrete, i.e. historical past, and the equally concrete, i.e. historical future. When the concrete here and now dissolves into a process it is no longer a continuous, intangible moment, immediacy slipping away; it is the focus of the deepest and most widely ramified mediation, the focus of decision and of the birth of the new. As long as man concentrates his interest contemplatively upon the past *or* future, both ossify into an alien existence. And between the subject and the object lies the unbridgeable "pernicious chasm" of the present.[36]

The problem, now an *aporia*, is that "the truth of becoming is the future that is to be created but has not yet been born," that although "reality is the criterion for the correctness of thought," nevertheless, "reality is not, it becomes—and to become the participation of thought is needed."[37] Try as he did to overcome oppositions and contingencies through dialectic, Lukács found himself returning to the present in the revealing form of a "pernicious chasm."

The point of this illustration is not to degrade or undermine the power of dialectic as inquiry (rhetoric and dialectic are, after all, complementary methods). Rather, it is to show what happens when dialectic is forced to confront the plurality of worlds in their immediate, historical existence. Even such a relentlessly self-critical thinker as Lukács (who endorsed, in principle, a pluralist ontology)[38] was driven to search for the correct tendencies for a whole picture within each provisional array of choices. In its more apocalyptic moments, rhetoric has shared a similar dream: to move from its own unfinished perspective to the emerging totality. The great temptation for rhetoric, as for Lukács's vision of history, is to see its euphoria as successfully lodged in the pivotal unfolding and final transformational phase of this totality. But then, like history itself, its duty would be done; and with a perspective no longer partisan, its own worldly existence would be over. Fortunately for the facts of the matter, rhetoric's lofty ambitions are invariably compromised by reminders of its more earthbound task, which is to open up projects for the sanctioned actions and partisan interests of others.

And so we come to the more practical faith of dialectic's counterpart. It is that provisional forms of agency may be found and articulated within successions of appearances. Grasped in unfolding episodes, shared by implicated audiences, rhetoric may—through its various affiliative inferences and dissociative devices—provide definition, impetus, and direction to history in the making, even as we wait impatiently for the heroes and villains to be named later. Rhetoric's material is thus the configuration of appearances, whose resonances of *thanatos* (the "yawning abyss," the "pernicious chasm") so tormented Lukács; these are moments of present choice construed as a contingency—a unique particularity about which something *may* be done. The central virtue of rhetoric is "perspicuity" writ large: *phronēsis* refigured as *kairos*—proper choices at propitious moments.[39]

Rhetoric in the Army–McCarthy Hearings

No single example of rhetoric could match the conflict and the frustration of Lukács's dialectical quandary. In part this is because the rhetorical struggle over the meaning and definition of appearances is literally ongoing. It is also because, as an art of the commonplace, rhetoric does not usually find the same sorts of drama and collision of great forces in its subject matter as there were in our earlier illustration. But one serviceable exemplar does come to mind: an episode that may have marked a rhetorical turning in the repressive cold war era in the United States in the 1950s. I refer to a justly famous exchange during the Army–McCarthy hearings of 1954.[40] Joseph McCarthy, junior senator from Wisconsin, and his Senate subcommittee, together with the still influential House Un-American Activities Committee, had succeeded in combining a virulent form of anti-Communist paranoia with a style of witch hunt political invective. The result, given the ideological climate of the times, was to question the loyalty and character of many distinguished American citizens. In many sectors of American public life (including the entertainment industry, civil service, unions, and surely politics) reputations were tarnished, careers ruined. Meanwhile McCarthy and his ambitious associates (Roy Cohn and G. David Schine) were able to build by this means careers of great power and influence.[41]

In many ways, the conspiratorial demagoguery of Joe McCarthy embodied rhetoric at its least attractive and least responsible. Full of bluster and innuendo, completely ruthless in their methods, and unhampered by any interest in the truth, he and his colleagues postured and bullied their way into the highest offices of the nation. During Eisenhower's first term as president, McCarthy's increasingly sensationalist charges—of Communists in the State Department, a "soft" Secretary of Defense, and the implausible claim of Communist infiltration of the armed services— had a chilling effect on his own party. But it was only McCarthy's extravagance that finally moved a reluctant oppositional bloc into action.[42]

The Army–McCarthy hearings were convened in 1954 to investigate charges that McCarthy had used improper influence to get special treatment in the army for his supposed surveillance operative Private G. David Schine. McCarthy retorted, characteristically, that the Army itself had singled Schine out for special attention, because it had something sinister to hide. During the two-month period of the hearings, daytime television viewing increased by 53 percent.[43] There is no decisive evidence that exposure to the hearings, by itself, caused a dramatic shift in public opinion about McCarthy. But it is perhaps not too much to say that these televised hearings provided ordinary people with a kind of improvised forum for examining alternatives to the junior senator's increasingly monologic speech.

The rhetoric of conspiracy and paranoia poses one of the more direct challenges to the integrity of appearances. For in this discourse, what presents itself as public, visible, knowable, and benign is always a lie. For the conspiracy theorist or (in McCarthy's case) demagogue, only the hidden is true. And the hidden is always private, invisible, removed from our grasp, and—above all—thoroughly malignant.[44] Of course, the atheistic, ruthless, demonic image of cold war communism fitted this typification perfectly.[45] Moreover, once we cease to trust appearances and begin to view the tendencies of the world with extreme suspicion, other rhetorical implications follow immediately. For one thing, pluralities of appearance dissolve. What look for all the world like differences of opinion, checks and balances, tolerance for eccentricity, are magically transformed into "fellow traveling," or unwitting service to this grand antagonist. Closely related to this is the kind of license to kill often granted to those whom we trust to read our deeper truths. The niceties of ethics, decorum, and due process then become less important than in normal times; for if, as McCarthy frequently intoned, "This is a war" and, what's worse, a war against a "brutalitarian force," then virtually any means necessary to defeat this horrific enemy are permissible.

The outcome of a successful conspiracy rhetoric is a kind of counter-deliberative stance, almost a nightmarish parody of the dialectical thinking discussed earlier. This discourse can never really prove anything, because its ordinary materials (that is, of the world) are lies. Hence it arouses not faith, but only radical suspicion. It can suggest no provisional judgment or action because the particulars of the world have already been appropriated. They are part of the false unity controlled by the enemy. Thus it appeals not to optimism, but to a kind of phobic vigilance. Finally, this discourse must beg, and eventually circumvent, the whole question of virtue. For in a world without clear definitions of conviction, the defeat of a dishonorable antagonist must surely be honorable. But why can honor not defeat dishonor through its own morally superior qualities? And what finally sustains the affirmative vision of this great cause? Conspiracy discourse can call forth no sustaining sense of collective virtue because its primary emotive resource is the projection of virtue's absence: guilt.[46] The question is whether such a rhetoric of "anti-appearances" can be subjected to the force of prudential reason within the public realm.

There are many fascinating rhetorical episodes throughout the hearings. The "cropped photo" incident shows that McCarthy was not above doctoring photographic evidence to imply military complicity in the preferential treatment he sought for his own operative;[47] this suggests more anxiety regarding the phainomena than one might at first expect. The senator's abusive and cantankerous manner gradually brought his character and motivation into the spotlight. The most powerful rhetorical proof, as Aristotle noted, is ēthos—the character of the speaker as it is manifested through the speech (*Rhetoric* 1356a5–15). And in a world view without any room for proof, the fate of McCarthy's cause finally came to depend on his public character.

The pivotal exchange took place between McCarthy and the attorney representing the Army, Joseph Welch, in the last week of the hearings. Welch had been examining Roy Cohn, McCarthy's chief counsel, about the number of Communists in the Army Signal Corps. Parodying the alarmism of conspiracy rhetoric, Welch had just finished urging Cohn to turn over the names of all those traitors to the FBI by sundown. Cohn, after playing along with this for a time, then made the mistake of noting that J. Edgar Hoover probably knew about these security leaks already and probably had the names of all the offenders. The modest trap had been sprung. "Then what's all the fuss about if Mr. J. Edgar already has everything under control?" In a kind of microcosm of his modus operandi, McCarthy snapped: "Mr. Chairman, in view of that question . . ."; to which the chairman, Karl Mundt, replied: "Do you have a point of order?" McCarthy then retorted: "Not exactly, Mr. Chairman, but in view of Mr. Welch's request that the information be given once we know of anyone who might be performing any work for the Communist party, I think we should tell him that he has in his own firm a young man named Fisher—who has been for a number of years a member of an organization which was named, oh years and years ago, as the legal bulwark of the Communist Party."

The ensuing scene, as McCarthy prepared for the rhetorical kill, was described by William Manchester as follows: "Welch looked stricken. A hush had fallen over the table. Smiling, licking his lips, his words freighted with sarcasm, McCarthy went on: 'Knowing that, Mr. Welch, I just felt that I had a duty to respond to your urgent request. . . . I have hesitated about bringing that up. But I have been rather bored with your phony requests to Mr. Cohn here that he personally get every Communist out of government before sundown. Therefore . . .'"[48] McCarthy rambled on. He wasn't sure if Welch knew that "his man" was a member of the party. In fact, McCarthy and Welch had agreed not to bring the matter up on condition that some incriminating data about McCarthy's chief counsel, Cohn, was also kept off the record. McCarthy wasn't sure why Welch would want to "foist" Fisher onto this committee; in fact, as McCarthy well knew, the truth was the opposite.[49] Through all this, Welch appeared sad but stoically resigned. When the tirade was over, Welch struggled to respond as McCarthy frivolously ignored him. After several attempts to speak through McCarthy's interruptions ("I can listen with one ear," the senator said at one point)[50] and interminable haggling by McCarthy over documents incriminating Fisher, Welch finally began his response:

"Senator McCarthy? You won't need anything in the record when I finish telling you this. Until this moment, Senator, I never really gauged your cruelty or your recklessness. Fred Fisher is a young man who went to Harvard Law School and came into our firm, and is starting what looks to be a promising career with us. When I decided to work for this case, I asked Jim St. Clair, who sits on my right, to pick someone else to work with us, to work under you, that you would like. He chose Fred Fisher and they came down on the afternoon plane. That evening, after we had made a little stab at trying to see what the case was about, Fred Fisher and Jim St. Clair and I went to dinner together. I then said to these two young men: 'Boys, I don't know anything about you except I've always liked you. But if there's anything funny in the life of either one of you that would hurt any aspect of this case, you speak up quick.'

And Fred Fisher said, 'Mr. Welch, when I was in law school and for a period of months after, I belonged to the Lawyers' Guild' (as you have suggested, Senator). He went on to say, 'I am Secretary of the Young Republicans league in Newton, am the son of a Massachusetts Senator, and I have the respect and admiration of my community and I am sure I have the respect and admiration of the 25 lawyers at Hale and Dorr.'

And I said, 'Fred, I just don't think I am going to ask you to work on the case. If I do, one of these days that will come out and go over national television and it will just hurt like the dickens.' So, Senator, I asked him to go back to Boston."

By this point in Welch's statement, there was an eerie hush throughout the hearing room. Other than flashbulbs from the Press and McCarthy nervously shuffling papers, there were only silent murmurings. Welch then paused briefly before his own quietly definitive peroration: "Little did I dream that you could be so reckless and so cruel as to do an injury to that lad. It is true that he works for Hale and Dorr. It is true that he will continue to be with Hale and Dorr. It is, I regret to say, equally true that I fear he shall always bear a scar needlessly inflicted by you. If it were in my power to forgive you for your reckless cruelty, I would do so. I like to think I'm a gentle man. But . . . [lengthy pause] that forgiveness will have to come from someone other than me."

A scene of some confusion followed these words. Mundt wanted it placed on the record that Welch had never attempted to use Fred Fisher as counsel for the Army. McCarthy himself, completely oblivious to what had transpired, continued to insist on introducing documentation incriminating Fisher. Only after a brilliant flourish in which Welch said to

.a very nervous Cohn: "I did you, I think, no personal injury, Mr. Cohn"—
to which the response was "No, sir"—"I meant to do you no personal
injury and if I did I beg your pardon,"[51] did the contrast become clear.
McCarthy could not apologize, because he did not even recognize his
offense. His own callous lack of regard had become one of the phainomena in Welch's array of "proofs." Once more, McCarthy went back to
Fisher; to which Welch responded: "Let us not assassinate this lad further, Senator. You have done enough. Have you no sense of decency, sir,
at long last? Have you no sense of decency?"

There is, of course, no real answer to such a question. As an initial
query, it would have appeared intemperate. But in rhetoric, the particularity of kairos is critical; and as the final, exasperated gesture in this
dramatic exchange, Welch's question proved to be conclusive. Everyone
in the hearing room except McCarthy knew the answer.

Earlier, I described the hearings and this exchange as marking a rhetorical turning in the repressive cold war climate of the 1950s in the
United States. Many prominent civic groups were forced to reconsider
their "Better dead than red," extremist approach to dissent in light of
McCarthy's own abusive tactics. This does not mean that the approach
ever disappeared from the American scene. But by the end of 1954,
McCarthy had been censured by the Senate; and thereafter he ceased to
be a major force in American politics.[52]

What we have in this remarkable exchange is not the clash of great
oppositional forces in search of a grand totality, but rather an agonizing
moment of particularity, with all its resonance. The issue is no longer the
imagined evils of communism generally. It concerns a particular individual who is not even present at the hearings, the absent Fisher. In terms
of McCarthy's world view and strategy, Fisher's absence or presence does
not matter; if he is, or has ever been, in league with this demonic force,
he is an enemy without rights. Yet what finally made Welch's vilification
of McCarthy so effective was that, in showing Fisher to be an innocent,
or at least harmless, individual, as opposed to a type, he demonstrated
that McCarthy's injury to him was both dastardly and unnecessary all at
the same time. This was, in other words, a contest over appearances.

It is worth considering how Welch managed to emerge with a definitive
advantage. He spoke in a private voice about the endangered, absent character, Fisher. Instead of proceeding through overt argument (an approach
which had been fatal to McCarthy's legion of earlier victims), Welch
·simply related a string of anecdotes, a tale. And note the theme of this

tale. The whole point is one of disclosure, devotion to craft, truth telling, and respect for the hidden. If great rhetoric is always about rhetoric, then so is this quaint and outwardly ordinary discourse.

With what appears to have been extreme reluctance, Welch violated his own trust with Fisher in order to bring this private character into sharper public focus. Fisher is described as someone with a promising future who was handpicked for the job of Welch's associate counsel; yet he has already been forced to withdraw from this public role because of his possibly damaging association with the Lawyers' Guild. For McCarthy, private realities and motives were always sordid and suspect; and there was no complicating this Manichaean opposition with the complexities and ambiguities of real personal life. By contrast, consider Welch's story. St. Clair and Fisher come down on the plane; with Welch, they take "a little stab" at the case and go out for dinner. Welch then, in a fatherly way, asks if there is "anything funny" in the life of either one. Fisher tells him the truth. Welch makes a painful, but honorable, decision out of devotion to the case. It is almost as if the entire aura has been inverted. Welch's every word, phrase, and nuance—"anything funny," "hurt like the dickens," "young lads"—place him in the world of the uncontroversial and ordinary. The word choice makes certain features stand out; it also demystifies McCarthy's sense of intrigue, presenting us not with co-conspirators, but with ordinary professionals making honorable decisions without guile. It cannot but affect our own mood as "hearers": we are made to feel almost as if we are invading another's privacy in the mere witnessing of this tale.

But now consider the theme. Fisher has already returned to private practice. He has been left on the sidelines not because he was guilty of anything, but because, given the climate of the times, he might appear to be guilty and thus damage the case. In this alternative construal, what is hidden sometimes needs to be respected as private. It is not always a malignancy that threatens the republic. Welch seized not only the moment, but the power to define. In investing Fred Fisher with the tones of real life—"Secretary of the Young Republicans" and "son of a Massachusetts Senator"—Welch was able to employ his own privileged access to transform Fisher's ordinariness into a quality of ēthos. Accordingly, he added to this configuration of appearances an alternative impetus, direction, and mood. Whether Fisher was actually honorable or even totally innocent, he was at least harmless. Yet he has been harmed. What cannot be overlooked is the forensic theme of the story. Fisher's very absence helped to reinforce McCarthy's own culpability. It was as if the senator had reached randomly into the private sector to incriminate someone. He was, in his own words, bored. And obviously he wanted to upstage Welch's bit of showmanship. But at what cost! What McCarthy has done for sport, we have been made to overhear in human terms, to understand in shared disturbance.

Powerful as the theme of Welch's story was, he made certain that the point was not lost. Three times he stepped outside this construction of events to address the moral theme directly to McCarthy: "I never really gauged your cruelty or your recklessness," followed by "Little did I dream that you could be so reckless and so cruel" and "If it were within my power to forgive you for your reckless cruelty." The voice was solemn and oracular, a kind of Greek chorus intoning the mood of events. Welch thematized the episode tragically, in light of the irreversible damage frivolously inflicted upon another. But more than this, he was able to make Fred Fisher a kind of metonym for all the labeled victims needlessly damaged by McCarthy's unscrupulous conduct. Finally, as a classic ad hominem argument, this discourse framed and underlined McCarthy's own conduct with a lethal and irrefutable coherence. Indeed, McCarthy's lack of remorse or even recognition of his culpability was used against him. Asking Cohn whether he, Welch, had harmed him was a further ingenious move on Welch's part. For Cohn also had something to worry about (his relationship to Mr. Schine). Nevertheless, Welch apologized, just to make the contrast clear.[53] Recklessness is utter disregard for the consequences of action for self and others. Cruelty adds to this a willful pleasure in the damage done. Repeated three times and punctuated by McCarthy's own lack of recognition, the lethal equation works like this:

Cruelty + recklessness × persistence = "Have you no sense of decency, sir, at long last?"

In a sense, Welch had also reinvented *and captioned* McCarthy the demagogue and presented him to others. Of course, he could not have done this without McCarthy's assistance.

I have dwelt at some length on this rhetorical episode to underline the contrast between a dialectical and a rhetorical approach to multiple particularities, or the plurality of worlds. There is a sense, of course, in which my choice of examples already presupposes contrasting analytic frames. But with both Welch versus McCarthy and Lukács, there is a heightened intensity of struggle, as well as genuine uncertainty about what the future might hold. In both cases, moreover, the meaning and implication of phainomena are highly ambiguous, to say the least. One suspects too that the very criteria that Lukács introduced to validate action could have been applied retrospectively to Welch's conduct (just as, conversely, Lukács could be judged and evaluated as a rhetorician). Yet, despite all these parallels, there is a clear contrast between the dialectical and the rhetorical approach. Instead of an expectation of action which validates its own relationship to an emerging totality, there is in the practice of rhetoric an invitation to struggle over the provisional meaning of appearances. Even as the demagoguery of McCarthy attempts to preclude effective response, it demands some sort of rejoinder. If the moment belongs to Welch, it is made possible only by a sense of participatory contest over uncertain but urgent particulars. In this case the operative mood is not necessity, but contingency. I have not traced every feature of our developing vocabulary of appearances; but perhaps I have said enough to show how qualities of unfinished particularity may be engaged through rhetorical definition. Having been defined with sufficient clarity, some rhetorical questions, when finally given voice, have already been answered.

CONCLUSIONS

This essay began with the idea that there is not one way, but rather a multitude of approaches to both methods and objects of inquiry, and that a failure to understand this is what led to the false sense of collusion between Aristotle's organon and the Enlightenment project of "First Philosophy."[54] After all, if the only way to answer our questions of inquiry were to yield analytic "simples" or large dialectical "wholes," then the legacy of the human sciences seems to be the rush to technical reason and the scandalous absorption in the human subject. This same false sense of collusion has also led to a misreading of rhetoric itself. In this misreading, rhetoric is the residue of failed philosophy, with the lesson that what we have become—through some uncharted diagnostic—is all that we might be. My own reading is rather different. It assumes that although we may be forced to be pluralists by necessity, there is no reason why we could not choose to be rhetoricians by design. I have searched Aristotle's organon for characteristic differences in the ways in which plural objects of inquiry are framed and constituted by the methods addressing them. Rhetoric may be included among these methods because, it *has* been argued, an opening for just such a method is created by the organon of Aristotle's basic works. What follows are some tentative conclusions.

First, it should be apparent that rhetoric is not some historical curiosity, originating in primitive civilizations or privileged social formations.[55] Neither is it a sophistical discourse of power. Based on our examination of questions in the *Analytica*, rhetoric is necessarily implicated by the available forms and subjects of inquiry. It is implied by the limit conditions for demonstrative analytic and totalizing dialectic. Apart from rhetoric, there is literally no systematic way of exploring particular, probable issues of choice and avoidance. In addition, dialectic and rhetoric are seen to imply one another. There is surely no logical reason why Aristotle would move directly from the *Topica* to *De Sophisticis Elenchis* without developing the art designed to sophisticate reason about particulars—namely, rhetoric.

Second, rhetoric is implicated in what we might term the modern crisis of dialectic. This is not necessarily a happy implication. Although there is a tendency throughout the founding vocabulary of dialectic to dissolve individual difference in general likeness and to move away from direct participation in worldly appearance, it is only in Enlightenment and post-Enlightenment dialectic that we detect a kind of temporal paralysis and exclusion of rhetoric. Dialectic may imply the possibility of rhetoric in theory; but in actual outcome it may preclude rhetorical practice. In our analyses of Lukács and Joseph Welch, the problem emerges clearly.

There is no question but that dialectic and rhetoric approach the plurality of worldly particulars differently, in accordance with their traditions. But dialectics of modernity, however sweeping in compass, seem unable to preserve a space for meaningful practical conduct unless they allow some cognitive possibility for rhetoric. This is not only because dialectic does not, in and of itself, offer a paradigm of meaningful practical conduct; it is also because rhetoric's own cognitivity is necessarily implicated in the practical directive consciousness of others. Rhetoric is the only art which creates meaningful public thought and action. When dialectic closes the circle of practical action by alleging that all reasoned thought is in the service of power or reification, it necessarily reduces rhetoric to false consciousness, and the materials of rhetoric and public life are devoured by critique. By materials, of course, we mean phainomena.

Third, neither rhetoric nor dialectic can do without the concept and elusive practices of reason. It is undoubtedly true that we have defined reason too monologically and too narrowly in the past. As social actors, we have been too ready to abandon the search for reason in the positions of others. Nevertheless, we cannot do without its regulative force and constitutive meaning, which guide our sense of implication. In my view, much of the misreading of both rhetoric and pluralism derives from fairly basic category mistakes with regard to the meaning and force of reason. Construed dialogically, reason admits to at least three distinct renderings:

(1) As technē, a methodological art of reflective inquiry and analysis. This is its central use in the organon and throughout the *Rhetoric*. It is a search for coherence and justification in thought and action. Those who practice reason as a technē enter into a community of thought in which claims are attended to, taken seriously, and critiqued.

(2) As a grammar of self-understanding, as in the view that the human being is a reasoning animal. So construed, reason is an essence which characterizes persons for themselves. It is part of a systematic vocabulary for explaining what it means to be human.

(3) As a product—that is to say, an outcome of human creative energies. This is the confounding sense of reason. Once we have the historical invention of the history of ideas, we can reflect back on how the reasons we produce intersect and inhabit our social formations. Reason may now be treated as rationalization, a manner of reproducing itself, an appearance. This is a devious sense of reason, because it allows for the collapse of technē and grammar into the surface condition of *thing*—a kind of reductio to reification. This is also why and how the radical misreading of both rhetoric and pluralism became possible. If we are to avoid further lethal reductions of our virtues and "goods," it is necessary that rhetoric maintain an ongoing affiliation with the more richly textured sense of reason as art and grammar. This is also because:

Fourth, the moral weight of appearances is not automatic. Although certain configurations—concentration camp victims or children being crushed by tanks—may seem to present compelling moral "messages" directly on their own, it is more likely the case that captions have already been formed through highly refined, but unspoken, cultural conventions. In general, it can be said that configurations of appearance require the dialogic test of participation and reciprocity, civic friendship, affiliative agency, solidarity, regard, even hope, in order to form and adjudicate articulate messages. This is also, of course, a traditional argument for the open forum implied by pluralism. Rhetoric in the Aristotelian vein presupposes certain guiding principles for the proper anticipation of, and participation within, appearances. These principles concern competence, performance, coherence, and distance. They are relational values, or "goods," characteristic of the traditional practice of rhetoric.

We turn our attention now to the archaic origin of these goods, not so as to mystify them or nostalgically bemoan their absence, but so that we may better appreciate the prospect for their recovery and cultivation in our own time. In due course, we will consider Aristotle's imposing vision for an ethic and an aesthetic of rhetoric as an activity that is ethically significant and a practice that is an art.

2

Rhetorical Reflection:
Toward an Ethic
of Practical Reason

When a sieve is shaken, the refuse appears;
so do a person's faults when he speaks.
The kiln tests the potter's vessels;
so the test of a person is in his conversation.
Its fruit discloses the cultivation of a tree;
so a person's speech discloses the cultivation of his mind.
Do not praise anyone before he speaks,
for this is the way people are tested.

—Sirach, 27: 4–7

Even earlier in the twentieth century, the public agenda seemed lost or abandoned. In an atmosphere of crisis, civic institutions could only repeat empty symbolic reassurances. The symbols were in fact empty, because there appeared to be no learned experience except failure for them to rest on. Resignation, cynicism, and hopelessness had become the order of the day. In the midst of this material and symbolic dispossession it seems almost fanciful to imagine a creative ethical option for speech. Around the world oratory flourished; but it was hardly the sort to revive hopes for participatory democracy. Imagine now a public figure, a man paralyzed from the waist down—an aristocrat, no less—surveying this same bleak landscape and somehow grasping its inventional possibilities: through speech, a political praxis for recovery, reform, and eventual empowerment. Imagine that.

With this chapter, we begin a serious exploration of the classical Greek tradition as a basis for understanding the roots of rhetoric as an ethically significant human practice. Our impetus for this exploration is modern: the conflict between partialist and impartialist ethical theories in our own time. But in the fragmentary texts of this tradition we find clear precursors of our sense of displacement and lost foundations.

Before there was any discussion of "cultural incommensurability," there was the conflict of two spheres in fifth-century Greece: *nomos*, the realm of culture and moral truth, and *physis*, the realm of nature and reality.[1] For centuries, Greek philosophers and statesmen had never doubted that the norms and customs of nomos were true, by nature. In other words, these two realms were seen to be one and the same. But all this began to change with the increase of contact, sometimes violent, among Greek cities and with other cultures. It also coincided with a decline in the power of *mythos* and the rise of a skeptical humanism that many of us find quite familiar. To the extent that the realms of nomos and physis are seen to be one and the same, the members of a culture are able to trust in a moral order that is not in question. But this trust is in direct proportion to a foreclosure of cultural alternatives. When these realms begin to separate, this raises the question not only of whether virtue may be taught, but also of whether the teaching possesses any binding power in the face of reflection.[2] The attempt to theorize rhetoric developed in response to concerns such as these, and so did rhetoric's ethically significant relational goods. Yet then, as now, the underlying issue for any purportedly *ethical* reading of Aristotelian rhetoric is whether we can distinguish between a culture of practical reason and a prophetic understanding of political ideology: a vision of the "right" ultimately reducible to the might of its authors.[3]

There is a disturbing modern corollary to this ancient separation of natural and cultural spheres. It lies in the search for a kind of Archimedean fixed point, or impartialist stance, to ground or erase uncertainty. Anything less than such a standpoint weakens the authority of judgments; a slippery slope winds downward to ethical relativism and political chaos. Then too, the argument goes, an absence of impartiality all too readily spells neglect for the strangers among us, those who challenge or disturb our familiar conventions. The impartialist view certainly has its attractions. If it were open to us, I suspect that most of us would want the foundations of moral discourse to be as firm and unassailable as possible.

But what we *want* is curiously irrelevant to the impartialist position. It would be fatal to the argument to find it merely confirming already fervently held intuitions. The aim of this position, I suspect, is to erase the boundaries between nomos and physis, to find a perspective so neutral that truths (moral and physical) follow *naturally*. One wonders what *virtue* would mean in such a system. Would we teach it or simply demonstrate it? The fact that, after two millennia, we might still wonder about these things suggests that there is usually good reason for questioning any proclamation of neutrality.

And once neutrality is debunked, what have we? There is a broad range of partiality, stretching from Nietzsche to the conservative Aristotelian. It is, after all, the classical Aristotelian who longs for solidarity, defers to the local, valorizes friends and family, and is convinced that strangers are barbarians. This is a caricature, but a recognizable one.[4] Not to be outdone, the Aristotelian of all political persuasions might reply that specific circumstances and particular argumentative conditions are prior to all moral judgment. Thomas Nagel and Bernard Williams have introduced the concept of "moral luck" to show that the very capacity to proclaim and endorse ethical imperatives depends on favorable states of affairs, states that are much more fragile and fortuitous than the position itself would suggest.[5] Martha Nussbaum suggests that this development is not something peculiar to irrational modernity, but rather is a characteristic of moral discourse generally. Such discourse, as the greatest of classical drama reminds us, is fraught with the tragedy that we can sometimes abide one universalizable norm only by violating another which is incommensurable.[6] And Peter Winch has forcefully stated what this might mean for the impartialist position on moral reasoning: "Spinoza maintained (in my opinion with some justice) that 'knowledge of good and evil,' maintained in a purely general way, is a confused form of awareness. In his view I can attain clarity only through a sharpening of my perception of the particular circumstances which characterize my individual presence in the world, a sharpening of perception which is at the same time a purification of my practical involvement."[7]

But if this be virtue, how may it be taught, other than by culturally equipping the already well endowed? And, in fact, this was frequently the way of rhetorical pedagogy. Winch and the particularists do not have the last word in this dispute. Indeed, there is a core misconception at the root of these issues. But what should be apparent, by now, is that rhetoric—in its most traditional of vocabularies, at least—is biased in the direction of the particular. This is what allows its operation to claim continuing ethical relevance (and controversy). It is also what makes its claims to theoretical generality and rigor dubious. I should also say that I share what I take to be the Aristotelian rhetorical tradition's predilection for building *toward* the general, rather than *from* the general—at least in ethical matters. This predilection may seem more intuitively obvious in the case of rhetoric than in Aristotelian ethics, where—until recently—Platonic understandings have prevailed.[8] However, we can be grateful to Martha Nussbaum for underscoring, in *The Fragility of Good-*

ness and her collection, *Love's Knowledge,* the priority of the particular for Aristotelian thought:

> The particular is constituted out of features both repeatable and nonrepeatable; it is outlined by the structure of general terms, and it also contains the unique images of those we love. The general is dark, uncommunicative, if it is not realized in a concrete image; but a concrete image or description would be inarticulate, in fact mad, if it contained no general terms. The particular is prior for the reasons and in the ways we have said; there are relevant nonrepeatable properties; there is some revisability. In the end the general is only as good as its role in the correct articulation of the concrete. But particular human contexts are never, if seen well, sui generis in all of their elements, nor divorced from a past full of obligations. And fidelity to those, as a mark of humanity, is one of the most essential values of perception.[9]

In pursuing this domain of particularity within the *Rhetoric,* I do not intend to answer all indictments of the partiality position on ethics. But at least as far as one such objection is concerned—the so-called favoritism for the local as implying a neglect of the *other*—I hope to demonstrate that this charge is fundamentally wrong-headed in the case of rhetoric.

ORIGINS OF RHETORICAL TRADITION

The prevailing ethical interpretations of Aristotelian rhetoric are usually rooted in Aristotle's other great works on the subject—the *Nicomachean Ethics* and the *Eudemian Ethics*—as well as the imposing ethical indictments of rhetoric offered by Aristotle's teacher. To be sure, these interpretative horizons are important, as Aristotle himself made clear. But in light of the aforementioned dispute about moral discourse generally, it is helpful to point to two important markers in the development of rhetoric as a practice that might account for itself: the Sophist, Protagoras, and the finest Athenian teacher of rhetoric, Isocrates. It is my contention that Aristotle could not have discovered and formed the principles of rhetoric as a theory until rhetoric had reached a certain level of development as a practice. And while it is undeniably the case that rhetoric's golden age had passed by the time Aristotle formulated his theory (this is clear from both Aristotle and the history of his contemporaries), a richly textured vocabulary had begun to take shape in Greece about rhetorical practice, its cultural meaning and value.[10]

Protagoras' Great Speech

As with most of the Sophists, what we have of Protagoras consists largely of fragments. There is his notorious secular humanist pronouncement, usually translated "Man is the measure of all things." We also have evidence of his powerful oratorical style, said to have held listeners spellbound. Perhaps most immediately to the point, Protagoras is usually credited—if that is the right word—with being the first of the Sophists to purport to offer wisdom for money. He thus serves as a most conspicuous dramatic foil to Socrates in one of Plato's greatest and most challenging dialogues, the *Protagoras*. It is perhaps ironic that a work of Plato should give us our most extensive textual embodiment of this Sophist. But while it is highly unlikely that the surviving language represents Protagoras's actual words, we can be assured that this is no mere straw man for Socrates as protagonist. As Guthrie observed, "When Plato puts into his mouth a speech on that topic, he has substantially reproduced Protagoras' own views, most probably as given in the work so named."[11]

So let us recapture the situation. Socrates, in that irritating way of his, has challenged Protagoras to defend the proposition that virtue can be taught and, more generally, to defend his profession. The connection between the two is straightforward. Should Protagoras fail to rise to the occasion, his own claims to teach wisdom are in jeopardy. What follows is usually referred to as "Protagoras' Great Speech."[12] Let us see why.

Protagoras begins in a rather cavalier manner by asking those assembled whether they would prefer a myth or an argumentative speech to illustrate his proposition. He settles on a myth, for its congeniality as an opening gambit. The myth is the story of Prometheus; and in Protagoras's rendering, we find something of the ancient Greeks' conception of an "original condition." It seems that in distributing various gifts and talents to the creatures of the earth, Epimetheus gave something of value to everything except the human creature. Hindsight being twenty-twenty, Prometheus stole from the gods cunning and fire and gave these to humankind: "And then soon, by his skill, he began to speak and to use words; he invented dwellings and clothing and shoes, coverings for the night and nourishment from the earth" (322b). But this was clearly not enough. For persons were scattered at the beginning, unable to cope with other creatures or with one another. They did not know how to gather together or avoid injuring each other, for they did not have *statecraft*.

So it was that Zeus sent Hermes to distribute *dikē* and *aidōs*—the senses of justice and shame—to allow for the possibility of deliberation. Moreover, when Hermes, who is surely the god of rhetoric, asked Zeus whether these qualities were to be distributed to some persons as specialties or to all, Zeus replied "Among all . . . and . . . let all have them in common. For there could be no cities if but a few had them, as it is with the other skills" (322d). This is the reason, Protagoras maintains, why deliberation in Athens naturally takes into account the views of all. Because everyone has the capacity for political excellence, all may be habituated in the life of public virtue.

The myth, of course, is an allegory for the more elaborate arguments of Protagoras. But although few in attendance would have been likely to grant this tale a literal truth, the recourse to figurative origins brilliantly attenuates the Socratic search for further reflective grounding. Protagoras effectively blurs the split between nomos and physis by suggesting that our very existence as humans is driven by an inclination toward justice and public virtue, even as this inclination may be realized only through a life in *common*. The arguments for his position are ingenious.

First, Protagoras contrasts political virtue's generality with the virtue of other, more specialized talents. To claim to be a gifted flute-player, for instance, when one is not would be foolish; but for a public person to acknowledge in all truthfulness that his character is lacking in civic virtue would be the height of absurdity. Why is false pretension to special gifts evidence of foolishness, but pretension to political excellence a necessity? The answer can only be that one can be deficient in musicianship without serious loss to one's humanity, but that "no one can fail to have at least some share of justice, or he would not be human" (323b). Put another way, to be deficient in civic virtue is *our own failing* precisely because it is *within our own capacity*.

On the question of training, Protagoras has another interesting contrast to offer. If political virtue were purely the outcome of capricious fortune, why should the absence of good character provoke anger and blame? By counterexample: "Who, for example, would be so foolish as to attempt any such thing with the ugly or small or puny? For men know, I think, that such things as beauty and its opposite are due either to birth or to chance" (323d). Where political excellence is concerned, people grow angry at each other's failings. Why? "It is clear that they do so in the belief that this is an excellence which can be acquired by practice and instruction" (324b). This, by the way, is why we punish those who have committed wrongs; not only because we believe that they were capable of doing otherwise, but also because we believe that the guilty may still be trained, through deterrence, to avoid bad conduct in future.

Protagoras offers his position as a postulate of democracy: "That it is quite natural for your fellow-citizens to recognize both smith and cobbler as competent to give advice on political questions" (324c). He is also able to explain why natural talents can not be passed from one generation to another, unlike political excellence. Once more, the difference is instruction: "As soon as the infant can understand what is said to it, nurse, mother, tutor and father himself vie with each other to ensure that the child will develop the best possible character, so that, whatever it does or says, they instruct it, pointing out that 'this is just, that is unjust; this is *fine*, that is *base*" (325d). Who is the person who is expert in this teaching? Protagoras's answer to this challenge resonates with a self-criticism worthy of Plato himself: "As it is, you are spoiled, Socrates: because each and every man teaches excellence as well as he is able, you think that no one does. Yet no more would you find one man who teaches people to speak their native Greek, if you were to look for one" (328a). Analogous to our individual acquisition of articulate thought is our immersion in a culture wherein the goods of public life are made recognizable and available for us in word and deed. For Protagoras, all this is proof of the proposition that virtue can be taught.

Protagoras' Great Speech is not without its problems. For one thing, teaching and training are construed so broadly as to encompass virtually the whole of culture in public and private life. Then there is the problem for the Sophist of professing as a talent and skill what everyone in fact does. Socrates makes much of this. But what is expressed memorably here is the sentiment that all our public practices presuppose that we are capable of acquiring recognizable notions of political virtue and acting on them. Embedded in our practices just as surely as we are wedded to our native tongue, our civic and rhetorical conduct is unavoidably ethical in its *significance*.

Isocrates' Antidosis

Despite the professions of the Sophists that they were capable of teaching wisdom and virtue, the greatest rhetorical teacher of the Greek tradition was a native of Athens who was wary of these grandiose Sophistical claims. Isocrates seems to have aroused the ire of philosophers and Sophists alike, although Plato managed to find a few kind words for him toward the end of the *Phaedrus*. Even historical biographer H. I. Marrou finds it difficult to offer much that is positive, writing of him that "in every possible respect—in power of attraction, radiance of personality, variety of temperament, depth of thought or in art itself—Isocrates is not in the same street as Plato: his work seems flat and monotonous, his influence superficial and even pernicious."[13]

If there is a grain of truth in this very French view, it raises the question of why we should devote even minimal attention to one so removed from the mainstream of classical philosophical issues. Yet Isocrates has his own unique and quite visionary contribution to make to our sense of an ethically significant rhetorical practice. Although possessed of a subtle and complex intelligence, he refused to engage in what he regarded as the hair-splitting, pedantic dialectics of his day. He is perhaps most renowned for his pronouncements on the centrality of speech itself to all we are in cultural life:

> Because there has been implanted in us the power to persuade each other and to make clear to each other what we desire, not only have we escaped the life of wild beasts, but we have come together and founded cities and made laws and invented arts; and, generally speaking, there is no institution devised by man which the power of speech has not helped us to establish. For this it is which has laid down laws concerning things just and unjust, and things honorable and base; and if it were not for these ordinances we should not be able to live with one another.[14]

Isocrates' pan-Hellenic optimism allowed him simply to sidestep the disjunction of nomos and physis in Athens. Since speech was formative of all institutional and cultural reality, there was no point in trying to step *outside* speech in order to justify its products and claims. Isocrates taught his students largely through his own elaborate rhetorical examples; and what he taught them was that great, ennobling themes bring quality to discourse as well as virtue to orator and culture alike.

It is a sturdy, enduring position, well suited to the developing rhetorical practice in Greece's golden age. But in one of his most fascinating teaching documents, the *Antidosis*, Isocrates finds this position sorely tested. Ostensively written as a document of self-defense in response to a court challenge and decision against him, he sets about reviewing and attempting to vindicate his reputation and his teaching of philosophy before what he construes to be a largely unsympathetic audience.

The problem is straightforward. Great and noble themes and lifelong dedication to the formative art of rhetoric have apparently not been enough in Isocrates' own case. Moreover, a succession of tyrants and abusive policies have left Athens far removed from Isocrates' transcultural ideal. In a situation more than vaguely reminiscent of our own, the problem is how to *use* rhetoric to help revitalize its significance as an ethical practice. The *Antidosis* is replete with procedural strategems and tactical reversals. At one point, Isocrates resolves to take no credit for the noble citizen-orators he has educated and all the blame for any who have fallen short. Yet, unmistakably, his faith in the integrity of this civic culture has waned; for "no one may rely on the honesty of his life as a guarantee that he will be able to live securely in Athens; for the men who have chosen to neglect what is their own and to plot against what belongs to others do not keep their hands off citizens who live soberly and bring before you only those who do evil; on the contrary, they advertise their powers in their attacks upon men who are entirely innocent and so get more money from those who are clearly guilty" (21–25). Whether or not this is an accurate portrait of his immediate situation, it certainly poses problems for one's choice of speech and audience.

Isocrates elects to address those remaining honest persons in Athens, those who have not been corrupted by the "sycophants" who seem to be everywhere. It is to these honorable exceptions, those for whom there is still hope, that Isocrates presents his most compelling defense of rhetoric as an ethical practice. He begins with a deceptively simple observation, which we might take as his own gloss on the nomos–physis problem: "My view of this question is, as it happens, very simple. For since it is not in the nature of man to attain a science by the possession of which we can know positively what we should do or what we should say, in the next resort I hold that man to be wise who is able by his powers of conjecture to arrive generally at the best course" (268–72). In this humbler vision, the Good is not implanted in our souls as some prior truth; nor is it forever removed from our ordinary lives. Rather, it is approximated most of the time in our ongoing attempts to do the best we can with what we have.

And what arts best equip us for this most human of efforts? Isocrates hesitates to tell us, for he is sure that we will not believe him. Carefully distinguishing his view from that of the Sophists, he writes: "I consider that the kind of art which can implant honesty and justice in depraved natures has never existed and does not now exist, and that people who profess that power will grow weary and cease from their vain pretensions before such an education is ever found" (272–76). In other words, virtue can never be arrived at as some intended content of a pedagogical practice. "But I do hold that people can become better and worthier if they conceive an ambition to speak well, if they become possessed of the desire to be able to persuade their hearers, and, finally, if they set their hearts on seizing the advantage—I do not mean 'advantage' in the sense given to that word by the empty-minded, but advantage in the true meaning of that term" (275). As he proceeds to elaborate on the virtues deriving from the rhetorical arts, it becomes quite clear that these qualities are not intentional *objects* of the enterprise, but rather *by-products* of an acquired rhetorical competence. They are, in other words, goods of a practice.[15]

His argument on behalf of these rhetorical goods is carefully measured and compelling. To speak or write discourses that are worthy of praise and honor, for Isocrates, literally requires that we support causes "which are great and honorable, devoted to the welfare of man and our common good" (276–77). Anything less, he makes quite clear, will yield only perishable discourse. Moreover, the one preparing a discourse, in selecting edifying examples and noble actions and precedents, "will feel their influence not only in the preparation of a given discourse but in all the actions of his life" (278). Isocrates goes on to insist that *character* is the strongest source of persuasion "and that the argument which is made by a man's life is of more weight than that which is furnished by words" (279). In direct proportion to our desire to persuade, then, we find ourselves striving to be honorable in the eyes of those whom the community values. Finally, Isocrates wishes to argue, consistent with the entire tenor of his pedagogy, that true advantage comes not from the short-term edge one may gain in manipulating, or taking advantage of, one's fellows, but only to those who are righteous and faithful and "most conscientious in their dealings with their associates, whether in their homes or in public life" (282). That is, true advantage comes from taking one's craft seriously.

Isocrates thus describes a rhetorical practice which is fully integrated into the life of a civic-minded human being who tries to do the best he can in public life. In this pedagogical vision of rhetoric, he does not insist on virtue or the good as a precondition for a *true* rhetoric; nor does he undertake to teach us what the virtues are so that we may know them. Isocrates purports only to teach the practice of rhetoric, since it is foundational to what our noble cultural themes, our gods, and our governments are all about. In a way that neatly reverses the Aristotelian tradition, Isocrates treats ēthos not as a component of rhetorical argument, but as its unmistakable by-product. Learn the practice of justification through speech, he seems to be saying, and you will be justified. Master the practice of rhetoric, and virtue will follow.

We cannot know with any certainty how effective Isocrates' arguments were with his contemporaries. Moreover, while I personally find this justification of rhetorical practice convincing, it is surely not the way we usually conceptualize the area of persuasion today. Consistent with the position of Protagoras, we still blame one another for our moral shortcomings, and we are surely willing to punish our fellow citizens for their wrongdoings, however skeptical we may be as to the educational benefits of punishment. But the aggrandizing sentiments of Isocrates are likely to be most effective in a grand age, when the accomplishments of the logos are conspicuous and resplendent for all to see. In our less accomplished period, we might expect the observations of Protagoras and Isocrates, different as they are, to return ironically, in a blaming of rhetoric for the mean-spiritedness and short-sightedness of culture. This may be why, eloquent as they are, Isocrates' sentiments are no substitute for the philosophical justification of rhetoric as a practice.

Perhaps we can now appreciate that at one time the arts of public discourse were thought to be conducive to ennobling virtues of character and culture. The question is whether rhetorical practice might once again become instrumental in the cultivation of such goods; or, in language which both Isocrates and Protagoras would recognize, whether we can teach virtue to rhetoric.

ARISTOTELIAN RHETORICAL TRADITION: THE ETHICS OF A PRACTICE

By almost any standard of judgment, ancient or modern, Aristotle wrote *the* book on rhetoric.[16] I will be arguing throughout this study that Aristotle offers the first, and perhaps the only, philosophical justification for what rhetoric *must* be if it is to be a fully realized, artistically significant human practice. While this is no Sophistical appropriation of rhetoric, Aristotle presents his subject as material for instruction and even mastery. And while the expressed differences with Isocrates are pronounced, if not quite as significant as he claims, there is one abiding agreement: that the development and sophistication of rhetoric as a practice allows advocate and audience alike to develop important relational goods and virtues.

In this first reading of Aristotelian *rhetoric*, I will attempt to show how rhetoric moves from being an ethically significant form of activity to a *practice:* an activity with internal standards of excellence that, if achieved, yield conduct that is ethical.[17] In teaching us possibilities for practical reason in a community of multiple goods, virtues, and authorities, Aristotle's *Rhetoric* provides our first sustained exposure to the norms of rhetorical culture.

In an initial defense of rhetoric, Aristotle establishes a line of argument that moves from its ethical significance to its capacity for an ethical quality. Central to this position is the prominence of practical reason in the optimal conduct of rhetoric. Rhetoric as practical reason provides us with a manner of engaging the particularity of appearances. Specifically, it presents audiences with appearances as particular contingencies in which they share an interest. The argument for rhetoric's ethical propensity thus turns on the mutual regard that speakers and audiences must have for one another, given the simultaneous condition of being a witness to the construction of proof *and* an agent vulnerable to the partisanship of others. The preferred condition of audiences in this classical understanding of rhetoric is one of civic friendship, in which a partiality of regard is the better part of prudential reason.[18] Within this reciprocally manufactured rhetorical culture, it is possible to take seriously the interests and needs of what would otherwise be mere projections of self. As a practice, then, rhetoric possesses the agonistic tendencies of logos: to contend, contest, and thus perfect the mutual capacity of speaker and audience for responsible conduct. Rhetoric may thus be seen as the principal art responsible for the shape and coloration of public character.

RHETORIC AS DYNAMIS AND TECHNĒ

Perhaps the most basic question confronting rhetoric, in light of its uncertain status in Greek culture, was whether systematic investigation of its practice and operation was even possible. Recalling the futility of Sophistical claims, as well as Isocrates' well-known reluctance to theorize, Aristotle's opening rationale for systematic rhetorical inquiry requires careful scrutiny. Following the remarkable pronouncement that rhetoric is the counterpart of dialectic,[19] Aristotle explains that both are methods dealing with what people in general know and do. But how so? Is it because we are gifted with these talents, subject to their facility, trained in their craft? Note the way Aristotle puts our uncertainty to his own uses: "Ordinary people do this either at random or through practice and from acquired habit. Both ways being possible, the subject can plainly be handled systematically, for it is possible to inquire the reason why some speakers succeed through practice and others spontaneously; and everyone will at once agree that such an inquiry is the function of an art" (Rhetoric 1354a).[20] In refusing to take sides regarding whether nature or training is the ultimate source of rhetorical excellence, Aristotle leaves the question open and calls for his own systematic inquiry. Further, he assures us that this will be a serious business, an epistēmē, a search for what is available to guide our judgment in practical matters.

What is not clear, and in fact has caused considerable confusion, is the meaning of art as Aristotle applies that notion to rhetoric. In his first full discussion of the status of rhetoric, Aristotle describes it as a technē: a body of rules that may be known and applied through the exercise of reason. This introductory statement (reminiscent of Aristotle's defense of ethics in the Eudemian Ethics [1216b5–25])[21] conceals its confusions nicely. But, several passages later, when Aristotle attempts to define rhetoric, he describes it as "the ability in each case to see the available means of persuasion" (Rhetoric 1355a, 25–30). Here what was previously regarded as a technē is referred to as a dynamis, a potential for doing, a power in its nascent state.

Attempts to reconcile these apparently conflicting conceptions have caused no end of difficulties for Aristotle's interpreters, ancient and modern. Typically, those who wish to emphasize the integrity of rhetorical theory stress the importance of rhetoric as dynamis, whereas those who regard rhetoric as the ongoing technique of influencing others stress technē. But the latter view does not hold up very well, for many reasons. For one thing, the equation of technē with technique simply does not work. The very idea of a form of conduct admitting to the ordered supervision of a technē is no small claim. Ethics, for instance, is not treated as a technē by Aristotle.[22] So it is significant that Aristotle allows deliberation a measure of system and rigor that ethics cannot hope to achieve. All this suggests that the very idea of rigor *through* technē is what opens up the possibility of a rhetorical theory in the first place.

But there are other problems. Rhetoric as a faculty or a potential alone would be unteachable, analogous perhaps to the gift or natural power which some orators mysteriously possess. On the other hand, rhetoric as only technē, without any recognition of its potential and power, could easily degenerate into a logistical code for those with easy access to others. This is what the less scrupulous of the Sophists were accused of offering their students. A sense of dynamis preserves rhetoric's capacity for critical reflection. In this light, it is interesting that, recently, some philosophers have sought to retain the concrete emphasis of technē while attempting to magnify the cognitive importance of the contents of persuasion. Witness Paul Ricoeur on the status of rhetoric as technē:

> Rhetoric's status as a distinct technē poses no great difficulties. Aristotle was careful to define what he calls technē in a classical text of his *Ethics*. There are as many different technai as there are creative activities. A technē is something more refined than a routine or an empirical practice and in spite of its focus on production, it contains a speculative element, namely a theoretical enquiry into the means applied to production. It is a method; and this feature brings it closer to theoretical knowledge than to routine. The idea that there is a technique for producing discourse can lead to the sort of taxonomical project that we will consider in the next study. Now, is not such a project the ultimate stage in the technicization of discourse? Without doubt this is so; however, in Aristotle, the autonomy of technē is less important than its linkage with other disciplines of discourse, especially that of proof.[23]

Ricoeur provides us with a fascinating, albeit skewed, depiction of rhetoric as a *practice* in this passage. Yet he is undeniably equivocal as to the origins and destiny of this so-called speculative element. It is difficult to see how one and the same feature can raise technē above the routinization of technique while at the same time representing an ultimate stage in the technologizing of discourse. Presupposing the degeneration of technē in his very explanation of the concept, Ricoeur's treatment must also be presupposing a further reflective dimension that identifies the qualitative features and norms of a practice even as these same features and norms may find themselves neglected. More than simply a

technique or a colorless method for moving others, rhetoric as technē is
an art that must itself be produced, moved into actual existence.

Rhetoric, within the justificatory context of book 1, retains the concrete emphasis of technē while attempting to include the reflective capacity to identify the possible materials of rhetoric in real settings. The
passage in question is the aforementioned 54a11, in which Aristotle is
about to define the art of rhetoric. Grimaldi notes:

> At the same time he will shortly speak of rhetoric as *dynamis*
> (55b25), and this particular aspect of rhetoric plays a prominent role
> in the treatise. What, then, is the relationship between *technē* and
> *dynamis* when used of rhetoric? Rhetoric considered objectively, or
> in itself, is a system of rules of principles derived from experience
> (cf. *An. Post.* 100a6–9). These rules constitute the *technē*, the art of
> rhetoric as it can be known by the mind. Furthermore, still looking
> at rhetoric objectively, if we take the relatively simple definition of
> *dynamis* as 'that which so contains everything necessary to a thing
> that it can come into existence' (Trendelenberg, *Elementa*, p. 44),
> then there is a way in which all these principles and rules also con-
> stitute rhetoric as *dynamis*. For they represent all that is necessary
> for rhetoric to exist. When the principles are set into motion by
> actualization (*energeia:* 'that which brings the necessary things into
> existence,' ibid.) rhetoric ceases to be a *dynamis* and exists in fact.[24]

This intricate discussion is critical to the status of rhetoric because, as
Grimaldi suggests, rhetoric is not just a complex of techniques, or even
a set of practices to be assembled and coded. In a brilliant synthesis of
the prevailing pedagogical stances on rhetoric (the gift of nature versus
the acquired skill), Aristotle presents his practice as a powerful capacity
(dynamis) that must be defined in thought before it can be enacted and
enacted in order to exist. It is not only that the rhetorician studies what
is a capacity of human nature—that is, the direction of human agency
through discourse—but that this systematic study, this technē, is also a
potential that must be prodded or coaxed into existence in order to be
realized.

The question is *how*? How are we to find and develop the capacities
that warrant and establish rhetorical study? There may be an exemplar
in the way in which Aristotle proceeds when dealing with rhetoric's
methodological counterpart. Here he is discussing dialectical method:
"We shall be in perfect possession of the way to proceed when we are in

a position like that which we occupy in regard to rhetoric and medicine and faculties of that kind: this means the doing of that which we choose with the materials that are available" (*Topica* 101b5–10).

Throughout Grimaldi's reading of the *Rhetoric*, the capacity for bringing the rhetorical into existence is found in a developing knowledge of what might be recombined within the speaker, the subject matter, and especially the audience to achieve desired goals:

> But the correct exercise of either *dynamis* demands a knowledge (*epistēmē*) of the body of principles proper to each *technē*. Rhetoric viewed subjectively or in the person, is the power to actualize the principles which reside in one who has mastered the system of rules and therefore possesses the knowledge (*epistēmē*) of rhetoric, and with it the requisite *dynamis*. When the person actualizes this *dynamis*, he exercises the *technē* of rhetoric. Rhetoric as a *dynamis* within a person is the possession of the rules and the principles which constitute the *technē* and which consequently endow the person with the capacity to see all the elements in a subject which can lead to the desired goal of the speaker.[25]

On Grimaldi's reading, Aristotle has brought together the practice of rhetoric, its "art," with the reflective imagination demanded by its most severe critics. The result is a justification of rhetoric rooted in its own modal status—that is, its possible and potential manner of existence—rather than its state-of-the-art quality of performance. This aspect of the argument is important for those tempted to invoke the degenerate state of current rhetorical practice to disparage the possibility of a contemporary rhetorical tradition. For once we accept the *possibility* of improvement that an art might bring, the unsatisfactory condition of actual practice only serves to dramatize the urgency for reform. Interestingly, Aristotle follows this account directly with a sustained diatribe against the horrible state of existing practice. Moreover, by equating his own stipulative sense of what rhetoric optimally is with the notion of potential (dynamis) as a powerful capacity for doing, he allows us to appreciate the dilemmas of any position that disjoins conceptions of logos from conceptions of power.[26] Aristotle offers a convincing argument that the reason embodied by language is one of the most important sources of power available to the human being. Given its theoretical ideal and its own mode of possibility, then, rhetoric possesses undeniable ethical significance. This is precisely because the actual state of its practice may vary.

This view of rhetoric as a practice with a reflective dimension may help shed additional light on the famous four-part justification of rhetoric. Often thought to be an incongruous bit of idealism in the midst of an otherwise Sophistical study of technique, each step toward justification may be viewed instead as arguing for a more cogent relationship between technique and the reflective ideal of good judgment. In step 1 (the tendency of truth and justice to prevail over their opposites), Aristotle attributes a natural power to truth and justice; yet he shrewdly reasons that the occasional failures of truth and justice to prevail must be found in our own deficiencies of technique (*Rhetoric* 1355a). This is a fascinating ambiguity, suggesting at once the existence of a truth and justice and at the same time a rhetorical complicity in their by no means certain success.

Step 2 helps to clarify this position by allowing that even knowledge in exact form will not be enough to persuade some audiences. We must employ topoi of common opinion with some audiences, even if we already have the knowledge to determine proper judgment. Step 3 is of particular interest in this light, for it includes Aristotle's famous appropriation of the *dissoi logoi*—arguments on the opposite sides of a question. This is typically regarded as a way of forming more proper, moderate judgments where matters are uncertain; but that is not what Aristotle exactly says. He says that we must not use rhetoric *in practice* to argue false conclusions, but "in order that we may see clearly what the facts are, and that, if another man argues unfairly, we on our part may be able to confute him" (ibid.). What this suggests is that the dissoi logoi are helpful even if we have already formed a proper judgment; for it is only by taking the opposite viewpoint that we are able to see what the facts themselves are.

Step 4 completes Aristotle's argument elegantly by bringing us from the power of truth and justice to the power of the logos itself. In an argument quite reminiscent of Protagoras on the indispensability of political excellence, Aristotle remarks that it is shameful to be unable to defend oneself through rational speech, more so than to be unable to defend oneself through physical prowess. Why? Because rational speech is more integral to our being human. As to the dangers thereof, Aristotle characterizes rhetoric in a way that makes its ethical significance transparent. He says: "And if it is argued that great harm can be done by unjustly

using such power of words, this objection applies to all good things except virtue, and most of all to the most useful" (1355b). Thus, the power
of the good (its dynamis) is brought together with the power of the logos,
so that the ethical significance of a practice may be made available to
civic life. This is a philosopher's vision of rhetorical practice.

AUDIENCE AS RHETORICAL AGENCY

Echoing the earlier sentiment of Plato, Aristotle allows that rhetoric is
not easy to practice; but the aim of rhetoric is a kind of discovery which
enables us to come as near to persuasion as the case allows. An appropriate, related question, however, is how shall we realize an optimal
practice of this art? As Aristotle envisioned the matter, rhetoric literally
could not come into existence without a certain type of hearer, what
we understand as the audience. This may be why Aristotle observes, at
the beginning of book 2: "But since rhetoric is concerned with making a
judgment (people judge what is said in deliberation, and judicial proceedings are also a judgment), it is necessary not only to look to the argument
that it be demonstrative and persuasive, but also to construct a view of
himself as a certain kind of person and to prepare the judge" (1377b21–
24).[27] Aristotle cautions that to pervert or manipulate the character of a
judge would be analogous to warping a carpenter's rule before using it;
this is how important reliable audience judgment is in the *Rhetoric*. As
Grimaldi notes, "He is quite aware, in other words, that one is always
speaking to a person, who is a complexus of reason, feelings, emotions,
and set attitudes."[28] Aristotle made the point directly: "A statement is
persuasive and credible either because it is directly self-evident or because it appears to be proved from other statements that are so. In either
case, it is persuasive because there is somebody whom it persuades"
(1356b25–28).

Our second claim, therefore, is that the potential of rhetoric is best
realized through a prescribed form of engagement with an audience as
an agency of the art. To clarify this position, we need only amend Aristotle's observation in the *Nicomachean Ethics:* "The origin of action—
its efficient, not its final cause—is choice, and that of choice is desire and
reasoning with a view to an end" (1139a30–32). From this reconstructed
perspective, it is the rhetorical audience (the "one who decides") that
functions as the efficient cause of the enactment of rhetoric as practical

art. Here too is an important difference from typical conceptions. More than a necessary inconvenience accompanying the institutional presence of discourse, the audience literally *decides* the fate of discourse. And in doing this well or badly, the Aristotelian audience becomes *decisive* to rhetoric itself.

In a quite subtle but persistent way, the whole emphasis of the *Rhetoric* is on the action and agency of others as an audience in the formation of character and the rendering of judgments. This is obvious enough in the most logocentric of Aristotle's devices—the enthymeme (to be discussed shortly). But this evocation of agency is present throughout the *Rhetoric*, in the markers for character, or ēthos, and in the often unstable territory of emotion, or pathos, as well.

Aristotle is emphatic that ēthos is more than an intrinsic character trait of the speaker. As he repeatedly insists, it is the character of the speaker as presented or made manifest by the speech. Over and against the depersonalized contemporary notion of reproducing "the body" through discourse and the introverted notion of the self that this notion seeks to replace, Aristotle gives us something that is still recognizable as a delineation of the *public person.* Moreover, while he acknowledges, along with Isocrates, that personal character is often the strongest source of persuasion, he clearly regards ēthos as a mode of proof, rather than just an impressionistic aura of credibility and trust. And the components of ēthos quite obviously derive from the norms of competence, regard, and virtue held by his own culture. In chapter 1, we noted that the primary emphasis of Aristotle's treatment was the implication of an advocate's character for the public awareness and avowal of his advocacy. The ethics of Aristotelian rhetoric confirm one's public character through the conspicuous recognition and inferences of the audience.

To recall our earlier example, only when a sense of honor is available can honor itself be accorded. This may well be why we feel a sense of collective shame when we have placed our faith in a public figure who then misleads us, who is not what he or she appears to be. It is an embarrassment to have been taught "virtue" by a charlatan.

Now I turn to the difficult territory of pathos, or emotion. Again, conventional readings of Aristotle must be regarded with caution. Gadamer sees the discussion of pathos as trafficking in the excitation of emotions. Ricoeur sees it as the worst sort of manipulation of technique.[29] Indeed, the treatment of emotion raises serious questions about Aristotle's regard for the audience as an agency of judgment. Are we to tread lightly lest we warp the carpenter's rule while simultaneously sampling this glossary of pleasures and pains? Silvia Gastaldi echoes the prevailing view when she observes: "In his rhetorical treatise . . . Aristotle confines himself to a descriptive analysis of passions: ethical evaluation is completely lacking here."[30] I will argue that, to the contrary, Aristotle's treatment of the emotions is entirely consistent with his regard for the audience as an agency of logos and judgment. The rich vocabulary of pathos offered in book 2 of the *Rhetoric* could be applicable *only* to creatures capable of responsible moral choice. Moreover, Aristotle applies this vocabulary in a revolutionary way: to the public consciousness, the other as our own addressee.

Virtually any of the fourteen passions could be used to illustrate this point. I will take an example which allows us to depict the moral as well as the *inventional* power, or dynamis, of emotion as a mode of proof: the case of pity. In book 2, Aristotle says:

> Again, we feel pity when the danger is near ourselves. Also we pity those who are like us in age, character, disposition, social standing, or birth; for in all these cases it appears more likely that the same misfortune may befall us also. Here too we have to remember the general principle that what we fear for ourselves excites our pity when it happens to others. Further, since it is when the sufferings of others are close to us that they excite our pity (we cannot remember what disasters happened a hundred centuries hereafter and therefore feel little pity, if any, for such things). (1386a30–40)

Aristotle concludes this remarkable discussion by stating: "Most piteous of all is it when, in such times of trial, the victims are persons of noble character; whenever they are so, our pity is especially excited, because their innocence, as well as the setting of their misfortunes before our eyes, makes their misfortunes seem close to ourselves" (1385b). This is one of the passages that, arguably, are behind the repeated references to the *Rhetoric* when, in the *Poetics*, Aristotle attempts to explain the nature of tragic pleasure. It is also possible to detect that same partiality to those near and dear (in class, birth, age, and character) that has received strenuous criticism from the Kantian universalist position. But who can deny that there is something more important—even transformational—going on here as well? For it is rhetoric that removes us from the immediacy of familiar appearance, thereby allowing us to formulate conditions for appreciating the needs of others. So, "what we fear for ourselves excites our pity when it happens to others." How? Not quite a virtue, not exactly an individuated passion, pity becomes—through rhetoric—a form of proof.

Here rhetoric clearly does more than traffic in the "excitation of emotions," as Gadamer put it. More than simply a spontaneous awareness of what is happening to an *other*, there is a doubly reflexive move, from awareness of our own emotion (fear) to a recognition of what may be involved when it is others who are suffering. Here emotions are themselves relational, allowing the sense of recognition we require whenever we are taken outside our own immediacy: from the neighborhood to the moral community. It may also be apparent that we would not be able to make the move from fear for ourselves to pity for others *without* the intervention of rhetoric. Even in the greatest of tragedy, Aristotle counsels that rhetoric as the art of thought constitutes sympathetic awareness of the *other* as governed, like us, by fate, chance, and reversal. Without rhetoric's intervention, we would have only the partiality of immediate interest, the familiar locale. We would end where we started.

The larger portrait of audience offered by Aristotle's *Rhetoric*, then, is of an agency capable of character, of "social emotions." Despite Aristotle's absorption in particulars, this is clearly offered as more than an empirical observation; it is a normative construal of what an audience is *as a capacity*. The best—indeed, the only—contemporary depiction of this capacity that I can locate is that of Henry Johnstone as he attempts to explain the mode of reflection engendered by rhetorical address itself. He writes: "The wedge of rhetoric separates the person to whom a thesis is being addressed from that thesis itself; it puts him over against the thesis, causing him to attend to it as an explicit idea that he might previously have been unaware of because it figured only implicitly in his experience."[31] The only elaboration I can offer here is that this mode of reflexivity is entirely consistent with Aristotle's own normative construal of an audience. To really think *as an audience* cannot be a morally neutral activity. Aesthetically speaking, it may be to see people in assembly as better than they are, thereby allowing us to address what is best in them. Ethically speaking, it is to address them in such a way that they and we may become better than we were. Such an interpretation is entirely consistent with what we earlier called a "practice." But whatever the other merits of this reading, it should now inform our understanding of a less speculative issue: namely, the substance of rhetoric as practical reason.

RHETORIC AS PRACTICAL REASON

If the point of a practical art is actually to *do*, rather than to know, what is sought as an outcome, then what does rhetoric actually do? A frequent modern answer (usually accompanied by mild disdain) is that what rhetoric does is *persuade*. Ricoeur goes so far as to proclaim that Aristotelian rhetoric sealed its fate two thousand years before its alleged demise due to its "overburdening content—witness Book II of the *Rhetoric*, which abounds in what Kant would have called 'popular' psychology, 'popular' morality, 'popular' politics."[32] But this is a partial truth at best and inflated far beyond its weight. The invocation of Kant is as revealing as the apparent aversion to all that is popular. As Nussbaum points out in a perceptive rendering of exactly the same material, Aristotle is interested in a sense of the Good that is applicable to ordinary people, as well as to philosophers and kings. Moreover, he was sufficiently sensitive to the particular circumstances of good and bad fortune to realize that even kings require prudent awareness of these same particularities if their public character is to be judged worthy of respect and emulation.[33] In order to be competent in the arts of civic life, we need to know more than what an abstract good state might be. We must be aware of what the multiplicity of goods are as they appear to the character of our fellow citizens. To engage these ordinary convictions rhetorically is also to judge: to make the best anticipation of what the character of those assembled might become.

Although considerable attention has been devoted to the forms of argument and kinds of appeal prescribed by Aristotle's *Rhetoric*, we are still entitled to ask what is distinctive about the manner of making inferences introduced at this stage in the discussion. Although the evidence is inconclusive, some textual indicators suggest that practical reasoning is discussed and practiced throughout the *Rhetoric* in ways that are quite different from Aristotle's other treatments of the subject.

We should recall, first of all, that the quality marking excellence in practical reasoning is a kind of prudence or "moral sight" (phronēsis, or practical wisdom). Throughout the *Nicomachean Ethics*, this quality is treated as a virtue that is acquired by the particular citizen and then strengthened through the choices he makes. As Howard Gold writes: "Ethics-politics is in principle phenomenologically embedded, and cannot be explained unless reference is made to particular actions and their particular characters of realizing the good for a particular man."[34] Although Aristotle in the *Nicomachean Ethics* never tires of observing what men in general aim to accomplish, his region of application is always the individual person. Even in his model of practical reason, a revised version of the syllogism, he seems to be offering a variation of his own teleological framework for understanding the solitary actions of an intelligible human agent. As MacIntyre observes:

> Aristotle's account of practical reasoning . . . has a number of key features. The first is that Aristotle takes the conclusion of a syllogism to be a particular kind of action. . . . This account returns us to the question of the relationship between practical intelligence and the virtues. For the judgments which provide the agent's practical reasoning with premises will include judgments as to what is good for someone like him to do and to be; and an agent's capacity to make and to act upon such judgments will depend upon what intellectual and moral virtues and vices comprise his or her character. The precise nature of this connection could only be elucidated by a fuller account of practical reasoning than Aristotle gives us; his account is notably elliptical and in need of paraphrase and interpretation.[35]

But elliptical or not, Aristotle's account of practical reasoning is the fullest treatment we have from the Greek tradition. What may be in need of paraphrase and further interpretation is the connection between this reasoning process and the practice of rhetoric.

MacIntyre's interpretation of practical wisdom seems fair and balanced in light of Aristotle's notorious equivocations throughout the *Nicomachean Ethics* between individual excellence and culturally sanctioned virtues. But it raises the critical and not altogether unexpected question of why we need a separate art which treats deliberation as an identifiable discursive form and the audience as "one who decides." The answer must be that there is need, at times, to firm up and complete our own reasoning practice through the intervention of competent, interested others. Thus it is that rhetoric, as distinct from all other arts and modes of inquiry, implements practical reason through the complementary participation of someone else: namely, the rhetorical audience. Throughout the

Rhetoric, Aristotle characterizes the judge (as one who renders a verdict) as an agent capable of phronēsis. In discussing the ends of deliberative discourse, he observes: "It may be said that every man and all men in common aim at a certain end which determines what they choose and what they avoid. This end, to sum it up briefly, is happiness and its constituents" (1360b5–10). Earlier, this was the aim of individual action, *eudaimonia*. However, the point of rhetorical choice is to open the judgments of character to those who would judge. Where social virtues are concerned, it is others who must enact and thus complete the choices available.

Perhaps the most interesting—albeit speculative—evidence for the collective character of practical reasoning in rhetoric comes from Aristotle's treatment of the virtues. When Aristotle treats virtue as dynamis in the *Rhetoric*, rather than *hexis* or acquired disposition (the way he typically treats it in the *Politics* and the *Nicomachean Ethics*), he seems to confuse one and all. Grimaldi struggles with the passage thus: "This definition of virtue as *dynamis* disturbs both Spengel and Cope, who rightly point to passages in the *Nicomachean Ethics* (and specifically to 1106a4–12 and 1106b36–1107a2), which deny that virtue is a *dynamis* and assert that it is a *hexis*. But even if the statement in our passage were a careless mistake on Aristotle's part, it would hardly justify Cope's conclusion (pp. 159–160) that there is a vast difference of approach between the popular *Rhetoric* and the comparatively scientific *Ethics*."[36] In response, Grimaldi introduces numerous counterexamples that allow him to conclude that "the meaning of *dynamis* here is not so obviously contradictory as it has been assumed to be."[37] But if my own analysis makes at least intuitive sense, the meaning of dynamis is not what is really at issue. Rather, it is the status of virtues as relational goods for the *practice* of rhetoric. With regard to the single agent, who is so central in the *Nicomachean Ethics*, it would make perfect sense to regard virtue as a character trait strengthened by dispositions toward right action (or hexis). But consider the more expansive conception of practical reason which informs the rhetorical treatment of virtue:

> That is why forensic pleading and debating contests are pleasant to those who are accustomed to them and have the capacity for them. Honor and good repute are among the most pleasant things of all; they make a man see himself in the character of a fine fellow, especially when he is credited with it by people whom he thinks good

judges. His neighbors are better judges than people at a distance; his associates and fellow-countrymen are better than strangers; his contemporaries better than posterity; sensible persons better than foolish ones; a large number better than a small number. Honor and credit bestowed by those whom you think much inferior to yourself—e.g., children or animals—you do not value. (*Rhetoric* 1371a5–15)[38]

While there may be reason to quarrel with Aristotle's specific gradations of value, the passage is fascinating. In rhetoric, there are no qualities of character that may reasonably be cultivated by means of an individual's solitary action. To the modern mind-set, which is all but saturated with ideas of autonomy, this is a difficult concept to grasp. But for Aristotle, virtue construed rhetorically is a relational good, a good which confers good things through others; conversely, what is called virtuous must itself be "worthy of praise" by others. Note too the clear identification of these relational *others:* the kinship and friendship of peers in a community. It is clear from the above passage that not just any others will do. But whatever the accreditation of those who judge, the quality of value must be conferred on the individual, in a judgment which implicates the character of the judge. I suggest, then, that virtue in the *Rhetoric,* far from being a concept that is somehow confused or mistaken by Aristotle, is in its nascent state a dynamis, a powerful capacity awaiting propitious realization. How is it implemented? In the same way that deliberation is completed: through the adjudication of a reasoning, competent audience that confirms, qualifies, or denies the allegation of virtuous qualities on behalf of some other person, action, or project— thereby ensuring virtue's enactment for itself. This is why it may be said, without recourse to figurative language, that by judging we help to perform the virtues of public life. The account I am offering may also help to explain why Aristotle gives so many apparently incompatible characterizations of different virtuous qualities throughout the *Rhetoric,* while remaining adamant about the purpose of reasoned deliberation.[39] Each of the divergent characterizations of a given virtue might literally become real for the audience that must decide.

Further support for this interpretation may be found in Bitzer's important reading of Aristotle's enthymeme. Bitzer offers impressive evidence that the premises requested by the rhetorical advocate are notions of popular conviction already available to the rhetorical audience.[40] I have previously described a contemporary variation of these notions as *social knowledge*.[41] My only qualification of Bitzer's analysis is a suggestion that the convictions of the audience *about attributable qualities of virtue* (as dynamis) are not always fully formed as premises in advance of their enactment within an enthymeme. When they are indexed in time through the volition of common assent, the utterance gives them a new facticity. In this sense, Bitzer's single example of an enthymeme with an abstract conclusion—namely, "Let justice be done!"—is no longer abstract, once its conclusion is uttered.[42]

Finally there is the question of how virtues, here construed as qualities ascribed to, and eventually performed by, the *other*, might be viewed as both relational goods *and* goods that are internal to the practice of rhetoric. The short answer to this question is that rhetoric is a relational art. A more serious, comprehensive answer must await closer engagement with the purpose or dynamis of the art.

Contrary to its recurrent usage in the *Politics* and throughout the *Nicomachean Ethics*, practical reasoning in the *Rhetoric* does not function to prescribe or explain the conduct of persons as individual moral agents. Rather, through the direct participation of a suitably involved audience, this formulation of rhetoric both justifies and qualifies the conduct of advocates, as well as those who are addressed. Pivotal to Aristotle's understanding of rhetoric, then, is its peculiar inculcation of cognition, ēthos, and emotion in the decisions and acts of collectivities. The norms and conventions of a culture thus find themselves employed as premises of both recognition and inference. The norms of social knowledge that apply to membership of groups are the selfsame norms of enthymemes. As these expand or contract, they impinge directly on the lived reality of culture, including its extensiveness.[43] In summary, rhetoric in the classical sense provides an important inventional capacity for the conventions, emotions, and cognitions necessary for affiliation in a community of civic life.

For the stalwart moral agent, phronēsis may be something imaginable to stoic autonomy on a case by case basis. But for the rest of us—and that is a lot—it is imaginable only where premises of thought are permeable to the interests of others in an atmosphere of civic friendship and public exposure. So positioned, we may begin to appreciate and address the real materials of rhetoric. Rhetoric is about something that has always troubled philosophy and ethics. This something was not invented by the postmodernists. It has been with us all along. It is called *contingency*.

RHETORIC AND THE NARRATIVE
OF HUMAN CONTINGENCY

Although it is a commonplace among interpreters of Aristotle's *Rhetoric* that the art of rhetoric addresses unsettled matters, few terms within the Aristotelian lexicon are as complex and elusive to contemporary understanding as "contingency." Within the text itself, we are given some minimal assistance when Aristotle construes contingency as "dealing with the probable" or those things that "may be one way or another" or, in another place, uncertain (1357a). Yet it is clear that in saying this, Aristotle does not mean to imply the flipping of coins or the foretelling of futures.[44] What exactly he did intend will probably remain a mystery to rhetoricians and classical scholars alike. But although there may be no definitive answer, the expanding uncertainty in our own time suggests that it is worth reopening the question.

Consider what happens to rhetoric if contingency is construed *only* in material terms. If contingency is placed squarely and solely in the world of events, as things that may be about to happen, then the substance of rhetoric must always be receding from the imminent uncertainty of chance and fortune toward the eventual facticity of historical truth. Rhetorical practice would then be no more durable than the latest weather forecast. On the other hand, if contingency is understood as an attribute of propositions alone, then rhetoric would be nothing more than a subset of logic and, in all likelihood, a flawed logic at best. The answer, if we are to preserve the possibility of rhetoric, must be that there is a broader understanding of contingency, an understanding that is consistent with our broader ethical understanding of rhetoric. We will begin by considering an initial understanding of contingency and then look at its importance in light of the unfolding narrative moods of human action.

In his original formulation, Aristotle distinguished the contingent from both the necessary and the impossible. The contingent is neither something that is necessarily the case nor something that could never be the case. Rather, it is something which sometimes is and sometimes is not the case. It is something whose truth is, to use Sarah Waterlow's term, "intermittent."[45] Interestingly, Aristotle adds that contingency is presupposed on the very notion of voluntary agency, since it makes no sense to deliberate over things which are going to be the case anyway or things which could never be the case. What is left for us to consider is a relationship among propositions whose truth is determined, if at all, by perishable circumstance, incomplete knowledge, and fallible human action. Aristotle's aim is to deal with such matters as reliably as possible. This is one reason why we are given both his ethical treatises and a rhetorical treatise.

A more difficult question concerns the relationship between contingency and ethical choice. We might approach this question by considering the way in which contingencies intrude on our most consequential, character-forming judgments. These nagging particularities appear as the whole range of material that Bernard Williams, Thomas Nagel, and others describe as "moral luck."[46] If only my draft lottery number had been higher, I wouldn't have had to agonize over the character-forming decision of whether to serve in the Army. If only I had passed out on the couch, instead of trying to drive my loyal, attractive campaign worker home, my character would not have been forever marred by this tragic episode. And so forth. In Robert Bolt's *A Man for All Seasons*, Thomas More struggles to arrange contingencies so that he will not be forced to betray his king.

This intrusion of the contingent into our moral lives is complicated further by the fact that much of the time we have no way of knowing in advance whether "mere contingencies" will prove to be decisive for our public vindication. As I was writing an earlier draft of this book, a tragic—or, perhaps, sinister—event occurred in which U.S. naval forces shot down a passenger airliner from Iran, killing all 290 persons aboard. Pentagon spokespersons claimed initially that the jet was descending and approaching the vessel that fired upon it and that it was outside the proper air corridor for domestic air travel.[47] In other words, casual matters of circumstance, episodic contingencies, combined to give naval officers the impression that they were under attack by an enemy plane. The event, thus described, was—as the American president put it—a tragic, but "understandable" mistake. But suppose, as now appears, that most—even all—of these descriptions were inaccurate: that the plane was in its proper air corridor, that it was taking off and was not approaching the naval vessel. What we now have is something more consequential for those involved. Gross negligence? Criminal conduct? It is not my intention to pass judgment on a still unresolved puzzle,[48] but only to suggest that the most casual of contingencies may turn out to have critical ramifications for the judgments we make.

We will return to these matters in the next chapter when we examine an aesthetic approach to contingency. What needs to be mentioned here, however, is that there is an ambiguous but important middle ground between the utilitarian reduction of all moral matters to the calculus of probability and the forced dichotomy of choice into serious and trivial matters. For some contingencies are so interlaced with our collective moral agency and our developing public character as to defy the rule of calculation alone. This middle range of contingencies is addressed and defined by rhetoric. Thus rhetoric may become an art as well as an instrument for what Charles Taylor calls *strong* evaluation.[49] It does this by sorting through conflicting accounts and alternative construals and weighing contending versions of actions and events as more and less likely stories to be woven into the unfinished texture of our lives.

As Aristotle conceived of rhetorical conflict, the audience is engaged in a manner that allows it to see more clearly and act more judiciously. This may be why he was able to present the major issues of both deliberative and forensic discourse as "resting points" of difference and disagreement, for that is what each issue must amount to (1417b–1418a).[50] It is also why he treats the very best audiences as a kind of extension of self, capable of weighing the merits of practical alternatives.

Viewing the *Rhetoric* as an ongoing narrative construction allows us to envision the audience as something more distinctive than the popular contemporary models of "target," "market," "mass," or "voyeur." The rhetorical audience escapes such reductions by taking on the responsibility of a social agent engaged in a practice of formulating and adjudicating proofs on difficult, but inescapably public, practical matters. In more modern language, the audience remains in, but not entirely *of*, the emerging human story that is charted and thematized by rhetoric. This is because the reflective judgment of the audience remains pivotal to the story's outcome.

Finally, by placing this narrative frame within the context of our earlier discussion, we are permitted an even broader interpretation. Edwin Black, who has also taken issue with Aristotle's "rationalism," has presented considerable evidence to the effect that *krisis*—or judgment—is among the most central aims of Aristotle's *Rhetoric*. There is no reason to dispute this finding.[51] In fact, the *Rhetoric*'s foremost recent interpreter, William Grimaldi, states it even more emphatically: "The rhetorical methodology so constituted has one primary objective: to enable the person to whom the spoken or written word is addressed to make a judgment."[52] This means, as we have seen, that the audience, a self-interested collectivity, is clearly conceptualized by Aristotle as an agency capable of deliberative insight.

But, given the numerous cross-references between the *Rhetoric* and the *Poetics*, there may be a secondary meaning of krisis in the *Rhetoric* that is also important. For krisis also depicts the moment of dramatic reversal (occasioned by conflict, after all) within a tragic poem (*Poetics* 1455b–1456a). To return to our narrative concern, namely, of what conflicts is Aristotle's *Rhetoric* the scene? We can now approach this question through another: namely, how is ethical character portrayed in the *Rhetoric*? Quite emphatically, character is construed in Aristotelian rhetoric as ēthos, one of the most enigmatic concepts in the entire lexicon (*Rhetoric* 1366a–b). Aristotle regards ēthos as the most powerful source of persuasion of all. Yet he seems to regret this and wish that it were otherwise (1377b). His treatment of ēthos regards it as a type of proof. But if ēthos is to be something other than an inartistic proof, it must be generated through the resources and devices proper to the art itself.

This may be why Aristotle insists that ēthos is the character of the speaker "as presented in the speech" (1356a). Neither communication scientists nor classical commentators have ever known quite what to make of this pronouncement. It seems to me, however, that Aristotle is regarding ēthos, since it is a proof, as a matter for judgment. It simply will not do to have a reputation as a likable guy, a nice person, or even a great communicator. Unless these qualities are manifested through discourse, through what we say, the residual effect is not a *proper* rhetorical proof. Aristotle here recognizes something that contemporary cultures often overlook. Even though our senses of decency, competence, honor, justice, and the good are often invoked and easily outraged, the character of public figures is not something that is constant or prior to rhetorical success.[53] Rather, character in public must constantly be re-formed and performed through the rhetorical choices we make in engaging responsible others. Thus the conflicts framed by rhetoric are not about the *real* nature of the good, the honorable, the just. Nor is the dynamis of virtue portrayed through the belated recognition of a tragic flaw, a moment of decisive reversal, an audience experience of pity and fear. Rather, in the ongoing story line of rhetoric, audience and advocate together engage urgent unsettled matters through recurrent, but reflective conflict. What may or may not be good or noble or just in the particular case is settled (for *now*) through the engaged decision of competent others. These others are competent precisely because they are able to recognize and enact the relational goods of civic friendship, practical reason, and hope. In rhetoric, the character of audience and advocate can be formed only through reciprocal engagement; and the proximate goods or virtues of rhetoric as a practice are thus enacted. As MacIntyre notes, there is a Sophoclean insight here: namely, "that it is through conflict and sometimes only through conflict that we learn what our ends and purposes are."[54]

Perhaps Aristotle had something like this in mind when he gave the dynamis of rhetoric the ennobling ends of judgment and discovery. Rhetoric, as we have encapsulated it here, may not manifest some predetermined truth; but it does attempt something which, in our modern day and age, may be more important. For it reaches out toward the definition and realization of proximate value *in* truth. It also provides the beginning of a synthesis of the impartialist and partialist positions. As we have noted throughout this reading, rhetoric is unavoidably biased toward the particulars—the persons, materials, and interests that are close at hand. But it works through these nearby phainomena to establish a mode of reflection involving something more general, emergent, and unfolding— the virtues and convictions of culture and an interested audience necessarily involved in unfinished episodes of public life. So, like practical theories of classical origin, rhetoric helps to transform those painstaking particulars of choice and accountability into a meaningful cultural story, thereby making public character, once more, a *possibility.*

We have been probing Aristotle's *Rhetoric* in search of the ethical goods it locates within rhetorical practice. While we have only begun to approach the interpretative community that this unlikely document forms with the modern reader, our search has allowed us to identify some features of rhetoric that might be of value to contemporary communities. It has been my contention throughout that the Aristotelian tradition not only offers a basis for understanding the goods internal to rhetorical practice, but also provides a constitutive vocabulary for recognizing, engaging, and recreating the worthier qualities of rhetorical conduct today. So it seems appropriate to ask whether this vocabulary possesses sufficient dynamis to ground and guide our own critical apprehension of rhetoric. Are there recognizable rhetorical occasions and artifacts wherein practical reason and civic friendship find expression, wherein a kind of audience agency is found and formed? Beyond this question lies the more fundamental one of how the constitutive ethical grammar of Aristotle's *Rhetoric* might work toward identifying the components and markers of a practice: the issues, audiences, institutions, and conventions—in short, the phainomena—relevant to the direction of contemporary human agency.

The profusion of rhetorical advocacy in contemporary life is undeniable: from self-help books to commercial sales to public relations, advertising, and television preaching. Coaches are now motivators; celebrities are political evangelists; and media anchors are mediators. Most of what results is deservedly perishable. But in rhetoric, unlike some of the other, finer arts, there is usually some relationship between competence and popular success. It is part of the very meaning of rhetoric, and surely some indicator of its ethical significance, that it must play to the crowd. Even granting that there is mediocre rhetoric in abundance, it may be that we have found little of promise because we have not known where or how to look. The question persists: does Aristotle's highly prescriptive vision of an ethical rhetoric identify any qualities that may still be appreciated and cultivated within contemporary practice? In light of our analysis in chapter 1, the question may be rephrased thus: might the particularities of our own cultural appearances form the basis for an ethical rhetoric, so that a public character might be performed, recognized, and judged? I now consider this question in what Burke might regard as a comic frame and then, in chapter 3, a tragic frame. Though the association is less than exact, I am linking the comic frame with the traditional ethical concern with invention and the tragic frame with the traditional aesthetic concern with judgment. The ironies of usage suggest limits to both ethical and aesthetic world views.

Rhetorical practice as envisioned by Aristotle invents and then invests its audiences with several significant relational goods. Beginning with the conditions for conduct that might be ethically significant, rhetoric calls its audience to a kind of "hearing, in attendance." As willing witnesses to what will be said "in their name," members of the audience leave the shelter of their various autonomous selves and embark on the prospective stance of an incipient collective actor. The audience is thus readied to participate in the unfolding meaning of a rhetorical message in all its immediacy and expected consequence.

Now, if we are to keep close to the parameters—what we might call the "friendly confines"—of the Aristotelian paradigm, the relational goods of rhetorical practice should be recognizable in an institutional context. For this is where we find the conventions and affiliative bonds that allow inferences to be constructed and enacted. However, this need not imply that all such practice is conservative or elitist. For one thing, if institutions are to be open, they require more than the ceremonial repetition of their collective virtues. Their openness must be tested. Barring civil war, the only plausible way of doing this must make some reflective use of rhetoric. I hope to show that there is no contradiction between viewing rhetoric as a normalized, institutional practice and admitting within it the possibility of new orders of realization. On a very basic level, rhetorical inference is always expanding the boundaries of the commonplace to admit and transform new information and ideas. This, I need hardly add, is inventional. Aristotle demonstrated convincingly that such a process goes on whenever audiences are moved from fear to pity in tragedy. And Grimaldi's treatment of book 2 suggests that a similar inferential movement occurs through all the morally significant emotions. Rhetoric not only engages; it also invents public moods.

ROOSEVELT'S INAUGURAL AS THE FORGING OF A CIVIC CULTURE

To pursue this line of thought in practice, I want to consider an important, but less well-remarked discourse in twentieth-century American political history: Franklin Roosevelt's first inaugural address.[55] It must be said immediately that this is one of the more canonical speeches in American public address; indeed, its iconic status may be one reason why it has not invited close readings. The common reading, according to the opinion leaders of the time, is that the speech constituted, all by itself, a rhetorical "cure" for the hard times of the depression. People who heard the speech still say that its early magical invocation ("The only thing we have to fear . . .") left them suddenly resolute and confident, almost embarrassed to have ever felt differently. To this felt transformation may be added the chronicles of the court historians,[56] journalists of the time such as Walter Lippmann, who wrote that, within a fortnight, the nation had been transformed. Will Rogers wrote that the nation hadn't been as happy in three years as it was on Inaugural Day.[57] Within a week, the mood in Washington and in Congress was completely different: confident, enthusiastic, perhaps inspired. Modern scholarship on the speech has drawn useful attention to its figurative devices. Halford Ryan Ross, for instance, notes Roosevelt's use of scapegoating, the rhetoric of war, and the carrot–stick approach to Congress.[58] But what no one seems to have remarked on is the significance of these or any other tactics for the sophistication of a civic sense.

To try and get at this significance, I will again employ Aristotle's sense of participatory inference and blend it with a perspective from modern pragmatics. We tend to think of rhetorical utterances as provisional answers to more or less ambiguous conflictual cultural questions. But a precise understanding of the occasion of a rhetorical utterance, such as an inaugural ceremony, or what Bitzer calls the "situation," may imply a set of fairly specific criteria for an apt response. To understand the question is to be able to come up with a proper answer. Most rhetorical utterances can be collapsed, rather neatly, into this pragmatic frame.

But great rhetoric, and in particular the *ethical significance* of great rhetoric in Aristotle's sense, is rather more difficult to capture within the pragmatic frame. To find or uncover the contributing elements to a great or eloquent discourse, we must enlarge the focus of the cultural-historical question that the speech seeks to answer. We are now on the unsteady terrain of cultural ēthos, viewing the heritage of our shared appearances from a longer view. I cannot say for certain that great orators always shared or sought this larger horizon. Nor does it much matter. But all great rhetoric seems also to be about its own definitive institutional context: as Pericles' funeral oration is about Athens and the *polis* and Lincoln's Gettysburg address is about the future of the republic. It is thus of interest that crisis has tended to evoke memorable addresses: Gettysburg, Lincoln's second inaugural address, and the great words of Webster, Frederick Douglass, Jane Addams, and Roosevelt. It may be that the very polarization of historical forces invites deeper thematic linkages to the agency of our times. I do not know. But to test the heuristic power or dynamis of rhetoric's classical vocabulary, it is surely critical to reconstruct the historical problem that Roosevelt was addressing, whether consciously or not. Then we may better appreciate the inventional power of his answer.

From my own study of this period in American history and its rather stark juxtaposition with earlier identifiable historical moods: the Roaring Twenties, the Progressive Era, and Social Darwinism, I suspect that what underlay the question addressed by Roosevelt was a concern with the changing American conception of work and its relationship to American character and power. Social Darwinism, in both its older and its newer forms, has held sway over differing social classes not only because of its scientific pretensions,[59] but also because it offers an outlet for ambition, a way of escaping the nether regions of class structure.[60] In equating hard work with success and success with justice, the inequities of class and culture can be overtaken through greater striving. With progressivism came the awareness that not only were some inequities undeserved; they were also institutionally reinforced. With this came a commitment to public activism through newly participatory political channels. It was a brief glimpse of possibility overturned by the Great War and the consumerism of the Roaring Twenties. What needs to be remembered, however, is that nothing progressivism ever offered rhetorically came to grips with the honorific value attached to work.

One sees in the 1920s a gradual, somewhat disturbing replacement of the so-called work ethic with what might be called a consumer ēthos.[61] Here one works to afford images of success that provide appearances of achievement in an otherwise hierarchical system. This devalues the instrumental power of work, at least where noninflationary measures of success are concerned. But what is missed is the fact that you could take away all the toasters, radios, and cars and find that you needed to work, period.

The Great Depression challenged existing rhetorical conventions. It deflated symbolic resources and bankrupted political speaking. As the capacity of the democratic collectivity to inform and persuade itself was thrown into jeopardy, existing commonplaces of political thinking were put to the test, and new forms and avenues of thought and action were called for. The language of tradition provides a way of appreciating the power of alternative responses to this unprecedented situation. With the fiscal collapse and three long years of the Great Depression prior to the election of Roosevelt, one might have expected some attempt to change official doctrines about work, character, and social influence. But no attempt was made. Hoover never budged from the official stance that government's mission was to encourage a climate favorable to business and thus—the free market intact—prosperity. In one of the ironies of understatement in historical commentary, Samuel Eliot Morrison cautions us not to be too hard on Herbert Hoover. He writes: "We should remember that some degree of F.D.R.'s success in dealing with the depression is owed to Hoover's proving that conventional methods had failed."[62] It was, one must concede, a most convincing proof. But with the conspicuous failure of conventional government and the loss of useful, honorable work by over thirteen million people, an accompanying feeling of helplessness, impoverishment, and powerlessness had begun to emerge. This, in sweeping and truncated form, is the fundamental problem that history presented to Franklin Roosevelt.

How could Roosevelt bring together the essential ingredients for character, confidence, and a practical constituency for a workable political recovery? It must be said that this was not an idle question as regards Roosevelt's own political power. Although a highly charismatic man, the remaining bastions of concentrated wealth continued to oppose him. And although his margin of victory over Hoover in 1932 was huge—more than seven million votes—it is safe to assume that a good deal of this margin came from dispossessed, virtually powerless people. They could vote, certainly; but many could not even live in the residences they claimed as their own.[63] Recall too that the much discussed mass society had become a social reality by 1933. Roosevelt's alleged constituency consisted of society's victims, its lost generation.

Roosevelt is the rhetorical exemplar of the depression era, a public figure who had to reclaim both his own public character and that of his audience. Only a rhetoric at its fullest capacity, one that can overcome the material obstacles impeding affinity among speaker, audience, and public, can work in such a situation. The challenge was typified by Roosevelt's personal situation, in that he was from a class that had been more caricatured and resented during the early years of the depression than any other; and he was severely handicapped in a society which defines disability as grounds for marginality, for being shut up in the home and out of public life.[64] If his rhetoric were to overcome these disqualifications, it would have to fashion a mediating definition of the public that glimpsed political motive as moral authority and political will as transcending class interests. Perhaps most astonishing, Roosevelt was able to transform and present his own handicap as a sign of vigor, recovery, and renewal. As he did so, he created a reciprocal bond with the public. He did this first by creating a discourse wherein people could respond reasonably to the depression instead of treating the prevailing appearances as signs of doom and secondly by projecting the capacity of people to act constructively as a collectivity, rather than as separate interests pulling in fractionated directions, trying to save themselves. Finally, he was able to redefine in practical terms the constitutive vocabulary detailing the duties and obligations of government. A politics of *praxis* replaced the rhetoric of restraint, principle, and legalistic imperative embodied by Hoover. Roosevelt's rhetoric was thus able to reconstitute in the public a sense of its own character, its responsibilities in light of that character, and the language of practical reason in a reformulated public sphere. But how?

The genius of Roosevelt's first inaugural address was its conception of a powerful, political praxis from the unlikely ingredients of social victims. I cannot give a complete reading here, but will focus on the profound inventional implications of his practical inferences. Roosevelt, as is well known, was a figurative genius. The very resonances of "new deal" served to lighten the burden of dread afflicting the public with a gamelike association. There was nothing wrong with the rules; it was just that we were getting bad cards. And Roosevelt, dealer to the hilt, would shuffle them again. Still, slogans only go so far. On Inauguration Day, Roosevelt introduced his statement by repeating the oath of office not in increments, as dictated by the chief justice, but as a whole. He then moved directly to his own remarkable choice of context: "I am certain that my fellow Americans expect that on my induction into the Presidency I will address them with a candor and a decision which the present situation of our Nation impels. This is preeminently the time to speak the truth, the whole truth, frankly and boldly. Nor need we shrink from honestly facing conditions in our country today. This great Nation will endure as it has endured, will revive and will prosper."[65] This proem frames the more famous declaration: "So first of all, let me assert my firm belief that the only thing we have to fear is fear itself—nameless, unreasoning, unjustified terror which paralyzes needed efforts to convert retreat into advance."

The remarks are so apparently uncomplicated and so blunt that we might overlook their accomplishment. Already Roosevelt has brought together his notion of audience expectation, rhetorical situation, and occasional propriety under his own definition to charge him to speak the truth ("frankly," in a subliminal bit of punning). Truth telling becomes an act of courage. Moreover, there is no need to hide from the truth. Why? Because we *will* endure, we *will* revive, and *will* prosper. Already, the audience has been made complicitous in what is to come. The remarks are so forceful that we might almost miss the word "revive" (not "survive" as some transcriptions have it). This is our clue that things have gone seriously wrong: we have somehow lost consciousness. Now comes the ringing declaration. But note the qualifiers: nameless, unreasoning, unjustified terror. There is also the reference to paralysis (interesting in light of Roosevelt's own condition) and, more important, a clear anticipation of the "war" imagery that Ross correctly highlights.[66] Roosevelt, in doubling up and reversing our relationship to fear, would have us transform cowardice and psychosis under fire into a form of readiness or vigilance. The declaration is energizing, as if in acknowledging our condition, we are freed from its grip. But more is needed than simple recognition.

A marvelously subtle enthymeme follows, which connects Roosevelt's own ēthos to power *through public support.* "In every dark hour of our national life a leadership of frankness and vigor has met with that understanding and support of the people themselves which is essential to victory." And then: "I am convinced that you will again give that support to leadership in these critical days." Note the casual way in which the category of frank and vigorous leadership refers back to the beginning of the address, where he says he will "address them with a candor." But more important, Roosevelt does not conclude the enthymeme in the expected way, as if to say "Well, here I am." Rather, he simply assumes that public support will energize his own leadership. It is as if he is offering a disenfranchised people a new partnership in power: you support me, and I, emboldened by your support, will be candid and vigorous. Together, we are strong. Note that "dark hour" has become "critical days," once the linkage is made.

This successful linkage ("In such a spirit on my part and on yours") allows us to "face our common difficulties." Here the speaker makes a fascinating equation: "They concern, thank God, only material things. Values have shrunken to fantastic levels; our ability to pay has fallen; government of all kinds is faced with serious curtailment of income; the means of exchange are frozen in the currents of trade; the withered leaves of industrial enterprise lie on every side." And so on. The equation is between material things and seasonal things. Material things are distanced colloquially from some apparently more ethereal realm, through "thank God." But then notice the imagery: "shrunken," "fallen," "frozen," "withered." These are, as Roosevelt notes later, "dark realities." But they are seasonal. This speech was delivered in March; and it is difficult to overlook the inference that Roosevelt envisions a material and seasonal change, as certain as the fact that winter gives way to Spring.

There follows one of the most important disjunctions in the entire discourse. Roosevelt intones:

Yet our distress comes from no failure of substance. We are stricken by no plague of locusts. Compared with the perils our forefathers conquered because they believed and were not afraid, we have still much to be thankful for. Nature still offers her bounty and human efforts have multiplied it. Plenty is at our doorstep, but a generous use of it languishes in the very sight of the supply. Primarily this is because the rulers of the exchange of mankind's goods have failed, through their own stubbornness and their own incompetence, have admitted their failure, and abdicated. Practices of the unscrupulous money changers stand indicted in the court of public opinion, rejected by the hearts and minds of men.

Then follows his famous pronouncement that "The money changers have fled from their high seats in the temple of our civilization. We may now restore that temple to the ancient truths." This is a rather grand statement, equating the persona of FDR with the biblical role of Jesus. When I have discussed the speech with students, some have recognized the scapegoating but have expressed concern regarding the harshness of Roosevelt's words. Remember, the juxtaposition of the opening sentences: "failure of substance" with "plague of locusts." I myself wonder why the biblical plague was invoked as a counterinstance. Were the allusion purely literal, I suspect that many in Roosevelt's audience might have preferred locusts to this prolonged misery. But obviously, the allusion is not literal. Roosevelt, in the pre-Dust Bowl depression, wants to distinguish between a hostile natural world turned against man by a vengeful Deity (as punishment for wrongdoing) and a harmonious nature ready to offer her bounty as our just harvest, but foiled by human rulers of the most evil sort. So interpreted, we as victims have done nothing to deserve our fate. The problem is not nature, but *human* nature. More important, Roosevelt ingeniously interprets this undeserved malevolence as having occurred in the past. With the election, a kind of marker event, we have already driven the evil rulers from power. Interpreting this development retrospectively allows Roosevelt to read the recent election as the power of his own constituency *already exercised*. This may be why he is able to refer to a court of public opinion and make the figure more powerful than a mere cliché.

As for the scapegoating, it is indeed harsh; and Roosevelt reaped antagonism from business throughout his political career. But it is worth noting, I think, that Roosevelt has not only fixed the blame; he has terminated the punishment as well. With the money changers' loss of their high seats, presumably this chapter is closed—and with lessons learned, as well. What are these timeless truths? Here, Roosevelt addresses the historical question squarely: "Happiness lies not in the mere possession of money; it lies in the joy of achievement, in the thrill of creative effort. The joy and moral stimulation of work no longer must be forgotten in the mad chase of evanescent profits. These dark days will be worth all they cost us if they teach us that our true destiny is not to be ministered unto but to minister to ourselves and our fellow man." The words may seem a bit arcane in our largely post-Christian world. But they are thoroughly biblical and probably would not have sounded arcane to Roosevelt's listeners. Moreover, they represent the finishing touch on a double response to Social Darwinism. Not only are the most successful not necessarily the most deservedly successful—after all, they rigged the rules and have stolen our money—but beyond this, the very idea of working for massive material success is wrong. In other words, we have two kinds of work: the mad chase for material success and the morally stimulating absorption in the process of working. In thirsting for work of any kind, Roosevelt's audience had probably abandoned the dream of speculative riches long ago; so the vision is appropriate. But more than this, it completely reverses the hierarchy of success and failure originally proffered by Social Darwinism. And in an era beset by massive unemployment, it does not abandon motivational ambition to the earlier doctrine.

The remaining half of the speech is devoted to Roosevelt's activist agenda for putting people to work. This is where the war allegories are most pronounced. But it can be said that, at this point in the speech, Roosevelt has already invented through his own figurative devices a constituency to lead the battle for recovery. In example after example, he links popular support to public effort: a general is only as strong, after all, as his army. In a characteristic form of address, which seems to speak *through* the people *to* others, the president concludes:

If I read the temper of our people correctly, we now realize as we have never realized before our interdependence on each other [sic— one of the few awkward constructions]; that we cannot merely take but we must give as well; that if we are to go forward we must move as a trained and loyal army willing to sacrifice for the good of a common discipline, because without such discipline no progress is made, no leadership becomes effective. We are, I know, ready and willing to submit our lives and property to such discipline, because it makes possible a leadership which aims at a larger good. This I propose to offer, pledging that the larger purposes will bind upon us all a sacred obligation with a unity of duty hitherto evoked only in time of armed strife.

By any measure, this is a remarkable—even a startling—statement. Roosevelt is inviting the people to enter his own regime of discourse, wherein submission and sacrifice and, yes, discipline are transformed into instruments of power. In return for this sacrifice, presented in an almost contractual sense, is the pledge of a larger vision that will bind this newly empowered people together in a sacred trust, like an army. It is interesting, in light of the binge mentality of the Roaring Twenties, that Roosevelt has blended a language that resonates with cures or recoveries from forms of dependency. He has named and admitted our condition, banished our fears, and called for our submission to *discipline*. Very subtly, he is also performing a figurative gesture that millions have only dreamed of witnessing in person. He is offering them work.

Roosevelt employs this language of his new regime as a wedge against conventional politics. After praising the simplicity and flexibility of the Constitution, he thunders: "But in the event that Congress shall fail . . . I shall ask the Congress for the one remaining instrument to meet the crisis—broad Executive power to wage a war against the emergency, as great as the power that would be given to me if we were in fact invaded by a foreign foe." This passage shocks contemporary audiences, and even in its day it was a considerable gamble. We learn from William Manchester that the First Lady herself was chilled by the remarks.[67] Also, it is not a carrot-and-stick approach to Congress at all—where is the carrot? No, in this speech (prophetic in many ways of Roosevelt's stormy second and third terms) Roosevelt places all his confidence in the audience. Had the audience gasped in disbelief or shouted disapproval, the utterance would have lost much of its impact and its inventional capacity. But in fact, as many commentators have remarked, the passage elicited the most impressive ovation of the speech.

Charismatic authority surfaces when conventional channels and procedures have collapsed. This, surely, characterizes the period from 1929 to 1933. Yet Roosevelt's genius was not to disband a politics of normalcy, but instead to employ the threat of a destabilized counterinstitutional rule as a way of making the institution perform. He could not have done this without the newly energized constituency of formerly powerless people.

As if to recognize his and their accomplishment, Roosevelt sums up his mood and goals in most unusual language: "We face the arduous days that lie before us in the warm courage of the national unity; with the clear consciousness of seeking old and precious moral values; with the clean satisfaction that comes from the stern performance of duty by old and young alike. We aim at the assurance of a rounded and permanent national life." I have asked students over the years to explain the peculiar choice of adjectives here. Most of the time, they miss the mark; the magic of eloquence is like that. The call to a "rounded and permanent national life" is an elegant—even Apollonian—vision of the polis restored. But "warm courage" and "clean satisfaction"—what can these mean? Let us suppose, however, that you have been out of work and have watched your family torn asunder and lost your home. You have endured every indignity. It is March. Can you imagine anything you would rather be than clean and warm? In endowing the virtues of public conduct with the glow of personal intimacy, Roosevelt invented and empowered a meaningful rhetorical constituency in 1933. He did this in a manner utterly faithful to the ethics of the rhetorical tradition, by linking the virtues and civilizing norms of public character to the actions undertaken in its name.

We have been examining a discourse from a time and circumstance far removed from the relative security of the Aristotelian polis. Indeed, each of Roosevelt's rhetorical choices involves issues of personal and public good in a world in which tradition can no longer be invoked with unquestioned authority. Invention is always a relational process. Usually it connects some traditional, or at least recognizable, sense of what rhetoric is with some more or less focused picture of unfulfilled possibilities. This could not have been done quite as forcefully with Roosevelt's discourse without seeing it as a piece in a larger frame, a frame that even Roosevelt may not have glimpsed completely at the time. To sense invention at work here is to suggest the profound interplay of these mysterious factors and the way they came together to produce a unique utterance, an utterance that crystallized and animated the power of a still unfinished history.

But what sort of krisis attends this instance of contemporary rhetorical practice? It does not appear to be the sort of judgment that would point fingers or sharpen conflict. Ethos is seen to be a quality of atmosphere, rather than an earned component of engaged moral conduct. And issues, to the extent that they admit of a moral dimension, are treated with a circumspection that borders on evasion. But at the same time, the people addressed by this modern leader are vulnerably complicitous: they must decide who they are willing to tolerate as their own representatives, as custodians—for a time—of their interests. The people invoked by Roosevelt are capable of being more than creatures of the marketplace or of professional roles and specializations. They must accept, without being unduly sentimental about it, that humans are capable of being better than their own found condition. Secondly, they must accept that, in one way or another, what people say and do on their behalf will ultimately reflect on them and even on us.

IMPLICATIONS FOR RECOVERY: TOWARD A RHETORICAL SENSIBILITY

As James Boyd White noted, the greatest rhetorical texts demand—through their engagement—an improved self-understanding.[68] They teach us how to read and practice them. I hope to have shown some ways in which Aristotle's *Rhetoric* does this. But, perhaps more important for our larger purposes, the *Rhetoric* also instructs us in how we might move beyond its initial formulations so as to enlarge the materials, focus, and prescriptive direction of the art. George Kennedy gives us the clearest indication that this text invites not the reverence for orthodoxy so frequently found among scholars and students, but a much more open and heuristic reading: "There is thus a theoretical art of rhetoric standing behind or above the productive art of speech-making. . . . Neither does the *Rhetoric* define persuasion. These and other ideas are implicit within Aristotle's thinking, and given world enough and time he would doubtless have worked them out in a logical fashion. . . . Aristotle would not have objected to the further refinement of his ideas by his successors, ancient and modern."[69]

In this initial, "ethical" reading, I have sketched a broad outline of the Aristotelian rhetorical heritage in light of contemporary understanding. From this outline, I hope to draw forth a first approximation of norms that might inform a rhetorical culture. I will consider four interrelated implications of this preliminary reading: first, the status of rhetoric as a *practice*; second, the position of the audience as a form of *agency*; third, the significance of phronēsis as an overarching rhetorical virtue; and fourth, the power of such a rhetoric to engage the problem of partiality and universality where the world of appearances is concerned.

Rhetoric as practice

The order in which I have listed the implications may seem strange. For the status of rhetoric as a practice is very much determined by its relationship to the audience, its cultivation of phronēsis, and so forth. Yet it is important to begin with this, primarily because it allows us to specify the senses of "practice" we may claim for rhetoric. Earlier in our discussion, we turned to Aristotle's own distinction between the theoretical and the productive sciences. In the productive science of ethics, for example, the point was not so much to know virtue for its own sake as to become virtuous through action. Aristotle's distinction provided an important corrective to the Platonic attempt to subsume all activities, crafts, and sciences under his own monistic theoretical terminology. At the time, we noted that the placement of rhetoric in such a schema was problematic. For rhetoric admits to both a theoretic quality and a certain form of power. Moreover, Aristotle nowhere explicitly says that the aim of rhetoric is to persuade. As near as we have been able to determine, the aim of rhetoric is to *practice* judgment (to enact krisis) where certain sorts of problematic materials are concerned. Perhaps that is what it means to be rhetorical.

But this still leaves unsettled just what sort of practice rhetoric is. The modern tendency is to take rhetoric as simply a pragmatic exertion of power through discourse or any manner of partisanship uncovered in discourse. Both conceptions assume that rhetoric is achieving its aims only when it is covering over its *true*—(that is to say, "false")—intent. But if my earlier attempt to read rhetorical practice has been at all convincing, it should admit to a broader understanding than this. Some idea of this understanding is suggested by Alasdair MacIntyre's useful distinction between goods that are *internal* to a practice and those that are *external*.[70] His specific example is chess. He argues that there is a recognizable difference between goods that are only casually and contingently related to quality play (such as paying a child to play or perhaps the publicity accompanying great success for an adult) and goods that are fundamental and integral to the mastery of this complex game ("analytic skill, strategic imagination, and competitive intensity").[71]

The distinction becomes serviceable for rhetoric provided we remember two things: first, that the goods internal to an activity are not necessarily the reasons why one seeks to master it. For example one does not play chess only to acquire and sophisticate these goods; one also plays to win. Still, with the acquisition of skill comes an appreciation for the well-played match, regardless of results. Second, and despite the singular focus of MacIntyre's repeated examples, the goods that are cultivated are not always localized within the autonomous agent alone. There is an unmistakable pedagogical sense in which improved performance by the other improves the quality of play, one's appreciation for the game, and perhaps the resolve of one's opponent. This means that we should not confuse goods that are internal to a practice with virtues that are somehow solitary and ultimate. It is worth noting that two of MacIntyre's own interior goods—strategic imagination and competitive intensity—require another person in order to be practiced and thereby cultivated. They are, in other words, *relational goods.* This does not mean that they are inferior to other goods, any more than that they are inferior to the self. Neither is implied by virtue of being internal to a practice. This is pivotal for rhetoric.

We are now in a position to claim that the goods or qualities *internal* to rhetoric are necessarily relational. Like competitiveness and strategic imagination (which mastery of rhetoric is also capable of providing), they require some *other* in order to be practiced. But beyond this, some very important civic qualities—such as civic friendship and a sense of social justice—are actively cultivated through excellence in rhetorical practice. These qualities are not merely distinctions for the autonomous agent to master; they are attributes of the body politic. Aristotle's original conception of rhetoric and its operation thus provides the outline of a most intriguing form of activity, one with its own distinct goods. Truly, we have been introduced to a *practice*—that is, a coherent, creative activity admitting certain standards of accomplishment.

Audience as agency

First among the implications of rhetoric's central ethical features is the special manner in which the rhetorical audience is conceived. Although this tends to grate on modern sensibilities, Aristotle was emphatic that not everyone, at every time, is capable of engaging in ethical conduct. While we have good reason to question his particular exclusions—

namely, women, slaves, and barbarians—there is a larger truth to the
point he is making. In the courts and in our own public relations, we
regularly allow as an extenuating circumstance whether a party is *in
any position* to engage in ethical conduct. Usually, this is taken to be
a comment not on the innate capacities of the individual, but on the
circumstances in which the person finds him or herself. But of course,
there is more to the problem than this. Aristotle's cultural reports are
all too easily converted into categorical prescriptions.

The larger question, however, is what it means to be a member of a
rhetorical audience in the first place. In this light, it is interesting that
we pay so little attention to how we characterize and treat the public
domain of human action. By "we," I mean theorists, scholars, and opinion
leaders of communication practice in what are supposedly citadels of *vox
populi:* namely, the recent Western democracies. By the public domain,
I refer not only to individual conduct with social significance, but also
to how people act as membership groups. The very word *act* seems to
strain against our understanding of the collectivity. This may be because
our most common image of the group, where messages are concerned, is
as a *target* or a message *consumer.* This is the audience as victim or as
some kind of collective digestive tract for messages. While we may justifiably protest Aristotle's exclusion of important social groupings from
the realm of the ethical as his own culture understood it, our own systematic exclusion of virtually all collective groups from this realm goes
virtually ignored.

Aristotle's way of characterizing an audience may have something of
value to offer us. The audience is more than a target, more than a consumer. It is midway between a public and a constituency—a kind of
collaborative agency for making ongoing judgments. Aristotle was emphatic that deliberative discourse was the highest form of discourse because it admitted to the best arguments. This was because its audience
knew its own shared interests better than anyone else. Even for forensic
and ceremonial judgments, it was the recognizable ēthos of an advocate or, better, a pair of opposed advocates, in light of common opinion
and value, that determined the material of argument. In generating an
atmosphere of civic friendship, rhetoric cultivated conditions wherein an
audience might accomplish or accommodate goods beyond itself. It also
envisioned a *language* of engaged community, in which positions were
taken, differences expressed, and inferences conjointly created. Most important, it included a lexicon of values, wherein civic ideals and ordinary

convictions must eventually come together so as to reflect, refine, and extend one another in the unfinished world of the practical.

This may be why Aristotle presents us with so many conflicting conceptions of the good, the honorable, and the just. These are the annotations of civic virtue that we must come to terms with in order to ground conduct consistent with the stated aspirations of public life. All this is a way of saying that such a vision of audience ascribes to it the capacity for ethically significant and then ethical conduct. This fits well with the ideal of a practice discussed earlier. Here judgment is not some cognitive yardstick that privileged communicators (like ideal readers or audiences) mysteriously possess, but rather a genuine potential available to anyone who cares enough to align themselves seriously with the implied convictions of others.

Such a vocabulary of characterization, however powerful, cannot guarantee that the public audience will somehow spring to life. Rhetoric is, above or beneath all, an art of chance and circumstance. But Aristotle has given us a vocabulary with which to accommodate the language of practical reason to issues in moral deliberation and judgment. In adopting this vocabulary, we are placed in a culture of justification, where occasions for judgment are recurrently available.[72] Even in his own time, it is likely that many such occasions were not appropriately engaged. But that is not the point. If one is committed to the possibility of human agency where collective conduct is concerned, it does not matter that rhetoric does not work optimally in every case. Character is possible only because it is possible to fail.

Phronēsis as virtue

If the autonomous agent could be given a moment to rebut my narrative thus far (and I suspect most of my readers are autonomous agents), he or she would properly say, "What's in all this for me?" It is tempting to dismiss this monologism of late capitalism (on *ad hominem* grounds, of course). But it has a point and deserves a serious response. So far I have been intent on highlighting all the features of an *ethical* reading that emphasize the collective, collaborative aspects of virtue: its public capacity, its attribution of agency to others, its regard for their interests, and so forth. To the tradition of philosophy that is steeped in the principle of human autonomy, such an emphasis is likely to smack of the worst sort of special pleading. And in order that we have our innuendos properly in place, let me add that the worst sort of special pleading by my own political lights is neoconservatism. Is this all just another call to absorb the self within the polis? What of the individual's own character?

We have already noted that Aristotle's primary preoccupation, throughout his masterful treatments of ethics, was with individual character, with how it is formed and trained and how virtue is acquired and strengthened. If we accept D. S. Hutchinson's careful exposition of virtue in the *Nicomachean Ethics*, it becomes apparent that virtues are acquired dispositions or traits of character which provide reasonable guidance to feelings.[73] Virtues are acquired through choice and training, whereby they become stable traits of mature individuals. It also becomes apparent that of the five intellectual virtues, one, phronēsis, deserves special attention. This is because, as MacIntyre and Ronald Beiner remind us, it is the master quality of practical wisdom, or prudential judgment, which makes possible the proper exercise of other virtues.[74] The question naturally arises, how is phronēsis to be cultivated? Here Aristotle suggests that deliberation about choice and action is the way to cultivate this superordinate virtue. Indeed, a proper appreciation of *all* the virtues can best be cultivated through deliberative civic conduct. Obviously, audiences can not cultivate proper judgment all by themselves. It can only be advocacy of ēthos, pathos, and logos which provides the initiative and hence the opportunity for ordinary people to transform themselves through choice, action, and proper judgment. It should now be equally obvious that the individual agent would be unable to cultivate qualities of phronēsis if left entirely to his or her solitary devices. This is why Aristotle was so emphatic that ēthos, as proof, is made present in and through speech to another.

Just as an advocate makes certain options for choice and judgment available to an audience, so the converse is true as well. It is rhetoric, properly practiced, which allows the rhetorician to become a more accountable moral agent—in other words, literally to cultivate phronēsis. Aristotle's oft-cited justification for considering both sides of a case needs to be examined in this light. We have only to consider what might happen should we be involved in a decision without concern for the weight of argument on opposing sides, or, to choose an almost opposite case, be so involved in one side of the issue as to hear only the same arguments over and over. In one case, we have moral indifference; in the other, moral fanaticism. Either way, we have the thoughtlessness that blinds both the individual and the collectivity to their own moral accountability.

This is not to propose the polis as some sort of model for political modernity. Despite all the talk of democracy, Athens was a city-state in which slaves were legal and neighbors were illegally plundered. Equally obvious and problematic is that Aristotle had no way of dealing rhetorically with the phenomenon of exclusion—what modern theorists understand as alienation. Rather, I am making the more modest suggestion that political systems which practice radical inequity and exclusion are themselves fearful of the rhetorical audience, for very good reasons. As we shall see later, the rhetorical audience can, through its very presence, confront us with issues and choices that are morally compelling. From this perspective, the normative ideal of solidarity is not some abstract precondition for rhetorical discourse, but one of rhetoric's richest performative accomplishments.

Partiality and universality

At the beginning of this chapter, I suggested that the debate between the partiality position on ethics—that we hold special obligations and duties to those near and dear—and the position of impartiality was fundamentally misconceived. My reason becomes clearer in light of the foregoing analysis. There can be little doubt that the force behind our moral pronouncements must depend on some more generalizable postulates of meaning and validity (at least some sense of consistency) if such language is to be taken seriously. But just as obviously, the autonomous agent who must reduce every such pronouncement to its abstract preconditions before offering a decisive response will either never respond or will respond in a vacuum of complete analycity. In practice, which is the only context in which most of us act meaningfully, we interrupt the indefinite extension of our obligations in order to preserve and savor our small moral victories. We could be made aware of their larger reach and implication through a more seasoned, exacting dialectic. But it would not matter. Either we would exhaust our own altruistic energy in the inability to help everyone at once, or we would act alone and ineffectually—since we would have nothing more pertinent than our imperatives by which to guide anyone else. There is a further, more embarrassing point, which must be apparent to any reflective civic-minded person.

Modernity, for all its universalizable talk of duty and right and obligation, lacks ēthos. In practice, modernity yields action that is partial and
selective when it occurs at all. That is why its platitudinous talk is so
easily dismissed as pompous special pleading. It is also why we must
find a way to reintroduce the particularist side into all that is reflective
within practical reason.

On the surface, I am taking the partialist side in the controversy. This
is because rhetoric is avowedly partialist in the way it views issues, the
world, and the other. It is also because moral problems arise only from
the particularity of agents situated in an incomplete picture. They can be
resolved only through a willingness to extend our own energy through
an unfinished, imperfectly understood episode. But if rhetoric is biased
toward the partialist stance, a larger possibility can be claimed for it
where ethics are concerned. We are drawn to our larger obligation to
the innocent victim, the needy stranger, by our ability, as Schopenhauer
sensed,[75] to see the other in ourselves. From our own family, perhaps,
we come to an awareness that others, of different races, religions, and
social castes, have families too. It can only be because we sense our complicity in the interests of others that such obligations can be recognized
or acquire practical force.

This is why the debate, as it stands, is fundamentally misconceived.
For Aristotle, partisanship, an excessive allegiance to locales and persons
that are near and dear, is not a bias inherent in rhetoric itself. Rather, it is
part of human nature. Thus it is not a problem to be transcended through
abstraction, but a universal feature of being human and *therefore* a resource to be used. If larger civic obligations toward the generalized other
are to be engendered, we must first see the other in ourselves. To develop
such a sense, we need to be drawn out of ourselves. And to enact this
phase of moral development, we must employ the only art capable of
presenting others to ourselves as both potential victims and potential
moral witnesses—that is to say, as audiences. Aristotle's richly textured
conception of ethical practice in rhetoric gives us some sense of how this
might be done. His advice is incomplete, as is the art, the world view it
presents, and the world in which it thrives. When the great hermeneutic
theorist Hans-Georg Gadamer writes of rhetoric's "universality,"[76] this
is what he seems to intend: the inevitability of and incompleteness of
partisanship in every culture at every time. He regards this universality
as an ethical problem; whereas we could just as well think of it as an
aesthetic promise.

3

In the Horizon of Necessity: Tragic Rhetoric and Public Character

Anyone who ever had a heart
Wouldn't turn around and break it

Anyone who's ever played a part
Wouldn't turn around and hate it.
—Lou Reed, "Sweet Jane," 1969

Most of the time we are unlikely to consider modern political life as supplying us with the materials for an *art*. Caricature, perhaps, as in the political cartoon or the made-for-television cartoons we know as docudramas. But the high drama and oracular vision once associated with the grand art of statecraft seem today as far from our experience as hooped skirts and horse-drawn carriages. Perhaps this is as it should be in an age that is suspicious of grand designs. But not so terribly long ago it was otherwise. A patriarchal aesthetic of politics exuded grace, poise, and propriety; it also flirted boldly with impending disaster. It was not with us for very long, and its departure is no longer lamented. But before liberal activism became the material of low comedy such activism may have been fated to reacquaint itself with its once tragic condition. Not much has been made of that moment, either now or in its unlikely year of 1983. It did not disturb the prevailing cynicism and resignation of the time. But with its passage is raised the question of what, other than grief, scandal, and buffoonery, the rhetorical arts of politics are supposed to depict.

In this chapter we will explore the origins and limits of rhetoric's aesthetic heritage, beginning, as we must, with the newfound prominence of aesthetics. A primary reason for rhetoric's rediscovery in the humanities is the recent widespread fascination with the aesthetic dimension in all textual inquiry. Thus Richard Rorty was able to proclaim that literary criticism was the new philosophy;[1] and from across the galaxies Herbert Marcuse titled his final work *The Aesthetic Dimension*.[2] Whenever an analytical comic and a dialectical tragedian tread the same novel path, it is a sure sign that something peculiar is going on. And what seems most peculiar to me is that the identity and meaning of rhetoric—what rhetoric *is* and *does*—seem to fall out in quite different, even incompatible, ways in each of its recent aesthetic configurations. To note examples from only one recent aesthetic tradition, that of literary hermeneutics, Gadamer reads Aristotle as a pre-Kantian idealist and construes rhetoric as the universal linguisticality inhabiting all cultures and traditions.[3] Robert Sokolowski, in *Presence and Absence*, regards rhetoric as an inferior four-term relationship in which disclosure must be adapted to another party.[4] Ernesto Grassi, who somehow finds Plato of the *Phaedrus* and the younger Cicero to be philosophical compatriots, is thereby able to convert rhetoric into a primordial mythic oratory of disclosure.[5] Who is the ultimate prototype for this orator-poet-statesman? Why Dante, of course. And what is disclosed? Something called "the brutality of being."[6] My point is not to caricature philosophical positions, but rather to take note of the frequent caricatures of rhetoric that have accompanied this latest aesthetic turn. One of the most disturbing excesses of transcendental hermeneutics is its uncontested tendency to decontextualize the rhetorical tradition. Once the very meanings of rhetoric are placed within an indefinitely large hermeneutic circle, to be read primarily in light of present awareness, these same meanings are up for grabs.

There is a further irony. Despite the flattering attention that philosophy has paid recently to both art *and* rhetoric, a glance at the roots of Western tradition suggests that artists and rhetoricians both have every reason to be nervous. Wherever traces of Platonic cosmology are encountered, rhetoricians are bound to address and redress the uncomfortable tension between the possible worlds of the poetic linguistic imagination and the realistic limits of social knowledge.

The character of rhetoric demands a turn to history for its proper understanding. We return, then, to the problem of reading. Mine will be a controversial reading, and, not surprisingly, there is an antagonist. Against the readings of Gadamer, Sokolowski, and Grassi, I want to suggest that the very conception of an aesthetic of rhetoric is, for Aristotle, rooted in the tension of justification. Far from being dependent on an already agreed-upon cultural ēthos, rhetoric's aesthetic status is a product of the unimaginably severe Platonic indictments; it exists, if at all, as a creature of doubt. What emerges from Aristotle's aesthetic discussion, fragmentary though it is, is a sense of rhetoric as intrinsic to a conflicted, indeterminate human nature—a rhetoric not of being but of becoming.

In the discussion that follows, several interim conclusions will become apparent. First, the aesthetic status of rhetoric is directly related to what audiences are able to discern about their own human condition. Art and appearance are *one* in Aristotle's view. Second, Aristotle presents his increasingly specific discriminations in a way that applies the poetics of rhetorical craft to the reality of civic life. As a public language, rhetoric is bound up in the way in which a political culture articulates its own best and worst intuitions about character. Third, this conception of rhetoric has clear ethical and aesthetic features. It is concerned with the proper arrangement of form, issue, style, and norm, so as to create and enact the most perfect sort of rhetorical practice. Moreover, it is interested in this perfected practice because it promotes judgments which help to articulate the superiority of truth and justice.

A REREADING OF POETIC AND RHETORIC

> What I mean by reading is not skimming, not being able to say as the world saith, 'Oh yes, I've read that!' but reading again and again, in all sorts of moods, with an increase of delight every time, till the thing read has become a part of your system and goes forth along with you to meet any new experience you may have.
> —C. E. Montague, *A Writer's Notes on His Trade*, 1930

I now turn away from the new aesthetics of philosophy and toward two foundational philosophers of aesthetics. The aim of this hermeneutic step is to recapture the uncertain mimetic foundation for the relationship between rhetorical and poetic discourse. In doing this, I hope to demonstrate the special senses in which rhetorical language is still the language of an art, while pointing to the historical problems afflicting the aesthetic rehabilitation of rhetoric. It is worth remembering that rhetoric begins its disciplinary history in a good deal of aesthetic trouble. My reading begins with the well-known, yet underestimated Platonic indictments, which, for their very seriousness, are relevant not only to Aristotle's mimetic theory of poetic discourse, but also to the aesthetic predicament of philosophy.

PLATO'S INDICTMENTS

Until recently, it was common practice to offer a rather benign interpretation of Plato's attack on art practices, as if the assault were intended merely to provoke or amuse. Even through the radically revisionist lens of Derrida, the self-reflexive indictments of writing are really a call for truer, more reflexive speech. The call is to be taken seriously, but not too seriously. With Eric Havelock's *Preface to Plato*, Edgar Wind's brilliant *Art and Anarchy*, and a host of related accounts, the burden of interpretation has now shifted considerably.[7] The indictments are simply too pervasive, too unrelenting—even shrill—to be taken as dialectical sport. Sporting antagonists do not propose banning or exiling their friendly rivals. It will become apparent, for instance, that Aristotle took his teacher's indictments of aesthetic practice very seriously. He had every reason to do so.

As for Plato's own ferocity, we can only speculate as to the reasons for it. Greek art was undergoing a revolutionary transformation in accuracy during Plato's youth, in the fifth century B.C. The enigmatic Apollines began to take on expression, then gesture, then a more naturalistic, life-like posture, as if animated by their own secular creators.[8] Although not all would agree, Gombrich argues persuasively that the narrative character of Homeric story telling was responsible for much of this transformation; the sense of an eyewitness recording how, as well as what, sequences of actions occurred could now be found throughout all the plastic arts.[9] In Havelock's terminology,[10] the Homeric spell of mythos had begun to enrapture all Greek culture's most formidable productions. So, while there is an undeniable metaphysical cast to Plato's antagonism, there is also some historical reason for its urgency.

Plato himself subscribed to a uniquely mimetic theory of creation, believing among other things that the universe depicts objects that are modeled on eternal and timeless principles.[11] So, in applying the term *mimēsis* to art, all that Plato was acknowledging was that most artists and practitioners of discourse are dependent on some relationship of depiction, representation, allusion, or manifestation with reality whenever they practice their craft. So far, so good. The problem comes when we try to discriminate among more and less successful instances of art, given this construal of its mission.

It must be said that for Plato there was no real problem. Since he believed that form, the ultimate meaningful essence of a thing's identity, was absolutely, timelessly real, it followed of necessity that all objects of social appearance could only be shadows, illusions of this more profound, hidden truth. From this compelling vantage point, all art, being among other things the invention of appearances, must be twice removed from its ultimate ground of being; it must be an imitation of an imitation, as it were. The test is unfair—only *true* philosophers pass—but it is relentless in its application. Art is not simply to be critiqued and discounted by contrast to these absolutes: the Beautiful, the True, and the Good. It is to be banished from the kingdom of the ideal.

These metaphysical features of the Platonic indictments are now commonplaces in the history of aesthetics and philosophy; and their very extremity has often been invoked as reason for easy dismissal of the arguments themselves. However, we do not have to look very far to find echoes of the Platonic indictment of appearances in more contemporary places: not only in Tertullian, for instance, but in Dostoevsky and Tolstoy,[12] people with every reason to be friendly to the cause of art. This attack on art has far-reaching implications, implications that transcend the ironies of contemporary aesthetic philosophy and challenge the place of rhetorical language within an aesthetic of appearance. As we prepare to consider Aristotle's aesthetic approach to rhetoric, it is worth asking why Plato's attack has been so powerful and so enduring. Several reasons come to mind.

First, the attack has a certain degree of credibility, even with respect to creative aesthetic practice. It is a common perception that art which appeals primarily through its lifelike resemblances—that is, photo-realism and environmental art—is not of great or lasting quality. Moreover, this perception is based on an insight that art teachers have shared for generations: that to create anything, even a primitive aesthetic resemblance, the artist must first have some integrative concept. If one tries to draw a portrait, even a cartoon, on the basis of a part-by-part, line-by-line reconstruction, the result will never be satisfactory. It may look correct at first, but sooner or later the figure will emerge on reflection as distorted or merely shallow. The artist requires a schema, an abstract figurative structure, a form. The essentials must cohere before the finer details can make any sense. And in some conspicuous cases, where the essentials do not cohere, the finer details do not much matter. As Gombrich noted long ago, "making comes before matching."[13] To anyone who has ever been misled, the attack on appearances will make some intuitive sense—hence its universality.

Second, and still more troublesome, Plato did not offer his indictment as a single sweeping dogma designed to decimate all the arts indiscriminately. Rather, his own monistic vision of Truth was adapted differently to the sensory appearances represented by each type of art under discussion. In every case, Plato seems to have hit his target squarely. The rhythms of music, for instance, are like a narcotic that numbs the mind. They are, as Kafka later believed, a hypnotic disturbance that distracts us from other more reliable voices. Lyric poetry is attacked in several of Plato's dialogues, but most savagely in the *Republic*, for lying communicatively to the imagination of its hearers.[14] With all due respect to Grassi's tyrannizing image of the poet as orator, among Plato's charges are that poetry is crippling to the mind, a poison to the soul, and a danger to the state. This is not a friendly challenge, a playful goad intended to stimulate some higher response. The problem with poetic art is exemplified by its mythic monologic form. In striking contrast to the dialectical method of question and answer (which Socratic reflection introduced), the poetic is a single, continuous stream of discourse that cannot be interrupted. Sometimes the muse takes over, the poet becomes possessed, and a primitive (and irrational) form of truth is approached. But most of the time, the rhapsody simply goes on, and on. With pictorial art, the argument is adapted toward yet another form of lie. Here the trickery is that of false witness, the misleading of vision through the acquired techniques of distance and perspective. In a revealing passage in the *Republic*, Plato has Socrates ask:

> Does a couch differ from itself according to how you view it from the side or the front or in any other way? Or does it differ not at all in fact though it appears different? The same magnitude, I presume, viewed from near or far does not appear equal. Why no. And the same things appear bent and straight to those who view them in water and out, or concave and convex, owing to similar errors of vision about colors and there is obviously every sort of confusion of this sort in our souls. And so scene-painting in its exploitation of this weakness of our nature falls nothing short of witchcraft, and so do jugglery and many other such contrivances.[15]

There is much of interest in this passage, not least the implied use of architectural criteria to delimit the plane-surface arts of painting and design. But although there are clearly analogies to other art forms, the brunt of his attack falls on the sensory mode most characteristic of painting—namely, vision.

But, as I have already suggested, Plato saves his most elaborate and far-reaching indictments for rhetoric, which is presented as a veritable synesthesia of sensory deceptions. Rhetoric lies to us through sight, through sound, and through deceptively pleasing images. Through its pretence of a fidelity to ordinary resemblance in all manner of "tongues," rhetoric seems to come closest to expressing a universal language, a kind of ongoing, benumbing confusion of thought. But it is not mere artifice. The charges are more serious than that. Alone among all the arts, and least forgivable, rhetoric lies *cognitively* by applying a language of universal forms (namely, Justice, Honor, the Good, and so forth) to a world of perishable, changeable particulars, divergent opinions, and misleading appearances. Rhetoricians purport to teach what may only be discovered, and they exploit the short-sightedness and wishful thinking of the citizenry. Since it is always better that a painful injustice be endured than perpetrated, the rhetorician finds him or herself in the worst sort of double bind, fated to be either the victim of his or her own craft or the instrument of terrible victimage.[16]

As we tally the damage wreaked so far, the force of Plato's conceptual onslaught becomes clearer. Rhetoric and the other arts are initially conjoined, but by a process of exclusion. They are at the margins, on the outside looking in, exiles from the cognitive kingdom. As exiles, they are excluded from Plato's body politic not only by the same optimal language (a "speech" of mind?) but also by the mutilations of each other's forms of discourse. Since Plato was so absolute in his own mimetic criteria and so scrupulously discriminatory in applying them to each genre of art practice, the deceptions of art cannot even be reconciled with one another, let alone with Plato's standards of Truth, Beauty, and the Good. Plato seems to be insisting that the varieties of aesthetic experience are so confused, so distorted, so removed from the Truth, that the arts cannot even tell each other the same, consistent lie. A language of true mimēsis should not require a further metalanguage for social translation. This specific aspect of Plato's indictment remains one of the most powerful obstacles to a language of art practice, even to the present day.[17] It may be one reason why the disparate voices of twentieth-century art practice seem to have joined in a common language only when they have *rejected* the world of ordinary appearance.[18]

Third, although Plato's attack radically fragmented the communicative discourse of aesthetics, the force of his indictments was not to dismiss the arts as transparent fallacies. Rather, as we have seen, the fifth-century revolution of resemblance in art made many of these so-called deceptions powerful and socially effective. The same may be said of rhetoric, which, in practice, was capable of making the weaker case *appear* to be the stronger. So it seems that the social urgency and single-mindedness that can be detected throughout Plato's charges arise not from the failures of art practice, but rather from the fact that it does its job too well. We do not exile from our midst someone who can be outwitted by society's own devices. This implication should not be lost; the whole attack on deception in art would be pointless were it not for public gullibility. Plato does not mean to imply that ordinary Greeks were going around trying to shake hands with statues. What he means is that the coloration, themes, and messages of contrived appearance— their very materiality—constitute a way of making present something about culture that is at odds with the real Truth and false to ourselves. Here, then, is a first ominous negation of the *language* and reflective capacities of ordinary appearance. This is the legacy of aesthetic philosophy confronting Aristotle.

ARISTOTLE'S *POETICS*

Those familiar with Aristotle's works will readily concede that they are not easily forced into the category of poetry. For all their complexity, the methods of this great philosopher were not designed to smooth over or transcend difficulties. This is one admittedly small reason why Aristotle was more than Plato's student, and why he became a pivotal figure in the foundational understanding of Western thought. If Plato was a poetically gifted philosopher with little sympathy for poetry, Aristotle was, in Richard McKeon's words, "a literal-minded scientist with an understanding and appreciation of art."[19] Aristotle's *Poetics*, for all its rigidity, was for centuries the single most coherent statement about the language of aesthetics available to Western thought. I turn to this treatise not only because it offers a forceful response to the Platonic challenges, but also because it presents a fascinating aesthetic departure from the more predictably Aristotelian placement of language within the public world. Since Aristotle's vision of aesthetic discourse depends on a conception of mimēsis that is radically different from that of Plato, we might expect the author of the *Poetics* to dwell on what had been rendered most suspect by the Platonic indictments: the integrity of ordinary life and the capacity of persons to recognize aesthetic quality within the languages of the poetic. Inevitably, such a reappraisal has critical implications for the imitative capacities of rhetoric as well.

Although we have only an incomplete form of this monumental work, the remarkable depth and rigor of what remains are due largely to Aristotle's concrete intuitions about form, substance, and the world of action. Richard McKeon makes the distinction concisely: "Aristotle professes continued attachment to Plato's philosophy of Forms, but not to the supposition that they exist as models separated from their occurrence in matter."[20] Because Aristotle believed that matter achieved intelligibility through form, his prescriptions regarding the creation of human form are powerfully coherent. As an illustration, consider the six architectonic parts of the highest poetic form, tragedy: plot, character, thought, diction, music, and spectacle, an array that Aristotle claims is exhaustive. Each component is the formal cause of the one that follows it and the material cause of the one that precedes it.[21] There are wonderfully felicitous implications of this ordering. Consider the fact that there is no formal cause of plot (perhaps the author, life itself?) and no material cause of spectacle—as theorists of mass society everywhere now know, it is made up of nothing. More constructively, plots are made out of characters: what they do, think, and express. Therefore, the material of plot is character, and the material of character is thought in its various aspects. Interestingly, we are referred to the art of rhetoric at this critical point. And consistent with this reference is the fact that character, as Aristotle sees it, is given form through action—in this case the sorts of actions that characters are given to perform in enacting the plot. Thus it is plot that provides aesthetic shape to the form of characters as these are disclosed through tragedy.

Equally coherent intuitions may be found about many other aesthetic concerns throughout this prodigious work. But since one aim of the *Poetics* is to recapture the integrity of aesthetic discourse within the now uncertain practices of ordinary life, I will concentrate on a three-step argument that Aristotle offers to counter the Platonic inhibitions on aesthetic discourse. These steps include the justification of poetic, the concept of cathartic pleasure, and the paradoxical aesthetic relationship between rhetoric and poetic.

Very early on in the *Poetics*, Aristotle presents us with a view of mimēsis that seeks to ground aesthetics as a valid form of human experience. Some commentators find Aristotle's discussion confusing, because it alludes to both didactic and hedonistic justifications for the mimetic impulse. Thus the opening passage reads: "The creation of poetry is generally due to two causes, both rooted in human nature. The instinct for imitation is inherent in man from his earliest days; he differs from other animals in that he is the most imitative of creatures, and he learns his earliest lessons by imitation. Also inborn in all of us is the instinct to enjoy works of imitation" (1448b5–10).[22] The question has been, of course, whether the pleasure of mimēsis might not conflict with its cognitive value. As has happened so frequently (in readings of Aristotle's *Rhetoric* too), the presumptions of faculty psychology—the rational and emotional aspects—have impeded a proper understanding of Aristotle's point. Consider what happens if we read these same words in light of Plato's most severe criticism: namely, that artistic practice is a distortion of formal truth and hence a deception. The undeniable fact that we learn from at least some activities that involve imitation *and* derive pleasure from imitative works raises difficulties for a philosopher who idealizes knowledge while disparaging art. Anyone familiar with Plato's dialogues must admit the possibility that some art is conducive to knowledge. So the rejoinder is begun.

On the matter of deception, Aristotle's subsequent words bring forth one of the most fascinating counterexamples in the history of aesthetics, the still debated pleasure we derive from painful resemblances: "What happens in actual experience is evidence of this [this instinct to enjoy imitative works]; for we enjoy looking at the most accurate representations of things which in themselves we find painful to see, such as the forms of the lowest animals and of corpses" (1448b10–13). The example is devastating. For if, as Plato claims, artistic practice deceives too well, then why would the depiction of painful objects not cause pain, as these same objects typically do in real life? The answer can only be that we recognize that the depiction is not the real thing. But let us pause for a Platonic rejoinder; would that not make art something even worse than deception: *failed* deception?

No. If this were the case, it still would not explain our pleasure. That pleasure seems closely related to the *eudaimonia* which consumes Aristotle's vision of the productive sciences. It seems akin to an awakening understanding, a recognition (or discovery, as Aristotle later explains) that this resemblance is not to be confused with the thing itself and that—even if painful—the creativity of depiction is somehow elevating and therefore worthy of appreciation. It is the pleasure of disclosure: in the light of what is absent, as well as what is present. What attracts us is surely not the graphic detail of resemblance or the reminder offered by worldly allusion, but a recognizable tension between our precise, found condition (created or not) and its undeniably generalizable character. And what on earth could this be but *form?*

The aesthetics of recognition, which, after all, is a kind of seeing, affords us the pleasure of learning. If Plato were hostile to pleasure, as rumor has had it, then it is difficult to imagine even this philosopher's opposition to the pleasure of coming to know. This is what makes Aristotle's final cut so decisive: "The reason for this is that learning is a very great pleasure, not for philosophers only, but for other people as well, however limited their capacity for it may be. They enjoy seeing likenesses because in doing so they acquire information (or find themselves inferring); they reason out what each represents, and discover, for instance, that 'this is a picture of so and so'" (1448b13–20).[23] The defense of learning through resemblance and difference cuts deeply. It is as true of the political cartoon as *The Blue Boy.* Along the ladder of inquiry, it runs from the search of "inquiring minds" for scandal about celebrities through the how-will-it-end suspense of narrative adventure to the *Wohin gehst du?* of contemporary inquisitors. We derive pleasure from learning, regardless of whether the kernels of knowledge are savory.

In contemporary terms, we might characterize the knowledge that Aristotle is alluding to as self-knowledge. There is no doubt a flicker of self-reflection in every resemblance. But we should add immediately that such knowledge assumes a minimal level of competence in ordinary civic actors as well—the ability to distinguish piety and pretense from good will, to critique in civic friendship what is said of our fellows. In this, Aristotle may well have been too optimistic. For between friendship and just anger there is but a small difference and a fundamental human capacity—the ability to discriminate between the mask and the face. In one forum, we might experience aesthetic pleasure; in another, rage and political disgrace. But in each, propriety defines character and the margin for hypocrisy at the same time.

With this minimal assumption, then, Aristotle is able to offer the elitism of Plato a final ironic thrust. For it is scarcely consistent to claim, as Plato had, that untutored slaves may be taught geometry, while ordinary citizens cannot be trusted with art. If my reading of this elegant justification makes sense, pleasure and knowledge are not at odds. Moreover, the integrity of aesthetics comes to rest on our ordinary capacity to distinguish the image from the object. In his definitive, final touch, Aristotle portrays the public sense of recognition in a manner that is unmistakably akin to dialectic. The seeing of likeness and difference is, after all, the pivotal ground of distinction in Plato's own dialectical method of collection and division.

In retrieving a foundation for aesthetics, then, it is worth noting that Aristotle does not make the poet a preternatural founder of community, but one of its members. There are no divine orators here, but only people who share our burdens of appearance. So the justification of the mimetic impulse is as close at hand as our own everyday practice. The aesthetic condition is rendered in terms as fundamental and as problematic as the human condition, in a tension that anyone can recognize—between work and world, between what is other and what is at hand. Even this minimal competence of audience as actor may be called into question, of course. Audiences of ordinary persons may not be capable of recognizing an art forgery from the real thing, for instance. And, given the complexity of restricted, aesthetic codes, they may not be able to recognize the real thing as art either. The capacity of the public to be duped in a variety of complex, cynical schemes seems to have become one of our modern commonplaces. Still, audiences have usually survived their duplicitous masters and proved capable of recognizing rhetorical impostors, those pretending to an affiliation and interest that is not there. Sadly, this needs to be demonstrated anew in every age. But, given the general thematic base of both rhetoric and aesthetics—that is, the imitation of action—such a minimal and renewable capacity for enlightenment is considerably better than nothing.

But, more than the simple fact of recognition, there is the nature of aesthetic experience itself. This too is pivotal for the classical understanding of created form. In all of Aristotle's work, the *Rhetoric* included, form is eventually addressed in its most perfected aspect. The concept of perfected human form has been the goad to many a perishable metaphysical insight, just as it has unleashed all manner of romanticism in contemporary aesthetics.[24] The picture is no less striking and every bit as memorable for this Aristotelian aesthetics. The theory of cathartic pleasure presents us with one of Western literature's most profound statements about the relationship between our personal and our human condition. I now turn to this difficult subject.

Why is tragedy the highest form of poetic discourse? Many reasonable answers emerge within Aristotle's own opus. Tragedy involves nobler, more expansive characters and actions, bigger issues, greater virtues and vices. At its best, the tensions and reversals of tragedy enlarge life's panorama. In keeping with the Aristotelian modalities, it might be added that the form of the tragic plot is also of a higher order, involving fateful *necessity*. It is certainly opposed to the less formally pure relationships of contingency, probability, possibility, and even chance. We shall see later on that this is artfully disguised complexity on Aristotle's part. Still, there is a superior coherence involved in the unfolding of tragedy. Then there is the matter of theme. If it is, as Socrates alleges in the *Gorgias*, better to endure a painful injustice than to perpetrate a similar evil, Aristotle (after preparing the way in book 7 of the *Nicomachean Ethics*) may have the last word by allowing for a form of discourse that enacts and perfects the experience of just such a painful event (like Socrates' own death) only to illumine its meaning for the aesthetic witness. Once more, on Plato's own implied criteria, this may be the most complete poetic form. These reasons for the aesthetic superiority of tragedy become, like the power of the art itself, increasingly speculative. However, they all point toward the conclusion that Aristotle regarded the dynamis of tragedy as truer and more universal than other embodiments of poetic language. Still, the nature of this tragic dynamis contains unlocked mysteries, as does the unnamed engine that drives the drama.[25]

In his discussion of "Further rules," Aristotle equates the tragic effect with "an appeal to our Humanity" (1456a20–22). As is well known, Aristotle believed that the truths of poetic were of a higher order than the truths of history. This is because poetic is concerned with *universal truths*, such as are found in tragedy, whereas history is concerned only with the particularities of action and event. (It remained for Hegel to discover that history, once idealized, could be made to reveal universal comic truths as well.) Aristotle's earlier account makes the more compelling case: "By universal truths are to be understood the kinds of things a certain type of person will probably or necessarily say or do in a given situation; and this is the aim of poetry" (1451b1–5).

But what of the appeal itself, its language and its message? In Aristotelian mimēsis, form as recognition may emerge dialectically through a felt sense of what appearance is *not*—that is, the thing itself. But with tragic pleasure the moment of recognition and discovery is truer than with other forms. Why? It is undeniably more painful; yet it is still experienced as aesthetic gratification. Again, why? To even begin to answer these questions, we must explore the more basic issue of how action in the particular is related to this overarching form of action as completed. Clearly—and despite the efforts of ardent revisionists—Aristotle was no determinist. He allows that an action may have multiple causes, including chance, fortune, will, passion, and circumstance. In the *Nicomachean Ethics*, we learn that character is not something intrinsic and integral to the self, but rather something made up, a kind of performative accomplishment (1139a32–1139b10). It is comprised of the actions that each of us undertakes. Yet, for all this, the form of tragedy—which is, after all, the form of action—becomes in its most perfected state a kind of necessity. Aristotle's example of the greatest tragedy, Sophocles' *Oedipus Rex*, may provide a clue to his larger position. The perfectly symmetrical plot of *Oedipus*—his curse, his crime, and its fateful consequence—seems to affirm the triumph of necessity in its most rigorous, irreversible form. Yet, even in this timeless work, there are multiple curiosities, from the vantage point of Aristotle's strictures for poetic excellence. For instance, there are improbable elements—by which I mean, as I suspect Aristotle did, elements of thought or character that do not appear appropriate to a particular situation. Examples include Oedipus's ignorance regarding the manner of Laius's death and the enactment of the Delphic oracle. These may be affirmations of poetic truth for Aristotle, examples of his astonishing dictum that "Probable impossibilities are to be preferred to improbable possibilities" (*Poetics* 1451b8–11). Even so, the ignorance of Oedipus is given mild censure even by Aristotle.

There are other problems. Despite MacIntyre's protestations of Aristotle's "Unity of the Virtues" doctrine and its aesthetic correlative of a heroic tragic flaw, Oedipus seems not to have such a flaw. If anything, he is unaccountably afflicted with what modern writers such as Nagel call "bad moral luck."[26] Of course, Oedipus's own character is directly related to all that happens; and, to put it mildly, there are regrettable lapses in timing. But this is a man of knowledge, whose very pursuit of knowledge is his ruin. One can imagine a comic version of *Oedipus* in which the hero, not being a "detail person," simply elects not to pursue the matter any further. No harm, no foul. Ignorance has long been a convenient vehicle for such interim happy endings. But this is clearly not what Aristotle or Sophocles were after.

Although the flaws of Oedipus are hardly those of a virtuous Aristotelian character, Aristotle gives us the most important accompanying discourse ever offered for a proper understanding of this work. And critical to that understanding is the fact that Oedipus is a willful human agent who makes contingent choices every step of the way. Although he acts without full knowledge—and arguably, the insufficiency of his reason is what drives him on—he acts with the best evidence available and even with a limited sort of vision. This contingent quest for truth, trapped as it is by unfolding necessity, is nonetheless triumphant. S. H. Butcher goes further still in his reading of Aristotle's *Poetics*. He writes: "The incidents of every tragedy worthy of the name are improbable if measured by the likelihood of their everyday occurrence—improbable in the same degree in which characters capable of great deeds and great passions are rare. The rule of probability, as also that of 'necessity,' refers rather to the internal structure of a poem; it is the inner law which secures the cohesion of the parts."[27]

What is Aristotle saying with this choice of example about the relationship of action and character to necessity? The relationship of action and character to necessity is far too complex and mysterious to be resolved with a single example, even one as great as Oedipus. But what Aristotle and his commentators seem to be suggesting is that action, viewed from the interiorized stance of the actor as particular agent, is always conceived as particular and contingent. Rhetoric, as the art of thought, provides the meaning of this particularized stance as it invents speech on occasions of uncertainty. But it is this same particular, viewed in light of a sequence of particulars from the retrospective formal unity of the plot, which then becomes subject to necessity. Conversely, necessity comes about only as the accumulation of contingencies. This may be what Wittgenstein had in mind when he observed, "Every tragedy could really start with the words, 'Nothing would have happened had it not been that . . .'"[28] Thus it is that poetic, as the imitation of an action, "is an expression of the universal element in human life."

The gap between deliberately formed opinions, judgments, and actions and the narrative reversal and judgments of necessity is one of the fundamental lessons of Aristotle's tragic view. Here is Martha Nussbaum on this theme:

The great tragic plots explore the gap between our goodness and our good living, between what we are (our character, intentions, aspirations, values) and how humanly well we manage to live. They show us reversals happening to good-charactered but not divine or invulnerable people, exploring the many ways in which being of a certain good human character falls short of *eudaimonia*. (In the extreme case, some of these ways may include damage or corruption to the originally good character itself. In such cases, however, it is important that the change should come not from deliberate wickedness, but from the pressure of external circumstances over which they have no control. Thus the damage will still display the gap between being good in deliberately formed intentions or values, and managing to live out a fully good life.)[29]

Nussbaum concludes: "Aristotle's belief that the gap is both real and important illuminates his anti-Platonic claim that tragic action is important and a source of genuine learning."[30]

It is the experience of this distance between the contingent and the necessary, a distance marked by the retrospective consideration of *any* action, that helps create the mysterious appeal of tragic pleasure. And of the appeal itself? Recalling perhaps his own dialectical grounding of form, Aristotle says: "Tragedy is the representation not only of a complete action, but also of incidents that awaken fear and pity, and effects of this kind are heightened when things happen unexpectedly as well as logically, for then they will be more remarkable" (1452a). In purifying and enacting a poetic form of human action's necessity, tragedy presents us with the single feature of human life that cannot be imitated or expressed away, the feature that is present even in its absence. As a recurrent element of plots, it is enacted through the character who must provoke, resist, recognize, and finally endure his or her fate. As a passionate recognition, it is the sense that the power of individual action is finite and that *this finitude is itself universal.*

By naming this particular recognition *katharsis* (a removal of pain in spirit),[31] Aristotle alludes to a powerfully rhetorical aspect of the tragic passion, an aspect with medical, musical, and even religious analogues. For it is not simply that tragic katharsis provides an insight into the plight of dramatic character. It also suggests that our recognition of fate heroically encountered and endured is liberating in a lofty way to the individual consciousness, now trapped in an ensemble of others. Indeed, for its part, the audience—that great, inarticulate personality—becomes for a time a witness to the *otherness* of individuated consciousness and to the limits of what each of its lonely embodiments might do. Here Aristotle's tendency to theorize from the best example of each category helps to reveal, through aesthetic performance, a tacit moment of recognition, from hero to community. I know of no better description of the *rhetorical* aspect of this process than that offered by Butcher:

> Applying this to tragedy we observe that the feelings of pity and fear in real life contain a morbid and disturbing element. In the process of tragic excitation they find relief, and the morbid element is thrown off. As the tragic action progresses, when the tumult of the mind, first roused, has afterwards subsided, the lower forms of emotion are found to have been transmuted into higher and more refined forms. The painful element in the pity and fear of reality is purged away; the emotions themselves are purged.[32]

It is interesting that, as Butcher turns to the *Rhetoric* to explain pity and fear, he finds himself referring to the morbidity of fear in *reality*. Although the ambiguity of katharsis may defy a complete understanding, its destiny is clear enough, its truths available for recognition. Here is a little notation from Wittgenstein: "A hero looks death in the face, real death, not just the image of death. Behaving honourably in a crisis doesn't mean being able to act the part of a hero well, as in theater, it means rather being able to look death *itself* in the eye. For an actor may play lots of different roles, but at the end of it all he *himself*, the human being, is the one who has to die."[33] Now if one were to come upon this message, say, in a fortune cookie, it would hardly liberate or reassure. Recognition of the sort hinted at in the anecdote, if it is to be genuinely powerful, must also become *public*. Where tragedy is concerned, recognition must be accompanied by a sense that one's self-discovery or knowledge is embedded in the human condition. This is what Aristotle seems to have recognized as universal about the perfection and limits of poetic form: that the witnessing of collective fate is available to no other form that transcends the ordinary understanding of individual consciousness. What remains to be shown is that such an act of tragic witnessing includes a powerful rhetorical motive that might also be preparatory to the reemergence of a public sense.

The unfathomable tension between appearances as particularities of action and action framed retrospectively by necessity has therefore a rhetorical counterpoint. This counterpoint invents virtue and character in the reflective recognition and relational movement of self *through* audience; thus we ourselves are constituted in a terror of recognition. Considered aesthetically, then, rhetoric is the art of thought.

TRAGEDY AS EULOGY: A MODERN EXAMPLE

In our discussion so far, I have drawn attention to several curiosities in the *Rhetoric*. Beginning with the Platonic indictments of both rhetoric and poetic and moving through Aristotle's quite different approach to mimēsis, we now find ourselves struggling with what, in this foundational theory, is the highest form of aesthetic experience: the tragic katharsis. Here, not only is the construction of *doxa* and logos of character itself a rhetorical task, but the emotional synthesis and release of passion (in the tragic emotions of pity and fear) are also discussed by Aristotle in the *Rhetoric*. Symmetries of omission and proportion between the *Poetics* and the *Rhetoric* persist. In the *Poetics*, only a brief allusion to comedy survives—as Burke recognized, comedy is the most characteristic deliberative orientation of rhetoric. However, in the *Rhetoric*, the least complete and—many would argue—least rhetorical form of discourse under discussion is the discourse called ceremonial, or "epideictic," the form that bears closest resemblance to the genres of the *Poetics*.

No single example can bring together all the mystery and paradox surrounding the aesthetic language of rhetoric. But the traditional rhetorical form of the eulogy comes close. Here is a ceremonial, literary form designed to praise or exalt the virtues of a human life before an audience that Aristotle describes as "spectators." Although the life of the subject is over, the speech is oriented retrospectively toward the present, in an artful celebration of what has come before. Aristotle is quite clear that the eulogy has no *ergon* beyond that of presentation and display. To some commentators, this implies diminishment or pointlessness, as if Aristotle did not know what to do with this form of speech. More likely, this lack of instrumentality locates it more decisively within the realm of an aesthetic language, to be appreciated less for what it does and more for what it is. But this is surely not the end of the story.

In her monumental recent study, *The Invention of Athens*, Nicole Loraux argues convincingly that the Athenian funeral oration and the rise of a public culture are inextricably linked: "Because in the fine death it is still the city that conquers nature, the political oration seeks to go beyond the common fate of mankind, and it is significant that the Athenians chose the setting of the public funeral to reaffirm the omnipotence of the *polis:* to replace man with the citizen, even in death, is certainly the ultimate achievement of the civic imaginary."[34] Loraux has grasped perfectly how aesthetic pain can prepare us for the invention of public rhetorical meaning. But, curiously, she never alludes to the larger implications for an aesthetics of language. She is aware of the numerous analogues in Greek tragedy, when these same emotions are evoked by masters such as Euripides and Aeschylus and even Sophocles. But oddly, she makes no mention of the theory of tragedy and the most definitive emotional preparation of katharsis. Despite the numerous connections that Aristotle himself makes between eulogy and poetic form, there are no citations of either katharsis or the *Poetics* in Loraux's remarkable study. While it is possible that the poetic associations of eulogy might have undermined the *political* aspects of this form which she sought to underscore,[35] my suspicion is that the method and theme of the original poetic theory could only have strengthened her argument.

It is generally agreed that there were no great eulogies on the occasion of John F. Kennedy's untimely death. Although there were continual shocked allusions to this material of high drama and tragedy, the usually reliable means of discourse production merely sputtered, as if too stunned by the harsh reality to reach for proper perspective. The real meaning of grief, the lingering trace of absence, is found not in the newsworthy moment, but in memory. So it was that, on 22 November 1983, twenty years later, friends, family, and fellow citizens of the fallen president gathered again in Trinity Church to remember. Though Kennedy in death would always be a heroic, youthful, martyred figure, much had changed for those he left behind. In those twenty years, there had been more assassinations, including those of civil rights leaders and his own brother, and a war (some said *his* war) gone terribly wrong. Within the nation there had been scandals, political aimlessness, and a sharp turn to the right—a further, ironic heritage from 1964, perhaps. Outside the nation, there were new geopolitical weapons, terror as an instrument of national policy, and lapsed commitments and convictions on human rights and disarmament. Inside the national institutions, a proud imagery of rhetorical rebirth had been painted; more emphatically than ever, this was a media age. Here there was an almost desperate belonging. But outside the comfort of a binge economy was the cynicism of scarcity.

It should be added that this cynicism had also come to color the popular understanding of John Kennedy himself. In light of our speculations regarding the deterioration of public langauge, it is interesting that most of the discourse surrounding the Kennedy legacy still seemed, and seems, nostalgically "modern."[36] From gothic rumors of conspiracy to the scandalized affliction of celebrity, the boundaries of myth and contemporary normlessness were beginning to close.

This portrait is far from complete, but we may assume it to be broadly consistent with the contextual and historical experiences of the friends, family, and Kennedy Democrat churchgoers in attendance at the November 1983 anniversary. Of course, there were some official curiosities as well. The president of the United States was also in attendance: Ronald Reagan, a symbol to many Kennedy Democrats of much that had gone wrong in the twenty years since Kennedy's death. The principal speaker was Senator Edward Moore Kennedy. Having emerged as a spectacular failure in the 1980 presidential primaries, Kennedy seemed resigned to his iconic role as oppositional voice. At the time of this address, he was still the most articulate opponent of everything the sitting American president represented.

The only other peculiarities which require notation are stylistic.[37] This speech was not exactly a eulogy, but more a discourse of commemoration and tribute. Nonetheless, the *epitaphios* theme and form were quite similar, as was the arrangement of topics. This speech was made, further, in the context of a Roman Catholic Mass. In itself, it is not unusual for an epitaph to be presented during a religious service. But this commemorative epitaph was spoken not prior to the Consecration of the Mass, but after the redemptive rituals of Consecration and Communion. This *was* unusual and may have reflected the retrospective character of the occasion. Finally, this service and discourse marked the conclusion of a weekend commemorative spectacle in which imagery of grief and martyrdom were everywhere. The Kennedy docudramas (on the Cuban missile crisis and the assassination), the revered press conferences, "Thank you, Mr. President," Rod Serling's worshipful "Years of Lightning; Days of Drums," even the old conspiracies—all were aired again. In the midst of the most traditional rhetorical and ritual forms were the inevitable trappings of modernity. But Kennedy's speech was able to rise above this "spectacular journalism" in my judgment. In alluding to the unfulfilled potential and personal limits of a public human life, it managed to mourn the passage of its own New Frontier rhetoric. For an instant, it renewed the forgotten promise of public life generally.

Kennedy's *exordium* acknowledged the uniquely public aspect of the occasion, even as he maintained a kind of stewardship over its meaning: "From this church, on a cold winter morning, nearly a quarter of a century ago, John Kennedy went forth to his inauguration as President of the United States. Now we, his family and friends, return here on the twentieth anniversary of his death, to remember him not in sadness, but in joy, and to share that joy with a nation and a world that shared our love for him."[38] The statement is simple, respectful of history's fateful assertion, yet definitive on the key question of mood. We return, as Kennedy did not. But we have come here not to mourn, but to share the joy of remembrance with a world that now joins our gathering. This is to be a somewhat belated Irish funeral. In the language of tragic destiny, to go forth is to return, of course; but this was the more interiorized view of the actor, with a generous spirit, not to be outdone in grace or recognition.

As the younger Kennedy spoke of his brother, one was reminded that perhaps no contemporary American had been more mystified in death. The manner of the late president's passing, the visible celebrity of his family and position—all this made access to his character difficult, especially in a forum such as this. Detractors of Kennedy's legacy usually stressed its dependence on all that seemed inconsequential in modern politics: charisma, media management, and the political fluff of image making. In a compressed narration of his theme, Edward Kennedy was able to turn the spectacle of grief to his own larger purposes:

> He came to the Presidency by the narrowest of margins. But when he was taken from us, our planet was more united in grief than it ever was in grandest design. Moscow wept with Boston, and with Dallas. In the years that followed, the feeling for him has not dimmed, but deepened. And today, far from this church, in lands where hardly anyone speaks his langauge, they still hear his call. His presence continues to be so powerful because ideals can be shown far more vividly in one life, than in all the lofty theories.

In mystification, there is ambiguity. And here it is the direct sensual communication of experience that links this man's life to a global constituency. Note the elegance of the contrast—from the narrowest of margins (no doubt, the Chicago precincts) to an entire planet—and the language: "plans," "designs," "lofty theories" of "language" are all on one side (as, probably, are the anti-Kennedy academicians). But on the other side, "grief," "wept," the hearing of a "call." And then, a "powerful," "presence," "shown" "vividly." Here is the instantiation of character in a direct and vast address.

So far, Edward Kennedy had done in words what he had been unable to do in life; he had used the almost mythic force of his brother's legacy, while eluding its deeper burdens. But now there were difficulties. To show the ideals of this life required some sort of language of ideals. This was a treacherous path, for two reasons: first, Kennedy's own New Frontier language of idealism, parodied even by sympathizers, was now sadly dated; and second, to employ the only remaining official language of civic virtue would be to recast this commemorative tribute into what Nicole Loraux claims is the real ergon of every eulogy: a tribute to the virtues of the body politic. But in light of the government in exile mentality of Kennedy followers, this would seem an unlikely choice.

This second alternative—a turn to Kennedy's more human side—had obvious pitfalls as well. For one thing, if even some of the rumors are true, the real private JFK was a character with more than his share of *hamartia*. Any speech based on the notion of concrete disclosure must at least raise this issue if it is to be taken seriously. Then there was the most serious problem of this option for the speech as a whole: for how would Kennedy be able to sustain this celebratory mood of joy, if he were to tell us once more the concrete story of his brother's life?

Nonetheless, Kennedy chose this second option: "He has been made a legend, but we remember him as a man." He would deconstruct the mythic Kennedy in order to present us with a more concrete reality. To my mind, a mark of the speech's importance, if not grandeur, was the way it did this while simultaneously rekindling the language of virtue and its public possibility.

The body of the speech presents a deceptively simple internalized ergon, a movement from the personal character trait to the public virtue. These outwardly directed disclosures would become—inevitably *must* become—somber were it not for the gentle bits of humor that punctuate the narrative. Kennedy begins with one such anecdote of family debunking: "We treasure him most as a son and a brother, husband, father, uncle, friend [note the outward movement even here—from the familial to civic friend]. He took issues seriously, but never himself too seriously.

Indeed, his family would not let him. After his election, when we were all at dinner one night, Dad looked at him and then turned to Mother and said with a smile, 'He may be President, but he still comes home and swipes my socks.'" All the humor was of this homespun order, designed to humanize the portrait of Kennedy while providing gentle relief from the weightiness of the theme. Of course, this is also an anecdotal commonplace of the Irish funeral. The stories are all ones we have heard before. Partly for this reason, we get the illusion of disclosure and the reassurance of familiarity with this extended civic family.

Wisely, the surviving Kennedy chose this moment to tackle the most difficult personal question. In a masterful synthesis of the general, the personal, and the Catholic, he observed: "And the qualities that made us love him were the same human qualities that attracted millions who never met him at all. He knew historians would write of him, but his truest history is written in the hearts of people everywhere. They forgave him his shortcomings because he gave us a sense of what human beings, despite their imperfections, can aspire to do. He challenged us to do better, but he also remembered that none of us, including himself, would ever do as well as we should." With this passage, Kennedy expanded further the strangely privileged relationship that all his hearers felt with this most human of public figures. Note the marvelous past-tense reciprocity between for*gave* and *gave.* Here, the ethereal charisma of Kennedy the public figure is deconstructed to reveal a fallible corporeal being. It doesn't matter what the historians say or, by implication, what his actual trespasses may have been. We are none of us perfect. To rise above his imperfections was surely part of Kennedy's call. Surely we and he must have had them. Here, it must be added, there is a great rhetorical advantage for the eulogy over the tragic soliloquy. The soliloquy employs a first-person disclosure to condense dramatic tension in the hamartia or actual flaws of character. The eulogy, as a classic ceremonial genre, is able to merge qualities of character with the virtues bordering on them for the purposes of amplification. Hence this would-be disclosure works as a tribute. The flaws do not even need to be spelled out in order to be forgiven.

But here a tension in mood is unavoidable. Joy is caring, but not readily compatible with forgiveness. To forgive, we must first be injured. Moreover, it is only the darker side of this life, its premature retribution, that renders further forgiveness unnecessary. This passage could not possibly work with, say, Joe McCarthy or even Edward Kennedy himself. Technically skilled as the words are, they gain credibility only through an absurd event. Equally so, their moral: Kennedy's own unnamed flaws are invoked as a lesson that he has been carefully teaching us all along.

We move now to the confirmation proper, a memorable series of personal images conjoined with imaginative public equivalences. Here ēthos is reconstructed, and a fresh and sensually real Kennedy is created anew before our wishful eyes. The graphic enthymeme which targets this expectation follows:

> In his leadership there was the same fine mix of elements as in his life. Walking along the beach at home, he said to me when I was very young, "On a clear day, you can see all the way to Ireland." In later years, the sweep of his vision reached from the soaring distances of outer space to the narrowest corners of human existence. And some day, when human beings look back from the stars towards a glistening blue earth, suspended in the sky, they will know that it was John Kennedy who first set them on their way.

It is a beautiful series of images: the distant nostalgic past, transformed metaphorically into a global vision and then inverted prophetically in a Copernican shift of consciousness, with Kennedy's own legacy at the core. In its sweep and grandeur, it exhibits a personal quality that is almost, well, Kennedyesque. And so consciousness itself is made to project outward, like Kennedy's and like our own public longing. Perhaps lost amidst the stylistic riches is the relative lack of color devoted to the more public version of Kennedy's qualities.

But the lexicon is a worthy one, and it continues: "And he had courage." Here Kennedy's endurance of sharp physical pain is publicly enlarged to include his sensitivity to the pain of others and his belated but emphatic civil rights conversion. The passage is noteworthy as Edward Kennedy's first conspicuous innuendo vis-à-vis the current administration. John Kennedy "rejected the cold affliction of indifference"—effective—"and the comfortable erosion of concern"—less effective, at least to those who have experienced the process of erosion. "He never summoned us to indifference." Of course, there would be no point in bringing in the alternatives to Kennedy's public character were it not for the fact that a representative of the political alternative was in attendance.

From courage, we move to compassion, which was "at the center of his soul [though] he never wore it on his sleeve." Here Edward Kennedy's voice broke as he told of the natural way in which his brother cared for and watched over his retarded sister, Rosemary. This is generalized to include the human family. And so from compassion to strength: no personal anecdote here (although the PT 109 example was probably ingrained in the public consciousness); instead, we move outward to virtues of design, things we do not do naturally so much as through a kind of acquired toughness. Understandably, this is followed by a testimony to John Kennedy's independence of mind ("which our parents, by their strength, instilled in all of us"). Kennedy's shift on the highly publicized missile gap is here invoked as an example of resisting external pressure and acknowledging what one has learned. It must be noted that these tensions of word and deed are common to the eulogy form. It is but another case of the speaker who wishes to stress a person's virtues equating qualities of personality with "qualities bordering on them." Put another way, the same matters of fact, decision, and reversal are now the tributaries of character and may be read quite differently in light of other virtues or vices.

The circle of interpretation has boundaries, of course; and it is hard to imagine anyone invoking Kennedy's resistance to pressure without the counterexample of the Bay of Pigs springing to mind. This failed invasion of Cuba was planned and plotted before Kennedy assumed command; and even the least sympathetic accounts present Kennedy as a reluctant, pressured accomplice. This conspicuous Kennedy failure becomes, in the forgiving light of memory, a misstep which represents his ability to admit error and concede defeat. After regretting that his brother's wisdom could not have survived to rethink America's course in Vietnam, Edward Kennedy overextends a bit with his maxim that "It is never an easy thing for the powerful to admit a mistake. But he showed us that it is perhaps the essence of greatness in Presidents that they can." In denying externality of ergon to the eulogy, Aristotle may have been expressing more than an antiquated intuition. Once we know that Reagan had recently recalled the United States peace-keeping force from Lebanon—after committing himself to the long-term importance of its mission *and* after 246 marines had been killed in a terrorist explosion—Kennedy's maxim of statecraft could easily have been dismissed as special pleading.

The last personal/public quality should be one to transcend the others; and it is: *growth*. Here we find the first genuine limit to the outward projection of disclosure:

Some say he grew in office. I believe he achieved a rare and noble height. And at the summit of his City on the Hill was America the tolerant. He had adversaries, but never enemies. And his likely opponent in 1964, Barry Goldwater, was also his good friend. His power was tempered with poetry. His activism with the deeper truth of art. He was tough on the pompous and the irrational, no matter what their place or rank. He was gentle with children, his own and others. And during the most serious discussions in the Oval Office, he was never too busy to take a call from Caroline, or to pause for a moment to play hide and seek with John.

This odd lexicon of liberal verities seems to exhaust the secular imagery of character only to turn back on itself once more. After scaling the heights (and appropriating Ronald Reagan's favorite anecdote about the City on the Hill), we find ourselves back with the private mortal man, the man whose growth must *necessarily* come to an end. The passage is followed by two compressed bits of Kennedy humor; but it is finally too late for this.

As these qualities have moved outward, they have become public virtues, but virtues no longer apparent in the practices of public life. They survive not as real civic verities, norms of public conduct, but only as the abstractions of one person's memory. In the harsh light of a post-Kennedy world, they disappear. As the language of Loraux prepares us to acknowledge, this commemorative address becomes a tribute to a polity which, like Kennedy, no longer exists. The younger Kennedy's language, a masterful transformation of public conventions, must now break with itself before the darker episode of history which now intrudes. In speech, as in life, Kennedy must die.

The gap between these passages might have been decades, or of a still painful regret. But now America's most conspicuously *political* family must publicly verbalize its loss. The eulogy has become a tragedy as the brothers are joined in death. And as survivor of this lost dynasty, Edward Kennedy speaks more slowly, from somewhere far away, in a mournful staccato rhythm: "What a wonderful combination they were! The two were one with purpose and vitality, in their capacity to dream dreams and renew our vision. Robert Kennedy had a valiant part then, and he has it on this day. To the end, he lived out the meaning of our brother's unfinished life. Among their greatest legacies are the people they brought into public endeavor. The happy few. The band of brothers on the new frontier have become a multitude who are still in the arena, at the center of the struggle." The caisson is approaching now. With the invocation of

Henry V ("the happy few"), the band of brothers has found its flaws, and its abrupt interruption is underscored. This was the end of any comic relief and the first of several memorable images of loss, *peripeteia*, and the transcendence of public will. As if to mingle our own destiny with his larger design, Kennedy intoned: "All of us in this church may not gather all together again. But for those who share the commitments, the compassion, and the high hopes of John Kennedy, there will never be a last assembly."

In summing up the public man, we are left with paradox and mystery: "this man, who had every gift but the length of years. He was an heir to wealth who felt the anguish of the poor. He was an orator of excellence who spoke for the voiceless. He was a son of Harvard who reached out to the sons and daughters of Appalachia. He was a man of special grace who had a special care for the retarded and handicapped. [Kennedy's voice broke again here.] He was a hero of war who fought hardest for peace. He said and proved in word and deed that one man can make a difference." Then Edward Kennedy concludes, as if in an afterthought (and without apparent conviction), "which is why his thousand days will be remembered for a thousand years or more."

Between days and years is the still moment, which is now upon us: "As Jackie wrote after that brave and bitter weekend, 'His high noon kept all the freshness of the morning. And he died then, never knowing disillusionment.' And he himself wrote, after our brother Joe was gone, 'Through it all, he had a deep and abiding faith. He was never far from God. And death to him was less a setting forth than a returning.'" Then, with a tone approaching defiance: "John Kennedy had faith strong enough for any fate. He made America young again, and the world seem new again." But we, the surviving friends, family, and citizens must remain within a world neither young nor new. Kennedy apparently sensed that decades and distances have been a protection, a mask of stoicism for our own disillusionment. If Edward Kennedy's words reopened the wound, they also did much to erase the distance. "So it is that on this anniversary, the span of time since November 22, 1963, does not seem like a matter of decades, but of days. And over his memory, and his meaning, death has no dominion. What he did and believed will endure. And in the end it will prevail."

In this remarkable passage, our capacity for undergoing this torment is entwined with our capacity to erase the distance between past and future, so to face and overcome historical (and *ethical*) mortality itself.

We have come to a point of stasis, where opposed forces of abstract virtue (memory) and fateful concrete existence (destiny) arrest each other in a still moment of temporary rest. In this moment, we may quietly measure our pain:

> Inevitably, we cannot forget the pain of his loss. On bright summer afternoons at Cape Cod, or in this waning season of the year, how often we still think of him in all his vigor, and say to ourselves, "We miss you Jack, and always will." But in the darkness, we see the stars and how clearly we see him now. We have known other great men and women in our time, in other countries and our own. Yet there was a spark in him so special that even his brief years and his early passing could not put it out. He made us proud to be Americans. And the glow of his life will always light the world.

On the printed page, these lines approach *bathos*, an excess that will not abide the ebbing of emotion. But in the context of the almost mythic Kennedy stoicism ("Kennedys don't cry"), it captures a powerful public moment of restored grief.[39] The entire statement is a scarcely cloaked sob. This is no longer the language of memory, but a more powerful, immediate language of grief and mourning. The injury and the burden have returned, to be realized and taken to heart all over again. It is at this pivotal point that Edward Kennedy's peroration was able to reenact his brother's inaugural address theme (and language), even as it managed to find within this tragic katharsis a moment for awakening the promise of public life:

> For him, on this day, twenty years ago, the journey came to an end. For us here, and others everywhere, there are promises to keep and miles to go before we sleep. Now his appeal summons us anew, not merely to remember him, but to rededicate ourselves. *The unfinished quality of his life symbolizes the unfinished agenda of America.* As the torch is passed to each succeeding generation, I believe that those who seek peace and justice, those who join the forward march of the human pilgrimage on earth will say of John Fitzgerald Kennedy, "He has never left us. And he never will." (Emphasis added)

With this masterful conclusion, Edward Kennedy was able to do rhetorically what Aristotle envisioned of the highest poetic art: to elicit from the deepest sense of human loss an affirmative human moment. This is the essence of tragic pleasure.

I have spent so much time on Kennedy's speech because it encapsulates that virtually lost form of discourse marking the boundaries of rhetoric and poetic. Only time and generations to come will tell whether Kennedy's speech deserves to be included in the pantheon of great rhetorical texts. Perhaps the least that can be said of it, in the present context, is that it is an emotional *au revoir* for liberal rhetoric. The test of its longevity will also mark the intersection of what we have been discussing so far: rhetoric as action (the ethical tradition) and rhetoric as language (the aesthetic tradition). Herein lies our paradox. For this speech, like the greatest of tragic discourses, presents a perfected version of human action before an audience of spectator-witnesses. And in each case, the real-life subject is absent.

But now the existential difference asserts itself. Kennedy's life is part of ongoing history. The speech thematizes the meaning of his life and makes it part of our cultural memory. But the life and the speech intersect in ways that *Henry V* the play and Henry V the historical being do not. There are other important similarities and differences. In the poetic tragedy, logos survives praxis. Poetic is, after all, the imitation of an action. In a very real sense, the fall of historical but fictionalized actors in the world of poetic represents the triumph of the word over the deed. Note, by contrast, how frequently the speaker of an encomium must profess the inadequacy of his or her "mere words." But the world of poetic *is* a world of language; and what is left unexplained in this world is exactly *how* such characters fall and such triumphs occur. In the greatest poetic tragedies the action which occasions disaster and defeat is internal to the machinations of the plot—a didactic construction of an author. In the complementary world of rhetoric, something that is not part of the world of words must finally be made to intrude. Kennedy's death is what the speech is about.[40] Whatever mimēsis occurs within the speech is occasioned by his nonbeing—indeed, by the anniversary of his nonbeing. I am tempted to defer to the more romantic linguistic metaphysicians on the question of whether Kennedy's prolonged absence is more real than, say, Hamlet or Henry's prolonged presence. But in the interests of contrariness, let me offer an answer that is tentative, but affirmative. For any reader—and certainly any witness—of the Kennedy speech, the late president's importance as a character is absolutely indispensable, not despite his tragic and irreversible loss, but *because of* that loss. For without the loss of Kennedy, there would be no speech.

But now we must be as precise as possible. I am not suggesting that Kennedy the man is somehow of secondary importance here. Exactly the opposite is true. Baudrillard, Foucault, and radical subjectivity to the contrary, anyone in Trinity Church would gladly have exchanged all the eloquence surrounding this event for the real-life return of its subject. Lincoln would have traded his address for the fallen soldiers at Gettysburg; Zola his appeal, for Dreyfus himself. And here, there may be a pivotal lesson: that even in the most poetic of rhetorical forms, there is a triumphantly intractable existential reality anchored to the discourse, which inexorably shapes its meaning.

This reality also helps us mark and define what is the quintessential aesthetic quality of rhetoric as a language. The quality is *propriety*. The overriding emphasis of Aristotle's rhetorical aesthetic is the transformation of what is available as proof into what is *proper* to the occasion, audience, speaker, and subject. This is emphatically true of Edward Kennedy's speech in Trinity Church. Even as the speech brings Kennedy to life again in our memory, it does not and cannot subordinate him completely to our imagination. Kennedy may be praised, and is, for his courage and his grace. It would be difficult to fathom his character being praised for, say, piety, humility, or temperance—even in a Catholic Mass. To personify a character, even a great character, is also to live within its limits. Whether intuitively or otherwise, Aristotle grasped that there are similar, moral limits to the language of aesthetics itself. This could be what prompts S. H. Butcher's sensitive, but troubled reading: "Aristotle, in respect to the delineation of character, is still on the border-land between morals and aesthetics. Mere goodness does not satisfy him: something, he feels, must be infused into it which does not belong to the prosaic world. But what that is, he does not tell us. He has no adequate perception of the wide difference that separates moral and poetical excellence of character."[41] If we have learned anything of value about the relationship between rhetoric and poetic, we may be grateful for Aristotle's lack of perception. Perhaps we can see, with this exploratory reading, why the cathartic possibilities of aesthetic language continue to intrigue and provoke contemporary thought. But beyond what may be an ineluctable puzzle for philosophy, the aesthetic status of rhetoric is another unsettled legacy of the tradition. I have shown that there are certain mimetic paradoxes in the relationship of rhetorical to poetical discourse throughout Aristotle's original discussions. Following our detailed analysis, we are now in a position to spell out some of these paradoxes.

Earlier, I stressed the questionable aesthetic status of discourse that purports to interpret and guide ongoing human conduct in real life—in other words, practical, situated speech. We have grappled with several conceptual approaches to the language of this art, including the still forceful Platonic indictments. Not surprisingly, these indictments were found to depend on an inclusive, monistic cosmology which rejected ordinary social *appearances.* The rich conceptual alternative supplied by Aristotle in the *Poetics* does much to reacquaint us with the power and limits of mimēsis as far as appearances are concerned. But it affords no reliable guide to the mimetic status of language which encounters real-life problems and decisions—that is, the language of rhetoric.

There is, I believe, a troublesome explanation at the core of this difficulty. Whether deliberate or not, the implication of Aristotle's rhetorical *and* poetic theories (when placed side by side) is to give us a double standard for appreciating and engaging the mimetic status of rhetorical discourse. Aristotle appears to conceive of the qualities of rhetorical discourse one way when placing them within the interpretative horizon of an *ethical-political* theory of action—the predominant emphasis of the *Rhetoric*—and quite another way when placing them within the perspective of an aesthetics of language—which, Butcher notwithstanding, is the predominant emphasis of the *Poetics.* As a great many commentators have noted, Aristotle believed that action (praxis) was superior to making or creating (*poiēsis*). This may be one reason why he seems to derive the value of poetic from its capacity to depict human action.[42] Recall, however, that the cognitive integrity of poetic derives from our ability to distinguish the depiction from what is depicted. So poetic language and action could never be the same thing. At the same time, Aristotle construes poetic truth to be more universal and truer than historical truth (what men have actually done) and places credible impossibilities on a higher aesthetic plane than implausible fact (*Poetics* 1460a25–30). He values myth more than, say, news. So what are we to do with a language that gains meaning only from the world of perishable history and that rarely endures longer than what men have actually done?

There can be little doubt that rhetoric would itself structure and guide the way people act on real social concerns—the "public endeavor," as Kennedy put it. The speech that instructs and implicates collective human conduct is also a formidable instrument of character. This is its ethical-political dimension. Yet, in the *Poetics*, Aristotle is adamant that the highest form of necessity could transpire as a sequence of events alone: "For where would be the need of a speaker if the required effects could be conveyed without the use of language?" (1456b5–10). Here both rhetoric and poetic are largely subservient to the mute force of necessity. This is consistent with Aristotle's notion that the purest *form* of discourse would be a demonstration, with no need for affect whatsoever.

The above represents Aristotle the *logician*, however, and is not necessarily the best way of integrating the *ethical* and the *aesthetic* in our reading of the tradition. To conclude this investigation into the aesthetics of Aristotelian rhetoric, it may be useful to summarize what each of our readings might lend to both the persistence and the recovery of rhetorical *norms* in our own cultural practices.

Our reading of Aristotle's *Rhetoric* through a predominantly ethical-political lens was designed to emphasize rhetoric's importance as a formation of action. This is because action tends to mark off and define the realm of ethically significant activity. Central to this ethically significant activity of rhetoric is the cultivation of practical wisdom, or phronēsis, through forming and acting on the best available arguments in practical settings. The formation of argument itself depends on a special relationship between the character of the speaker, ēthos, and the capacity for judgment, krisis, which must be cultivated in an audience. Emotion, pathos, is described in intricate detail throughout the *Rhetoric*, but its primary purpose is to place the audience in a proper frame of mind to judge the merits of a case. Aristotle does not provide much detail about what this proper frame of mind might be. But it is clear that the speaker and the audience are each regarded as moral agents, bound together in a relationship of civic friendship, in which each party is accountable to the other and to the common good. For Aristotle, then, the ethical domain of our rhetorical norms derives from the situatedness of praxis in a culture. To do what is proper in this ethical sense is to do and respond to what we are called on to do, in character and in response to the recurring constraints of rhetorical settings.

Aristotle makes rhetoric in tragedy the discursive art that is decisive for the aesthetic experience of necessity. If, ultimately, he is ambiguous on the hierarchies of poetic and rhetorical language (as I believe he is), this must be because of an essential tension in the way that form is situated within the world of collective action. Aristotle assumes that actions are particular, perishable, and to be recorded without further specula-tion. Without a consuming theory of history, the chain of particulars is potentially endless and surely unfinished. And rhetorical coloration, "in every effort to prove or disprove, to arouse emotion (pity, fear, anger, and the like), or to maximize or minimize 'things' " (1456a35–40), amounts to an aspect of social mood that is contingent at best. In other words, were rhetoric to be lodged in one of Aristotle's poetic genres (as are, for example, epic and farce), it would most likely be comedy. After all, it is comic discourse that is immersed in the crowd, with persons not much better, and perhaps a bit worse, than ourselves. It is concerned with chance and fortune, good and bad moral luck, things that could turn out any number of different ways for no definitively good reason. The audience for such rhetoric would be an imaginative sort of agency/witness, and the audience's wishes, fears, and hopes would be formative ingredients of the plot. In the midst of early modernity's pretensions, Kant was able to maintain in all seriousness that poetic sublimates emo-tions whereas rhetoric exploits them. But even if such a disjunction were well founded (which it is not), poetic sublimation still requires, as we have seen, some rhetorical mode of enactment. This is why, in the midst of Kennedy's tragic mood, there is the haunting call for re-demption. And through the material of every similar address, what is enacted is a comic hope, a happy ending, the mysteriously reduplicated wish that everything might somehow turn out all right after all. In the more action-oriented world of politics, the comic strain is far more obvi-ous. With the possible eccentric exceptions of Masada and Guyana, for instance, there has never been a willfully tragic social movement.

Other curiosities support this more symmetrical vision of rhetoric. Like comedic discourse in general, rhetorical discourse is concerned with contingency and possibility. Its limits are those of any hopeful action that rests on the reliability of an other. Poetically speaking, such dis-course may appear to be inferior to the higher form, the aforementioned necessity of tragic discourse. But like everything else about the Aristo-telian aesthetics of language, it is not nearly that simple. We should not overlook the fact that this superior, more philosophical universality of poetry is available to the arts only because poetic is one step removed from real action. It is, recall, a fiction, an imitation of the real. And within even the tragic view, it is rhetoric that is given the formidable task of constructing and expressing human thought for those who would undergo the brute force of necessity, *as well as* for those others who would witness this fate. So it is far too facile to claim simply that rhetoric exploits emotions. The audience for tragedy is not—yet—an agency of change. But it is surely a community of affiliation.

As we have seen, the emotional power of katharsis is an ergon that demands a rhetorical component. In its original Platonic meaning, katharsis is the soothing rocking motion we use to calm the fears and morbid enthusiasm of the very young. In poetry and in speech, rhetoric enacts this soothing motion as symbolic action: to express, redress, and so arrest this wildness of the soul. As Hans Robert Jauss senses, the conspicuous fall of the grand but flawed hero and the simultaneous taming of the soul are complementary aspects of an essential moment in the preparation of an emerging public sense: "If one combines Gorgias's and Aristotle's definitions, katharsis names the pleasure produced by one's own affects when they are stimulated by oratory or poetry and which can change the listener's and liberate the spectator's mind. Katharsis as the fundamental communicative aesthetic experience thus corresponds to the practical employment of the arts for the social functions of conveying, inaugurating, and justifying norms of action."[43]

Despite Aristotle's idealization of necessity in the discussion in the *Poetics*, it is apparent that the krisis and peripeteia of tragedy are not the machination of events alone. More important is the fact that even the most perfected form of tragic action does not exhaust the possibilities of what people may do. If we discover amidst the available means of persuasion the limits of practical reason, the lesson of tragic discovery turns out to be equally profound and reflexive.

In Aristotle's remarkable vision, then, the grandest achievement of poetic discourse, counsels us to recognize the limits of what the heroic individual may do, as actor. By striking, but representative, contrast, the close rhetorical relation, eulogy, links the final interruption of the individual life to *the continuity* of public life. In Kennedy's words, "The unfinished quality of his life symbolizes the unfinished agenda of America." The mimetic paradox of rhetorical and poetic discourse is that the original conceptual limits of each form imply the aesthetic possibility of the other. For the imaginative realm of poetics, Aristotle describes the highest discursive form as one of fateful necessity (an ironic anticipation of the ethical imperative). For the more limited and perishable discourse of rhetoric, he describes it as one of comic renewal. Even as the stories of individual life all end in the same way, so collective life must and does go on.

BEYOND AESTHETICS: TRAGEDY AND SOCIAL HOPE

Rhetoric no longer mimes an ordered world, *if it ever did.* With the shattering of mirrors has come a mad scramble for interpretative authority. It is as if all the old Platonic indictments have creaked their way forward again, only to leave no promise in their wake. Appearances and orders are all we have. More confusing still, the dynamis of rhetoric and poetic seem to be changing places in our time. Postmodernist sages dream of the textuality of everyday life, and philosophers of poetic dream of the new polis—a regime of letters, of course.[44] But rhetorical practice which occasionally breaks the mold—that of a Jesse Jackson, a Václav Havel, or a Nelson Mandela—is relegated to the periodic coloration we are afforded in life after peripeteia. My rereading of the initial controversy over rhetoric and poetic may do no more than allow us to marvel at ironies such as these. But in the background of philosophy's poetic fascinations, more constructive implications may be found in the renewed interest of literary studies in the terminology, if not the original tradition, of rhetoric. In continuing my study, I propose some more guarded conclusions.

First, there are several quite different senses of rhetoric that ebb and flow in the course of the poetic and ethical applications of Aristotle. Most basic, there are the actual rules and techniques of discourse practice. This is rhetoric as technē, as discussed in the initial sections of book 1 of the *Rhetoric* and alluded to as the "art of thought" in the *Poetics.* This rhetoric is embodied in patterns, arrangements, and arguments of language, and takes its models of performance from the original forms: deliberative, forensic, and epideictic. A second sense of rhetoric, however, is found in the prescriptive mission of invention, discovery, and judgment. In this larger sense, rhetoric is to practical reason—its systematic study—what philosophy is to reason generally. It can be shown rather easily that when either of these traditional studies abandons its cognitive method and object, it flirts dangerously with abandoning cognitivity. Finally, there is in Aristotle a largely unexamined sense of what it is about occasions, or episodes (my term), which invites the sort of reflective choice generated by rhetoric. Here we find ourselves talking about "rhetorical moments" as occasions of urgent practical choice, where incompatible options are forced on us, with only provisional understanding as a guide. This third sense is immediately obvious to anyone who has ever been placed in a public dilemma. What may be less obvious, however, is that it marks the most important narrative turning points of the tragic plot. Here is the singular, fragile connection, then, between the aesthetics of narrative and the theory of rhetoric. The most critical aspect of rhetoric, which is revealed by this last sense, is that rhetoric does not cease when settings for prospective action are closed. In fact, rhetoric conceived *tragically* involves the invention of thought for characters whose options are foreclosed. This also constitutes a reasonable contemporary definition of religious rhetoric.

In the growing literature of rhetorical studies, there has been a wealth of attention to the rules and genres of rhetorical technique, but proportionally less attention to the other senses of rhetoric revealed by the tradition. Thus, it may be that in the continuing scholarly concern with the degradation of practice and the highly variable status and integrity of rhetoric's philosophical standing, we are neglecting those features most important to a recovery of the art itself—namely, the changing concept and mission of practical reason and the expanding sense of rhetorical urgency in developing historical occasions. This third sense in particular needs to be examined more closely. For here, in the inescapable enactments of practical choice, is something vital to human conduct generally. It is no accident that the greatest poetry reminds us of its own limits in the midst of heroic peripeteia. That most agonizing and limiting form of the soliloquy teaches us that the poetry of solitude has never been enough to still history's other voices or even to form character in their midst. There is a premise here worth carrying forward. The public sense of rhetoric is not some recent ideographic invention of Jeffersonian Democrats. Further, it is more than a functional attribute of situations. Situations, like such Democrats, come and go. But rhetoric as a public affiliative art is always present to us in principle, because the autonomous individual, pressed far enough along his journey, is finally perishable. In other words, *rhetoric viewed aesthetically is an intrinsic feature of the human condition.*

Second, if rhetoric is part of what we, as historical beings, have become, it is worth examining whether and how rhetorical practice is already constrained by prior moments and motives of historical urgency. Part of such a pursuit would be a larger dialectical inquiry than I can undertake here. But it might suggest that much of our ambivalence about advocacy in private and public is probably a learned legacy of modern civic consciousness. If there can be civic friendship, then might there not also be civic anxiety and mistrust as well? A turn toward the core concepts of rhetorical tradition does not relieve us of the obligation to study the historical paradoxes afflicting modern prospects for recovery. But here the narratives of aesthetics may be of some assistance, in showing how the *ethical* and the *aesthetic* domain of rhetoric *together* can help to sustain the persistence and then perhaps the recovery of rhetoric in our own cultural practices.

The interpretative reading of rhetoric as a branch of aesthetics puts the predominant emphasis on the status of rhetorical discourse as a language art. We began with the ongoing problem of imitation and the status of created form within a world of shifting appearances. Broadly construed, rhetoric is an art of thought within the imitative context of poetic form. It creates and evokes emotions (pathos) not so much as a vehicle of proper audience cognition, but rather as an affiliative bond between perfected action and human response. Beyond the depiction of thought and the evocation of emotion, rhetoric provides the world of imitative discourse with a necessary tone and coloration, so that actions are plausible in light of an ongoing narrative. This means that propriety, rhetoric's principal aesthetic quality, is viewed compositionally, rather than situationally. Put another way, the appropriate is defined by factors internal rather than external to the text. An aesthetic reading defines the audience for rhetoric less as actor-judge and more as spectator-critic. Meanings within the aesthetic forms of rhetoric are primarily figurative and depend on the appreciative witnessing and reading of a critical audience. This reading too is a rhetorical act. Relatively speaking, and as marginalized by the greatest poetic discourse, rhetoric is a comic art.

But of course, it cannot be that simple. Each of these readings can be defended through the text of the *Rhetoric* itself, although each also depends on related evidence from other Aristotelian sources. The aesthetic reading, it must be added, can be supported through the emphasis of subsequent, post-Aristotelian rhetorical theory, which often emphasized the ornamental and figurative over the domain of ethical praxis. On the other hand, on the basis of our detailed analysis of the *Rhetoric* from both an ethical and an aesthetic perspective, we see that each reading implies the complementary necessity of the other, as a moderating force and influence—an antistrophos, to use Aristotle's term. Rhetoric understood only as an aesthetics of language readily degenerates into compositional stylistics. Its interest withdraws into text alone, as a largely verbal or semiotic phenomenon, and—in the disengaged applications of poststructuralist linguistics and deconstruction—it is able to reach and "read" the world, if at all, only by textualizing it. Questions of character, issues of substance, and imperatives for action are all bracketed in an exclusive preoccupation with this approach.

But rhetoric understood only as an ethics of action faces problems too. Not only does it idealize one particular orientation to Aristotle (since few theorists, ancient or modern, really share this view); it sacrifices much of the flexibility of rhetoric, especially on the level of invention and critique. Attending primarily to an optimalized notion of practice, it often has difficulty finding any real-life exemplars to fit its wishful formations. Moreover, and almost ironically, it is dependent on the actual state of things, insofar as history and the practical define its ultimate range of meaning and efficacy. Rhetoric as an ethical prerogative has important things to say about current events as well as the external constraints on the propriety of speech performances. But it usually has difficulty saying much of interest about rhetorical texts themselves, dependent as such texts are on a range of stylistic options in which this view has little interest.

My own view is that Aristotle's treatment of rhetoric as part of an aesthetics of language implies, as an unmistakable correlative, the moderating ethic of character and action. In part, this is because the highest thematized accomplishments of aesthetics return us, inescapably, to the ethics of character and action. Similarly, Aristotle's treatment of the ethical prerogatives of rhetoric leaves it in virtually a "tragic" condition, unless we can think of the heritage of that tradition in a way that is aesthetically inventive and transformational. So, if the ethical orientation to rhetoric is what allows us to envision norms for optimal communicative practice within a rhetorical culture, it is the aesthetic orientation that invites us to examine and appreciate actual rhetorical language with a view to creating and rethinking norms, thought, and action itself.

Earlier, I suggested that the aesthetic power of katharsis might prepare for a reemergence of the social collectivity. And with the practical use of reason having become technique and then technology in our own time, our more temporally conscious age has been given some epochal opportunities to test this thesis. In 1949, for instance, one of our most perceptive painters, Barnett Newman, observed: "The war, as the surrealists predicted, has robbed us of our hidden terror, as terror can only exist if the forces of tragedy are unknown. We now know the terror to expect. Hiroshima showed it to us. We are no longer then in the face of a mystery. After all, wasn't it an American boy who did it? The terror has indeed become as real as life. What we have now is a tragic, rather than a (unknown) terror situation."[45] Newman has given us a memorable portrait—in words and in his work—of what happens when the form of tragedy begins actively to engage the appearances of history. With the worldly and collective sins of reason has come an almost overwhelming sense of our own limits as well. The character of rhetoric in such a world is uncertain, at best. But in the midst of such uncertainty, we might remember that the experience of tragedy, even in its archetypal, perfected state, is not the final experience. It is only the archetypal *aesthetic* experience. The comedy of history does not stop. In some perverse but necessary sense, the murmuring of our survivors goes on and is rekindled. Similarly, an ethical sense of injury and of memory does not still the aesthetic impetus toward invention. In fact, as Aristotle's own memorable portraiture of emotion suggests, true, meaningful invention is likely to emerge only within an abiding sense of our own mortal and historical limits. Indeed, it is this sense that has always made possible and released a renewed and enriched sense of vital public life.

The exploration of this chapter confirms, then, that the lessons of poetic return us to the importance of rhetoric, but in a manner more humbling than the grand visions of contemporary aestheticism. Rhetorical form is situated in an ongoing tension between the creative insights of self—the intuitive recognition of our place in, our belongingness to, the world of appearances—and the generality of affiliations we share with our community of others. Far from grandiose schemes for ideal audiences, the disturbing reminder of the greatest poetic is that no individual can soar above the crowd for very long. With our reconciliation to the worldly order of necessity comes our reconciliation to the crowd as well. This sense is tragic, yet liberating, in a way that seems to defy the prophecies of mythic speech. Fredric Jameson provides compelling expression of this insight:

History is therefore the experience of Necessity. . . . Necessity is not in that sense a type of content, but rather the inexorable *form* of events. . . . Conceived in this sense, History is what hurts, it is what refuses desire and sets inexorable limits to individual as well as collective praxis, which its "ruses" turn into grisly and ironic reversals of their overt intention. But this history can only be apprehended through its effects, and never directly as some reified force. This is indeed the ultimate sense in which History as ground and untranscendable horizon needs no particular theoretical justification: we may be sure that its alienating necessities will not forget us, however much we might prefer to ignore them.[46]

In any given historical period, the norms which provide impetus and direction to what I have called a culture of rhetorical practice will themselves be more or less actualized, operative, and effective. Surely the art of discovering available means of persuasion needs to find the best available means for prolonging and perfecting its own existence. In the following chapter, we will examine the serious and foundational difficulties afflicting any attempt to carry forward the Aristotelian tradition of rhetoric. Then we will turn our attention to the larger project of recovering and resituating a traditionally derived theory of rhetorical practice. This project of recovery involves three pivotal steps:

(1) It must attach the traditional norms, derived from the legacy of rhetoric, to modern vocabularies for understanding the human condition.

(2) It must turn toward the constraint of dialogue and reciprocity in offering normative guidance for the ongoing practices of rhetoric. This is another way of saying that our prevailing vocabularies, whether we like it or not, will probably be communicative residues of modernism.

(3) It must provide an enlarged sense of the forum and occasions for rhetorical practice, so that the cognitive materials of decision and action may be able to achieve greater visibility and thus receive more competent judgment.

The first step will take us to the problems and possibilities of critical theory, especially the work of Horkheimer, Habermas, Blumenberg, and Arendt; the second step to the theory of conversation as language-action; and the third step to a broadened theory of rhetoric as intercultural performance. The aesthetic status of rhetoric needs to be confronted with the candor with which Jameson confronts history. Situated in the midst of that history, the horizon of rhetoric is as tenuous as its imitative promise is unfulfilled. *This is because rhetoric is the only art responsible for imitation and expression of public thought.* And nothing is more tenuous than that.

4

After Rhetorical Culture: The Spectacle of Modernity

We live in an age (perhaps the very first one) that does not understand metaphor, that thinks of symbols as abbreviations and life as politics; an age that thinks of science as religion and information as knowledge. Ours is an age curiously devoid of its own personal perception. That is not to say that many of us do not know a lot of things, but that the perception of connections between those things depends a great deal on faith that there *are* some connections. There are very few clues left in our society to serve as profound reminders that faith is a *part* of knowledge. . . . Perhaps the truth is as Julio Cortázar suggests in his short piece called "On Climbing Stairs": that we should climb them backward so that our vision would broaden and take in more rather than narrow and take in less. Perhaps the connections we would notice would be the metaphors we've lost.

—Keith Jarrett, from program notes for
"Serious Drinking and Inner Vigilance," 1987

It is a fact that not all stories are told. And if they could all be told, there is no imaginable forum that could encompass all the needs, themes, and moral concerns which deserve expression. Even if, as some of us once thought, the whole world is watching, its attention span seems limited to one thing at a time. This is, in less humble language, the modernist dilemma. It is all too easy to universalize wants, needs, interests, and norms. In a world of unequal chances, such categories exist only as a fragile language of development begging for yet another totalizing critique. What I want to suggest, however, is that such critique, the negative thinking of our time, also represents a form of exile: the self-imposed exclusion which refuses the most willing forms of attendance.[1] It does nothing to solve the *untold story* problem, but only adds another to their number. In this chapter I will tell the stories of two exiles: one from early Christianity, the other from what is commonly called late modernity. Each period was led to reject, for very good reasons, some aspect of ordinary life that is pivotal to rhetoric. Even if we cannot solve the problem of alienation and exile from rhetorical culture (and we cannot), we may at least begin to appreciate its futility.

A sense of loss is not unusual when investigating the heritage of a tradition. Among the many histories of ideas in which rhetoric holds a prominent place, there are few which do not invoke the mythology of "decline and fall" to explain the fate of the Greek tradition. In some versions, Aristotelian tradition itself is responsible for "the fall,"[2] having, together with Plato, ushered in the hegemony of reified reason. In other versions, such as the neoclassicism of MacIntyre,[3] the age itself is seen at fault, for failing to heed the lessons of Aristotle. To this, I would add an observation made by Donald Bryant nearly forty years ago: that the limitations of Aristotle's *Rhetoric* are primarily historical rather than philosophical.[4] Having celebrated Aristotelian rhetoric in the previous two chapters, it is time to face these limitations squarely. What, first of all, should we expect a rhetorical theory to do? Then, if our expectations are in order, what would it mean, practically speaking, to profess an Aristotelian view of rhetorical practice, especially in light (or dark) of both the promise and the predicaments of our age? This chapter engages directly with the major issues facing a serious reinterpretation of the rhetorical tradition and presents a broad outline for a path toward recovery.

TRADITION, PHRONĒSIS, AND NEGATIVE TELEOLOGY

Tradition as theory

Whether regarded as a work of philosophy, an adjunct to the theory of action, or a craft of language arts, there can be no doubt that the classical Aristotelian heritage constitutes an unusually coherent and systematic conception of rhetoric as a human practice. As if in response to the Platonic indictments, this rhetoric is able to offer a consistent account of what it does. First and foremost is its characterization of rhetoric as a practical activity. In a synthesis of art and craft, rhetoric helps to complete human judgments about questions of practical choice and conduct; it guides deliberate action. This means that rhetoric can be treated systematically and that it is a rational object of study. Since it combines pedagogy and philosophy, it is a worthy human technē.[5] To the extent that a culture's concrete normative assumptions, its conventional morality, equip its people with a workable version of the truth, Aristotelian rhetoric can be seen as providing a way for large numbers of people to come closer to a practical intelligence of human affairs. Taken largely on its own justificatory terms, this is the most critical contribution of Aristotelian rhetoric to an enlightened cultural praxis. But in assessing Aristotle's treatment as a *theory*, we find that several of its most attractive features become sources of troubling difficulties for any serious attempt to recapture its legacy.

Taking Aristotle's work seriously as *theory* requires that we consider it along at least the following dimensions: scope, clarity, coherence, and heuristic power. Let us consider each of these in turn.

Scope.   Aristotle's theory purports to be inclusive of all forms, proofs, occasions, and audiences that may be characterized as rhetorical. In quite explicitly ruling out *a-technic* proofs, as well as subjects treated by the exact disciplines and science, the theory established permeable boundary conditions for forms and subject matters of rhetoric. Unlike his own teacher (in the *Phaedrus*), Aristotle did not hold to a narrow, idealized set of criteria for what should properly constitute the *art*. This is why his detractors complain just as frequently about his sophistry as about his logocentrism. On the whole, then, this is a remarkably comprehensive theory.

However, its purported comprehensiveness presents the contemporary Aristotelian with something of a problem. Obviously a strict reading of Aristotle's criteria today would exclude many discursive and symbolic tactics that are arguably rhetorical: not only the nonrational appeal, but also the intradisciplinary rhetoric present in so-called social and natural sciences. The paradox, then, is that scrupulous adherence to the once comprehensive theory would limit contemporary theory to a quite exclusive subset of material. The other side of the problem is that comprehensiveness of the order achieved by Aristotle may well be unattainable in the electronic age.[6]

Clarity.   Notwithstanding certain ambiguities of operation (metaphor and examples being two of the most notorious cases), Aristotle's precision of definition and exactitude of description are almost maddening. His is clearly a theorist's rhetoric, rooted in the epistemology of discovery. Even where the practical functions of rhetoric are concerned, he puts demonstration, counsel, and argument to work in the service of judgment. Reasoning with clear exemplars—what we would today call "prototypes"—he aims to get as close to the exacting demands of truth as the case allows. Where there is ambiguity, as in the conflicting ethical and aesthetic criteria for competence in the performance of rhetoric, it could be argued that this is productive, since it effectively foreshadows the different emphases of rhetoric in different cultural contexts. But when we turn our attention to a revision of Aristotle, we find that his clarity is purchased at a price.

Aristotle insistently valorized one type of discourse—the political—over all others. He had least regard for the least clear of his cases—epideictic, the genre of his chief rival, Isocrates. He also based his remarkably copious lists of emotions, values, and received opinions on the "clear cases" of Athens and the pantheon of Greek poetry and drama. One could do worse. But in a multiple-horizoned, culturally diverse world like ours, clarity on the order of Aristotle can take the forms only of totalizing critique or canonical preachment. Other things not being equal, I prefer to avoid both these self-negating prospects.

Coherence.   Here I refer not only to the consistency of definitions, prescriptions, and postulates with one another—that is, internal consistency—but also to the consistency of these with the theorist's own assumptions and principles about the political, cognitive, and moral worlds of those who do rhetoric. Aristotle's "rough spots"—particularly epideictic and the refutative enthymeme—are offset by the remarkable congruence of artistic proofs with issues and ends of disputation and the dazzling interplay of his divisions across time, valued end, audience type, and genre. On the matter of consistency with other works and related assumptions, it is becoming apparent that the *Rhetoric* may be read, as we have read it, in light of Aristotle's organon, his *Ethics* and *Politics* and surely his *Poetics.*[7] But is it completely consistent with each of these? Surely not; although it is obviously the product of the same overall world view that produced and philosophically disciplined these other fields. Aristotle's *Rhetoric* values practical deliberation in an open forum about uncertain matters. He assumes, further, that we are likely to agree about most end values of disputation (the good, the just, the honorable), at least in general terms, and that our disagreements are likely to be over particularities of meaning or the proper means to achieve desired ends. This is all in keeping with an organic, developmental view of human nature as saturated with logos.

In an important sense, the value and resilience of the Aristotelian tradition turns on the fate of this human *essence.* This is because it makes little sense to describe and defend a rhetoric of ratiocination if the very concept of reason has been fully discredited. Several related questions confront the theorist who would retrieve Aristotelian rhetoric. If we assume that the centrality of logos is vital to the practice of Aristotelian rhetoric, can we recover this idea of reason and still defend it as somehow integral to human nature? I believe we can. Secondly, we must ask whether a rhetoric of practical reason can be defended *without* the foundations of Aristotle's developmental teleology. Here, our answer needs to be more guarded. If phronēsis is not to be reduced to wise guessing on the one hand or technical reason on the other, we must find some grounds for affiliating logos with the normative tendencies of modern critical reflection. Rhetoric may then be conceived as a kind of *creative reasoning*. Such an approach would also help to insure that a rhetoric of practical reason is worth recovering. This is the primary conceptual agenda of the remaining chapters.

Heuristic power.   Since we already know that we are far from the felicity conditions of so-called exact science, it is important to remind ourselves that rhetorical theorizing holds connective relationships not only among its own postulates and the prior conceptual commitments of its author, but also to the world of situated practice that it would explain and perfect. This is what I mean by the ambiguous term "heuristics." Here I would include not only the genres, forms, and strategies of ongoing persuasion, but even the situated argumentative stance of the theorist. In presenting a systematic vision of rhetoric, one is also making a claim about how we ought to conduct ourselves in the business of civic life. Admittedly, this is a murky area. The line between explanation and counsel is not always clear (although it becomes clearer when money is involved).[8] Moreover, from a theoretical standpoint, the line between conscientious reform and practical irrelevance is similarly blurred. But for all this, theory in rhetoric (from the Sophists to the modern day) has always been unavoidably practical and prescriptive. It provides what Kenneth Burke has called a "frame of acceptance" that privileges some means of production over others.

Aristotle provides one of the better examples of this heuristic quality. He was unmistakably disgusted with the real-life duplicity and flattery that characterized contemporary Greek judicial practice. He sought to purify language of its excesses and restore genuine virtue to the expression of ēthos through speech. His reluctant appropriation of the emotions sees them as a cognitively significant form of proof, useful for placing the audience (that morally significant human agency) in a *proper* state of mind. Finally, in diametric opposition to all his teachers, rivals, and even contemporary discursive practice, Aristotle sees rhetoric as inextricably linked with democratic civic practice.

The question that any contemporary Aristotelian sympathizer must ask, given the neoconservative appropriation of our subject, is whether such a reform-minded rhetoric is practicable. As I have proposed throughout this study, the key to any answer lies in first *envisioning* aspects of the practice in instances of contemporary rhetoric, for, if we can do this, we have exhibits for the possibility of reform. A second, far more serious issue has to do with the practical matter of squaring Aristotle's harmonious vision of order with our contemporary city-states, which are currently under siege.[9] Although a firm proponent of *dēmos*, Aristotle was conspicuously unresponsive to the plight of the exile, the barbarian, and the stranger, all of whom were left out of the civic picture. To ask whether a rhetoric of logos can make room for the discordant voices of these others is a little like asking whether Schubert's string quartets leave any room for Schönberg. There is no choice. It must.

Phronēsis and Logos

Although he was an alien in the Greek city-state of Athens, Aristotle shared many of the presuppositions of its so-called golden age. He believed that man's greatest gift and most distinctive excellence was reason. An avowed pluralist where the modes of inquiry were concerned, each of his many systematic inquiries is an expression of the power of logos. So, too, is the *Rhetoric*. Here Aristotle is confident that better— that is, more reliable, well-founded—judgments will result if logos is put to work in practical settings, examining problems of conviction, belief, and conduct in an atmosphere of uncertainty.

Prudence, or practical wisdom, is the preeminent political virtue in the Aristotelian lexicon. Although he was unable to isolate a reliable set of conditions for implementing this virtue, he did suggest that proper education, civic training, and deliberative practice would sophisticate natural prowess and so perfect the quality of phronēsis. I have extended his argument to say that the deliberative practice of rhetoric might go so far as to cultivate practical wisdom as a relational good for those membership groups and collectivities that are called to decide and act on civic matters. But the recovery of rhetoric requires that we reconsider this claim in light of an outwardly friendly amendment by well-intentioned Aristotelians. The amendment suggests that phronēsis, far from being a creature of training and procedure, is actually prior—and even necessary—to everything else, including practices of securing conviction, such as argument. Why make such a bold claim as this?

To answer this question, we must remember that some advocates of tradition have been embroiled in their own dispute with the forces of secularism. Over and against modernity's centuries-old claim that reason and argument are the *only* way to ground the universalizable norms of autonomy and justice, traditionalists have responded (mistakenly, in my view) with a heartfelt contradiction. Echoing their old nemesis of Gorgias and the boys, these defenders of the faith rejoined, in effect, that phronēsis cannot be taught. Either you have it or you don't. The intellectual consequences of this position appear to be, at best, paradoxical. If true—and who, ultimately, can determine this?—the rejoinder damages any procedural attempt to ground foundations for morality and culture. Depending on the prior presence or absence of practical wisdom, such an attempt is either unnecessary or ineffectual. Score one point for the "good" guys (were fortune so to favor them)—but at what cost? The entire value domain of good judgment, or prudential reason, now emerges as the intuitive property of certain favored subjects. Phronēsis becomes indistinguishable from good taste. Where civic life is concerned, normative content must be mystified if it is thought to exist at all. There is no other way of explaining how a group of more or less apt subjectivities can ever act in concert. Assuming that occasionally they do, there is the implicit, neoconservative hierarchy of "blessed" cultures (that are near and dear, with normative contents we recognize) over "foreign" cultures (those with primitive practices that we obviously do *not* recognize). This is the nightmare mutation of Aristotle, the polis state, which sends pluralists scrambling in their multiple directions.[10]

One of the most astute observers of the post-Aristotelian human condition, Ronald Beiner, has grappled with the problem of tradition's recovery in a way that I find instructive. In *Political Judgment* and other related essays, he has chronicled the limits of contemporary political discourse, as well as the collapse of civic culture which seems to be at the root of this problem. I cannot improve on his own statement of the difficulty: "Politics removed from the sphere of common judgment is a perversion of the political, and as such, cannot help but manifest itself in political crisis. It is precisely because there is a deep-seated political crisis in the modern world that we are obliged to inquire into what is involved in judging and what makes it possible for us to exercise this faculty."[11] Beiner's ambitious program for remedying this difficulty takes him back to Aristotle's *Rhetoric*, as informed by the ethical treatises and the primacy of phronēsis. He then attempts to synthesize the Aristotelian position with what he acknowledges to be the diametrically opposed position of Kant, as represented by Hannah Arendt's controversial vision of judgment. The synthesis is attractive for many of the same reasons that Arendt's own view of judgment attracts; it seeks and seems to preserve some room for reflection in cultural "dark times."[12]

However, in his more recent work, Beiner has made a subtle, but important, turn in the direction of more pessimistic Aristotelians. In an essay which traces the dispute between Habermas and Gadamer, "The Primacy of *Ēthos* and the Problem of Foundations," Beiner's aim (in part, at least) is to reduce the disparity between their respective positions.[13] He is quite persuasive in his claim that the similarities between these antagonists are more important than the differences. Each employs the Kantian language of German idealism both to frame and to articulate his arguments. More important, each relies on the whole process of acculturation (what Beiner and Aristotle call "habituation") in developing the mature human character. Without this sense of character and the normative content of culture, Beiner reasons, ethical judgment and practical wisdom would be lost.

Beiner's position is compelling to this point. But he goes further. In his haste to weld his own vision of phronēsis with that of Gadamer, Beiner wishes to claim that the necessary conditions for phronēsis are sufficient conditions for moral reasoning as well. He openly wonders what is to be gained by the "heroic theoretic labors" of Habermas to ground a critically reflective moral theory. In fact, Habermas's search for emancipation through reason is regarded as at odds with the more fundamental sense of judgment through the "*ēthos* of our very being as shaped by life in society."[14] He cites Gadamer approvingly on this point: "As Gadamer puts it: one cannot be convinced by argument to be virtuous."[15] Without arguing explicitly for the position, Beiner writes: "These given normative contents can only be supplied by ēthos, which in turn is a function not of reflective consciousness but of our very being as shaped by life in society."[16] This disjunction between ēthos and reflective consciousness is somewhat discomforting to any student of traditional rhetoric, Beiner included. After all, in the *Rhetoric* ēthos is treated less as a mode of being than as a mode of proof. Perhaps the most serious casualty of this revised position is the prospect, pioneered by Beiner's earlier work, for an art of civic discourse and judgment. When reflection and argument are split off from the very practice of ethical life, we are returned to the fateful spectacle of autonomous moral agents mindlessly acting out the situated life histories of their found condition. This sounds harsh. But what other inference can one draw from language such as the following: "One must act as if non-reflectively, embodying a sure sense of what is good and right; one must command a kind of practical assurance that even the strictest, most rigorous set of arguments fails to supply. This something is made available only by character and habituation, never by rational argument as such."[17]

Even in Beiner's reconstruction, the dispute over the sufficiency of phronēsis presents a fascinating replay of the ancient question, Can virtue be taught? Rephrased, the question now reads: May virtue be cultivated through reason, what Anscombe has called "the voice of *logos*"? Ironically enough, Habermas and Gadamer (and Beiner) seem to have switched conventional allegiances in their answers to this version of the question. While it may well strain credulity to say so, I would maintain that Aristotle of the *Rhetoric* is more compatible with Habermas than with these contemporary Aristotelians. For one thing, both Aristotle and Habermas plainly believe that logos and habituation have something important to do with one another.[18] In chapter 5, I will try to synthesize their positions further, at least to the extent that the *possibility* of an ethical consciousness might remain open to the practice of rhetoric.

I hope to have shown that the Aristotelian arts of phronēsis are notoriously difficult to defend without recourse to a larger vocabulary of reason. In fact, the continued possibility of phronēsis is best defended by pursuing this unlikely encounter between the legacy of traditional Aristotelian rhetoric and the discourse of emancipatory reason. To prepare the way for this encounter, we must return to the centrality of logos in Aristotelian rhetoric. First, we must resituate phronēsis within the larger grammar of reason which makes it possible. Second, we must ask whether reason can still be defended in an age which gives it little credence.

Aristotle's rhetorical ideal of krisis (or judgment) does not make sense without the expressed centrality of logos in all its forms. We should not confuse this "reason" with logic or the faculty of rationality. As we expand the figurative possibilities of practical intelligence, it is worth remembering that the enthymeme was designed not to be a distorted or flawed syllogism but rather a mode of participatory reflection on cultural norms. It is a form of logos designed to allow the audience to persuade itself. For Aristotle, the cultural values of an audience's way of life—its phaimonena—form the boundary conditions for possible effective argument. But these are neither univocal nor etched in stone. By taking a normative precept that is accepted in one context and considering it in light of a novel subject matter or issue, it may be possible to take a different slant on the sedimented cultural verities of our time. And, for a time, it may even be possible to reanimate and redirect the world of appearances. I will develop this notion further in chapter 6, since it provides a way of looking at the inventional contribution of actual rhetorical practice. At this stage, I want only to suggest that the enthymeme provides an ideal of reflective consciousness that is still worth pursuing. Here is Victor Turner in a somewhat similar vein:

> Any society that hopes to be imperishable must carve out for itself a piece of space and a period of time in which it can look honestly at itself. This honesty is not that of the scientist, who exchanges the honesty of his ego for the objectivity of his gaze. It is, rather, akin to the extreme honesty of the creative artist who, in his presentations on the stage, in the book, on canvas, in marble, in music, or in towers and houses, reserves to himself the privilege of seeing straight what all cultures build crooked. All generalizations are in some way skewed, and artists with candid vision "labor well the minute particulars," as Blake knew.[19]

Without some cognitive ideal such as Aristotle posited, rhetoric would be little more than the art of crooked thinking. The more pressing question, of course, is whether a cognitive ideal of reasoned reflection can still be taken seriously in the wake of the largely discredited Enlightenment project.

Although it will strike some inquiring minds as an archaic notion, there seems to me to be nothing preposterous in the proposition that humans have an innate capacity for logos. Essences are, as Wittgenstein observed, "expressed in grammar."[20] To say that *Homo sapiens* is a rational animal simply predicates something of the subject, human being, that is essential to it as a class or species. As Anscombe observes, such a definition need not contain all the relevant information about its subject to be an adequate definition. Human beings are also featherless bipeds. Since the proposition is self-referential, it is unlikely that *any* definition would contain enough information to (like a mathematical definition) exhaust the full meaning of its subject. The condition of adequacy for our logocentric proposition may be met if, as Anscombe says, there are no animals other than humans who satisfy it. The definition according to a capacity cannot be refuted by counterexamples of irrationality, mental disorder, rash behavior, or whatever.[21] The only further consideration relevant to our logocentric view of human essence is whether it comports with our understanding of each other in the shared appearances of real life.

Experiences differ, of course. But it may be helpful to reintroduce this whole amorphous process of acculturation which Beiner, Habermas, Gadamer, and almost everyone else connote by the term "habituation." Over and against the idea of rhetoric as a neutral force, directed to calculative ends, is Aristotle's conception of rhetoric as an evocative engagement with the other's capacity for reflection. Here is Martha Nussbaum on the centrality of reflection in Aristotelian habituation:

> We can embark on a program of habituation and training that is not simply a type of behavioral manipulation. Praise and blame are from the beginning not just pushes, but appropriate modes of communication to an intelligent creature who acts in accordance with its own view of the good, to reach out for more appropriate objects. . . . And if we think of what actually happens when one educates a child, Aristotle's insistence on the centrality of intentionality and selective attention seems far more empirically right. . . . It offers us an attractive account of the natural animal basis for the development of moral character.[22]

In the crafting of rhetoric specifically, Aristotle repeatedly instructs us to comport ourselves within the best potentials of ourselves, our issues, and our audiences, to cultivate ēthos and character in one another and to reach out toward truth in human affairs. He could not have done any of this without appreciating and addressing our human capacity for logos. Neither can we.

Yet logos, this human capacity for reason, is more than a simple reflective awareness of what is human about us. For just as our species distinguishes itself *by* distinguishing itself—that is to say, by inventing essences of us—so we are also (as Kenneth Burke long ago noted) the proud inventor of the negative, both the "thou shalt *not*" and the "that which is *not.*"[23] Reason's complicity in all manner of partisanship is well known. In rhetoric, it is unavoidable. We must now turn our attention to a final set of problems for a rhetoric of practical reason, a vision wherein reason has been reduced to an instrument of repression.

Negative Teleology

In a series of important studies, Hans Blumenberg has explored the residual implications of mythic and pre-modern world views for the problem of legitimacy of the so-called modern era.[24] Unlike Castoriadis, who believes that the very concept "development" is at the root of the difficulty,[25] Blumenberg finds a more complex relationship between secularization and the nagging normative questions and answers prompted by myth. Critical to this relationship is Blumenberg's suggestion that secularization does not spell the end of teleology; it merely represents the symbolism of progress and redemption in a different form. Nor is it the case that modernity is somehow cursed with this residue of outmoded forms of thought—as Acton argued in *The Illusion of the Epoch.*[26] Rather, to paraphrase what is spelled out in a painstaking, subtle manner, it is part of our historical condition to inherit questions from previous ages that our own age may be ill equipped to answer. To exclude such questions from consideration is not only unreasonable; it would deprive each generation of a compelling motive for inquiry—hence the continuity and the ongoing, symbolic goading of our makeshift teleologies.

Surely these provisional goads lack the Apollonian splendor of past visions. Indeed, Blumenberg goes so far as to find the essential character of symbolic forms not so much in their link with a perfected human quality (reason, autonomy, "species being") as in their connection with our deficiencies of biological adaptation, instinct, and so forth. So much for the a priori sufficiency of phronēsis. In all its diversity, this "Darwinism of words"[27] is what allows the human project to go on and, yes, to go forward. Blumenberg situates rhetoric in the midst of this project, as our ongoing way of constructing what he calls "provisional teleology," holding ourselves accountable within a measured span of time for the questions and provocations we inherit from the past, as well as for expectations and hopes we project forward, for now.

I introduce Blumenberg's position not to argue its superiority to other available prescriptions for normative development, but rather to argue for the ubiquity of teleological thinking generally. Even the numerous scenarios of decline and fall mentioned earlier, studies such as Horkheimer and Adorno's *Dialectic of Enlightenment*, MacIntyre's *After Virtue*, McCarthy's *After Philosophy*, Stout's *Ethics after Babel*, and Tracey's *Plurality and Ambiguity*, assume some intelligible baseline of normalcy as a margin for their own schemata of decline.[28] Insofar as they present us with an emergent path of intelligible influence with normative implications, it can be said that the modality of potential is alive and well. We are less likely to grasp the normative *content* of such visions, however, primarily because they are portraits of diachronic influence gone wrong.

This discovery provokes several more specific issues. If Blumenberg's project is still relevant, then we must ask how we might motivate ourselves and others, given the normative residues of numerous failed grand designs. For those not situated in settings conducive to reflection (and that includes much of the world), how are normative themes constructed in the first place? For the citizen, how is readmission to the arenas of deliberative culture to be gained? And for both, how do we extract, mediate among, and reflect on the normative content of culture so as to make sound political and moral judgments? In offering an overall direction for answering these questions, I wish to steer a course between two unsatisfying alternative positions. The first is the previously discussed "Either you've got it or you haven't" position in which phronēsis stands (or sits—whichever is proper) alone. To be fair, the hermeneuticist can and has argued that socialization is not the proper concern of the philosopher.[29] But whatever the virtues of that position for philosophy, it is hardly a viable option for the art and pedagogy of rhetoric. The second position is the supposedly morally neutral, "normless" position of Foucault, according to which we are repressed into a favored regime of discourse. This regime, depending on our locale, either gives us an illusion of autonomy and reasoned participation or leaves us on the sidelines, marginalized and removed from the dominant culture. This latter position, from which Foucault eventually struggled to extricate himself, would be dangerously arbitrary were it not also flagrantly contradictory. It is Callicles speaking again, still imagining that there is no difference between the rule of might and the rule of the better argument.[30] I will examine this position briefly at the conclusion of this chapter.

The position I am arguing here is that a critically reflective rhetoric is necessary in order to mediate among the normative contents of any community. On a practical level, such mediation can be mastered only by those with access to channels of communication, competence in employing the symbols of affiliation, shared interests in the implications of action, and so forth. But in a larger sense, membership in a rhetorical culture is potentially available to anyone able to acquire a rhetorical sensibility. The criteria for such a sensibility, as derived from the Aristotelian tradition, are both egalitarian and logocentric. At a minimum, we must be capable of recognizing and reading the modalities of our cultural phainomena; which is another way of saying that emergent social appearances must be grasped in both their complexity and their *modality*, their unfinished quality. Beyond this, one must be capable of participatory inference in the available topoi of rhetorical forms. In the remainder of this chapter I will consider the problem of exile in light of these criteria for participation in a rhetorical culture.

Lest the argument be misunderstood, I should make it clear that I am not claiming that there are no real exiles or outcasts from modern culture; nor am I suggesting that all exile is self-imposed. Rather, I am making the more complex claim that the culture of practical reason is not the cause of exile and marginality. Although hierarchy is a fact and technologies of risk and welfare are not equitably distributed, it is the reflection of reason which brings these matters to our attention. In the culture of critical reflection, there is no reason in principle for reason as a practice to rule anyone out. The Sophistical understanding of rhetoric, typified by instrumentalism, has tended to conceive of rhetorical practice in such a way that power is a precondition of any effective participation. In attempting to essentialize and recover the rhetorical tradition of Aristotle, I am interpreting and presenting the notion of rhetorical competence as a power in its own right, potentially available to anyone.

I will now introduce two figures who at first glance, could not be more different from one another: Tertullian, the second-century Montanist monk, and Max Horkheimer, the twentieth-century critical theorist. However, both are persons whose form of life and *form of consciousness* kept them from participating in a reflective rhetorical culture. For each, the prevailing political culture was exclusionary in the extreme. For Tertullian, it was the decadent spectacle and pageantry of second-century Rome; for Horkheimer, the imposing tyranny and degradation of a Fascist state. Given the lifeworlds of the time, it is not realistic to suppose that an enlightened rhetorical consciousness might somehow have spared either figure his torment of exile, let alone overturned the prevailing political regime. Yet, without being unduly clinical, we may still find these voices from the margins instructive. First, they tell us something about argument in its most desperate, marginalized state. As one commentator has noted (with evident understatement), Tertullian presents us with a form of exhortation that is not especially consistent with its sources;[31] yet, there is no question but that the decadent condition of his own lifeworld has robbed him of any reliable commonplaces. Second, each figure's characteristic consciousness includes features which work against a more forceful rhetorical stance. For Tertullian, as an early and very zealous Christian, it was the interiority of truth and the autonomy of soul, or self; for Horkheimer, the reification of reason added to the accelerating failure of late Enlightenment assumptions. Third, in an ironic way, these forms of thought are pivotal antecedents of the turning points of modernity itself—so much so that much of contemporary thought has fastened itself on the figure of the exile as a distinct, anti-rhetorical type. This is another way of saying that from a traditional rhetorical perspective, the consciousness of late modernity has exiled itself from the components of a rhetorical culture.

We will begin with Tertullian, who invented what may be the first rhetorical criticism of mass culture, *De Spectaculis*. Tertullian possessed all the resources of the logoi,[32] but for him the appearances had lost all modalities of agency and transformation. Thus the first form of exile emerges through a stance of radical opposition, but *without* the rhetorical resources of cultural appearances.

EXCURSUS ON TERTULLIAN: RELIGION IN EXILE

To understand the peculiar situation facing this early Christian apologist, we need to acknowledge the epochal importance of Christianity itself, as well as the extraordinary repression faced by the Church from the extended reach of the Roman Empire. The early Christian consciousness presented the human condition with a very different rendering of its place, meaning, and mission than anything that had gone before. Central to this Christian consciousness is the idea of incarnation, the phenomenon of God becoming man. The Incarnation has been explained from a variety of perspectives. But, unlikely as this might seem, one of the fathers of modernism has put it best. From the inclusive perspective of Hegel, the central meaning of the Incarnation is that the Divinity, once an ahistorical and absolute Other, has now come into the world as a secular instantiation of self: a human being. In his momentous *Phenomenology of Spirit*, Hegel wrote:

> That Absolute Spirit has taken on the shape of self-consciousness inherently, and therefore also consciously to itself—this appears now as the belief of the world, the belief that spirit exists *in fact* as a definite self-consciousness; i.e. as an actual human being; that spirit is an object for immediate experience; that the believing mind *sees, feels,* and *hears* this Divinity [in Christianity]. . . . The self of the existent Spirit has in that way the form of complete immediacy. It is neither set up as something thought, or imaginatively represented, nor as something produced, as is the case with the immediate self in natural religion, or again in religion as art. Rather, this concrete God is beheld sensuously and immediately as a self, as a real individual human being; only so is it a self-consciousness.[33]

This justly famous account of revealed religion is a helpful first approximation to the appeal of the Christian doctrine of the Incarnation. For God to become man, for the absolute to assume human form, represents a powerful condensation of the divine other in the immediacy of human life; indeed, Truth itself is now humanized. Although the idea was prefigured in some of the exilic and post-exilic Hebrew texts, Christianity gave its adherents a mimetic human consciousness that possessed an articulate interior dimension. Christian doctrine revolves entirely around this momentous fact, to such an extent that the entire project of "the good life" for the human being has now changed, and changed decisively. The parables of Christ, the two great commandments, and the entire metaphor of Godly transformation in the Nativity, the Crucifixion, and the Resurrection point to man's inner condition as the key to salvation. As Herschel Baker observes: "Although Christ's teaching was, as he believed, based on Judaism, it emphasized personal holiness and minimized ritual. His was a gospel of self-sanctification. What matters it to a man if he gains the whole world and loses his own soul? The kingdom of God is within. The very essence of primitive Christianity was its *inwardness*."[34] While this tenet of primitive Christianity may seem all but obvious to the modern mind, we should not neglect its rhetorical implications. They are momentous. Prior religions and prior Western cultures had assumed a benign compatibility between private and public consciousness. But here was a religion proclaiming that good works, even public virtue, were not enough to gain entrance to "the Kingdom of God." The mystery of the Incarnation and the inwardness of faith present a form of consciousness that is a complete, holistic vision—literally a new way of defining the meaning and value of human life.

Yet Tertullian's own situation can scarcely be attributed to the influence of this revolutionary Christian doctrine alone. As a newcomer to Christianity, Tertullian had a convert's zeal. Moreover, the extreme—even radical—nature of his pronouncements may be attributable to a personality described by some contemporaries as "harsh and intemperate."[35] Perhaps, too, his continual doctrinal battle against excesses of emotion derived from what some have described as his own state of constant irritation. But there is obviously more to it than this. For the fact of the matter was, and is, that Christ has not returned. And Tertullian, like many early Christians, was forced to rely on the interiority of faith to withstand the prevailing world of contrived appearance, the imposed culture of the late Roman Empire.

As to the character of this imposed culture, it was as it has been burlesqued by countless "spectacle" films which portray chariot races, gladitorial contests, lions and Christians, bread and circuses, the pageantry of surfaces. Consider, then, the plight of a newly converted Christian symbolically removed both from his native land, Carthage, and from this alien presence, this Roman hegemony of pagan ritual and play. Some sense of Tertullian's isolation is conveyed by the way he responds to the Roman vocabulary of public virtue. Perhaps the closest counterpart to the Greek notion of honor was Roman *gloria*. As Dennis Groh has written, "*Gloria* was one of the important words in the Republican political vocabulary. To Cicero the word meant more than *fama*, which was a neutral term; *gloria* was the praise given by all men, but especially by the *boni*, to the deeds and reputations of great men who served the state."[36] But for Tertullian, this same virtue is a passion, a category of lustful desire. And in his notorious discussion in the *Apologeticum*, he idealizes true Christians as "being frozen in relation to every passion of glory and dignity."[37] Contrasting this with Aristotle's treatment of honor's *phainomena* in the *Rhetoric*, we can better appreciate the extremity of Tertullian's displacement.

In a world where the truth can no longer be seen through the natural attitude, only a special attitude is sufficient for salvation. On one level, then, *De Spectaculis* is an exhortative epistle designed to counsel the Christian faithful to avoid all pagan ritual, whether circus, show, or contest. But on the level that concerns us here, Tertullian's polemic suggests a desperate rhetorical struggle between the new consciousness of Christianity and the decadent surface of ordinary life. It is the first mass-culture critique. The author is infused with the presence of a new truth, which takes Christ's incarnation in the most concrete way, as imbued with the mystery and interiority of faith. Although consistent with this truth, Tertullian's message is so extreme as to be, from an Aristotelian point of view, unimaginable. It is a rhetorical attack on the world itself.

The document takes the form of an epistle, the early Christian rhetorical form used to interpret and underscore the new message of Christ for the faithful; it is a kind of address to the soul. But from the beginning, Tertullian's *De Spectaculis* is not a message of reassurance. Stern and vexatious in tone, it begins with the assumption that those to whom it is addressed already have an approach–avoidance relationship with God. They are guilty of taking pleasure at the public shows, and their guilt is such that it cannot be mitigated, even by ignorance: "For such is the power of earthly pleasures, that, to retain the opportunity of still partaking of them, it contrives to prolong a willing ignorance, and bribes knowledge into playing a dishonest part."[38] Note that, for Tertullian, ignorance is no accident; it is willful, manipulated by a knowledge that is bad faith.

There follows a fascinating section in which Tertullian confronts "the views of the heathens, who in this matter are wont to press us with such arguments as these: That the exquisite enjoyments of ear and eye we have in external things are not in the least opposed to religion in the mind and conscience; and that surely no offence is offered to God in any human enjoyment, at any of our pleasures which, with all due reverence secured to Him, it is not sinful to partake of in its own time and place. But this is precisely what we are ready to prove." The particular heathen argument that Tertullian chooses to engage is not unlike the contemporary hedonism which some will recognize as the secular humanist position. Of course, this argument is given added weight by the fact that Christians are far from the dominant culture in Carthage and are subject constantly to the pressure of normalization. To the extent that Christians are permitted to participate in the public domain, why is it wrong to follow the same norms and sanctions as everyone else? If this means an occasional ceremonial pleasure, so be it. Tertullian's response, which occupies the body of the text, is most revealing of his own radical Christianity. He claims, in effect, that true obedience—that is, obedience to one's inner nature—must also govern one's public, or external, conduct. Here, in other words, propriety has no place. More than simply a doctrinal dispute, we have in the vision of Tertullian a radical clash in forms of life.

To Tertullian's adversaries, the world and its pleasures are intrinsically good and may be put to any human use whatsoever. (Modernism usually adds the codicil "so long as no one gets hurt!") The result is a doctrine of poetic license, in which liberty and the libertine are easily confused. Tertullian has difficulty even taking such a position seriously—his exposition is ironic throughout, as if the hypocrisy of his opponents were all but self-evident. But he wastes neither time nor energy in going about the task of refutation.

> We must not, then, consider merely by whom all things were made, but by whom they have been perverted. We shall find out for what use they were made at first, when we find for what they were not. *There is a vast difference between the corrupted state and that of primal purity, just because there is a vast difference between the Creator and the corrupter.* Why, all sorts of evils, which as indubitable evils even the heathens prohibit, and against which they guard themselves, come from the works of God. Take, for instance, murder, whether committed by iron, by poison, or by magical enchantments. Iron and herbs and demons are all equally creatures of God. Has the Creator, withal, provided these things for man's destruction? (Emphasis added)

Tertullian is familiar enough with the strictures of classical argument to recognize in his opponents a confusion of material and efficient cause. Although his own argument wanders somewhat toward the end, its path is clear. Having created the world and its objects, God maintains proprietory rights, as it were, to their proper use. For man to kill or raise idols or indulge in heathen rituals (like the shows) is to misuse God's world in a serious way, by replacing Divine authorship with the indulgence of human artistry. This argument, I suggest, could only be presented from the stance of a radically *new* Christian consciousness.

As we have seen, this new consciousness *individualizes* the redemption of Israel as a "Kingdom of God within you." Another hardly orthodox creed, that of Athanasius, puts it thus: "one, not by conversion of the Godhead into flesh, but by taking the manhood into God." Of prime importance for Tertullian is the fact that man himself is an artifact of God;

and with the human *becoming* of God, our own inner nature is now directly accountable to and *for* the divine. In the all-or-nothing world of this vision, our every desire and thought may be an occasion of sin or salvation:

> Man himself, guilty as he is of every iniquity, is not only a work of God—he is His image, and yet in both soul and body he has severed himself from his Maker. For we did not get eyes to minister to lust, and the tongue for speaking evil with, and ears to be the receptacle of evil speech, and the throat to serve the vice of gluttony, and the belly to be gluttony's ally, and the genitals for unchaste excesses, and hands for deeds of violence, and the feet for an erring life; or was the soul placed in the body so that it might become a thought-manufactory of snares, and frauds, and injustices?

To which Tertullian answers, "I think not."

As we can see, Tertullian's argument rests on his interiorized Christian notion of human guilt and culpability—of sin. In the foregoing passage, he clearly equates evil thought with evil action. In the questionable company of hands, feet, belly, genitals, and the rest, there is the soul, the interiority of the Christian self, the "thought-manufactory of snares, and frauds, and injustices." The link between murder and the evil pleasures of the shows is now transparent—if not convincing. To the radically Christian consciousness of Tertullian, the deed and the inward entertaining of the deed are equally malevolent. This is why he includes the plotting of evil in the lexicon of *acts* distasteful to God. Now it might seem that there should be a dialectical opposite to this inner corruption, which would presumably derive from the serenity and solace of a pure spirit. And indeed, there is. But because the phainomena of the world have been, as it were, stolen from the creator of their meaning, the self, or soul, may never be at peace. The following claims thematize the remainder of this tract: that "Satan and his angels have filled the whole world"; that "the places in themselves do not contaminate, but what is done in them, from which even the places themselves, we maintain, become defiled"; and that "the polluted things pollute us."

The centerpiece of Tertullian's polemic emerges when he turns away from the feasts and rituals and launches into a sweeping indictment of theatrical exhibitions. So far we have struggled with an ambiguity that the above passages can only underscore. The world, as the creation of God, cannot be intrinsically evil. Yet, its use may be perverted in such a way as to render the very objects of appearance sinful. In a kind of malignant reversal of pragmatic humanism, the act can corrupt the situation in which it occurs. Now it might seem that the theatrical exhibitions would be immunized against the force of these indictments; for unlike some of his other targets, the dramatic arts only depict, rather than enact, the excesses of Roman culture. But recall that, even for Aristotle, the material of plot is *thought*. For Tertullian, any performed action addressed to thought must finally erase the imposed distance between the act *suggested* and the act *committed*. And, if this were not enough, the very concept of aesthetic pleasure (derived from the recognition of this difference) must therefore be evil: "For as there is a lust of money, or rank, or eating, or impure enjoyment, so there is also a lust of pleasure. But the show is just a sort of pleasure." Indeed, so serious is the risk of this defilement that even witnesses to the crime become co-conspirators.

We are all familiar with the circularity of arguments rooted in an acceptance of the ordinary world. But when the world of common experiences is rejected as relentlessly as it is by Tertullian, we are entitled to ask, with equal insistence, why? And if this negation (like the *common sense* of the pragmatist) is circular, then its core—whether pathology, doctrine, or principle—surely demands further discussion. Critical to Tertullian's indictment of the shows is his remarkable interpretation of aesthetic pleasure. The following passage, which reveals the new Christian consciousness as fatal to the poetic quest, has received virtually no attention in rhetorical theory:

God has enjoined us to deal calmly, and gently, and quietly, and peacefully with the Holy Spirit, because these things are alone in keeping with the goodness of His nature, with His tenderness and sensitiveness, not to vex him with rage, or ill-nature, or anger, or grief. Well, how shall this be made to accord with the shows? For the show always leads to spiritual agitation. For where there is pleasure, there is keenness of feeling giving pleasure its zest; and where there is keenness of feeling, there is rivalry giving in turn its zest to that. Then, too, where you have rivalry, you have rage, and bitterness, and wrath, and grief, and all bad things which flow from them— the whole entirely out of keeping with the religion of Christ. For even suppose one should enjoy the shows in a moderate way, as befits his rank or age or nature, still he is not undisturbed in mind, without *some unuttered movings of the inner man. No one par-*

takes of pleasures such as these without their strong excitements;
no one comes under their excitements without their natural lapses.
(Emphasis added)

To better appreciate the force and finality of these remarks, we might
do well to consider the uneasy condition of Tertullian's new consciousness. The earlier classical indictments and defenses of art were all
grounded in assumptions of an *imitative* relationship between a work
of art and the world of common experience. Since Plato believed that
the world itself was but a pale approximation of the true Forms, he was
able to attack art as a distortion of truth, a deception that could not be
entrusted to an untutored audience. For all this, the Platonic attack is
launched entirely on the cognitive level. Aristotle understood this and
was able to reestablish the integrity of art (as well as rhetoric) by defending the ability of the average person to discriminate between appearance
and reality. He settled the matter—temporarily, at least—by noting that
such discrimination is a form of learning, which "is a great pleasure." For
Aristotle, pleasing resemblances may be distinguished from the world
of common sense. Art is defensible because it is important, but not
too important. It may be trusted because its power may be resisted. Put
in modern terms, it was Aristotle who first *disciplined* both art and
rhetoric.

We have already seen how drastically the new consciousness of Christianity has changed this aesthetic landscape. Recall that God has actually
entered the world of experience and has radically altered its meaning by
becoming man. The world of common sense fact has become the unfinished product of God himself, the only true artist. Hence the true
meaning of this world is no longer commonly sensible at all. Rather,
the world's significance must now be regarded in the light of the transformed significance of human life itself—that is, through the inner voice
of faith. But there is a major complication: since God the Son is no longer
materially present in the historical world, the interpretation of appearance is far from settled. The world of experience may be taken to heart or
left behind as a matter of faith. A dissonant chorus of voices and visions
clamors for the soul's attention. The private soul must make room for
the one, true message, a message that is both interior and absolute. This
message is in constant need of validation because it is in constant danger
of being abandoned.

If my reading so far is credible, there may be a terrible insecurity at the root of Tertullian's emotional lexicon. Even in a state of pleasureful well-being, the spirit will not remain calm. On this slippery slope of moods, one thing indiscriminately leads to another. The great modern invention of the self may trace its exact origins to this predicament. The self must long for the refuge of the infinite while living in mortal terror of each small comfort: "Still he is not undisturbed in mind, without some unuttered movings of the inner man."

Thus it is that Tertullian's consciousness frames an indictment of the culture in which he finds himself that calls into question the very nature of worldly meaning. He concludes: "Would that we did not even inhabit the same world with these wicked men! But though that wish cannot be realized, yet even now we separate from them in what is of the world; for the world is God's, but the worldly is the devil's." But where does this leave the *audience?* If private consciousness must be in a state of constant receptivity to the voice of God and if the rather minimal condition of encountering the public world is bidding welcome to evil, then the *true* Christian would seem to live permanently at odds with all public life.

In the final, scathing section of Tertullian's *refutatio*, he grapples with the most visible, persistent, and consequential accoutrement of Roman spectacle: the amphitheater, or *circus maximus*. Curiously, Tertullian uses this occasion to deny the mediating impact of occasion itself. In terms which utterly negate any possibility of *propriety* as a factor in choice, Tertullian declares: "Never and nowhere is that free from blame which God ever condemns; never and nowhere is it right to do what you may not do at all times and in all places." To the absolute pervasiveness of spectacle, Tertullian has juxtaposed his own equally pervasive injunction. If human sight is sinful, the sight of God is judgment and retribution. There can be no dispensation and surely no forgiveness.

But within this first mass culture, the final, most serious victim is the soul of man. The soul's subjective response is trapped in desperate rhetorical complicity with the shows: "Seated where there is nothing of God, will one be thinking of his Maker? Will there be peace in his soul when there is eager strife there for a charioteer? Wrought up into a frenzied excitement, will he learn to be modest?" And then: *"What will you do if you are caught in that heaving tide of impious judgments?"* (emphasis added). We can only speculate as to how Tertullian's audience responded to these rhetorical questions. But the questions seem quite shrewdly designed to address the *private* self, that aspect of us that takes personal exception to the rule of mass response.

Tertullian brought together in *De Spectaculis* the central tenets of the new Christian consciousness—the Incarnation, the mystery of interior faith, and sacrifice—in an unprecedented rhetorical assault on the mass culture of his contemporaries. But in his powerful final words, he makes the extraordinary acknowledgment that his attack has been based not on a philosophy of art, but on a fervently held social doctrine. More-over, the power of this doctrine must possess a rhetorical force that is all its own. Like the drama and pageantry of decadent pagan Rome, Chris-tianity had an aesthetic appeal. So the choice of visions, of orthodoxies, finally becomes a confrontation of two competing stories. Tertullian's ringing summation leaves no doubt as to which has the superior "plot":

> If the literature of the stage delight you, we have literature in abun-dance of our own—plenty of verses, sentences, songs, proverbs; and these not fabulous, but true; not tricks of art, plain realities. Would you also have fightings and wrestlings? Well, of these there is no lacking, and they are not of slight account. Behold unchastity over-come by chastity, perfidy slain by faithfulness, cruelty stricken by compassion, impudence thrown into the shade by modesty: these are contests we have among us, and in these we win our crowns. But would you have something of blood too? You have Christ's.

This final dramatic peroration is undeniably powerful. But it is puz-zling too. On the surface of things, Tertullian is grappling with the alleged false consciousness of his fellow Christians. But for all the irony, the venomous sarcasm designed to shame "normalized" Christians, the appeal seems to grant too much. After this relentless negation of interior "sin," have we come to our final defense of Christianity on the shal-low basis of life-*style*, the most prurient sort of aesthetic grounds? Must blood lust be the ultimate resting place of this case? So it would appear. Yet I suspect that something more remarkable is at stake in this final reversal.

In the world of this time there were two different kinds of blood: a blood of circulation and bodily maintenance and a blood of nourish-ment, of emotional and *spiritual* sustenance. Owen Barfield describes it this way:

The word *blood* is a particularly striking example of such a shift of meaning, since it is a substance with which, as it swings to and fro from heart to lung at the centre to visible complexion and sensitive skin at the periphery, we can still in some measure feel ourselves to be united by an extra-sensory link. We can, for example, both feel within ourselves and see through the curtain of another's flesh how instantly it answers to fear and shame. Thus we still partici-pate "originally" in our own blood up to the very moment when it becomes phenomenal by being shed.[39]

There can be no firm proof, other than intuitive experience, for what I am suggesting. But it should be remembered that until very recently the heart was regarded as the holistic center of sentimental life, the root metaphor of the emotional self.[40] Its blood, regarded subjectively, is our interior *life*. In Hebrew thought, the heart was the seat of the will and was often used for "sense" in general. To be given a "new heart" by Christianity was to have one's will transformed. It seems unlikely that Tertullian would undermine the force of this entire interiorized ad-dress with a peroration appealing only to public plot. What seems more credible and—even today—quite powerful is the way in which this final appeal juxtaposes the phenomenal blood shed through the pagan spec-tacle with what may be the last interior refuge of participation: the blood of sustenance and salvation, the interior redemption of faith, sacrifice, and now shame. This is rhetoric which, in Owen Barfield's words, indeed sees "through the curtain of another's flesh" in making its final call to worldly renunciation. It is a rhetoric of blood. But we are also shown how far removed from the collective figurations of public life Christian con-sciousness has become when one's own blood is what defines the forum of ultimate appeal. Convincing or not, it is some measure of the distance we have come from the classical affiliation with public appearance.

Implications

In its own time, Tertullian's *De Spectaculis* had a modest influence on controversies involving early Christian dogma. It was read widely by theologians and, in retrospect, may be seen to have anticipated Ter-tullian's own flight from Roman orthodoxy in favor of more extreme heretical doctrines. But this tract is also an oddly compelling antecedent to the contemporary tradition of "anti-appearances." We might think of the "mad monk" as a parable and precursor of world views wherein the subject is isolated, appearances are irretrievably damaged, and the prospects for human agency are lost. In other worlds, at other times, such a condition has lead to a desperate solace in the refuge of aesthetics. But for Tertullian, virtually alone on these bleak margins, aesthetics is itself complicitous in this condition. The arts have entered into, permeated, and become indistinguishable from the cultural landscape. In one of Tertullian's most memorable pronouncements, he says that "Satan and his angels have filled the whole world." By polarizing his options into the desperate extremes of spectacular consumption or spiritual exile, Tertullian offers us a powerful antecedent to the contemporary hegemony of the culture industry. At the same time, his own peculiarly modern consciousness became through such relentless antagonism, its own worst enemy.

Tertullian's early Christian consciousness may seem an unlikely harbinger of modern thought. However, Tertullian is the first historical figure to confront the full implications of the aesthetic stance as a world view. That he did not concern himself with the assumptions of art as a profession is because he knew full well that much of the known world had already begun to see art as the consuming preoccupation for leisure time. Art as creative project had been replaced by art as encounter for mass consumption. This may be why the brunt of Tertullian's attack was the *life-style* of aesthetics, rather than the integrity of its theories. We should not lose sight of the fact that Christianity's transformation of life is what makes Tertullian's radical antagonism possible in the first place.

Tertullian's tract also presents us with the first systematic critique of art as mass culture. As we have seen, in the original formulations of art, the question of art's cultural value was left open, largely because of diametrically opposed conceptions of aesthetic influence. Plato's mimetic theory assumed that a gullible audience would mistake the dangerous fabrications of art for the real thing. Aristotle's synthesis of a didactic and a cathartic theory celebrated the potential of serious art for purging human terrors through a recognition of our common fate. Of course, these foundational conceptions of art carried over to offer conflicting views of the place and integrity of rhetoric. For all the rampant psychologism in modern communication theory, it is interesting that the most prominent conceptions of popular cultural influence *on audiences* are still polarized between the ancient truisms of a mimetic and a cathartic interpretation. But in Tertullian's portrait of the aesthetic audience there is neither imitation of message nor katharsis through dynamis, but only the false consciousness which comes from losing the soul in the distraction of the crowd. This unique portrait, like his larger position on aesthetics generally, would not be plausible without the radically new faith which gives it force. Extreme as Tertullian's commitments may seem, they are different only in intensity from those of his colleagues.

Although the message of Christ introduced a new redemptive possibility into the world, with the departure of Christ the world darkened. God left the Holy Spirit with man (the interior consciousness of faith) and the Church as his visible sign. But the story was left unfinished, and Christ did not return.[41] Longing for a return of the *sight* of God, the early Christians were consoled through the interior message of faith. But that message, as Tertullian realized, could flourish and be heard only in an atmosphere of calm. Moreover, the Church's interiorized message and exteriorized rituals must compete with many other visible signs for attention and belief, particularly the spectacles. Thus it was that the early Christian evangelists disparaged the created things of the world and lived in a self-imposed exile from its artifice.

Finally, it must be said that Tertullian's extreme Christianity afforded him a profound appreciation of the diabolical impact exerted by these pagan spectacles. More than any of his contemporaries, he understood that the evil of spectacle is exerted through the emotional power wrought by sight (*aesthēsis*, now the claim to eyewitness authenticity). Further, since God is regarded as the only true author, evil is experienced as a theft of meaning, the worldly being substituted for God, the passionately inconsequential for spiritual truth. In short, as an alienated believer only too aware of the tyranny of mass culture, Tertullian teaches us through his anger about the true victim of spectacle. In an ironic reversal of the Incarnation, the real victim of the spectacle is this fragile new historical creation: the interiority of the self, the soul of man.

However, a disabling irony accompanies this war of the senses. For Tertullian, as we have noted, an act—even in ritualized performance—may corrupt the very context in which it occurs. Thus the enlarged arenas for aesthetic communication—the theaters and forums—are themselves corrupted insofar as they offer the occasions for performances as entertainment. For the audiences of these spectacles, the participatory enactment of social ritual may be virtually equivalent to the so-called real thing. In enacting the idealized symbolism of evil (hubris, greed, lust, or whatever), we entertain its collective possibility. For Tertullian, such participation is a form of social engagement for which we are individually accountable. Rather than engaging in the interiority of private communion with the divine, the soul is levelled and lost in a collective identification with passionate excitement and lust and a distraction from the real. The real, recall, cannot be of this world, given how corrupted it has become. We now see how far we have come from the unfolding *public* moments of disclosure in Greek civic life. In this melancholic homelessness of the soul within the pageantry of crowds, Tertullian has captured most memorably the rhetorical experience of spectacle. But he has also irretrievably dismissed all prospects for positive human agency in public life. There is no longer any core of sense to be shared, any common theme to be unfolded, any public symbol of affiliation, any way to speak. With the final, fatal corruption of the forum, the world may not be reanimated: "Not that any harm is likely to come to you from men: nobody knows that you are a Christian."

Modern culture has taken the aesthetics of the profane far beyond the mad monk's wildest dreams. This may be one reason why it is tempting to think of Tertullian as a forerunner of modernism as critique. As appearances have themselves become cultural transpositions and the arts an alternative orthodoxy, diffident culture critics like Baudrillard emerge as postmodern Tertullians without faith.[42] To give a last homiletic spin to this excursus, it may be worth remembering that Tertullian has rejected the whole worldly realm of images and signs in favor of a privileged voice that only the private person may hear (through inner speech, the unconscious, faith). His is a most spirited indictment. Yet the contemporary reader will also recognize a tone of exasperation, bordering on futility, in much of this radical negation. Why? Because the imagined power of Tertullian's ideal speech cannot compete with the superior power of the world that has visibly become *what is*, the given. I do not mean to suggest that all exiles are but figurative. It is just that Tertullian, in his extremity, has lost the dynamis of reason and any part-to-whole relationship between imminent constituency and the larger community (in a microcosmic form, its audience). The devaluation of public consciousness must inevitably devalue and dismiss any criteria for denial; it must consume the self as author with every fervent pronouncement. In the wake of such interiority of truth, the enhanced scope of rhetoric proportionally increases its impotence; and the line between inspiration and fanaticism must become blurred.

We live in an age of almost obsessive disengagement, albeit trapped in a spectacular rhetoric all our own—a rhetoric that is justifiably condemned as shallow and devoid of rational warrant. And much like Tertullian the apologist, we hanker after a vision of the truth that is somehow both privileged and interior at the same time. However, a serious displacement of all rhetoric (including our own) follows directly from the devaluation of public consciousness and from the displacement of our power for its transformation. Here we have reason as technique of refutation, but nothing more. The power of definition and hence engagement is gone. Modernity as political subjectivity is thus ushered onto center stage: an interior voice without a vision.

This first homiletic excursus should remind us of the need for critical cultural rhetoric to preserve some place for an other in the articulation of its own discourse. Otherwise, it is likely to be its own first victim. Audiences no less than private selves may be presumed capable of recognizing the difference between the mask and the face, especially when the face is their own. Most important, the *given* in any specific culture (be it comprised of icons, imagery, technology, symbols, signs, or faiths) must somehow have engaged our consciousness to be where it is. Similarly, it must be engaged by us, if only to suggest what we may yet become. As Tertullian recognized in principle but could not articulate in practice, the last civilized hope for such engagement is rhetoric.

EXCURSUS ON HORKHEIMER:
ENLIGHTENMENT IN EXILE

To study the ideas of an age rhetorically, we must do more than convert or reduce them to the persuasive imagery of a culture. Otherwise, we find ourselves raging against the same insuperable obstacles as our heretic monk. Such a stance is contradicted with our every attempt to make clear, grounded discriminations about quality in the world of thought and action. To study the ideas of an age rhetorically, then, is to ask in the most demanding way imaginable about the real-life implications of a body of thought. For whom? First and foremost, for those who take the ideas to be true. But we also must include those who are the legitimate or accidental heirs of a tradition as well. Specifically, what does a given concept of the world, the age, the self, the culture, imply for the possibility of rhetorical conduct?

This is what I now wish to ask about the historical episode of reason's greatest resurgence—*the Enlightenment*. How could it come to appear retrospectively to be the arch-enemy of normative cultural practices? I am thinking here of works such as *The Dialectic of Enlightenment*, the *Tragedy of Enlightenment*, the more recent writings of Ronald Beiner, MacIntyre's broadside against the entire Enlightenment project, and even the late nineteenth-century pronouncements of Nietzsche and Kierkegaard.[43] Now it will not do to make of the admittedly vain pronouncements of Kant, Voltaire, Hegel, and Descartes a modern faith at odds with the world. Becker's "Heavenly City" notwithstanding,[44] the architects of this modern edifice clearly intended and crafted their product as a worldly vision, in no way contrary to generalizable principles of freedom and autonomy.

Instead, I want to take the less equivocal step of arguing that the more radical indictments of Enlightenment thinking are themselves misconceived. In reacting against dominant Enlightenment presuppositions, contemporary thinkers have often confused form with substance, even as they have replicated the most specious features of late Enlightenment thought in their own radical reaction. Finally, I wish to argue that even if the voice of logos must ultimately depend on faith, it is a faith worth entertaining in light of its less inviting alternatives, which constitute a form of exile from which there is no obvious return.

At their most arrogant and inclusive, the postulates of Enlightenment reason come across to the late modern reader as at once naive and even repellent: a tragic protagonist waiting to take the fall. Here is that old hedgehog Isaiah Berlin offering them in summary form: "that human nature is the same in all times and places; that universal human goals, true ends, and effective means, are at least in principle discoverable; that methods similar to those of Newtonian science, which had proved so successful in bringing to light the regularities of inanimate nature, should be discovered and applied in the fields of morals, politics, economics, and in the sphere of human relationships in general, thus eradicating vice and suffering and what Helvetius termed 'interested error'."[45]

This preemptive vision was even then framed in irony, of course, by the fact that there were as many different inflections of unchanging human nature as there were Enlightenment cultures. Between the association of ideas across the dark rumblings of *Geist* and the shining citadels of Voltaire lies a vast landscape, within whose terrain the only commonality was probably the pre-reflective confidence with which reason itself was attached to each program. For all this, rhetoric (of a sort) flourished during this period, albeit in a precarious way. It is worth asking what happened. The stirrings of reaction were evident, first in Italy, then in the Prussian and Germanic cultures. It is the latter reaction which concerns us here: what it took as questionable, what it left unquestioned, what it left unresolved.

There is a sense in which the Enlightenment consciousness helped to institute the conditions for its own refutation. Primarily it did this by identifying itself—a First Philosophy, after all—with a privileged period of history, a period which was seen to be a major advance over previous civilizations and historic eras. Previous periods of world history had envisioned reason as consisting in aspects of a technē: the reflective arts of analysis, appraisal, and judgment through which claims were engaged, critiqued, and corrected. Then, too, reason and a grammar of self-understanding were seen as interdependent. Reason thereby becomes (as it still is, for some analytic philosophy) part of a systematic reflexive vocabulary for what it *means* to be human.[46] Yet there is a third sense of reason, marked most definitively perhaps by the application of the term "project" to the Enlightenment. This is the sense of reason as something produced in time, with a life of its own: reason as a product. This sense is made available to us, of course, by the first two senses. We learn over time that we may reflect back on the reasoning we have created in the past, and even that we may look back on previous grammars, previous definitions of the species, and so forth. In a benign way, this sense of reason as *product* is at work in every history of ideas ever written. Yet obviously and undeniably there is a less benign way whereby reason—in reproducing itself—becomes rationalization. This is presumably what Richard Bernstein had in mind with his befuddled dialectical observation that reason as emancipation and reason as reification go hand in hand.[47] Historically, reason as product has been associated with terrible episodes, and atrocious crimes have been committed in its name. Bombs have become "smart," missiles "patriots"; and otherwise reasonable people commit, permit, and tolerate this quotidian of mad reason. Reason as art and reason as grammar are thus conflated and levelled into the tragic fate of reason as faits accomplis production *within* history. Reason is thereby discredited.

Our second textual excursus examines reaction to the late German Enlightenment by some of the pivotal figures in what was to become German social theory. In my view, the entire utopian impulse of modernism as critical theory is founded on disillusionment with the pretensions of the late German Enlightenment: first, Kant and Hegel; then, of course, the first real rebel children of the Enlightenment, Marx and Freud. But what is most striking in this reaction is not what is overturned, but what is still taken for granted. Consider at least some of the failed assumptions of German romanticism that helped to usher in the modernist moment. Among these are:

(1) the autonomous ego as knower,
(2) the autonomy of reason as a faculty,
(3) a dialectical vision of progress through historicized reason,
(4) an idealist conception of knowledge and truth,
(5) a terminus to the project of inquiry that is final in the sense of being absolute or, perhaps, absolute in the sense of finally *Being*. [48]

Throughout this study, I have been concerned with the rhetorical position of the exile, the person who either cannot or will not participate in the prevailing appearances of the speech community. For reasons of consciousness, cultural temperament, or historical condition, such people find themselves excluded from the dominant conceptions of God, meaning, and political virtue. How are they to invent discourse, to speak, listen, and judge? With the barbarism and genocide of mid-twentieth-century Europe, we were confronted with a world very different from anything ever dreamed of by the classicists, a world that seemed to defy attitude and choice, a world that took Kant's notorious "scandal of reason" to nightmarish extremes. In some quarters, at least, the prevailing culture exiled the voices of its own conscience. Understandably, no one alive at the time emerges from this dark period of history completely unscathed. This too is part of our legacy. For those in the critical theory tradition, crisis has been fixed in the latter twentieth century, so much so that to many the very idea of hope coming from the world of ideas is a sure sign of intellectual fatigue or failure of nerve. In Owen Barfield's prophetic terms, we are all exiles now.

> O dear white children casual as birds,
> Playing among the ruined languages,
> So small beside their large confusing words,
> So gay against the greater silences
> Of dreadful things you did: O hang the head,
> Impetuous child with the tremendous brain,

> O weep, child, weep, O weep away the stain,
> Lost innocence who wished your lover dead,
> Weep for the lives your wishes never led.[49]

I now turn to Max Horkheimer's powerful essay "The End of Reason," because it represents one of the clearest examples of relentless dialectical critique in counter-Enlightenment vein. It is a critique that in its brilliance and sweeping compass seeks to meet this vast historical crisis head on. The essay, published in 1941, but written piecemeal three years earlier, begins with several dark, apocalyptic pronouncements:

> The fundamental concepts of civilization are in a process of rapid decay. The rising generation no longer feels any confidence in them, and fascism has strengthened their suspicions. The question of how far these concepts are at all valid clamors more than ever for an answer. The decisive concept among them was that of reason, and philosophy knew of no higher principle. It was supposed to order the relationships among men and to justify all the performances demanded of them. The church fathers and the guiding spirit of the Enlightenment agreed in their praise of reason. Voltaire called it "God's incomprehensible gift to mankind" and "the source of every society, institution, and order."[50]

There follows a series of equally extravagant observations about reason from Origen and Kant (who predicts its eventual triumph over retrogressions, darkness, and deviations). Horkheimer concludes that "from this ideal of reason . . . the ideas of freedom, justice and truth derived their justification. They were held to be innate to it, intuited or necessarily conceived by it."

The urgency of Horkheimer's words reminds us that this essay was not written at a time of historical tranquility or bourgeois leisure; it exudes crisis. Still, there are several initial curiosities to be noted. This is already a totalizing statement. Horkheimer does not say, for instance, that the fundamental concepts of *German* civilization are in the process of rapid decay, though the immediate political context of the remarks is unavoidable. Further, he specifically locates the exigence of his inquiry in the "suspicion" and displaced "confidence" of "the rising generation." The claims that are made on reason's behalf seem sweeping, naively utopian, an invitation to historical reversal. This is likely to be a tragic narrative. Still, we must look closely at how Horkheimer allows the personified character of reason to perform, if only to better understand its eventual fate.

Horkheimer next makes a connection that is critical to reason's fate, in the observation that "The philosophy this world produced is essentially rationalistic, but time and again, in following out its own principles, it turns against itself and takes the form of skepticism." This is the dark side of the Enlightenment: that reason, unavoidably immersed in the process of critique, finds its own optimism suspect. Horkheimer locates the paradox of reason in its attempt to abandon the fetishes of belief (namely, the gods, utopias, souls) while maintaining the same standards of cognition as skepticism. While not even Kant (!) was able to defeat skepticism, rationalism was still losing all but the most empirical attachments to its doctrines. So Horkheimer finds that in the present day skepticism has emerged victorious: "Skepticism purged the idea of reason of so much of its content that today scarcely anything is left of it." Moreover, "none of the categories of rationalism has survived. Modern science looks upon such of them as Mind, Will, Final Cause, Transcendental Creation, Innate Ideas, res extensa and res cogitans as spooks, despising them even more than Galileo did the cobwebs of scholasticism."

These stark pronouncements presuppose a number of less obvious background assumptions: that reason is consubstantial with rationalism, that its resources may be depleted with the passage of time, that it may be identified with the happenstance of successive events, and so forth. It would be misleading to label these assumptions stratagems, since their overall effect is to entrap the arguer; but they are surely rhetorical in the classic sense of constituting thought within a tragic frame. Indeed, Horkheimer finds that the "grammar of everyday language" has succeeded in adapting the animistic fetishes that once accompanied rationalism to decadent political reality. Such reason tells us that "duty demands," "life calls," and so forth. In a monumental bit of understatement, he observes that this reason "does not suffice to propagate freedom, the dignity of man or even truth."

Horkheimer's tract is intended to show how reason has reached this terrible condition, as well as, I suspect, to protest what can no longer be averted. While conceding that "reason has not been cancelled altogether from the vocabulary of those who are up to date," Horkheimer regards its most conspicuous surviving traits as the pragmatic, means–ends, efficiency thinking of contemporary technical organizations. Of course, he has one technical organization more in mind than any other as he writes. Indeed, he finds that three of Locke's four degrees of reason (he omits "final cause") may be located, without amendment, in modern techniques of war: "When even the dictators of today appeal to reason, they mean that they possess the most tanks. They were rational enough to build them; others should be rational enough to yield to them. Within the range of Fascism, to defy such reason is the cardinal crime." This is Callicles returning triumphant in demonic Nazi form. Ironies notwithstanding, Horkheimer's aim is to show that the new barbarism is only a more pronounced version of the old, that reason and efficient adjustment to social power arrangements have always gone hand in hand.

This theme, reminiscent of themes discussed at length in *Dialectic of Enlightenment*, inspires Horkheimer to undertake a remarkable reconstruction of previous historical stages of reason and their relationship to prevailing arrangements of power. Employing an odd amalgam of early Marx and late Freud, Horkheimer claims that reason is essentially a social category of use, which induces the individual to subordinate his or her own instinctual interest to that of society whenever these interests are at odds. He finds that "even Greek idealism was to a large extent pragmatic in this sense and identified the good and the advantageous, the beautiful and the useful, and putting the welfare of the whole before the welfare of its members." For "the individual was nothing apart from . . . the whole." From the auspicious origin of the polis, we are taken through the medieval towns to the rise of the nation-state, wherein "rationality in the form of such obedience swallows up everything, even the freedom to think." This last statement, although extreme, is crucial for the larger theme that Horkheimer wishes to explore. For as long as the thinking subject may dissent at least in thought, reason can reserve for itself some measure of autonomy. But in a striking series of excerpts from both dissenters and supporters of the French Revolution, Horkheimer finds that "patriotism . . . is that national reason of which I speak; it is the abnegation of the individual." As part of the Jacobin reaction, Mathiez wrote that the prevailing reason "admits of no contradiction, it requires oaths, it is made obligatory by prison, exile or the scaffold, and like religion proper it is concretized in sacred signs." Horkheimer's conclusion stresses the dramatic ironies in this, perhaps the Enlightenment's greatest embarrassment: "The basic unity of the period obliterates differences of opinion. The enthusiasm of the counterrevolution and of the popular leaders not only joined in a common faith in the executioner but also in the conviction that reason may at any time justify renouncing thought, particularly of the poor."

We find in these words the extreme consequences of reason as a form of historical accommodation. But even the most tortured reappropriation of categories would find it difficult to confine reason to such foreclosure of reflection alone. This is, to be sure, a great evil. But it is difficult to see how an awareness of the contradiction is even possible without the continuation of reflection by means of critique: in other words, by another form of reason. All this is to say that reason is hardly the univocal category that Horkheimer has presupposed so far. There are many different forms and voices of reason, Horkheimer's included. At times, we must concede, it is terribly difficult to hear them.

The body of his essay constitutes an attempt to link the succession of reason's forms to this barbaric stage of history. Central to Horkheimer's analysis is a sweeping, but dubious claim. The role of reason has always been to reconcile the individual to the collectivity in light of divergent systems of values, goods, and ends in view. This is why Horkheimer can observe that rationalists, absolutists, and empiricists are all correct in exactly the same duplicitous way:

> Owing to this contradiction, the appeal to the universality of reason assumes the appeal of the spurious and the illusory. Reason's claim to be absolute presupposes that a true community exists among men. By denying the reality of universal concepts and pointing to existing reality instead, the empiricists are right as against the rationalists. On the other hand, the rationalists are right as against the empiricists in that, through what is implied in their concept of reason, they uphold the potential solidarity of men as an ideal against the actual state of affairs in which solidarity is asserted with violence and catastrophe.

Of course, this latter idealist sense of rationalism is precisely what sustains the circling of reflective dialectic and continues the process of critique. This is why Horkheimer is forced to allow that the ideal rationalism is either a lie or a lost form of historical reason. In fact, he concludes that "thinking in terms of mere existence, of sober self-preservation, has spread over the whole of society." His brilliantly pessimistic conclusion is that "all men have become empiricists."

There follows a dizzying array of rationalistic forms, together with their implications for mass consciousness. Nominalism leads to the triumph of pluralism: the diversification of end states in contemporary secular democracy. Horkheimer sees this as the unbridgeable gap between science and value: "It is regarded as a matter of subjective preference whether one decides for liberty or obedience, democracy or fascism, enlightenment or authority, mass culture, or truth." What once were regarded as virtues are here reinterpreted as "attributes characterizing individuality. Poise, rank, propriety, gallantry still are what pragmatism mistakes them to be, habitual forms of the individual's adjustment to the social situation." By imitating the norms from an already deformed, victimized stance, "power is made to appear as eternal." Clearer now than before is the fact that reason's practices—as presented here, at least—are each a form of rhetoric—rhetoric construed as rule and domination. And although the motive behind each form of rhetoric is a kind of self-preservation—here is the autonomous ego again—the actual practices of reason cancel out this motivation in the most contradictory ways imaginable:

> This self-preservation may even call for the death of the individual which is to be preserved. Sacrifice can be rational when it becomes necessary to defend the state's power which is alone capable of guaranteeing the existence of those whose sacrifice it demands. The idea of reason, even in its nominalistic and purified form, has always justified sacrifice. During the heroic era, the individual destroyed his life for the interests and symbols of the collectivity that guaranteed it. Property was the institution that conveyed to the individual the idea that something of his existence might remain after death. At the origin of organized society, property endured while generations passed away.

Again, note the reification of reason in Horkheimer's own appraisal: "*The idea* of reason . . . has always justified sacrifice." Of course we offer reasons to justify sacrifice. Sometimes sacrifices discredit, by their terrible cost, the original justification. Sometimes the victims are not around to tell. Sometimes ultimate costs are invoked as an ultimate investment requiring still more ultimate costs. Once reason becomes, as it were, a self-proclaimed historical episode, irony and tragedy abound, to say the least. But in the midst of Horkheimer's luminous recognition is the intrusive fact that this collapse need not have been as fateful or as final as he presents it here.

Horkheimer's relentless negation of reason quickly slides into an indictment of reason's cunning, the duplicitous purposes to which the arts of reason have been put. The origins of critical theory's notorious aversion to rhetoric may be found right here, in "that injustice which made language the servant of gain. The muteness of men today is largely to be blamed on language which once was only too eloquent against them." Here is yet another familiar, albeit somewhat unlikely, indictment of reason. In its capacity to manipulate and outwit the other, reason takes those who are least adept in its ways and means and dominates their fate. If we assume that the practices of reason are themselves correlated with unequal power relationships, then we see that Horkheimer is here raising the age-old specter of an art which may make the worse case appear to be the better and so deprive an audience of its own apparent interests. There is a response to the charge, of course, which Callicles recognized: namely, that the force of the better argument may also restrict power against the weak and afford to the dominated an avenue of power; that is, that it may become a source of liberation as well. Here the horizon of barbarism surrounding Horkheimer seems to rule out this possibility.

Perhaps it is this relentless logic of association that brings Horkheimer to his next, still more elemental topic: *childhood*. Complaints about children rejecting authority and ignoring demanding studies in favor of flashy technologies and physical display may be as close as we get to truths which transcend history. Some of what Horkheimer says has these familiar tones. But childhood is also a social symbol, one that is historically affiliated with a kind of reason; and Horkheimer is preoccupied with the historic fate of this symbol. Once again, he is sensitive to the rhetorical functions of the symbol, even in its most protected state: "Childhood becomes a historical phenomenon. Christianity inaugurated the idea of childhood in its glorification of the weak, and the bourgeois family sometimes made that idea a reality. During the Christian era up to the Enlightenment, however, reason operated on the child as an external compulsion to self-preservation which crushed everything that could not defend itself." During the Middle Ages, Horkheimer generalizes, art and sculpture revealed the secrets of hierarchies involving children, namely "who could with impunity beat whom." But it is the Enlightenment appropriation of childhood as myth which is again the focus:

Children who in the Christian world suffered the tortures of Hell were, in the Enlightenment, rewarded with the Christian heaven.

Happiness shall be theirs because they have been chosen as the symbols of innocence. In his adoration of his children, the enlightened businessman of the 19th century could mourn his lost childhood without becoming superstitious. Children symbolized the Golden Age as well as the promising future. The rationalist society gave children legends and fairy tales so that they might mirror hope back to their disillusioned elders.

Then, to insure that the sober theme is not lost: "The child ideal reflected the truth within the lie that kept the underlying population in line, the utopia of eternal happiness." Horkheimer paints such a bleak picture of this hope that it is difficult to imagine how history could make matters worse. But it does and has: "They can do without this utopia today."

Horkheimer was confronted in Nazi Germany with a terrifying perversion of the childhood myth: the mystification and cultish worship of German youth as a political act, the extermination of Jewish youth as a still unfathomable technical project. The symbolic weight of these activities may be what provokes a remarkably inventive—but I think false—synthesis of Freud and Marx. In a state which has become a fatherland ruled by *der Führer*, the superego has been appropriated by the dominant social arrangements: "During the heyday of the family the father represented the authority of society to the child and puberty was the inevitable conflict between these two. Today, however, the child stands face to face with society at once, and the conflict is decided even before it arises." In this process, too, reason becomes a passive accomplice: "The world is so possessed by the power of what is and the efforts of adjustment to it, that the adolescent's rebellion, which once fought the father because his practices contradicted his own ideology, can no longer crop up. The process which hardens men by breaking down their individuality—a process consciously and planfully undertaken in the various camps of fascism—takes place tacitly and mechanically in them everywhere under mass culture, and at such an early age that when children come to consciousness everything is settled."

It must be said that Horkheimer readily admits his deviation from the Freudian position. The magnitude of the historical crisis has been such as to alter radically our understanding of the human unconscious. Universal determinants of personality and character have themselves become historically specific phenomena: "Since Freud, the relation between father and son has been reversed. Now the rapidly changing society which passes its judgment upon the old is represented not by the father but by the child. The child, not the father, stands for reality. The awe which the Hitler youth enjoys from his parents is but the pointed political expression of a universal state of affairs."

As an indictment of prevailing social practice, Horkheimer's diagnostic is a powerful precursor of Frankfurt's studies of the *Authoritarian Personality*. But it is not difficult to see here also the conceptual confusion that takes hold when the autonomous ego becomes the locus of freedom, while reason remains a historic category. As an instrument of repression, reason, the voice of "many," will inevitably overwhelm the lonely individual. In the dark nightmarish realm of the immediate, Horkheimer has drawn the curtain on cultural difference and then banished even the possibility of redemption.

In this context it is interesting that the erosion of sexual taboos presents itself as a related topic. Now that the function of the superego has been dissociated from parental authority, it becomes the prerogative of the decadent state. And in an anticipation of Marcuse's "repressive desublimation," it is the state that removes all censors of what might otherwise be regarded as sacred or forbidden. The consequence? "Sex loses its power over men. It is turned on and off according to the requirements of the situation. Men no longer lose themselves in it, they are neither moved nor blinded by love." Here Horkheimer's longing for an earlier Victorian form of reason is almost palpable. However, since reason *in general* is our antagonist, Horkheimer cannot argue for an earlier stage of repression. He takes refuge in one of the few surviving strains of late German Enlightenment culture: a deeply melancholic romanticism.

> The sexual freedom prescribed by the population policy does not cure the anxiety of the world of sexual taboos but expresses mere scorn of love. Love is the irreconcilable foe of the prevailing rationality, for lovers preserve and protect neither themselves nor the collectivity. They throw themselves away; that is why wrath is heaped upon them. Romeo and Juliet died in conflict with society for that which was heralded by this society. In unreasonably surrendering themselves to one another, they sustained the freedom of the individual as against the dominion of the world of things.

At this point, it may be worth reminding ourselves of just how Romeo and Juliet surrendered themselves, just how they threw themselves away. Moreover, the accumulation of appearances—sacrifice, the rackets, strength, childhood, sex—now presents itself as more than a random succession of nightmarish images. These are the invariant components of culture itself, only given a perverse, lurid transformation. But this crisis imagery also presents a graphic depiction of Horkheimer's own dilemma. To reject all that this crisis culture has become, he must still find some horizon of difference, a conceptual terrain on which to stand. This may be why, in the midst of a diabolically bleak situation, the heroism of sacrifice seems quietly to have been reborn.

With love bidding a poignant farewell to reason, only one elemental reminder of reflection remains: "Pain is the means of calling men back from the noumenal world into which all empiricist philosophers and even Kant forbade them to penetrate. It was always the best teacher to bring men to reason." Horkheimer dwells on the most brutal features of reason's precarious reduction: torture and the terrible annihilation of self in this barbaric age. Yet with pain—perhaps *only* with pain—comes the last prospect for recognition. No longer does the rationalization of power get in the way. Here, in a last desperate moment, the possibility of a different sort of reason glimmers: "In the inferno to which triumphant reason has reduced the world, it loses its illusions, but in doing so, it becomes capable of facing this inferno and recognizing it for what it is." We seem to be on the verge of a resolution, or at least a moment of hope. But then: "Skepticism has done its job. Ideals seem so futile today that they can change as rapidly as agreements and alliances do." Through the forms of sacrifice, gangsterism, strength, childhood, sex, and pain, we have witnessed the mutation of reason in ever more elementary symbols. But far from being cathartic in effect, this reduction has only polarized primitive forces.

The last passages of Horkheimer's essay bespeak a pessimism that borders on the euphoric: "The terror which pushes reason is at the same time the last means of stopping it, so close has truth come." And then: "The progress of reason that leads to its self-destruction has come to an end; there is nothing left but barbarism or freedom."

CONCLUSIONS AND REFLECTIONS

Earlier I observed that no one emerged from the dark years of the mid-twentieth century entirely unscathed. Unlike several of the other, figurative exiles examined in this book, Horkheimer cannot be said to have been responsible for his isolation. Most persons of conscience who could do so fled. Those who remained either resisted or collaborated. Walter Benjamin took his own life. As one born after those years, I would be presumptuous in the extreme to suggest some superior vantage point that hindsight affords. In an era that deemed history the final arbiter of conviction, the exhortations of others to sacrifice and virtue were small consolation. And the heirs of the German Enlightenment tradition were entitled to ask whether the boundaries of moral community made sense anymore. Those familiar with the work of Horkheimer, Adorno, and Marcuse through the fifties and sixties have a general outline of their answer: not in this world and not at this time.

We need to remind ourselves, however, that Horkheimer's masterful essay is both a powerful cultural critique and a revealing exercise in late Enlightenment thought. If anything, the presuppositions of critique are made more obvious by the crisis atmosphere. So our interest in the ongoing conceptual relationship between rhetorical practice and culture might be usefully applied to this pivotal episode for the cultivation of social character and conviction, human purpose and agency, as generally conceived. Is there a space for innovation and invention, for temporary closure, accountability, and judgment? In the case of Horkheimer, I can imagine a simple, disingenuous response to such an inquiry along the general lines: "No, of course there were none of these things, because there were none of these things in Germany."

There is something to be said for this response, of course, as I have already indicated. Who can say how he or she might respond in some similarly desperate setting? Even so, I wish to claim that Horkheimer's critique brings with it certain features of late German Enlightenment thought which make it difficult to do anything other than end reason. Specifically, the notion that the possibilities of reason are encoded in the episodes of history *alone* has the effect of reifying the subject as victim, as well as placing Horkheimer's own reflection on the most ambiguous terrain. Add to this Horkheimer's unshakable conviction in the autonomous ego as the locus of freedom, and it is understandable that no real *community* of exiles ever developed. Of course, language in the public forum could not be trusted in the era of Horkheimer's critique. But one wonders, given the limits on social reflection, if the practices of reason could *ever* be held accountable in any promissory way. This makes a vast difference to the prospect of continuity or even vision in the midst of crisis. If we regard the work of reason as always in league with the exploitation of those without power and autonomous selfhood as the only conceivable locus and definition of freedom, then the public sphere will forever be poisoned, and solidarity will be impossible.

There are several striking instances of Horkheimer's critical double bind where the practices of reason are concerned. To take one example, Horkheimer wished to condemn the final degradation of reason when used in conjunction with the extermination program. He writes: "If reason has been purged of all morality regardless of cost, and has triumphed over all else, no one may remain outside and look on." We all understand what he means, of course. But consider the fact that reason, even in its earlier Enlightenment incarnations, possessed for Horkheimer a duplicitous morality at best, a lie to force compliance from the lower classes. So what standards of reason's morality can we possibly use to measure this decline? Add to this the further paradox that "no one may remain outside and look on." Where does this leave Horkheimer himself?

Horkheimer employed his own dialectical reflection in such a way as to create for himself one of the more remarkable aporia of modern thought. In its original Greek sense, the word *aporia* suggests the condition of being trapped without resources or reinforcements. This was, as Horkheimer well recognized, exactly the condition confronting speculative thought. Overall, his presuppositions engendered what William James might have called a tender-minded philosophy, one which was driven from the world's horrors and abuses.[51] Rather than decrying the Holocaust or the Gulags as irrational on the grandest of scales, he finds rationality itself to be impossible in such a world. The question is whether we can rescue Horkheimer's radical negation from its aporia. History, as we know, did not.[52]

Of all late Enlightenment thinkers, Horkheimer was probably the most provocative and insightful. The unhappy fate of his thought forces us to reflect on the consequence of any vision of reason that abandons all transcendental possibility. But for all this, some important correctives for the relationship of rhetoric and culture may be found in the work of Horkheimer's contemporaries.

It is interesting, for instance, that Arendt traces the experience of fascism in Germany not to the complicities of reason, but rather to the banality of evil, located ultimately in the inability to think, to reflect on the alternative possibilities of ordinary life.[53] For his part, Cassirer considers the Nazi experience to be a pathology of symbolic consciousness on a broad cultural level. Turning away from his own serious reflections regarding the world of myth, Cassirer was still able to regard what the

Fascists did as *bad myth*—in other words, as forcibly invented and re-vised myth, rather than myth that emerged as part of the succession of stories and cultural experiences of the time. Along the way, Cassirer also suggests the need to broaden our understanding of reason to include not merely the discredited philosophies of rationalism, but also the methods and modalities of reflection generally.[54] Ernst Bloch went still further, arguing that even in the worst moments of Nazi appropriation of mythic thought, there were moments of affirmation in taking our nightmares as well as our daydreams seriously.[55] In our own time, Hans Blumenberg takes the brute physical inadequacy of the human species, its inability to compete with strength, instinct, and so forth, as evidence that we are, through our own inherent deficiencies, fundamentally rhetorical creatures.[56]

There are critiques that might be directed at each of these visions. Cas-sirer, for all his breadth of vision and foresight, failed to bring clearly into focus the way in which a sense of negation and struggle might inform his own organic picture of reflection. Arendt's understanding of both think-ing and political judgment was never able to escape its Kantian origins. Bloch's vision of hope has a tendency to shade into mysticism and never engages difficult questions of choice and action on a political scale. But for all this, an alternative organic picture of culture that might be com-patible with rhetoric has survived both the failed project of modernity and the pessimism of the counter-Enlightenment.

There may be no more disturbing image in the history of culture than that of the suffering child. Surely, there is no more chilling image than that of the *corrupted* child. Horkheimer employs both, as compelling images of a culture that has been blinded to any principle of civility, a world that is beyond hope. Yet Arendt employs exactly the same image, that of the child to whom everything and anything may yet happen, as conclusive evidence of what she terms "natality," the rebirth of the new possibility, a culture of hope. It seems inappropriate—even pathologi-cal—to love and be deeply absorbed in your own child yet oblivious or insensitive to the fate of children generally. Beyond the mystery of the self, where care is difficult to measure, is the communicative fact of ex-ternalization. Emmanuel Levinas traces this notion directly to the idea of the child which mystifies and overcomes our sense of self by being real as well as other.[57] My point is that life's most painful image may still offer us a utopian moment, the possibility of a world in which children do not have to suffer. Of course, it may also drive us mad, as it apparently did Mahler, among others.

From the perspective of hindsight, it is possible to view the complexities of reason's abandonment another way. Clearly, the unfathomable historic atrocities associated with the Nazi seizure of power drove Horkheimer away from the critique of practical choice made available by an *ethical* stance, toward a more *aesthetic* refuge from the immanence of action and consequence. Appropriately and compellingly, he constructed from this stance its archetypal poetic form: a tragic narrative in which reason plays the central fateful role and finally has its fall. There is no room within this form, of course, for a return of comic possibility, a world of redemption after krisis and peripeteia. This is understandable, given the time at which the essay was written. There was time for only a glimmer of recognition. There was not yet room for hope. But for Horkheimer the tragedy never really ended, even after the war. With the heroic collapse of reason, it becomes the individual's fate always to recognize, but never quite to rejoin, the ongoing regenerative life of public thought.

Yet, in the midst of this tragedy, can we not also see the glimmering of logos painting its own reifications into a corner? In this narrative, reason has been personified as a character. But it has also assumed the form of a plot, in its most elegant variation as fateful necessity. Further, is reason not also the counsel, the theme, the thought, the "proof"? And what of the character of authorship? Is this story the product of events alone, or are these not also mediated by the anguished reflective soul of Horkheimer? And if *one* anguished reflective soul, why not more? My point is, predictably, a reflective one. Despite the desperation of circumstance, reason never disappears into a perishable content as long as the mediating artistry of its own form remains visible and effective. And this is what seems to have happened here.

This does not mean that the consciousness of late modernity has been conducive to a revival of logos—or the flourishing of rhetoric for that matter. Prefigured ironically by Tertullian's retreat from public appearances and his fragile refuge of solitude, Horkheimer's own faith in reason was betrayed so bitterly that the already small space of reflection itself closed. In our own time, the prevailing theorists of dark times and hegemony—people like Foucault and Baudrillard—profess the belief that the reflective space never reopened. Admirably, they deplore the reluctance of dominant cultures to make room for differing, dissident voices, for marginalized peoples to tell their own story. But there is never any systematic consideration of the reasons why dominant cultures should listen to, as opposed to vaporize, all "others." And it is difficult to see what would be achieved by such a hearing, even if it did occur. This is because these same theorists regard the normalized discourse of reason in dominant culture as itself a regime of linguistic hegemony and repression. Like the pessimistic Horkheimer, they see civility, decorum, the "rules of the game," as only a mask for an underlying condition of dependence. The conceptual knots begin to tangle; for there seems to be no real criterion of difference within the vocabulary of such critique between the marginality of the sidelines and the normalized field of play. The homeless beggar and the Fortune 500 chief executive are one in their oppression in the dubious refracted light of hegemony theory.

Horkheimer's legacy is not one of bad faith, however; rather, it is of a single imposing question. If reason is not reducible to the product domain, the materialized forces of history, then what on earth can it be? And rhetorical culture too, as realized in the practical consciousness of logos: what character traits does it possess? The question may be broached only rather cryptically at this point in our analysis. Reason, neither matter nor spirit, is an art. And rhetoric, its very close next of kin, is closest in spirit and practice to the child: always culpable, corruptible, and vulnerable to victimage—but also correctable. Too immature for the closure of great systems and as impatient as Greek youth with the grand inquisitions of philosophy. Playful, coltish, and coy. Not always trustworthy. Seducer and seduced. Capable, as were the Hitler youth, of great zeal and even greater crimes. But as surely as with every birth, always renewable, as are the new childlike possibilities of every age.

This is where rhetoric holds promise as something more than a cultural corruption. Mikhail Bakhtin, who was no stranger to oppression, wrote that the whole point of rhetoric was to argue from the viewpoint of the third party. As he put it, "profound individual levels do not participate in it." He added: "The court of arbitration is a rhetorical court. The extraordinary refinement of all ethical categories of personality. They lie in the border area between the ethical and the aesthetic."[58] This border area, of course, is the fragile territory which must be cultivated if we are fully to recover the lost rhetorical art.

5

Universal Pragmatics and Practical Reason: From Deformation to Reformation

Practical Reason can no longer be founded in the transcendental subject. Communicative ethics appeals now only to fundamental norms of rational speech, an ultimate "fact of reason." Of course, if this is taken to be a simple fact, capable of no further explanation, it is not possible to see why there should still issue from it a normative force that organizes the self-understanding of men and orients their action.

—Jürgen Habermas, *Legitimation Crisis*

Proclamations of reason's eclipse, like many a categorical dismissal, have shown themselves to be a bit hasty. Perhaps the life of practical reason, as a mode of reflection open to the collectivity, may be thought of as a generational phenomenon.[1] In any historical period, there are likely to be cultures in which reason and rhetoric have been poisoned. But it seems premature to pronounce any state of affairs, however extreme, as having eliminated forever the prospects for recovery. In the retrospection of dark times, utopian thought can appear foolish. But some such thought may be necessary if possibilities for reflection are to be reinvented. Here is Ernst Bloch: "The main thing is that utopian conscience-and-knowledge, through the pain it suffers in fact, grows wise, yet does not grow to full wisdom. It is *rectified*—but never *refuted* by the mere power of that which, at any particular time, *is*. . . . And so in ages of growing darkness at least a *horror vacui*, and in the ages of increasing enlightenment always a *plus ultra*, shows that Utopian consciousness is alive."[2] Bloch's implicit model of maturation without bitterness deserves to be taken seriously as perhaps another elusive guise of phronēsis.

However, a further issue is raised by Horkheimer's pivotal episode, an issue that is not so easily settled. For even if reason, like history, never really did *end*, there is every basis for supposing that the finality of its determinations is at an end. Once the forms and substance of practical reason are linked diachronically to the incremental successes and frustrations of history, we are reminded constantly of the *insufficiency* of reason.[3] The obdurate fact is that most so-called issues do not remain long enough on the agenda of public discussion for us to appreciate reflection's deficiencies. For issues that do persist, notorious "litmus" questions like abortion, the values parade themselves as a scandal of Enlightenment thinking, autonomy of "choice" going hammer and tongs at "sanctity" of life, defenders of "privacy" and advocates of "family" ritualistically dancing round each other in a poisoned public sphere.

No wonder that the veterans of the Frankfurt school were able to salvage the faculty of reason only as a last-ditch dialectic of entrapment—a dialectic that resists reification by immunizing itself against the world of production.[4] What was lost to logos was the only thing worth having in the practical world of rhetoric: the necessary impurity of its force and relevance. But there is one important philosopher who stubbornly resists the banishment of modernity and persists in animating the project of reasoned reflection as well. His work is the subject of this chapter.

While a myriad of studies have positioned Jürgen Habermas in modern philosophical tradition, a substantial burden of proof faces anyone wishing to appropriate critical theory for traditional rhetoric. I will undertake this task as a gradual courtship, rather than attempt to sweep the late Enlightenment off its foundations. In light of our tragedy of *exile*, it is important that Habermas belongs to the next generation. Although schooled in the conceptual traditions of Kant, Marx, Hegel, Freud, and the Frankfurt school, Habermas presents a unique and powerful synthesis of prevailing contributions from the human sciences. My claim here is that Habermas's project on discourse ethics, together with his practical placement of the public sphere, offers a basis for synthesizing the normative component of practical wisdom and a rhetoric goaded by emancipatory reason. Following some rhetorical amendments to the Habermas project, I will then explore an important illustration of the "public" as a rhetorical proposition: Mario Cuomo's 1984 address on abortion.[5]

COMMUNICATIVE ACTION
AND RHETORICAL PRACTICE

From his earliest work, Habermas has been interested in the public sphere and the possibility of reclaiming it through methods of social inquiry. But in order to address this project seriously, he has had to grapple with the failed interpretations of German Enlightenment thought, as well as their implications for the problems of social theory and practice. I will address both strains in Habermas's project here: the critical theory vision of the public sphere and the attempt to provide a communicative rationality foundation for morality known as *discourse ethics*. What seems to hold the two sides of Habermas's vision together temporarily is the theory of universal pragmatics.

The assumptions and structure of language as communicative action comprise the subject of universal pragmatics. To Habermas, the consuming mystery is that we are able to communicate with others at all. The key to this mystery must be that, in some respect at least, we are held accountable for what we say. Thus far, Habermas is roughly consistent with the action-centered world view accommodating performatives, a view derived from the successive generations of Wittgenstein, Austin, and Searle. But unlike the first people to engage in language pragmatics research (especially Wittgenstein), Habermas begins not with a substantive, imperfect world that provokes, defines, and occasionally corrupts speech, but rather, with demonstrably successful speech utterances that require certain extra-situational, or *idealized*, postulates for their complete analytic explanation. As Habermas noted in "What is Universal Pragmatics?," his first extensive discussion of these matters, "Whereas a grammatical utterance fulfills the claim to comprehensibility, a successful utterance must satisfy three additional validity claims: it must count as true for the participants insofar as it represents something in the world; it must count as truthful insofar as it expresses something intended by the speaker; and it must count as right insofar as it conforms to socially recognized expectations."[6] Already, we sense a leaning towards a prototype of Western-styled analytic speech in these conditionals. But Habermas was well aware that not every real-life utterance will satisfy each conditional fully. This may be one reason why he adapted Searle's distinction of types of speech act which would, in the most coherent of communicative exchanges, imply each obligation in every would-be performance. Hence we have:

(1) Constatives (which assert, narrate, report, or dissent) implying *truth*.

(2) Representatives (which reveal, admit, or express) implying *sincerity*.

(3) Regulatives (which command, warn, excuse, or exhort) implying *propriety*.[7]

Of course, the preconditional is that all utterances be comprehensible, so that we know what other obligations are incumbent on them. In some earlier and some more recent work, Habermas has shifted back and forth between the term "representatives" and the term "expressives." He has also allowed that indirect usages and intermodal inferences may be drawn as we move from one dominant type to another.[8] But he has been reluctant to back away from the purported universality of normative postulates underlying each type of utterance. In direct and instructive contrast to the contextualism of rhetorical-situationist thinkers,[9] Habermas draws the values of speech not from what is valued *in the world*, but from the very idea of a rational communicative form of action. Moreover, this is what has allowed Habermas to make the bold and melodious claim that the good life (of truth, freedom, and justice) is anticipated in every successful act of speech.[10] Working through a dialectical tradition (which American pragmatism has typically lacked) is what evidently grounds his brand of pragmatics in universalizable presuppositions.[11]

Those familiar with the language pragmatics tradition will recognize two further peculiarities in the Habermas version. First, he has combined the Gricean notion of conversational postulates with what Austin and Searle considered to be felicity conditions, or "institutional facts." The synthetic result? Validity claims. This terminology suggests a second critical shift: from conversation and meaning to argumentation and proof. As with many of Habermas's labors, there is a stunning insight here. This insight is that the very background of our "taken-for-granteds" in the linguistic turn contains a potentially universalizable normative content. This discovery becomes the procedural scaffolding for the Habermas vision of communicative rationality. Important as the insight is, though, it leads Habermas down some questionable analytic paths.

For Habermas, argumentation is the prototype for all successful and even problematic communicative action. This is how he is able to think of speech as a "successful accomplishment" in the first place. Indeed, if we construe argumentation as a process of sequencing discourse in such a way that some speech acts function as reasons for other speech acts, then Habermas's initial typology of utterances (constatives, representatives, and regulatives) implies idealized argumentative obligations to offer grounds, disclose motives, and exhibit norms.[12] And, lest the point be missed, there appears to be a more than casual symmetry across these three types of claims, three types of obligations, and the three types of interests which grounded knowledge in the earlier phase of the Habermas project.

But the Enlightenment philosopher in Habermas is inclined to ask how these value presuppositions of speech conduct are *themselves* to be grounded. Suppose, in the cantankerous fashion of Callicles, that one or more speakers persistently disagrees with these suppositions. Or suppose we were to happen on a cultural lifeworld in which these presuppositions were not informative of communication at all? Habermas has devoted considerable attention to securing the normative presuppositions of his theory of communication against a variety of skeptical and reductionist objections. For instance, he grants that not all instances of communication are consistent with his prototype. Whenever the validity claims discussed above are not mutually recognized and at least tacitly accepted, one may either break off communication *proper* (my term) and use force or cunning; or one may resort to reflexive argument (which he regards as "discourse") in order to reestablish the normative base necessary for the continuity of speech. But suppose that such argument is itself foreclosed for one reason or another. Suppose we are confronted with the situation of Habermas's own childhood or of Horkheimer in Germany. What then? This is where Habermas provides his ultimate, albeit highly controversial "original condition," a norm of interaction to which false consciousness and closed speech must finally submit. He argues that, should all else fail, the validity claims of discourse would themselves be sanctioned through understood agreement, given unrestricted, full, and fair discussion. This uniquely relational presupposition is what Habermas referred to as the "ideal speech situation":

> This freedom from internal and external constraint can be given a universal-pragmatic characterization; there must be for all participants a symmetrical distribution of chances to select and employ speech acts, that is, an effective equality of chances to assume dialogue roles. If this is not the case, the resultant agreement is open to the charge of being less than rational, of being the result not of the force of the better argument but, for example, of open or latent relations of domination, of conscious or unconscious motivations. Thus the idea of truth points ultimately to a form of interaction that is free from all distorting influences. The "good and true life" that is the goal of critical theory is inherent in the notion of truth; it is anticipated in every act of speech.[13]

A great many of the questions which have been directed toward the plausibility and coherence of this ideality notion seem to ignore the inescapability of some such counterfactual ideal as an impartial standard grounding all investigatory and demonstrative argument (such as formal and symbolic logic, mathematics and calculus, and whatever remains of philosophy). Habermas, well aware of the irony of origins, is reminding us that not just *any* set of circumstances is sufficient to produce the consensus on validity claims which make communicative action intelligible. Moreover, the absence of such a consensus *in fact* does not remove the possibility of such a consensus under optimal conditions. This is the major thrust of Habermas's argument. Questions about whether such a utopian setting could ever be attained historically also miss the point. For the point is that Habermas has offered at least a plausible candidate for a standard, one that avoids the problems of infinite regress and relativism that have plagued consensus theory.

So long as Habermas's project revolved around the continued sustenance of critical reflection, the postulates of communicative action provided a clear and powerful alternative to the failed autonomous identity paradigm which gripped and paralyzed critical theory for more than a generation. It might be added that, despite its Kantian proclivities, there is not yet anything in this conceptual system that would disown or marginalize the messy world of ordinary discourse. Indeed, some such strategic discourse might be necessary in order to intervene within the circumstances of ordinary life so as to concretize more reflective institutional formations. Put another way, we might grant that the vast preponderance of ordinary discourse deviates from ideal conversational postulates yet not necessarily be forced to dismiss such discourse as a cultural corruption.[14] Habermas seems to flirt with this more realistic posture throughout the complex presentation of his theory of communicative action and, more particularly, through the intersection of this with his theory of the public sphere. We will explore this promising synthesis in due course.

But first, there is the central problematic of this chapter. Despite its considerable promise, the Kantian *theoria* of this vision eventually seems to overwhelm its praxis. Throughout the development of the universal pragmatics theory, Habermas increasingly identifies validity claims with specific typologies of speech. To the extent that these typologies betray a hierarchy of rational *and ethical* significance, the theory tends to undermine the normative impetus and inventional power in the conduct comprising Habermas's own public sphere project. I now turn to these difficulties.

From the perspective sketched here, the problem is not so much the ideal speech situation. As long as we know this to be a postulated, counterfactual condition, then we can get along in real speech situations, what Bitzer calls *rhetorical* situations, without serious difficulty.[15] Rather, the core problem resides in a more basic derivation from language pragmatics. Recall that Habermas introduced the ideal speech situation as a way of dealing with a more fundamental objective: namely, to ground the normative validity claims associated with three types of performative utterances. Recall too that an intuitive claim of comprehensibility was presupposed, so that these other claims could be properly understood. This basic claim of intelligibility becomes a Gricean version of what was previously called the "locutionary" domain of utterances, the aspect of what is actually said in making or performing the utterance.[16] The illocutionary domain is now captured by the tripartite categories of constatives, expressives, and regulatives. The question is, what has happened to the perlocutionary domain?

Very early on in the universal pragmatics program, it became clear that Habermas wished to consider the perlocutionary as an entirely different sort of speech utterance, one that was oriented solely to success, at the cost of full disclosure. For good measure, he followed the speech act tradition in appearing to discount the figurative realm of what he called "symbolic action" as well: "It seems to me that *strategic action* (oriented to the actor's success—in general, modes of action that correspond to the utilitarian model of purposive-rational action) as well as (still insufficiently analyzed) *symbolic action* (e.g. a concert, a dance—in general, modes of action that are bound to non-propositional systems of symbolic expression) differ from communicative action in that individual validity claims are suspended (in strategic action, truthfulness; in symbolic action, truth)."[17] Habermas then adds, as if to further qualify his remarks, "My previous analyses of 'labor' and 'interaction' have not yet adequately captured the most general differentiating characteristics of instrumental and social (or communicative) action."[18] But by the time we reach the very important *Theory of Communicative Action*, there can be no doubt that Habermas has disjoined the illocutionary from the perlocutionary, both categorically and hierarchically. There is also no doubt about which category occupies the higher ground. In a careful reading of Habermas's recent discussions, Allen W. Wood observes:

"Habermas wants to identify the distinction between perlocutionary and illocutionary acts with the distinction he draws between 'orientation to success and orientation to understanding' (erfolgs und Verstandigungs-orientierung) [TCA:286]. He wants to understand this not as a distinction between two ways of looking at the same action, but as two different and mutually exclusive ways of acting."[19]

We are now in a better position to appreciate the difficulties that Habermas has with the tradition of practical speech I have called rhetoric. It is not simply that, according to certain idealized speech situation criteria, rhetorical speech is flawed and distorted. It is that rhetorical speech is assumed to be mainly strategic speech, oriented toward success. I say "mainly" because there are places in *Theory of Communicative Action* where he allows that rhetoric may be an argumentation *process*[20] and even the entire domain of the figurative claimed by Derrida.[21] At various times in its long, checkered history, rhetoric has of course occupied all these provisional dwellings. However, within universal pragmatics, rhetoric constitutes a crude subset of *perlocutionary speech*. For Habermas, this means that it is denied any of the reflective validity claims that he presupposes for the *illocutionary* realm known as communicative action.

Extending the implications of this position a bit further may explain why rhetoric could be dismissed as immature.[22] For if we accept Habermas's rather rarefied conception of argumentation as the prototype for a reason-based philosophy of communicative action, and if we accept the relegation of rhetoric to the nonreflective domain of strategy, then rhetoric could be seen as a flawed, transitory stage in the maturation of human nature—hardly the sort of thing to write a book about.

Carefully argued and comprehensive as Habermas's position is on most matters, I think he has made a serious wrong turn with this adaptation of language pragmatics and its implications for the derivation and placement of rhetoric. As Wood makes plain, Habermas's bifurcation of the "strategic-perlocutionary" and the "rational-illocutionary" is certainly inconsistent with the Austin–Searle tradition.[23] For Austin and Searle, the *locutionary,* the *illocutionary,* and the *perlocutionary* are all ways of singling out identifiable things we do with the same utterance. Of course, this does not yet speak to difficulties within Habermas's position. It could be, for instance, that Austin and Searle are wrong. But now we must look to the plausibility of cases; and here the troubles seem to multiply.

To be fair, Habermas wants to allow that there may be illocutionary and perlocutionary aspects to the same act, but he then wishes us to move to the dominant overall type of utterance and decide what it is. In this categorical realm, as in so many others, the cognitive reasserts itself through several further controversial distinctions: for instance, the perlocutionary is always parasitic (a corrupt derivative) on the more basic illocutionary form, and the perlocutionary always requires that the speaker withhold his true aim in performing the utterance.[24]

Despite numerous belated attempts to reinterpret the evidence, the split between illocutionary and perlocutionary communicative acts is simply counterintuitive for actual speech practice. Wood takes issue with many aspects of Habermas's distinction. He argues first that some per-locutionary acts display their aims openly—indeed, aid and abet their accomplishment through such display.[25] Wood reinterprets one of Austin's examples—"I'm sorry, Miss, I didn't mean to frighten you. I was running for a cab"—to show that orders and intended persuasions are not contradictory to one another.[26] But let us suppose that the intent had been to frighten. Would its disclosure have foiled the intended act? To use a slightly less sinister example, consider ghost stories. To a child sitting around a campfire, does the camp counselor's avowed perlocutionary intention of frightening make the fear any less likely? Is not the reverse true? Then consider the frequent cases in which uncertainty and ambiguity of intent are part of the very meaning of performance. In settings as varied as saber rattling and the quid pro quos of international jousting to the admonishments of higher education, we find language used to provoke and constitute a gray area of uncertainty that is sufficiently unsettled to subvert the overdetermined scenarios of calculative thinking. In fact, Hans Blumenberg sees the rhetoric of ambiguity as playing a critical part in *deferring* the regimentation of assigned roles to predictable outcomes. Such is his rather bleak portrait of liberal arts pedagogy.[27] In cautioning one and all to think again, our perlocutionary tone provokes hesitancy and caution, a mood which may be, in some charged settings, a preliminary to reflection.

Now Habermas's point about the manifestation of intent may be defensible in a more modest version—for instance, if we were to say that the manifestation of intent is not sufficient to accomplish a perlocutionary act. By saying, "My intent, with these words, is to ask you to marry me," I have, in an awkward sort of way, asked you to marry me. By saying, "My intent, with the word 'Boo,' is to scare you," I will probably not have the required perlocutionary effect. But this is true only if there *are* purely illocutionary and perlocutionary utterances; and we have already seen that there is reason to question this distinction. There is also reason to question the distinction where so-called strategic speech (such as bargaining and persuasion) is concerned. For here the incompleteness of initial intent is built into the process. Where bargaining is concerned, each party knows that the other's initial offer is not necessarily the final offer. The strategy of speech is qualified by a tacit understanding and acceptance of ambiguity. And, interestingly enough, it is redeemed by a certain reciprocity of strategy. The case is instructive for some cases of persuasion. For the most part, I will be unable to persuade you simply by manifesting my intent to persuade you. From a critical point of view, of course, we may infer from this fact a general suspicion of persuasion that prompts would-be practitioners to camouflage their intent by breaking down resistance and falsifying expectations. This would count as a withholding of persuasive intent and appear to be supportive of Habermas's overall point.

But it is by no means the only, or even the most obvious, case of persuasion in practice. I may address a jury with the obvious intent of persuading them as to my client's guilt or innocence. The intent will not be sufficient to achieve my desired aim, of course. But for millennia, theorists have observed that the seriousness with which I take my own persuasive cause will be a powerful instrument on its behalf. This is at least part of what we mean by ēthos. Then there is the complicated matter of *disputation*. Whenever there are two or more sides to be heard in a dispute, we quite justifiably are not moved by intent alone. We await the other point of view, the fuller picture that helps to complete our own reflective decision. Here too is a case in which the singularity of an individual's intent needs to be *exposed* to a longer, larger process or argumentation and reflective judgment.

Most perilously, there are the cases that the Habermas of *Knowledge and Human Interests* might have pointed to. Perhaps, as has been written of some enigmatic public figures, I don't fully grasp what my intent really is. I may await the uncertain sense of my public existence to help define me. While such cases may be unusual, they are by no means completely anomalous. Moreover, they are rivaled by other, morally neutral cases. Perhaps I advocate a position in public, literally to test whether it has the necessary support to carry pragmatic weight as policy. Perhaps I advocate a position to preempt a more dangerous version of the same position. In cases like these, it might be said that my intent is to be argumentative; or, in a more autonomous and restricted sense, that I have entered into a process of controversy as argumentation, at least in part, because I wish to allow others to help define and disclose my intent.

There is a further problem in treating the comprehensibility condition as the prototype for all communicative action. With this move, Habermas seems to be assuming that there are never prior conditions to understanding and, further, that comprehension may only take the privileged form of rational reconstruction. On the other hand, if Austin and Searle are correct in believing that symbolic acts have locutionary, illocutionary, and perlocutionary features, this at least allows that sometimes certain perlocutionary features of discourse may be prior to appreciating fully and thereby constituting some other communicative acts; for example, "Listen to reason, damn it!," uttered in loud, desperate tones. In the specific case of rhetoric, it may mean that the super-addressee is not only an extensional implication of locutionary acts; for, as we speak, this same idealized listener may become a creature of concern, suspicion, passion, and conscience. In Habermas's favorite contemporary paradigm, the institutional protection built into the legal system is largely one of suspicion: presumption, precedent, and burden of proof. And in self-important calls to conscience, such as "The whole world is watching," we are concerned with an audience-witness who not only knows what we mean but also cares about what we have experienced. If this intuition is sound, then it means that the idealized addressee evoked by our most passionate utterances must be a rhetorical creature, capable of being *moved* by discourse.

To sort out these emerging issues, let us now reexamine our opening probes from the perspective outlined at the beginning of this chapter, a perspective which suggested a dualism to the Habermas projects.

RECALLING THE PUBLIC SPHERE

In my view, Habermas's concern with communicative action finds its clearest application to our commonsense intuitions about practice when it is read alongside his earlier project for the transformation of the public sphere. There the particulars of context and choice emerge not as deformities, but as productive ingredients of participation and constraint: the two sides of institutional practice. There too the intervening horizons of setting and immediacy of need may influence shared understandings without disturbing or finally destroying them. It is in the public sphere that we are able to find, without desperate searching, a productive placement for the creative arts of reason, including those of rhetoric.

When we read Habermas's communicative rationality program in conjunction with his recently translated *Structural Transformation of the Public Sphere*, some fascinating parallels and contrasts begin to emerge.[28] For one thing, the knowledge-constitutive interests that Habermas pointed to in later research emerge here as historicized phenomena. One does not have to agree with the precise causality to appreciate Habermas's attribution of generalizable interests to a particular institutional practice associated with disclosure and publicity. Add to this the fact that these practices are seen as having generated norms which now transcend the practices themselves. Put another way, these norms may now be referred back to individual cases to assess departures and deviations from the prototype. Here is a typical illustration:

> Bourgeois culture was not mere ideology. The rational-critical debate of private people in the *salons*, clubs, and reading societies was not directly subject to the cycle of production and consumption, that is, to the dictates of life's necessities. Even in its merely literary form (of self-elucidation of the novel experiences of subjectivity) it possessed instead a "political" character in the Greek sense of being emancipated from the constraints of survival requirements. It was for these reasons alone the idea that later degenerated into mere ideology (namely: humanity) could develop at all.[29]

This is an interesting observation and one that is easily misread. What Habermas is suggesting is that the class interest and partisan base of bourgeois culture were able to generate and sustain a generalizable concept—namely, humanity—which itself transcended class interest. This same concept may therefore be referred back to actual practices as *criteria*, to show their deformations and distortions. Thus the institutional lifeworld is able to generate norms of critique that defy historical reduction.

While there is little in Habermas's gloss on classicism to distinguish the merely ideological from the merely rhetorical, the fact remains that a vital public sphere is impossible without partisan forms of expression as well as types of encounter wherein these same forms may be encouraged or at least tolerated. Throughout this work, Habermas acknowledges the way in which ordinary communicative practices clash, provoke debate, and eventually prompt reflection on the rules and principles for discussion. The so-called universal standpoint seems to emerge from a quite specific set of conditions.

From this friendlier strain of critical theory, then, we may derive the following important conception: *Rhetoric is the primary practical instrumentality for generating and sustaining the critical publicity which keeps the promise of a public sphere alive.* One might quarrel with Habermas's assertion that the public idea is a unique and unprecedented invention of the bourgeois Enlightenment. But regardless of historical accuracy, the fact remains that every major institutional practice associated with a vital public sphere—whether it be journalistic critique, café society conversation, political pageantry and performance, even public speech—seems to embody the creative strain of reason which we call rhetorical art. And despite Habermas's well-known reluctance to revert to philosophical traditions prior to Kant, there are unmistakable similarities between this valorized bourgeois public sphere and the less examined Greek polis.

Yet there is one final parallelism which places even this promising opening for rhetoric in jeopardy. It has to do with the remarkably prophetic critique that Habermas offers of institutional practices in modern public life. The entire conclusion of *The Structural Transformation of the Public Sphere* is a virtual catalog of abuses, distortions, and deformations of the original public idea; here is the anticipation of discussion as consumer product, of politics as gamesmanship and ritual, of public debate as public relations.[30] The critique is so trenchant as to make MacIntyre and Arendt look tame by contrast. Even granting the notorious barbarism of modernity's dark side, Habermas's critique here comes close to the aporia he quite properly critiqued in an earlier generation of critical theorists. We may concede that, not surprisingly, the worldly practices of speech, like Enlightenment morality, perhaps, have not lived up to their initial expectations. But the conceptual question is how the validity claims of normative reason (visible in a nascent state even at this early stage) intersect with real practices of speech, the speech which once made them possible.

There are really only two possibilities for an answer. The first suggests that these claims only work in the extremely rarefied realm in which the equally rarefied argumentation paradigm is applicable (science and perhaps legal reasoning). They must therefore be removed conceptually from everyday institutional practices and *surely* from rhetoric. But if this is true, then this duality has the practical effect of opposing rhetoric to argumentation. Further, there is the undeniable fact that rhetoric has always addressed practical questions through a language of value. What are we to make of this? Finally, we must wrestle with Habermas's still forceful critique of modern institutional practices. If the norms of ideality subsist in a wholly separate realm, then where did the norms for this critique come from?

The other possibility is that the ideality suppositions do intersect with everyday institutional practices, but in ways that have yet to be spelled out cogently. One way is already obvious, and that is as a form of critique. But if we are not to marginalize all ordinary decision-making conduct out of existence, we must clearly turn such critique in an affirmative direction. There is increasing evidence that Habermas wishes to do this. In recent work,[31] he has been unusually forthcoming in offering postulational directives for an ethical communicative practice.

On the basis of what he regards as the definitional interdependence of autonomy and solidarity, Habermas postulates that in any setting involving communicative action, the individual arguers or advocates are on their own, *but are bound by their own good faith to recognize their mutual embeddedness in a community of discourse.* This same bond of belonging requires from advocates as interlocutors the inalienable right to say "yes" or "no" and the overcoming of egocentrism and resistance to self-criticism.[32] This latter condition seems remarkably congruent with what Henry Johnstone has characterized as the reflective "wedge" interposed by the very fact of belonging to a rhetorical audience. It is particularly interesting that such codicils are now introduced as *necessary conditions* for an adequate discourse of ethical judgment.[33] Within this same communicative setting, what Habermas calls *discourse ethics* would require equal rights of individuals within argumentation (I assume we could append the conditions of the ideal speech situation here) and equal respect for the dignity of each participant within the process—presumably, the meeting of other good faith conditions of communicative pragmatics generally.[34]

In other words, Habermas is finally making room in his program for those persons (private or public) who must engage practical historical questions. For the first time, we are getting some conceptual guidance on the mediation of practical contingencies through his creative rendering of justice, solidarity, disclosure of the hidden, and his aforementioned relevance and propriety conditions. Without too much trouble, these same conditionals could be given a practical turn toward an ethic of audience engagement.

Examples such as these are evidence that Habermas wants to do more than set off argumentation as a remote, idealized sphere of discourse. He wants to find a way of motivating sound communicative practices. For all this, his own procedures as a theorist of discourse ethics continue to exhibit a deep ambivalence about the way in which everyday practices intersect differing lifeworlds. We need to identify this ambivalence before pressing forward with our revisions.

On the one hand, Habermas allows that "unless discourse ethics is undergirded by the thrust of motives and by socially accepted institutions, the moral insights it offers remain ineffective in practice."[35] On the other, he goes to considerable pains to distance himself from the partiality of practical arts of reason for particular institutional horizons. He states the difference bluntly in his 1988 Tanner lecture on "Law and Morality:"

> Neo-Aristotelians are especially inclined to an ethic of institutions that renounces the gulf between norm and reality, or principle and rule, annuls Kant's distinction between questions of justification and questions of application, and reduces moral deliberations to the level of prudential considerations. At the level of a merely pragmatic judgment, normative and purely functional considerations are then indistinguishably intermingled. . . . Ethics oriented to conceptions of the good or to specific value hierarchies single out particular *normative contents*. Their premises are too strong to serve as the foundation for universally binding decisions in a modern society characterized by the pluralism of gods and demons. Only theories of morality and justice developed in the Kantian tradition hold out the promise of an *impartial* procedure for the justification and assessment of principles.[36]

This is a reasonably accurate characterization of, say, the Beiner we discussed in chapter 4. But it is a much less apt characterization of Aristotle himself. With his concluding demand, the differences have been made fatefully clear. It is not simply that one position presupposes a substantive form of life and the other does not. Rather, Habermas believes that the Kantian position presupposes a lifeworld that is more in keeping with radically divergent world views which must coexist and clash in *modernity*. Secondly, Habermas believes that the Kantian position, with its distinction between justification and application, is a genuinely *impartialist* position, which will not play favorites in the world of moral choice. We are left with a fascinating conundrum which, in a sense, reflects the collision of nomos and physis in chapter 2.

If it is the case, as Habermas has conceded, that morality thrives only in an environment in which certain moral intuitions have already taken hold and been institutionalized, then it is simply not the case that his theory is without partiality. It presupposes a developed Western-style culture or at least a Westernized forum in which less developed, partialist cultural intuitions may clash with one another. This is in no way to deny that the Habermas postulates, norms, and validity claims are attractive, even compelling. But it is to insist that a certain partiality toward a developmental vision of modernity exists within the very fabric of this program. Shortly we will reconstruct Habermas's validity claims as a goad to the more context-bound, particularist choices that real human agents confront.

But this cannot be a one-way relationship. Despite its conceptual tension with the world of messy, real-life particularity, Habermas's earlier treatment of the concept of humanity makes plain that some practical interventions may be prior and necessary to the very moral intuitions which discourse ethics conceptualizes. This raises the inevitable question: Given that discourse ethics, at least in its most general frame of universalized morality, finds its existence dependent on a more or less compatible form of life, how can we justify political practices that are intended to alter or re-*form* power arrangements in order to better effect means for implementing the insights of discourse ethics? I have in mind not only the normal discursive engagement with practical problems like child care, environmental protection, neighborhood safety, but also demonstration, confrontation, and dissent. We are ready for a program of friendly rhetorical amendments. The amendments are designed to show just how ideality considerations figure in the world of institutional practices.

REVISING DISCOURSE ETHICS:
TOWARD AN EMANCIPATION OF RHETORIC

My objective throughout the next two chapters is to extend Habermas's revisions without damaging the core normative perspective of his project. In general, this friendly extension aims to decenter the autonomous speaking subject through a renewed acquaintance with the world outside: the contexts, audiences, and appearances which muddy, complicate, and constitute meaning in ordinary life. The amendments are therefore a reminder, rather than an overturning of foundations.

Habermas's privileging of cognitive understanding and his restriction of meaning to the redemption of autonomous intentions might be said to emanate from the same source. Habermas allows for no intervening horizon between the category of "form of life" (lifeworld) and that of "speech act" or utterance. This admittedly allows him to universalize validity claims without undue complication; but it ignores the troublesome fact that utterances do not admit to the "invariance claims" of truth in the same sense that sentences and propositions do. This is because they are embedded in episodes of potentially limitless complexity and variation. The same verbal composition—say, "I wouldn't do that if I were you"—could be an utterance of counsel, a threat, or a parental imperative, depending entirely on the episode which has occasioned it.[37] This is precisely the point. Utterances are occasioned and therefore "perform" validity claims; they are redeemed, therefore, not in an abstract, generalized realm of truth, but in the practical realm of decision and conduct. My suggestion is thus a simple mediation of reciprocity involving the intersection of ideality and practice. Just as Habermas purports to unmask normative content in everyday partisan discourse, it may be argued that, conversely, the ideality postulates of discourse ethics are unfinished and incomplete, at least in their counterfactual condition. They need to be performed, completed, and enacted in the world of practice if they are to leave their postulational character behind and become immanent and forceful. We are still able to retain this dimension of ideality that is so critical to the fate and resilience of practical reason, but as a *regulative* ideal implicit within the grammar of reason itself. This, at least, is the overall direction of my synthesis and revision.

Two very different contemporary rhetoricians figure prominently in this revision: Cháim Perelman and Kenneth Burke. Each provides a core insight that usefully complements the universal pragmatics and discourse ethics programs, even as these same authors provide renewed appreciation of the status and performance of rhetorical practice. There is, of course, much more to each of them than can be captured here. Perelman's key insight, entailed in his movement from a view of persuasion as *effect* to a reflective vision of conviction through the adherence of a competent audience, is that audience receptivity is a normatively significant condition.[38] Burke, as his legion of readers know, is the more earthbound, even whimsical, of the two. But his mix of Marx, Freud, dialectical thinking, and literary criticism leads to a much more tolerant, critical fallibilism where the imperfections of actual discourse practice are concerned. For Burke, the very meaning of *symbolic action* (recall that this was once a vulgar form, disparaged by Habermas's theory of communicative action) must include notions of identification and *division*,[39] struggle, and tension, as well as more inclusive modes of engagement—above all, an unfinished inferential quality that continues the ongoing ontological conversation of real life. For Burke, in other words, there is no contradiction ultimately between discourse practice that is always suspect and practice that is the best available embodiment of human civility. Good and evil are truly entwined in the world of Burke's particulars. Indeed, this is why we are always goaded toward a better life. We are, in his words, "rotten with perfection." But we will now turn to Perelman.

In two of his less renowned works, *The Idea of Justice and the Problem of Argument* and *The New Rhetoric and the Humanities*, Perelman offers an important grounding to the idealism of rhetorical practice.[40] Using the specific instance of the universal value of justice, he begins where modern theorists from Rawls to MacIntyre have foundered. There is a multitude of intuitively sound concrete approaches to justice, each of which is practically incompatible with the other. He makes this point with the following forceful words:

> It is always useful and important to be able to qualify as just the social conceptions which one advocates. Every revolution, every war, every overthrow has always been effected in the name of justice. And the extraordinary thing is that it should be just as much the partisans of a new order as the defenders of the old who invoke with their prayers the reign of justice. And when a neutral voice proclaims the necessity of a just peace, all the belligerents agree and affirm that this just peace will come only when the enemy has been annihilated.[41]

It is difficult to miss the irony here. The very universality which is attributed to the scope of justice as a quality may be purchased only by donning a mask of abstraction that hides the basic disagreements over what justice itself means. We are only able to agree on the value of justice in theory; for as soon as they line up over matters of human choice and interest, the partisans of justice share only a nominal agreement. The contrast with Habermas is instructive. Instead of regarding these worldly differences as deformations requiring redemption in the purer theoretical realm of practical discourse, as does Habermas,[42] Perelman finds in them evidence that theory is of limited utility in resolving practical questions of meaning.

Perelman's project begins with the demonstration that alternative construals of justice yield practical difficulty when placed in opposition to one another. Considering several marks of differentiation (equity, merit, works, needs, rank, legal entitlement),[43] Perelman is able to underline the difficulties facing any definitional system when it enters into the realm of concrete choice. Indeed, *this* is where the fundamental incompatibilities among systems disclose themselves to the sharpest extent. Here is his analysis: "If the idea of justice is confused it is because each of us, in speaking of justice, feels obliged to define concrete justice. The result is that the definition of justice carries with it also the determination of the categories regarded as essential. Now this, as we have seen, implies a given scale of values. In seeking to define concrete justice, we include in the same formula the definition of formal justice and a particular view of the world. Hence flow such divergencies, misunderstandings and confusions."[44]

For Perelman, justice is the principle aim of all practical reasoning, a broader conceptualization than that offered by the traditional theory of forensic discourse. Beyond the formal contrast of locus, however, is the more important end of rhetorical practice itself. For Aristotle's *Rhetoric*, at least, the end in view is not persuasion but *judgment* (1377b21–24). Edwin Black, in a detailed reconstruction of the *Rhetoric*'s use of the term *krisis*, found that the most precise analogy for its meaning and function was the judicial rendering of verdicts in a court of law.[45] So we find ourselves back in the realm of institutions again. Significantly, Perelman locates the critical determinant of the normative content for justice in the concrete inferences that *audiences* make as an ongoing part of the justification process.

As Perelman takes his inquiry forward, he decides on a formal principle common to all the varying notions of justice, expressing it as follows: "It consists in *observing a rule which lays down the obligation to treat in a certain way all persons who belong to a given category.*"[46] With this principle, we have arrived at a juncture critical to the entire project; for in order to actualize the formal properties of justice in real-life settings, we must undertake to follow the prescriptions of rules for application. Perelman believes that this process of rule formation and enactment provides the neglected stuff of contemporary practical reason: "In effect, we have seen that equality of treatment is linked to the fact of observing a rule. On the other hand, the category in question in the definition is the essential category, for it is the category that is taken into account in the application of justice."[47]

Perelman found the procedure of rule application to be analogous in form to the way conventions work within the practical syllogism:

(a) the rule to be applied, which provides the major term of the syllogism;
(b) the quality of the person—the fact of regarding him as a member of a given category—which provides the minor term of the syllogism;
(c) the just act, which must be consistent with the conclusion of the syllogism.[48]

Most immediately pertinent is the normative constraint exerted by the procedure of forensic argument. For Perelman it is that the entire process of judging well in concrete settings helps us to enact and make *more real* the virtue of justice. It is a performative microcosm of concrete justice itself. Consider the following: "The foregoing thoughts bring to light the kinship existing between justice and the requirements of our reason. Justice is in conformity with a chain of reasoning. *To use the language of Kant, we might say that it is a manifestation of practical reason.* It is in this respect, indeed, that justice stands in contrast to the other virtues. These, with their greater spontaneity, bear directly on the real, whereas justice postulates the insertion of the real into categories regarded as essential."[49] The innovation here is important. For Perelman, justice is the virtue that is primary *to* and constitutive *of* practical reasoning. And his explication of the rule of justice helps us to understand why. By apportioning comparatively meaningful properties to real persons in existent settings, those who reason through problems of justice also help to enact the virtue. It would not be an exaggeration to say that Perelman has shown us how to integrate the contemporary analytic construction of inference rule with the traditional architectonic virtue of phronēsis, the overarching prudential capacity to judge what qualities should be applied on their proper occasions; for in Perelman's developing inventional schema, that is exactly what the *practice* of justice amounts to.

The final step in Perelman's own reasoning process, optimally, would show how the rule of justice might also function as a rule for audience engagement in rhetorical practice. It must be conceded that Perelman never developed this theme explicitly enough to allow us to complete our formal amendment of universal pragmatics. Fortunately, however, he gave us a fascinating textual point of departure for the revision in his brilliant essay "Act and Person in Argument." Recall that the missing inferential link in the rule of justice notion is, for rhetoric at least, its glossing of the particular audience in favor of the editorial "we." Even the practical syllogism, clearly generalized beyond the classical Aristotelian formula, fails to stipulate just who is obligated to perform the conclusive just act. What is needed is a manner of thinking rhetorically, so that the essential qualities of persons—(their *character*)—may, as Perelman has implied all along, emerge through their own participation in the formation of discursive judgments. This is what we are presented with in the following important passage:

> In the relation of act to person, we understand by "act" anything which may be considered an emanation of the person; in addition to actions, these might be judgments, modes of expression, emotional reactions, or involuntary mannerisms. In this way, in placing value on a judgment, an evaluation is thereby accorded to its author. The manner in which he judges permits the judge to be judged and, in the absence of accepted criteria applying to the subject, it is extremely difficult to prevent the interaction of the act and the person in this area."[50]

Although the compass of this statement is extremely broad, Perelman seems to have already imagined that the joint construction and disposition of argumentative discourse must involve acts of both speakers and audience. More telling still, the character of judges (as those who speak and are spoken about) is marked and implicated in the judgments themselves. If this extension is sensible, then we have indeed moved away from the "collective narcissism of the speaking subject"[51] and implicated the addressee in the constitution of meaning, judgment, and therefore character. For Perelman, it may be said that concrete justice is enacted in part through the way we participate in forms of *justification*. Through justification, we justify our acts and thus ourselves. Much as Aristotle did with *deliberation*, Perelman prioritizes the forensic category as both a normative content and a process. We now have a way of appreciating the normative conduct of audiences, consistent with the *rhetorical* redemption of at least some concretized particulars in language use. Where we need to look further is to the figurative character of symbolic action generally. How are we to find, within this opaque, subjective material, any normative impetus to reflection?

This is where Kenneth Burke's genius enters the picture, along with his uniquely interactive notion of form. While not denying the importance of the speaking (or writing) subject, Burke allows that a performance of character can best be inferred from figurative discourse when its audience becomes, as it were, a complicitous *other*—when it acts as an affiliative agent of language. For Burke as *critic*, audience engagement takes on an identifiable shape, a *form*, through all figurative symbolic action. Burke's highly inventive deconstruction of the symbolic need not be explicated here. But the way in which the normative pervades all symbolic action deserves our attention.

Granting the recalcitrance of the world's facts, the "X that is not words," as Burke put it, his lifelong concern has been with how we might best participate reflectively within the world as symbolically configured. His word for what is recognizable within this figurative creation is *form*. And virtually from the beginning of his critical theory, Burke's vision of form has been rhetorical. In his revolutionary discussion of "Psychology and Form" in *Counter-Statement*, he observed: "And by that distinction, form would be the psychology of the audience. Or, seen from another angle, form is the creation of an appetite in the mind of the auditor, and the adequate satisfaction of that appetite. This satisfaction—so complicated is the human mechanism—at times involves a temporary set of frustrations, but in the end these frustrations prove to be simply a more involved kind of satisfaction, and furthermore serve to make the satisfaction of fulfillment more intense."[52] Many have marveled at Burke's constant invention of strategies and devices for individuating and extending form through its myriad discourse practices. Burke has sensed in the very impurity of symbolic action a motive of human continuity and purposefulness. Long before the postmodern condition was proclaimed, Burke's writing had addressed and, I think, surpassed its curious vision of propriety. He knew that the world of ideology could not be replaced by a *purer* language somehow removed from motive and partisanship. But he also realized that this same world demanded something more complex than even that greatest of texts, the *Rhetoric*, had envisioned as the logocentric substance of persuasion. There could be no krisis without identification. But he also knew that every identification was also a division or, in postmodern parlance, a repression, a deflection, or a difference. Through devices of repetition, dissociation, displacement, transposition, compensation, projection, convergence, and many many others, we enact our own figurative conversation with the others among us. There can be no moving out of the barnyard scramble. *This is because, for Burke, the negative is not a deformation or distortion, a problem to be resolved. It is intrinsic to our human condition as symbol-using animals.* Even in *pure persuasion*, the closest Burke comes to a rhetorical archetype, we act in and through the only anthropomorphic worlds we know—symbolically constructed ones.[53] In so doing, we "purify war." This, of course, is the kind of oxymoron that could not help but offend more formal senses of purity (not to mention German idealism). But in the very richness of its frustrations, we can see—by contrast with Habermas—what Burke is driving at.

Burke never makes the neo-Kantian turn of postulating the ideal conditions for all *real* sermonizing in language. The primary reason for his reluctance to universalize pragmatics is that he believes that a normative movement is already in progress within the very mechanisms and stratagems of symbolic action:

> By identifying such symbolic prowess with an "entelechial principle," I have in mind the notion that inherent in it there is the incentive to "perfect" itself by covering more and more ground. For such a potentiality is saying in effect: "Whatever the nonverbal, there are words for it, ranging all the way from the technically, scientifically couched analysis of a situation or process to a sheer expression of attitude, as with a poet's feeling that spring requires completion in a spring song, or a devout believer's gesture of reverence in his devout act of prayer."[54]

While the idea of entelechy, with its impulse toward perfectibility, recurs throughout Burke's work, it receives its clearest articulation in his latter preoccupation with the theory of symbolic action. The intricacies of that theory are less germane to our immediate concern than the fact that, for Burke, the world of the symbolic is analogous to a type of spirit inhabiting and animating our most mundane human materials. In an important essay in *The Rhetoric of Religion*, Burke writes:

> Words are to the non-verbal things they name as Spirit is to matter . . . verbal or symbolic action is analogous to the "grace" that is said to "perfect" nature. . . . A duality of realm is implicit in our definition of man as the symbol-using animal. Man's animality is in the realm of sheer matter, sheer motion. But his "symbolicity" adds a di-

mension of action not reducible to the non-symbolic—for by its very nature as symbolic it cannot be identical with the non-symbolic. . . . In all such cases, where symbolic operations can influence bodily processes, the realm of the natural (in the sense of the less than verbal) is seen to be pervaded, or inspirited, by the realm of the verbal, or symbolic.[55]

In addition to revealing something of Burke's own hierarchy, wherein the symbolic is clearly above the material, these excerpts insist on the operation of an animate force in the symbolic realm that is independent of both material reduction and instrumental control. A Burkean perspective reminds us that the normative substance for any procedural justification comes *not* from the rigor of procedure, but from the particularity of symbolic experience; and this normative goading is an ongoing operative force within all symbolic action. Burke thus helps us to take an alternative route, *through* the dramatism of artifacts, to understanding the unfolding *telos* toward visions of the true, the right, and the just. What this leads to is an erasure of the distance between ideal presuppositions *behind* utterances and the entelechial motives goading and guiding utterances as performed. Put another way, *utterances may now be seen as moving toward the implied directives of their own (logocentric) presuppositions.*

Thus far, I have tried to moderate the Habermas program for sustaining the reflective potential of reason. With Perelman, I have made allowance for the fact that audiences themselves may participate in a reflective manner, even through a sense of idealized justification. I have also raised the question of whether certain ordinary forms of inference within discourse admit to such a reflective potential. Recall that Habermas leaves this question open, to the extent that normative *content* needs to be extracted from ordinary discourse through a systematic analytic reduction. What he does not allow for in any explicit way is that such discourse *may come to reflect upon itself* or perhaps encounter in its own contexts other practical discourses emanating from positions and perspectives which may help to temper and moderate its claims. With Burke, criticism moves from an abstract plane to the more practical contextualized treatment of discourse types. This and the all-important repositioning of the *negative* have decisive implications for universal pragmatics and discourse ethics.

Habermas's postulates and validity claims—of truth, rightness, truthfulness, propriety, and so forth—may now be appreciated as powerful normative enticements, or goads, to the perfectibility of discourse practice. But this is not because these norms somehow hover outside history and spatiotemporal existence; such an a priori, "view from nowhere" is simply implausible.[56] Rather, it is because these same claims and norms, including autonomy, solidarity, and social justice, embody an extremely elegant process of idealization *as symbolic action* that we are inclined to follow their path. Perelman's vision of the rhetorical audience allowed the practical exercise of judgment to cultivate our recognition of a sense of the universal within the particular. It helped to enact the quality of justice concretely, even as it helped to individuate the character of the judge. Burke extends this participatory ideal through his own athletic skepticism with a myriad of symbolic forms and the ongoing entelechial adventure with language itself. So conceptualized, Habermas's ideals can be viewed as rules for a performative practice that may never be terminated; for this is the only way we have of even glimpsing the *form* of the rules in question.

My revision qualifies these postulates further by holding that they figure as cultural *modalities* of symbolic action, rather than ahistorical universals. In the historicized context of real communicative episodes and encounters, the status of these postulates is that of the "possibly, but not yet realized" domain of entelechy. In a searching treatment of Kant in his *Grammar of Motives*, Burke finds much the same sort of entelechial tendency throughout Habermas's own idealistic heritage:

> The entire pattern of thought in the *Critique of Pure Reason* stresses unification. Even the variety of data available to the intuitions of sense has an "affinity" in its manifoldness. This "affinity" I would translate grammatically as a gerundive: for if the manifold of sense can be unified by the concepts of understanding, then there is in this manifold a kind of "to-be-unitedness" that one could call an "affinity" among the components of the manifold. Reason aims finally at the most unified principle of all, the idea of God as the total unity that is the ground of all existence.[57]

Burke is able to disclose, even in these most scientized foundations of Enlightenment reason, an unfinished conditionality that demands some sort of noetic engagement. By a figurative extension, it is not unreasonable to construe Habermas's postulates as historical creations inferred from the partial and unfinished normative contents of real communication practice. They might yet be realized, in *part* of course, through ongoing rhetorical struggle as successions of claims and counterclaims about the properly individuated values of civic life.

There is, I think, increasing evidence that Habermas, in his theory of communicative action, has come to recognize and reflect an alternative derivation for the normative constraints on practices of civic discourse. In an initially puzzling section of his monumental project *The Theory of Communicative Action*, he offers an extensive analysis of the functional limits to money and power as steering mechanisms for the sociopolitical system.[58] The ostensive purpose of this analysis is to show that Parsons's theory of the social system places undue reliance on constructs— namely, money and power—that are themselves insufficiently grounded. So, in detaching us from our own linguisticality, money requires a further reflective level of constraint—namely, that of law. Where power is concerned, the structural asymmetry of those who command and those who obey requires a further level of reflective constraint; not surprisingly, this is the communicative domain of legitimation. The observations are well founded, but curiously positioned, and are developed at a length which seems, at first blush, to exceed their actual importance.

Much more is going on here than initially meets the eye. Habermas is not only dismissing two, far from prevailing paradigms of social cohesion. He is also going to war against two competing ways of modeling communication itself: as commodified signification (Baudrillard) and as a regime of discursively constituted power (Foucault). This is why it is so important for Habermas's own theory of communication that it demonstrate the further need of legality and normative integrity, of legitimation. However, this remarkably perceptive conceptual inversion also forces Habermas to descend, as it were, into the performative maelstrom of communicative action. In his inclusive treatment of the further steering media of the societal system, he now includes levels of what he calls *influence* and *value commitment*.[59] The former is clearly supposed to be rhetorical, while the latter is not. While it is not clear to me how hard Habermas is trying to discriminate these levels from one another, the fact remains that he seems unable to distinguish them when viewing them through the lens of actual practice. Both advice and moral appeals are now oriented to mutual understanding. Both rely on traditions, values, forms of social life—what I call "social knowledge."[60] Influence relies on consensus for its criteria of rationality, whereas value commitment relies on pattern consistency. We find Habermas conceding, whether by accident or design, that a domain of ideality may emerge from practice, in addition to being imposed on it.

REFORMING RHETORICAL PRACTICE: CUOMO ON ABORTION

> Let us too, echoing his uncertain tale
> Cry Sorrow, sorrow—yet let good prevail
> Let good prevail!
> So be it! Yet, what is good? And who
> is God? How name him, and speak true?
>
> —Aeschylus, *Agamemnon*

One intuition is inescapable. Rhetoric is the primary—indeed, the *only* —humane manner for an argumentative culture to sustain public institutions that reflect on themselves, that learn, so to speak, from their own history. The more difficult question, of course, is how rhetoric may do this in any normatively reliable way, given the severe difficulties and distortions in many of these institutions.

The short answer is that rhetoric helps to define and so constitute such a culture by expanding the reach and scope of validity claims in practice and also by inviting audiences to think figuratively about their own place and conduct in unfolding historical episodes. Lincoln was able to do this in a truly memorable way in the midst of his nation's greatest institutional crisis with his second inaugural address.[61] Closer to the present, discourse by advocates as diverse as Elizabeth Linder, Nancy Kassebaum, and Jesse Jackson has performed similar functions for our own, much-reviled public sphere. Discourses like these remind us anew of the possibilities for rhetoric in each age.

There is no issue haunting our contemporary political agenda that defies rational resolution as consistently as that of abortion.[62] As this essay is written, "right to life" advocates and "pro-choice" proponents present independent, absolute, and apparently irreconcilable visions of policy. Together, their advocacy offers more than a litmus test for political campaigners. For those interested in practical reason, the issue of abortion offers an insistent and disturbing counterexample. It is the case we often urge our students not to discuss in classroom oratory. But, as philosophers are wont to do, Alasdair MacIntyre has gone so far as to use the question as a paradigmatic case of essentially contested and incommensurable moral disagreement in contemporary life. Here is his analysis:

["Pro-choice" position]
Everybody has certain rights over his or her own person, including his or her own body. It follows from the nature of these rights that at the stage when the embryo is essentially part of the mother's body, the mother has a right to make her own uncoerced decision on whether she will have an abortion or not. Therefore abortion is morally permissible and ought to be allowed by law.

["Pro-life" position]
Murder is wrong. Murder is the taking of innocent life. An embryo is an identifiable individual, differing from a newborn infant only in being at an earlier stage on the long road to adult capacities and, if any life is innocent, that of an embryo is. If infanticide is murder, as it is, abortion is murder. So abortion is not only morally wrong, but ought to be legally prohibited.[63]

As the above arguments make clear, certain fundamental terms in the controversy are given an absolute rendering of value; these terms will *not* admit of qualification or compromise. Moreover, there is an ironic undertone to the values themselves. Those in favor of abortion's legality, liberals in many other matters, have chosen the libertarian catchword *freedom* as the grounding of their argument. Those adamant about abortion's immorality, and thus illegality—very frequently, though not always, conservative on other matters—have chosen *reverence for life*, a ground for pacifism and equal rights, as the core of their anti-abortion argument. This curiosity may simply be another indicator of the special status that abortion has held as an issue apparently immune to rational argument.

As the politics of the summer of 1984 grew more heated, both sides abandoned any pretence of argumentative civility. Placards, scurrilous charges, and street tactics interrupted the speeches of political campaigners. The Democratic party stalwarts bore the brunt of this activism. By conceding that abortion may be questionable as moral practice yet subject to legal protection, their *pure tolerance* position yielded much of the initiative and ground of discussion. But then politically neutral opinion leaders, traditionally removed from such controversy, began to get actively involved.

If there was a political exigence which occasioned New York governor Mario Cuomo's speech on the matter, it was probably New York archbishop John O'Connor's pastoral letter of 24 June in which he strongly urged members of his flock not to vote for anyone supporting legal protection of abortion. Of course, the abortion issue was by no means a settled matter even among Catholic theologians. But to the faithful, such a pronouncement had the practical effect of foreclosing an entire range of political options. To the governor of New York, the archbishop's pronouncement was tantamount to a personal attack, since Cuomo, a devout Catholic, felt obligated to enforce New York's relatively liberal abortion laws. There followed a vitriolic series of exchanges between Cuomo and both O'Connor and other members of the Catholic Church. These exchanges, in the heat of a political campaign year, only polarized the conflict. Then, on 13 September 1984, Governor Cuomo delivered an important address to the Department of Theology at the University of Notre Dame.[64]

As I have implied, the volatility of the abortion question is due to its having a legal dimension, a moral dimension, and an expedient political dimension all at the same time. While perhaps not unique in this respect, abortion also manages to blur domains or spheres of judgment which are typically disjoined in the Habermas program. Habermas quite explicitly regards the pragmatic, the ethical, and the moral realms as implying quite different grounds and criteria for reflection. He draws analogies (a bit too emphatically, in my view) between the pragmatic and the calculative, ends–means thinking of technical reason; the ethical and the individuated unity of a single human life and its character (here lurks neo-Aristotelian phronēsis); and the moral and judgments which imply an impartialist stance generalizable to all categories of persons at all times.[65]

The problem, given Habermas's pronounced resistance to meta-narratives, is what to do about questions which are contested *because* they are ambiguously affiliated with several differing realms and meanings of discourse. Abortion is, to be expedient, a political issue, involving advantages and injuries to the polity and even to politicians. To be more technically calculative, it is also undeniably a *medical* question, involving (as do all medical procedures) certain risks and benefits to all involved. Entailing the autonomous choice of the woman, it obviously implicates the ethical character of a unified individual life. Involving, as it does for many, a judgment which might be made more categorically about life itself, it may well partake of additional *moral* dimensions. It just will not do, as Habermas himself has attempted, to place the issue in one of the three categories and end the discussion.[66] The point is that people *really disagree.* Moreover, the issue is weighted with an ambiguity which seems recurrently to invite such disagreement. Our intuition, expressed abstractly, may now be rendered in a concrete way. I suspect that there are no ways of working through the public ambiguities of an issue such as this other than by means of rhetoric.

So it appeared, at any rate, to Governor Mario Cuomo.[67] A governor who is by political affiliation a Democrat, by ethical faith a Catholic, and by the imperative of definition the chief legal officer of the state must choose audiences carefully if he is to extend the range of consensus as far as possible. In short, our first attempt to instantiate a revised discourse ethics approach within practical reason must come face to face with the better part of political realism. In matters of rhetorical controversy, all audiences are *particular*, even as all symbolic action must reach out for a wider hearing. Cuomo's choice was reminiscent of John F. Kennedy's decision in 1960 to address the Greater Houston Ministerial Association: like Kennedy's, Cuomo's speech was directed to people who, on the surface, were least likely to be sympathetic, but who were most likely to give the speech a respectful, thoughtful hearing. The choice of an audience that is unsympathetic on doctrinal grounds but reflective by academic inclination as the preferred forum of policy discussion becomes particularly pertinent as the text proceeds. In Habermas's terminology, such a choice probably enhances the sincerity expectations for the speech along an expressive dimension. Beyond these initial choices, of course, was the fact that a successful performance here would be likely to engender favorable discussion by the opinion leaders who informally mark the pulse of agenda setting in mass society. Let us now take a closer look at the text itself, in light of the revision I have been attempting.

The form of the discourse is quite complex. Initially, Cuomo presented his intent as that of a visiting lecturer. But that intent was eventually displaced by a tone of increasing disclosure; and the cumulative effect is closer to that of a guarded, carefully honed apologia. Following informal introductory remarks, the governor articulated an overall theme which then functioned as the consuming principle of the discussion:

> In addition to all the weaknesses, all the dilemmas, and all the temptations that impede every pilgrim's progress, the Catholic who holds political office in a pluralistic democracy—the Catholic who

is elected to serve Jews and Moslems, atheists and Protestants, as well as Catholics—bears special responsibility. He or she undertakes to help create conditions under which all can live with a maximum of dignity and with a reasonable degree of freedom; where everyone who chooses may hold beliefs different from specifically Catholic ones—sometimes even contradictory to them; where the laws protect people's right to divorce, to use birth control devices, and even to choose abortion.[68]

Cuomo's words express a traditional democratic premise and a cautious variation on the classical justification of politics as the "master art." For Aristotle, politics was the primary or architectonic art, because it instituted the conditions whereby all other arts (and human goods) were possible. For the governor of New York, the role of the politician is still informed by the classical conception. He or she is to help create *conditions* wherein highly diversified convictions and actions may prosper. But critical ambiguities remain. The classical polis was grounded in certain common assumptions as to the proper ends of deliberative choice, as well as an elaborate notion of what it meant to be a citizen. The classical notion of the polis, in short, is precisely that pre-Kantian form of life in which Habermas had no interest. But in Cuomo's modern world a fascinating variation takes hold. For Cuomo, as for the Habermas who theorized the public sphere, certain considerations of expediency have to take precedent before *reflective disagreement*, the disagreement of controversy and participation, are even possible. It is almost as if he has been forced, through the constraints of the *vita activa*, to turn the hierarchy of Habermas's discourse ethics upside down.

Yet there are dangers of inclusion here as well. In the pure tolerance of pluralism, only the institution seems to be held in common. Within its bounds are any number of incompatible norms and values. Dignity and freedom are, of course, goods for virtually any polity; and it is interesting that Cuomo presents ethical postulates in a way which virtually concedes their Habermasian universality. But if faith provides us with any ultimate strictures, then it is surely the case that these same values are *instrumental* goods where matters of faith and morals are concerned. Shortly, even the speaker must concede that "insistence on freedom is easier to accept as a general proposition than in its applications to specific situations." What follows in this unusually forthcoming text is an attempt to translate abstract virtue into a code of concrete justice.

Acknowledging that the Constitution offers only ambiguous guidance on the substance of moral advocacy, Cuomo marks off a series of cases (contraception, the nuclear freeze, and abortion) where arguments from religious teaching and arguments for the good of public life tend to merge. What is most interesting about his use of these specific issues is his reluctance to invoke any validity claims related to truth. Instead, it appears that sincere, well-motivated persons are likely to differ about any number of these issues, and the problem facing us thereby becomes one of propriety—where to draw the line in the *grounding* of arguments. This convergence of sincerity and rightness is explicitly presented to this audience as a matter to be dealt with through *proper* argumentative procedure:

> No law prevents us from advocating any of these things: I am free to do so. So are the bishops. And so is Reverend Falwell. In fact, the Constitution guarantees my right to try. And theirs. And his. But should I? Is it helpful? Is it essential to human dignity? Would it promote harmony and understanding? Or does it divide us so fundamentally that it threatens our ability to function as a pluralistic community? When should I argue to make my religious value your morality? My rule of conduct your limitation? What are the rules and policies that should influence the exercise of this right to argue and to promote?

The point of these rhetorical questions (and there are a great many of them in the speech) is to suggest that there must be some boundary, however blurred, between the advocacy of a policy position on moral grounds and the official sanctioning of some moral positions to the legal exclusion of others. Moreover, Cuomo is sensitive to the fact that this boundary affects not only the implementation of policy, but also the way policy itself is argued and promoted by elected officials. But here is the beginning of a problem that will plague Cuomo's analysis. For if abortion is really believed to be immoral—that is, the generalizable impartialist position—then there is no imaginable way in which such a finding may be supervened by a propriety norm of advocacy. Put bluntly, if I really do believe that all human life is sacred and that abortion is the indiscriminate slaughter of human life, then I am duty-bound to do everything I can to outlaw such a practice. If there is a rule of justice powerful enough to mediate between these realms, it is a rule that must be enacted rhetorically.

The central argument that may be traced through Cuomo's entire address turns on the understood difference between personal moral *principle* and public moral *consensus*. After a brief narrative of the many different religious orientations characterizing the American heritage, he introduces the underlying premise: "Our public morality, then—the moral standards we maintain for everyone, not just the ones we insist on in our private lives—depends on a consensus view of right and wrong. The values derived from religious belief will not—and should not—be accepted as part of the public morality unless they are shared by the pluralistic community at large, by consensus. That values happen to be religious values does not deny them acceptability as a part of this consensus. But it does not require their acceptability either." With this apparently sensible premise, Cuomo echoes Habermas's escape from Hegel, at the same time as he presents another variation on the universal audience–particular audience duality. It is interesting, in light of Habermas's categorical disjunction of spheres for validity claims, that this practical example of rhetoric tends to do much the same thing, as a form of institutional packaging. Although there clearly is a tension between sincerity and propriety, Cuomo places "sincere" religious affiliations in the traditional abode of the *private*. This has the additional consequence of removing these convictions from the prospect of argumentative redemption. There is Burkean irony in this repositioning of religion's "secular salvation." And to make matters considerably more complicated, Cuomo does all this primarily on grounds which Habermas would recognize as those of *propriety*—what is right for the Church.

Perhaps unnoticed in the midst of the conceptual shuffling is the fact that Cuomo brackets the whole question of whether abortion might be, on some absolute scale, an immoral or even barbaric act. He does this on the ground that a pluralist society holds differing, even incompatible, ideas about such matters. And oddly for one who proclaims a fervent doctrinal affiliation, he dissolves the seriousness of this specific issue primarily on the grounds that these differences are ultimately differences of belief. It is only when he begins to draw analogies with an issue that is considered equally immoral and barbaric in the polarized differences it presents to us that the real contradictions of such a pure tolerance position begin to emerge. Note that these are *rhetorical* contradictions. Important to my analysis and emendation of Habermas is the fact that they can be perceived and engaged in *no* other way.

The practical question of a policy's morality has now been re-presented by Governor Cuomo as a procedural meta-question of *propriety:* should

I speak on certain matters? This takes on a special poignance because Cuomo is a politician trying to animate a secular pluralist morality with spiritual conviction, albeit one that is compatible with a consensual democratic tradition. We now recognize the uncomfortable fact that the aforementioned Habermas hierarchy of politics, ethics, and morality has been leveled. Public morality is grounded in a generalizable consensus that transcends the particularity of religion and ideological stripe. Although Cuomo does not employ Habermas's actual terminology, his operative conception seems to embody a synthesis of ideality postulates, given an audience endorsement for good measure. And within this widened sphere of public morality, we have what?

The answer is confusing. There are private matters of belief; these seem to be particularities of conviction that govern personal conduct, but nothing more. Then there are particular audiences who share core beliefs (this closely parallels Perelman's ground for agreements of value), and at least some of these core beliefs carry with them fundamental obligations governing the conduct of others as well. Cuomo is a member of such an audience, as are—presumably—the members of the Department of Theology at Notre Dame. In choosing to address this particular audience, the governor must have been aware that their own agreements had severe public implications. The premises of public morality allow the governor to stand at one level removed from his own immediate audience and even from himself. But they do not, I believe, afford him the luxury of transcendence. From the standpoint of the theology department, or even the fundamentalist Christian, a narrow position of absolute right and wrong could not possibly be overruled by consensus. For better or worse, abortion, in Cuomo's words, "is a 'matter of life and death,' and degree counts." So however narrow the principle, the authority of such a sanction extends outward and governs the potential transgression of every citizen. If there is to be a rule of justice that governs our argumentative conduct, as well as our policies, it requires clearer articulation than we have encountered so far.

It is Cuomo the man of practical politics who eventually defines the overarching rule for moral influences on policy judgment. In his important words: "The community must decide if what is being proposed would be better left to private discretion than public policy; whether it restricts freedoms, and so to what end, to whose benefit; whether it will produce a good or bad result; whether overall it will help the community or merely divide it. The right answers to these questions can be elusive."

In plain language, what is offered here is a majoritarian principle of social justice to guide practical reasoning in this otherwise volatile setting. Cuomo would have the community (that invention of social consensus) function as judge in proposed attempts to make moral code a governing principle for social policy. He even goes so far as to offer a list of topoi to help guide the resolution of disputes in elusive cases. To use the terminology of Perelman (as revised here), Cuomo's discourse is an attempt to characterize the collectivity in such a way that convictions of participant groups may be protected without these same convictions being endorsed as a governing rule for the conduct of all. The question we must ask is whether this principle presents itself with intuitive soundness to the pertinent audiences themselves.

It must be said that, among the most elusive questions in Cuomo's entire discourse, is *how* the community is to decide the numerous uncertainties attached to the abortion question. His own overall guideline is necessarily weighted in the direction of the classical deliberative stasis (that is, advantage and injury). Yet subsequent attempts to flesh out the parameters of this position seem less than elegant. As one illustration, consider what happens when he finally gets around to discussing the Church hierarchy's position on abortion. Here are his words: "But the differences in approach reveal a truth, I think, that is not well enough perceived by Catholics and therefore still further complicates the process for us. That is, while we always owe our bishops' words respectful attention and careful consideration, the question whether to engage the political system in a struggle to have it adopt certain articles of our belief as part of public morality is not a matter of doctrine: it is a matter of prudential political judgment."

I find these words curious for several reasons. First, Cuomo has clearly moved away from the stance of judging within the *community* among several conflicting positions to another more circumspect form of judgment as to whether to express a conflicting position in the first place. After all, once we decide *not* "to engage the political system in a struggle," there is no further problem. But that is only because there is no further controversy. Second, it is not clear who the "we" represents in this passage. The address is built on Cuomo's personal articles of faith, so it might refer to the Catholic governor. But "we" are not all governors. The statement is clearly more cogent as a personal conviction than as a guideline to all relevant audiences. Regrettably, this is the problem with much moral controversy. Third, even as a personal guideline, the statement appears to strain against the public consensus principle offered earlier. Put another way, the political system is already engaged in a struggle over the question of abortion. One wonders if public officials do much to help the *community* decide by a strategy of prudential nonengagement.

The remainder of the governor's speech helps to clarify some of these ambiguities through a series of argumentative overtures to this most difficult audience. He begins by disclosing his sincere acceptance of Catholic doctrine as a guide to his personal conduct: "As a Catholic I have accepted certain answers as the right ones for myself and my family, and because I have, they have influenced me in special ways. . . . As a Catholic I accept the Church's teaching authority. . . . As Catholics, my wife and I were enjoined never to use abortion to destroy the life we created, and we never have." One senses that this odd public testimonial, profession as *expression,* is designed to do more than simply bolster Cuomo's credibility. It seems to prefigure the *other* in this world of plurality as well. The Cuomo that is sincere in his own *private* morality recognizes the multitude of equally sincere others, some of whom are advocates of opposed positions. In such a world, presumably, it is the tolerance of difference that must maintain the secular upper hand. Fair enough. But there is something uncomfortable about this. Are all moral concerns, by this modernist definition, therefore necessarily *private* concerns? What of the barbarism and neglect we see all around us in the forms of social injustice, inequality, torture, and repression? Are these things just other cases of differences in opinion? Are there not more basic moral principles, without which these opinions are simply meaningless indulgences? The problem is instantiated in the way in which each statement of Cuomo's credo is followed by some nagging sense of difference within constituencies of the larger public forum. For example: "But not everyone in our society agrees with me and Matilda. And those who don't—those who endorse legalized abortions [sic]—aren't a ruthless, callous alliance of anti-Christians determined to overthrow our moral standards. In many cases, the proponents of legal abortion are the very people who have worked with Catholics to realize the goals of social justice set out by popes in encyclicals: the American Lutheran Church, the Central Conference of American Rabbis . . ." And the list goes on. Here is an attempt to recognize others as familiar extensions of ourselves. Larger commitments to social justice (if they really *are* larger) allow these differences to be placed in perspective. But it is interesting and a little disconcerting that even Cuomo presents these distinguished constituencies as "endorsing" legalized abortion. Understandable as Cuomo's need for distance may be, these proponents endorse (as does Cuomo) the legal protection of choice.

What Cuomo calls a "latitude of judgment" is then translated into a rule of *reciprocity:* "Certainly, we should not be forced to mold Catholic morality to conform to disagreement by non-Catholics, however sincere or severe their disagreement." The implication, of course, is that neither should we mold them legally in the reciprocal direction. At this point in the discourse, however, those fully immersed in Church dogma may well have stopped short of Cuomo's initial assumption. From a certain undeniably narrow point of view, the failure to ban abortion legally does indeed amount to a molding of Catholic morality in the public arena. What began as an article of faith could appear, in some quarters at least, as a defense of pure tolerance.

This admittedly extreme characterization acquires some weight through a most unfortunate attempt at figurative thinking following the reciprocity argument. Cuomo reminds his listeners that the Church showed "practical political judgment" on the question of slavery in the antebellum South: "The decision they made to remain silent on a constitutional amendment to abolish slavery or on the repeal of the Fugitive Slave Law wasn't a mark of their moral indifference: it was a measured attempt to balance moral truths against political realities. Their decision reflected their sense of complexity, not their diffidence. And as history reveals, Lincoln behaved with similar discretion." There is, of course, a measure of truth in this further attempt at bridging the division between religious and secular positions. But it is an odd secularist who projects historical relativism onto those who believe most adamantly in one, true story. In my view, such an analogy could only undermine the force of much that came before. Silence in the face of moral abomination is not easily characterized as heroic. The theology students and conferees at Notre Dame undoubtedly knew this, just as they knew that the prewar Lincoln was neither president nor bishop. The Lincoln who behaved with "discretion" before the war also proclaimed that "A house divided against itself cannot stand." And in the midst of that war's terrible denouement, pronounced: "If we shall suppose that American slavery is one of those offences which, in the providence of God, must needs come, but which having continued through His appointed time, He now wills to be removed and that He gives to both North and South this terrible war as the woe due to those by whom the offence came, shall we discern there any departure from those attributes which the believers in a living God always ascribe to Him?"[69] Surely Cuomo did not wish to imply that before the Civil War, slavery's morality was a matter of opinion best relegated to the private realm. Just as surely, he would not want to defend forever this divided house.

The less than surprising fact is that Mario Cuomo spoke much more eloquently as a man of practical action than as a moral and political theorist. His arguments against the Hatch amendment are strong—in fact, ironically reminiscent of the prewar Lincoln. His practical questions about the effects, social and otherwise, of banning abortion in a society that has virtually abandoned its obligations to social justice should be read by all who consider themselves civic reformers. Here is an example of his sentiments:

> Better than any law or rule or threat of punishment would be the moving strength of our own good example, demonstrating our lack of hypocrisy, proving the beauty and worth of our instruction. We must work to find ways to avoid abortions without otherwise violating our faith. We should find funds and opportunities for young women to bring their child to term, knowing both of them will be taken care of if that is necessary; we should teach our young men better than we do now their responsibilities in creating and caring for human life.

More profoundly than any recent public argument, the Cuomo statement is an indictment of those who believe that the right to life extends for only about nine months. Yet it is apparent that any practice of reasoning that attempts to be *ethical* and *public* at the same time encounters significant difficulties.

CONCLUSIONS AND IMPLICATIONS

In yet another restatement of his complex position, Habermas concedes that "the concept of communicative reason is still accompanied by the shadow of a transcendental illusion." Showing renewed confidence in figuration, he describes his concept as a "rocking hull—but it does not go under in the sea of contingencies, even if shuddering in high seas is the only mode in which it 'copes' with these contingencies."[70] By presenting his foundation as unstable and fallibilistic, subject to indefinite further revision, Habermas seems to be repositioning his communicative stance as that of a regulative ideal, rather than a detached a priori ground of validation. While this is entirely in the spirit of my revision, it will no doubt occasion hard-line defenders of Habermas to insist that this was what he intended all along. At the same time, hopeful rhetoricians can suppose that at last, he is coming around; and those weary of the tumult can wonder anew whether the game has been worth the candle. I believe that it has.

Habermas's own work—its capacity to absorb, refine, and respond to the revisions of others—is the best arbiter of the theory introduced thus far. But the enactment of practical reason is another matter. I have tried throughout this project to rethink practical reason rhetorically, through its characteristic *manner* of engaging collective thought. This meant that the discourse ethics program had to be moderated by the earlier Habermas project of a public sphere—real volatile controversy, partisan participation, and an uncertain forum for provisional judgments. While a single example can hardly be the prototype for testing this revision, the case of Cuomo on abortion helps to show that rhetorical engagements with such divisive issues may still be enlightening. Here are some of the morals of my story.

First, while Habermas presented validity conditions as presupposed by certain types of communicative utterance, in practice the actual encounter with an audience seems to define a convergence of such conditions through the nature of rhetorical performance and its enactment. If so, the choice of an audience may prove to be the single factor most conducive to the institutional realization of practical reason. Such an observation as this could have all the quality of a truism, given the pronouncements of neo-Aristotelianism and the so-called situationist formulation of rhetoric.[71] However, the special problems of moral argument in the public sphere seem to necessitate a choice of audience that will both challenge and extend the valued intuitions or social knowledge, lending meaning to ambiguities in an advocate's claims. The implications of such a finding are significant if we have been accustomed to criticism that simply assumes the perspective or world view of the audience in order to lend its verdicts pragmatic force.

In choosing an audience, we must presumably rest our judgment on something relevant but not reducible to the situation. If we conclude, as I have, that Cuomo's choice of rhetorical audience was particularly apt, then we must have in mind some intuitive criterion for what counts as a challenge and a grounding for the arguments in a moral controversy. Perhaps this is the sort of difficulty that led Perelman to the notion of a universal audience, Castoriadis to the notion of an "Imaginary Institution,"[72] and Habermas to the ideal speech situation. But it also suggests an intervention from the uninvited guest of neo-Aristotelianism. Ethical choice and character enactment always involve the mediation of generalizable principle with unique particular. This is what phronēsis *is*. In rhetoric, it may be the audience that lends juridical force to generality. But the fact remains that judgments about audiences, much like judgments *by* audiences, are neither certain nor absolute. They are probable. This does not mean that they are random or arbitrary, only that they are debatable.

Second, it is possible to detect some heuristic value in the figurative thinking of rhetorical form when it comes to the judgment of actual arguments. In Cuomo's speech we find a remarkable tension between the secular constraints of propriety (*his* version of phronēsis) and the privatistic relegation of faith to conditions of sincerity. One suspects that Cuomo's real view of faith and civic conviction is more complicated than this disjunction suggests. Why? Partly because the movement of the discourse as *form* is more densely layered than that. We are given a transposition of ideal, consensually based pluralism, only to find the virtue of *tolerance* manifested most emphatically in the spectatorial disengagement of faith from public discourse. This is the modern cultural lifeworld which, in the view of conservatives like MacIntyre, dare not speak its name.[73] And it must be conceded that the rhetorical results are far from eloquent in the classical sense of the term.

But this discourse must also be something more expansive than the mere manipulation of tactics for perlocutionary effect. The fact is that there is a larger position that Cuomo is trying to sketch, a position that would make room for the reflective space of public difference to be asserted with impunity and perhaps even with a kind of mutual forebearance. There are, of course, clear cases where Cuomo's vision of this sphere admits to confusions or glaring exceptions. The slavery illustration does not work. There are also inconsistencies. The same principle requiring the protection of personal morality from state or religious interference is apparently set aside in cases like the nuclear freeze issue or capital punishment. And while Cuomo wishes to be steadfast on the separation of Church and State, the principle seems dubious when applied to the right to employ religious arguments on political questions. Cuomo does not actually *deny* this right. But his repeated calls for wisdom translate all too readily into a call for *caution*—an inhibition of civic engagement.

There is more. If there is a bottom line to this controversy, it is found in Cuomo's refusal to abdicate the political expediency grounding of deliberative controversy in the face of moral challenge. If I may venture to complete our Habermas trichotomy, Cuomo apparently would regard it as *unethical* to do so. In the most recognizable generic antecedent to Cuomo's speech, John Kennedy as presidential candidate made the following pledge to the Greater Houston Ministerial Association: "But if the time should ever come—and I do not concede any conflict to be remotely possible—when my office would require me to either violate my conscience, or violate the national interest, then I would resign the office, and I hope any other conscientious public servant would do the same."[74] In offering to sacrifice his *public* identity, Kennedy prudently retained his subservience to a moral ideal. From this vantage, it is possible to see Cuomo's speech, skillful as it is, as a painstaking attempt to forestall the decisive conflict of conscience and expediency that Kennedy addressed. Moreover, it is only partially successful. What, then, are we to conclude about the rhetoric of public argument from an imposing perspective like that of Habermas?

From the Habermas perspective of discourse ethics, Cuomo's speech might be seen as an attempt to establish a consensual base for ethical public controversy, a base that implies ambiguous standards for sincerity and propriety, all the while bracketing the whole matter of truth. But from the revision of perspective suggested by Perelman, I believe that judgments are possible on the level of propriety of argument, internal and external consistency of rules, and plausibility of inference making, as well as more traditional criteria. And an even more telling range of evaluation is suggested by the more expansive revisions of Burke. For to the extent that we accept this larger reflective space for judging the expedient prioritizing of moral issues, even when we are disagreeing with the grounding of priorities themselves, we have *already engaged in the reflective cognitive movement of rhetorical judgment, as an implied audience.* In this larger episodic sense of reciprocal, inferential engagement, rhetoric *by definition* cannot be reducible to perlocutionary effect.

The shades of nuance and difference in even this volatile topic hold lessons, I believe, for both Habermas and MacIntyre. In practice, abortion—even if it *is* murder—admits many more qualifications, exceptions, and case-related justifications than the neo-Kantian postulates for extended normative discourse can ever include. This is not to side with one extreme or the other, but only to note the practical inconsistencies which inevitably accompany their public expression. The same could be said of murder too. But these practical truths surely need further discussion. To return to the beginning of my commentary, true reflexivity and true reciprocity need to be related if communicative competence is ever to have an articulate rhetorical dimension. If judgment is treated only as a faculty, it is unlikely that audiences will ever be lucky enough to share in the privilege. By contrast, if judgment is treated as an acquired competence, sophisticated through practice, the prospect for its democratization is considerably more promising.

Along with the all-or-nothing dichotomies of dialectic generally, there is a critical need in the Habermas lexicon for a theory of modality. I do not mean only the mediation of time and circumstance, although these dimensions are clearly important. I mean something as basic as the manner of affirming or denying propositions themselves. Propositions may be many things other than deterministically true or false. We have seen that they may be probably, possibly, contingently, potentially true—or false. To use the Habermas conditionals and postulates rhetorically would not be to dismiss deformations of partisanship wherever they are found. Rather, we would *temporarily* suspend our judgment of sincerity, propriety, rightness, and intelligibility of argumentative premises, in order to see whether and how they might be actualized through the experiences *of others* over the course of ongoing episodes.

The key rhetorical corollary to contingency is *plausibility*, a notion which allows that in public life the same verbal or nonverbal utterance may actually mean different things to different people. And, more radical still, it may even be that this is not such a bad thing. To echo and paraphrase McKeon's sense of a "productive ambiguity," it may be part and parcel of how a more public, collectivized sense of phronēsis really works, if it is to work at all. We will be exploring this alternative construal of rhetorical meaning in the next chapter.

For now, it suffices to say that Habermas continues to offer the world of rhetoric equal doses of inspiration and puzzlement. I have, in this chapter, attempted to bring the two Habermas projects closer together, through a rhetorical revision. So long as rhetoric is envisioned as somehow antithetical to reason in the grand style or as the unhappy residue of reason's historical embarrassments, such a revision is not likely to be welcomed in any quarter. But to the extent that we envision at least the possibility of a rhetorical practice which might be informed by a sense of justice, solidarity, disclosure, the particularity of audience interest, the forums of distance and disturbance, and the critical publicity of judgment, then a rhetoric informed by practical reason remains a live civic option for our age.

Finally, and paradoxically, the very problems of Cuomo's courageous speech help to illustrate the possibilities of rhetorical argument in addressing the moral dilemmas of our time. Rhetoric never promised to solidify deterministic, prima facie structures for moral conduct. In fact, and without too much difficulty, such a promise would shortly be recognized as a contradiction in terms. Rather, what rhetoric did, and does, promise is that interested advocates and agents may deal with radical contingencies in the human condition better through the shared disputation of practical reason than through other available options. Some rhetorical criticism has remained faithful to this promise, by allowing us to recognize and hear eloquence while seeing through and beyond its vision at the same time. In so doing, rhetoric might begin to repay Habermas's monumental contribution to the ethical mission of practical reason.

6 Rhetorical Coherence: Refiguring the Episodes of Public Life

The temporal structure of a future-oriented remembrance would moreover allow the formation of universalistic ego structures on the basis of partisanship for particular identity projections; for every position can come to agreement with the other positions it is confronted with *in the present* precisely in its partisanship for a universality to be realized *in the future*.

—Jürgen Habermas, "On Social Identity"

Rhetoric is the counterpart of dialectic.

—Aristotle, *Rhetoric*

Nobody admits to liking rhetoric very much. But almost everyone admits to having occasionally been seized and transported by a discourse which changed or influenced their life and priorities. It is a commonplace that such discourse is rare, the exception that proves our (usually untested) rule. But all practices need to have outstanding exemplars, touchstones of accomplishment. And virtually by definition, such outstanding cases will be rare. It is probably not possible to determine whether great or eloquent rhetoric is rarer now than it was in the various golden ages of the past. Nor do I think that the determination, could it be made, would be all that interesting. However, it *is* important to wrestle with the question of what makes for great rhetoric, if only to determine the extent to which it is possible in our day. Why?

Because first, no matter how infrequent its actual occurrence, the fact that there should be an occasional instance of great rhetoric *at all* is critical evidence that the practice may be perfected. Second, because I suspect that even the success stories to which we might point could be dismissed as preaching to the converted. A devil's advocate might say, for instance, that we are so well versed in the doxa, or cultural premises, of the rhetorical craft that we are already far down the road proposed by our revered text; we are, so to speak, its captive audience. As I understand the point made by widespread critiques of hegemony, it is that much of the Western cultural lifeworld is in exactly this place; it is a restricted, elite code for an already captive audience—hence the suspiciously political seating arrangements at the faculty club, the culture of misreading gathered together with the culture of misspelling.

The question I want to ask is a shamelessly modern one, framed by the divergences of conviction and lifeworld that most of us cannot help but experience. The question is, may rhetoric be *liberating*? May it, in other words, put us in touch with a range of issues and experience outside our normalized, received opinion, our doxa? And, paradoxically, can it do this *through* received opinion and the traditional resources of rhetoric?

In this chapter I offer three rather unlikely candidates as examples of eloquent modern rhetors: a politically ambitious black urban preacher; a disgruntled mother and sociologist; and a reclusive, avant-garde Czech playwright. In very different ways, each of them presented and captioned rhetorical episodes that are likely to have a continuing impact on the audiences of our age. Their utterances are now part of our still cacophonous public conversation. But what of this conversation—the utterances that inform and comprise its meanings? If conversation is to offer something more powerful than a metaphor for good reading, then further articulation of the relationships among rhetoric and conversation is needed.

From Habermas I have taken the admittedly optimistic thesis that even behind the closure of reasoned discourse a certain ongoing potential for logos remains. Habermas wouldn't put it this way, of course. But, as a legion of critics has gone to further and further lengths to dispense with rationality, Habermas has at least been tempted to broaden its definition.[1] It is now possible, for instance, to allow context and strategic factors to enter the picture, thereby making rationality clearer and more forceful. Although the admission of context is bound to cloud the claims of discourse ethics to impartiality, some such middle-range opening was absolutely necessary, if only to allow primitive distinctions between fiction and nonfiction to emerge.

In this chapter, I plan to take advantage of this opening—strategically, as it were—by filling in the middle ground between the "form of life" horizon proper (or lifeworld) and the symbolic acts which make up utterances. My argument in the preceding chapter was that the Habermas position needed to be fleshed out so as to account for the middle-range complexity and contextual variation of *all* utterances, not just *rhetorical* utterances.[2] However, once we make some room for *partisanship* within the world of communicative action, it is possible to provide additional clarity and direction for the normative impetus of rhetoric. If the overall direction, the entelechial tendency, of rhetorical practice is goaded by the generality of performed validity claims, then the practical guidance of rhetorical choice is always a *relational* matter, one that is discovered through the reflective prospects made available by rhetoric's encounters and episodes. As Aristotle anticipated (but wisely did not elaborate), rhetoric is the counterpart of conversation.

TWO GENRES OF COMMUNICATIVE PRACTICE

Probably no concept has been invoked more frequently as a paradigm for humanistic inquiry than that of conversation. At various times, writers as diverse as Richard Rorty, Alasdair MacIntyre, Kenneth Burke, and H-G. Gadamer have made much of this speculative allusion. Yet, with the exception of Gadamer, who employs it as a metaphor for hermeneutical understanding, very little speculative thought has been expended on the harder questions of what conversation is and *does*. This, broadly speaking, is what we are concerned with here.

My starting points and boundary conditions differ from those of universal pragmatics in *two* ways. First, instead of contrasting rhetoric as a type of *speech act* with more rarefied conceptions of argumentation, I view it as a reflective variation on recognizable discourse practices—for example, fictive literature and ordinary conversation. Second, I maintain that the moderating reflective tendencies within rhetoric are found not in the particular utterance of the speaking subject so much as in the mediation of expressed partisanship—as *dialogic controversia*. Within this dialogic controversy, it is the *enthymeme*, as a middle-range inferential prototype of rhetorical practice, that allows conduct to become obligatory through an entwinement of situated interests and perspectives. The end result suggests that the reflective capacity of rhetoric is embedded in the reflective capacities of conversation in general—not only conversation as argument-constituted communicative action, but conversation as the sloppy, playful, give-and-take of ordinary life,[3] distortions and all. Generally speaking, rhetoric emerges in discourse as a reflective and anticipatory choice among options imposed in a moment of uncertainty or contingency. The discursive impetus behind rhetoric is often intentional; it is always accountable, even as its successful enactment is always collaborative, bound up with the confirmation and commitments of others. Put another way, as long as conversation is possible, the horizon of rhetorical reflection remains available.

Following the lead of the Russian philosopher, linguist, and literary theorist Mikhail Bakhtin, we now consider conversation and rhetoric as the two primary genres of speech communication.[4] This generic distinction proves to be important, because it helps to restrain the impulse to allow one privileged discursive form (such as argumentation) to somehow constitute a rarefied, honorific embodiment of discourse practice at its best, thus relegating every other genre of communication to an inferior position. Instead, I wish to stress the interdependence of the conversational and the rhetorical genre. I also wish to suggest ways in which rhetoric may be restorative for certain issues and problems in coherence, rather than simply disruptive.

Our analysis of rhetoric and conversation begins with the historically dubious, albeit mythically rich, assumption that these are two interdependent discursive arts with analogous zones of emergence. For, as the opening words of Aristotle's *Rhetoric* suggest, these arts are lodged in a relationship of antistrophos; they are counterparts and hence complementary to one another. Despite their complementary relationship, however, these practices have acquired characteristically different approaches to the problem of *form*, just as they have acquired characteristic conventions, rules, and utterance relationships.

Since both conversation and rhetoric are distinctive instances of *natural* discourse (opposed to both pure literary fiction and artificially generated codes), we might expect their forms to be the product of historically inflected expectations, traditions, and conventions. If this intuition proves correct, then the implicit rules for communicating would undergo a discernible shift when rhetoric emerges within conversation, and vice versa. These acquired rhetorical conventions, in turn, might then suggest certain implications for the nature of meaning and accountability in rhetorical conduct. As the several illustrations in this chapter are designed to show, much is at stake in the practical collaborations provoked by rhetoric: the narrative continuity of episodes, the future of human relationships, and even the dignity and quality of public character.

In order to appreciate properly rhetoric's contribution to coherence in natural discourse, we must first demonstrate that rhetoric is not an accidental feature or a deformation of ordinary discourse practice. Instead, I wish to suggest that *rhetoric is an inherent potential of any shared discourse practice.* In making this suggestion, I am further distancing myself from specifics of the universal pragmatics position—in particular, its decontextualized privileging of cognitive-centered claims to truth in what Habermas calls "practical discourse."[5] The uncomfortable fact remains that ordinary discourse practice does not easily translate into claims to truth redeemable through argumentation. This is because, as we have stressed, utterances are quite unlike propositions, in that they are contextually embedded in episodes. Put somewhat differently, their privileged claims (if any) are to the *plausible,* rather than the true. Such an awareness seems to be the best available to the situated human agents who actually *do* the communicating. Beginning with this less paralyzing awareness of rhetorical interdependence or *mediation* among subjectivities allows us to appreciate emergent dimensions of conventional meaning that would otherwise be subordinated or missed entirely.

Although questions of origin are notoriously suspect, conversation and rhetoric typically occupy traditions of parallel longevity and significance within the historical development of discourse practices. According to Eric Havelock,[6] however, the oldest form of discursive consciousness was offered by neither conversation nor rhetoric, but rather by the mythopoetic discourse of narrative epic. Havelock writes: "The epic therefore is from the stance of our present quest to be considered in the first instance not as an act of creation but as an act of reminder and recall. Its patron muse is indeed *Mnemosūne,* in whom is symbolized not just the memory considered as a mental phenomenon but rather the total act of reminding, recalling, memorializing, and memorizing, which is achieved in epic verse."[7] The traditional sense of poetics, in other words, is found in the reenactment of experience through the spell of continuous discourse, as an extended monologue. Moreover, the *only* way to break the rhapsodic spell of words endlessly repeated was to separate the self (and the speaker) from the remembered word as an *utterance.* How was this to be done? According to Havelock, it "consisted in asking a speaker to repeat himself and explain what he had meant. In Greek, the words for explain, say, and mean could coincide."[8] However we characterize this primitive interference, its implications are provocative, to say the least. The interruptive question usually posits in tacit form the assumption "that there was something unsatisfactory about the statement and it had better be rephrased."[9] Note too that the tacit inadequacy implied by interruption need not be a concern for *truth.* In fact, we have in effect bracketed our concern with truth in the very act of attending to the "tall tales" of the traveling poet or storyteller. What is striking about this in light of our category of natural discourse is that this interruptive question is itself a reminder of *contextuality*, a "where was I" question that helps to reconstitute the form and content of poetic as dialogic conversation. Conversational dialogue, in Havelock's account at least, began with the very first quizzical "Say what!?" Thus "the poetic dream, so to speak, was disrupted, and some unpleasant effort of calculative reflection was substituted."[10]

Ironically, this very opening for logos and the dialogic openness of conversation are viewed by the founders of critical theory as the beginning of a new sort of hegemony, of reason and calculative thinking generally. Regardless of the merits of this charge, it is helpful in the present context to explain, however metaphorically, both dialogue and dialectic as forms of social usurpation of solo performance, as breakage or displacement that takes place through logos whenever some other responds in genuine confusion or disingenuous skepticism to a monologue.

Of course, with this interference and the prospect of rephrasing something comes a practical choice. And it is rhetoric, that practical collaborative art of logos, that makes "the unpleasant effort of calculative thinking" a worldly possibility. As Havelock concluded from his own investigation of poetic, "The story of invention belongs properly to the sphere of *logos*, not *mythos*. It was set in motion by the prosaic quest for a non-poetic language and a non-Homeric definition of truth."[11] Today this quest is likely to seem more quixotic than prosaic to many. But despite the mythopoetic overtones of Havelock's recounting of origins, an important original partnership between dialogue and rhetoric has been posited. Moreover, it seems that the selfsame capacity to differentiate person from message has also made possible public reflection with others, in addition to expansion of the world of actional choices. There is the ominous allusion to calculative reflection, but let us (calculatively) defer this for the moment and turn instead to a further speculative suggestion as to the formal, synchronic relationships between dialogue and rhetoric as discursive practices.

Much of what we have been able to discover about rhetoric can be identified as acquired traits of language use, specifically the performative dimension of messages that thematize the conduct of interested others. Since rhetorical messages anticipate an audience response as part of their very meaning, they also lend themselves to a kind of refinement and conscientiousness that ordinary talk seems to preclude. Conversation, to paraphrase Gadamer, is something we "fall into" rather than choreograph from the outset.[12] And once involved in its web of associations and

demands, we are less leaders of it than led. Of course, one may be, like
Samuel Johnson, a witty, gifted raconteur, a conversationalist par excellence. But the fact remains that eloquence in conversation is realized in
the mastery of the moment—what the Greeks called kairos. In rhetoric,
which often begins with the urgency of the moment, eloquence moves
beyond wit to the virtue of propriety—what the Greeks called phronēsis.

We can summarize and simplify the differences between rhetoric and
conversation by allowing that one presents itself as monologic, partisan, and directed outward to the attention of others, who then judge its
quality; this is the performative dimension of rhetoric. The other appears
to be dialogic, bipartisan, and directed only to those in the immediate
encounter, who may appreciate, but never fully grasp, the holistic form
itself; this is the emergent dimension of conversation. Figure 1 shows the
respective zones of emergence and the interpretative horizons implied
by the intersecting discursive genres of conversation and rhetoric. It may
help to explain the ways in which these two practices interrelate and
inform each other. Initially, we are interested in what might be called
synchronic relationships. Although each genre of discourse, as actually
enacted, takes on its characteristic qualities as a succession of utterances
over time, we are interested, first, in characteristic junctures of intersection and complementarity for these forms as prototypes of discourse
practice—that is to say, irrespective of their temporal priority. Note also
that although there is considerable overlap in this diagram to account for
rhetorical and conversational interrelationships, both the presumed impetus and the anticipated direction for each mode of discourse practice
are quite different.

Conversation seems to emerge from the conventions and norms for
talk within the culture.[13] Normally, we talk with people who share our
ordinary life conventions; or we have to improvise ways of speaking
across such conventions. Moreover, conversation emerges, in almost all
cases, from conventional styles of language usage: rituals of greeting, acknowledgment, "small talk"—everything that Heidegger disparaged as
"idle chatter." How richly nuanced, disclosive, or individuated meaning
becomes depends entirely on subsequent talk. This is another way of
saying that conversation as a practice is not a static, monothetic, fully
assembled phenomenon. In a sense not fully conveyed by the diagram,
it gathers its own contributed resources as momentum, either to raise
questions or to answer them, to provoke or entice further contact, to
amuse or divert, or even to pass the time. This is the polythetic sense

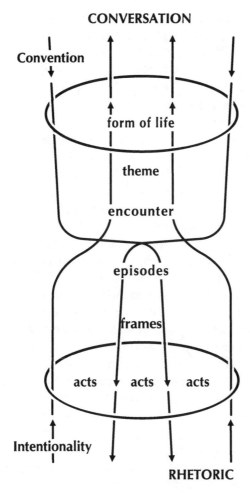

Figure 1. Conversation and rhetoric. This diagram, minus some directional flourishes added here, originally appeared in T. Farrell, "Aspects of Coherence in Conversation and Rhetoric," in *Conversational Coherence: Studies in Strategy and Form*, ed. R. Craig and K. Tracy. Copyright 1983 by Sage Press. Reprinted by permission of Sage Publications, Inc.

of a condensed, provisional dynamis, the localized teleology we find in every conversational episode.

And so, if it is not too grandiose a question, we ask about the destiny of conversation. For the most part, conversation is eminently perishable discourse, to be registered and forgotten almost as its fragments are generated. But then, as I think most of us can testify, there are the memorable exceptions, luminous moments of exchange, disclosure, or counsel that stay with us forever. Such conversations are instructively referred to as "memorable," even as one is recorded as such in the memorable film *My Dinner with André*.[14] Now and then a single conversation may have a decisive impact on one's life. When this happens, conversation not only leaves behind its conventional zone of emergence; it becomes an indelible part of that intentional consciousness known as memory.

By contrast, the impetus for rhetoric derives from intentional consciousness—the practical intent to shape discourse toward extrinsic goals. Such a construal of rhetoric is entirely consistent with the less flattering portraiture offered by idealist philosophy over the centuries. There is, to be sure, the sense of partisanship and wishful thinking that we have come to associate with purposeful rhetorical art. But this hardly exhausts the picture. We misunderstand rhetoric if we assume that it begins and ends as merely directive or manipulative discourse. The intentional consciousness precipitating rhetoric is not necessarily limited to that of the speaker. The social knowledge of an audience may be such as to invite or even require a discourse to meet its needs or aims, the urgent moment that may be captioned and completed only by appropriate words. And even where the intention of a would-be advocate provides an initial impetus for rhetoric, the transparency of contrivance and will is only the intrusive beginning of a much more subtle and complicated activity. In fact, rhetoric is able to accomplish its own dynamis and enact its optimal aims only if it is able to set initial intention and expectation aside so as to allow for preferable choices and judgments to be made. The essence of rhetoric's contribution to coherence, then, is a special mode of collaborative address and engagement with those very others whose needs and interests are also at stake. Indeed, our most emphatic sense of rhetoric emerges during those moments of urgency when choice can be deferred no longer and the cooperative regard for others is necessary, if meaningful conduct is to be possible. This is true whether we are trying to save the republic or salvage the evening.

When such moments arise, even the most forthcoming and reciprocally sensitized conversational partners must act outside the zone of immediately intelligible meaning in favor of the more opaque prospect of contingent and retrospective justification. So understood, the practical choices of rhetoric are redeemed extrinsically through the extenuation of circumstance. What, then, is the destiny of rhetorical discourse? Alone among discursive practices, rhetoric rests its fate and consequence not only on the experiences of the interactants, but on the mysterious accord of events as well. In a symmetrical counterpart to our diagrammed relationships, truly lasting rhetoric (rare enough, to be sure) abandons its initial horizon of intention entirely and becomes part of a culture's form of life, its ongoing conversation with history. Michael Walzer has observed:

> The shared understandings of a people, however, are often expressed in general concepts—in its historical ideals, its public rhetoric, its foundational texts, its ceremonies and rituals. It is not only what people do, but how they explain and justify what they do, the stories they tell, the principles they invoke, that constitute a moral culture. Because of this, cultures are open to the possibility of contradiction (between principles and practices) as well as to what Oakeshott calls "incoherence" (among everyday practices). And then it isn't always possible for interpretation to take the form that he prefers: a conversation, not an argument. [It is] right to insist that, "there is no mistake-proof apparatus by means of which we can elicit the intimations most worthwhile pursuing . . ." Indeed, there isn't; but that is not to say that the pursuit might not be (has not been) considerably more adventurous than he allows. And in the course of the adventure, conversations turn naturally into arguments.[15]

All I would add to round out this picture is that, in the course of the adventure, particularly eloquent arguments also turn naturally into conversation.

A second complex of differences follows from this initial distinction. There is a marked difference in the ways in which conversational and rhetorical discursive practices take on their respective characteristic directions. Even though figure 1 suggests that each conversation includes a potential rhetorical zone of emergence[16] (which involves reflective human agents), in practice conversations can appear to be virtually indeterminate in direction. At various junctures they may entail polite chatter, playful jest, embarrassing disclosure, task performance, advice and consent, philosophical dialogue, or relational confrontation. The reasons for this indeterminacy are varied. But they most assuredly derive from the almost random complexity of each party's personality, needs, competence, character, and even attention span. When these variable ingredients encounter one another, it is not surprising that prediction and control are early casualties. By at least recognizable contrast, rhetorical utterances usually have some end in view or destined point of resolution where we expect discourse to come to rest.

Accordingly, the sense of expectation and suspense in rhetoric has to do with both the manner of its actual unfolding—that is, how it gets where it is going—and the uncertainty of its impending denouement—that is, whether it will get where we suppose it to be going. This is a rather roundabout way of saying that conversation usually takes shape through an *emergent* sense of directionality, rhetorical discursive practice through a *foreordained* or *proposed* sense of directionality. This should not be taken to mean that rhetoric necessarily requires a *mis*leading or a withholding of intention. As we shall see, the very ordinance of rhetorical form requires a complex collaborative arrangement involving active participation with the audience.

Third among our preliminary contrasts between conversational and rhetorical discourse practices is the difficult matter of their respective boundary conditions. In earlier research, I have taken pains to establish that everything is *not* rhetorical.[17] From the preceding discussion it should be apparent that there are large chunks of the world that are not conversational either. What is fascinating is the inverted symmetry we find in relating each discursive practice's formal boundaries with the other's zone of emergence. Conversation, despite Gadamer's anthropomorphic characterization, never completely abandons the bounds of intentionality imposed and expected by each partner. We know this from the simple fact that meta-communicative utterances are always relevant, in principle, to any substantive phase of a conversation. Even if all participants are, to put it colloquially, on a roll, it is always possible to interject, "Wait a minute. . . . Time out! Back up. . . . There's something there I didn't quite get." While the question of intention never exhausts meaning, it remains readily available as a question. This is because, Gadamer notwithstanding, whatever spirit emerges within conversation would be impossible without the consciousness of the interactants.

For its part, rhetoric is always striving toward, but never beyond, the lifeworld yielded by cultural history generally. This very worldliness of rhetoric has been subjected to attack from the time of Socrates, through Kant, to that of Ricoeur and Habermas. Even in its most radical guises, the movement of rhetoric is always partisan and therefore *partial*, from the particular to the more general and holistic. It is also unavoidably immersed in the materials, experiences, and participatory norms of the given. Yet the practical limits which the world imposes on rhetorical advocacy in general are no greater than those imposed on any other ethically significant human courses of conduct. They are only more conspicuous, as when a candidate who is badly trailing in the opinion polls proclaims: "The people are responding to our message; they're on our side. The only poll that counts is the one on election day." More than most other forms of utterance, failed rhetoric does not leave its context quietly. It crashes and burns with the weight of the event, in full public light. But for all these embarrassments to rhetoric—its weak claim to pride—these same rhetorical characteristics offer an important inventional resource and reflective grounding for coherence in meaningful communication.

The differences between conversational and rhetorical discursive practices sketched so far are sufficiently pronounced to pose interesting questions about the coherence problems that each tends to encounter. We know, for instance, that the practice of intelligible, competent communication is largely (although not solely) a matter of acknowledging, following, violating, and sanctioning rules. Even the idiosyncratic departures from recognizable form in communication are communicative only insofar as they depart from some intelligible conventions. Yet, given the human origins and self-referential character of communicative conventions, it is not surprising that these stipulative constructs seem to defy the closure of our most elegant matrices. Some rules—for instance, the "third person reference" rule [18]—seem differentially prohibitive for cases of conversation and rhetoric, respectively. Still others—those governing turn taking, shifting topic, interrupting, and so forth—are applied and qualified in quite different ways in the practices of conversation and rhetoric. To complicate matters, there are times when the emergence of rhetoric in conversation poses severe, potentially irreparable coherence problems for the interactants. Yet at other junctures, virtually the same devices of rhetoric emerge in the nick of time, as it were, to retrieve and crystallize muddled sequences of informal discourse. In order to even begin to explain these curiosities, we turn now to the difficult problem of transformation, specifically when and why conversation begins to take on rhetorical features.

TOPOI FOR RHETORIC IN CONVERSATION

If we are to remain consistent with the synchronic features of discourse practices discussed so far, we should be able to locate junctures of tension or occasions within conversation where these characteristics of rhetoric might emerge. I would call these cases of premeditation, disturbance, and disputation, respectively:

(1) Premeditation: where the content and/or direction of a conversational sequence has been prepared in advance by at least one of
the interactants.

(2) Disturbance: where the definition or status of a developing conversational episode is contested, or at issue, such that the reflective practical choices of the conversants are invoked to determine
the outcome.

(3) Disputation: where the interactants openly disagree about some
practical matter outside the defined parameters of the conversational setting.

There is, of course, considerable overlap between the sorts of conditions envisioned by each type. But for our present purposes, what is most
important is that we suspend or sharply qualify our coherence expectations and our encounter conventions for many of these cases. There
is suggestive evidence that such tenuous junctures within conversation
offer inventional occasions for rhetoric.

Premeditation

To appreciate the rhetorical qualities of prepared discourse, we need attend only to the apparent discrepancy between its moment of origin
and its moment of expression. The great surrealist poet André Breton
once observed that the "speed of thought is not greater than the speed
of speech."[19] Far-fetched or not, this intuition may help to explain our
expectation of spontaneity in free-flowing conversation: the expectation
that thoughts will be triggered, formed, and articulated in the real-time
of an actual encounter. By recognizable contrast, discourse that has been
prepared in advance preempts this expected proximity of utterance formation and expression. In less formal conversational settings, at least,
we have a tendency to resist this sense of preparedness as manipulative.
Perhaps the corollary to Gadamer's mythos of falling into conversation
is that we feel inclined to alter our expectations whenever we sense that
we are being pushed.

To illustrate this clearly *rhetorical* variation, I pause to reconsider an
excerpt of real conversation that Frentz and I examined in our initial
language-action study. John Dean has just entered the Oval Office and is
addressing President Richard Nixon:

D: The reason I thought we ought to talk this morning is because, in our conversations, I have the impression that you

don't know everything I know and it makes it very difficult for
you to make judgments that only you can make on some of
these things and I thought that——

P: In other words, I have to know why you feel we shouldn't
unravel something?

D: Let me give you my overall first.

P: In other words, your judgment as to where it stands and where
it will go.

D: I think there is no doubt about the seriousness of the problem
we've got. We have a cancer within, close to the Presidency,
that is growing.[20]

In our first study of this passage we were intrigued with the implications
of Dean's remarks for the unraveling of an institutional form of life—
namely, that of the presidency. From the perspective of the presidential lifeworld, it is virtually impossible to read this passage closely and
not conclude that Nixon was well aware of the Watergate cover-up. Yet
it is also of interest as an illustration of premeditated discourse. Note
the way in which Dean imposes his own anticipated reasons and interpretations on the encounter. There is a reason why they are talking: "I
have the impression that you don't know" what you need to know, and
so forth. Dean has clearly thought this through in advance. Indeed, he
goes so far as to employ his own reading of previous conversations as
a contextual frame for the theme of the present encounter. But perhaps
most interesting, in light of our *interference* metaphor, is the fact that
the president twice tries and fails to interrupt this train of thought.[21]
Each time he tries to rephrase Dean's utterances so as to signal his (that
is, Nixon's) knowledge of what has transpired. Not just incidentally, this
clever bit of indirection would also relieve Dean of the need for any further unburdening. But in each case, he fails. Rhetoric, as initiated here,
seems to carry a temporary license not to be interrupted. And apparently
this relational convention is so strong that not even the president of the
United States is able to dislodge its force. The rhetorical features of what
I have called premeditated discourse find recognizable parallels in our
other two types of cases.

Disturbance

This second type arises when interactants are forced to attend to the
uncertain status or contested definition of their own accumulated con-

versational episodes. Perhaps there are unavoidable implications of the conversation for the real world of prospective action; or perhaps certain working assumptions of one of the interactants about the relationship are shown to be false. Perhaps a conversational turn has become, for some reason, painful or unsettling. But whatever the reasons, the status and defined meaning of the conversation themselves become contingencies, and "Where do we go from here?" becomes a practical question.[22] What is sometimes called a "still moment" of arrested momentum (the trope known as *ekphrasis*) then arises. As choice beckons, we abandon our equation of thought with spontaneous expression in favor of a more deliberative interpretative horizon: of proposal and attendance, of advocacy and complicitous other as audience. Here, for instance, is a telling exchange between H and S:

> *S:* Look, I just wish you would tell me what I've done wrong——I mean, you're so damned angry!
>
> *H:* Well, I'm not even sure I even remember one particular thing, what it was; it was everything; you just really pissed me off, that's all——Anyway, I don't want to keep going through it. . . . I'm——
>
> > *(interruption)*
>
> *S:* You're the one that keeps——
>
> > *(interruption)*
>
> *H:* I'm saying things I don't even mean. Look, ask me tomorrow ——I'm sorry, I just lost it there for a while.
>
> *S:* OK.

While not particularly elegant stylistically, the utterances in this episode have taken on a rhetorical burden that is not easily discharged. In fact, they place the conversation itself in an uncertain interpretative horizon. There is no explicit referent for "it," but unmistakably "it" is what has conjured forth this entire, apparently regrettable episode. In questioning his own capacity to say what he means, H is not only withdrawing one of the performative conditionals from the conversation; he seems to be proposing that a productive ambiguity be restored to the proceedings. And the implications stretch beyond this, suggesting that this entire episodic sequence be dropped or filed for indefinite future reference. S is thus no longer a spontaneous dialogue partner, but a potentially complicitous audience. In this capacity, S apparently assents to the proposal. Yet, as we will see later on, rhetorical content sometimes outlives the moment of its utterance. And even in this anxious episodic sequence, we might wonder whether "it" will return for another round of discussion.

This dimension of practical choice in rhetoric is not always limited to conventional implications for future, real-world conduct. Sometimes severe dislocation in levels of meaning or continuity of development force participants in dialogue to beat a hasty stylistic retreat, to withdraw as gracefully as circumstances allow. Again, a rhetoric of extrication (not pretty, just effective) seems called for. Here, for instance, is a case in which a relatively distant acquaintance has just disclosed a severe personal problem at length to an unsuspecting other party. After awkward silences and uncomfortable clichés of reassurance, the episode speeds to an ending:

> A: Well, look, I know everything's going to go a lot better for me now—just being able to, you know, talk this out with somebody makes me feel a lot better. I mean, I feel a lot more confident now.
>
> B: Er, ah, good, it helps I know to talk about these things, and I'm sorry I couldn't be more help, but . . .

Now it cannot be stated with assurance what has caused A to recover so promptly; but it may well have been an absence of indulgent reciprocity, with quick recovery as the best solution. The distanced version of reciprocity—"You've got your troubles; I've got mine"—is not totally satisfying as an explanation of this abrupt comic turn. But since the status of previous disclosure is clearly at issue in A's optimistic prognosis, I can only conclude that the practical choices of rhetoric are at work here, preserving conversational continuity and making room for the possibility of further choice. Rhetoric is, after all, a comic art.

Disputation

As the third type of rhetorical juncture within conversation, consider the disputational episodes that occasionally erupt within otherwise polite discourse. Here, for instance, is a facsimile of a late evening conversation:

> P: Well, it all really does sound wonderful and everything, but I have to say that these old world places get less and less at-

tractive when you actually think about living there. I mean, what you are is what your parents were, and that's it. And, as a woman, that just isn't enough for me. . . .

F: As a woman?

P: As a woman.

F: So it's better for you in the good old USA?

P: Yup, no question about it; I like the freedom.

F: Well, I just can't resist making this observation that years ago, when the women's movement was getting started, I said the problem is that this is just a bourgeois movement. I mean, once you get to wear a corporate white collar, you're just going to be another shill for the market economy.

S: Wait a minute! That's not fair. . . . P's just expressing satisfaction in what we've achieved. Women have helped liberate themselves. Blacks did it, the Irish even did it, for God's sake.

F: So, OK, jump all over me; I knew you would. All I'm saying is you're being narrow. One little victory and you're cheerleading for late capitalism. What about the poor, the single parents, *those* women? Plus, look, you're in public life now. That's what you wanted, so you can't hide. If you can't stand the heat . . .

(interruption)

S: I know, "If you can't stand the heat, get back in the kitchen."

(general laughter)

F: Alright, it was an unfortunate choice of words.

P: Admit it, she got you. You've just been skewered. . . .

F: OK, OK, I surrender. I mean, S is very witty . . . you know, for a girl."

(more laughter)

In the midst of all the bantering, a little debate has occurred, complete with disagreement, issues, punch lines, and even the defusion of timely humor. An odd sort of symmetry also characterizes this exchange, as the person first indicted, P, offers the final decisive verdict on F's position. And, as if to insure that there are no hard feelings, F concludes by parodying his own sexist position. As in the most developed rhetorical cultures, here the strength of a person's position is directly correlated with the skill of advocacy, one's ability to hold the floor.

In light of counterexamples like these, it is odd that we go to such lengths to avoid disputation within polite conversation. For years now, the ubiquitous Ms. Manners etiquette columnists have been counseling would-be interactants to always nod agreeably and try not to say anything contentious.[23] One is reminded of those pathological speech patterns wherein the patient always repeats the last word or phrase of the therapist's previous utterance. I would also hazard the speculation that the popularity of "trash-talk" and sensationalist panel discussion shows in recent years (Phil Donahue, Morton Downey, Jr., Geraldo Rivera) is that they fill a disputational void, picking up right where polite conversation leaves off.

For present purposes, the most important characteristic of disputational junctures in conversation is that they usually do not erode the coherence of discourse. In fact, when conversationalists begin to disagree *and* disagreements become heated, we begin to move toward all the rhetorical characteristics of our diagrammed continuum. We relax turn-taking rules. Whoever can hold the floor through eloquence, persuasive acumen, or just plain endurance tends to keep it, and extended episodic fragments are considered acceptable conduct for individual social actors. Something else happens with controversy in conversation in that, as each person says his or her piece, we begin to vary more freely the contexts and actions and even the times that are at issue. We vindicate our past pronouncements, tell stories in which the other is or was at fault, and defend ourselves through an improvised narrative that helps to apologize for or excuse our own lapses.

And something else: not unlike its technical definition, coherence is a quality worthy of appreciation in conversation only because of the constant prospect of interference. Any interactant at any time can destroy *any* conversation. Both conversation and rhetoric are collaborative arts. The very presupposition of intelligible form seems to require a benign conspiracy among interactants or else an act of faith. This is why the suspension of more immediate, short-term expectations (empathy or approval, for instance) forces us to reflect on form as an earned accomplishment. In keeping with scarcely recalled traditions, other more remote anticipations must be introduced. Perhaps as Dean sought to do with Nixon, each of us tries to "give you my overall first." We do not cease to collaborate, of course. We grant the extension and variation of urgency and accounting. But we also listen more critically, waiting for our opportunity to respond. We have slipped unobtrusively, but undeniably, into the mode of rhetoric.

THE RHETORIC OF CONVERSATIONAL COHERENCE

Our working assumption throughout this chapter has been that conversation and rhetoric are interdependent, but distinguishable, discursive practices. Despite the striking complementarity we have found within the emergence, interrelations, and transformations among these primary practices of discourse, the norms for appreciating rhetorical contributions to conversational coherence are not well understood. Moreover, the implications of such rhetorical contributions for appreciating responsible *public* or civic rhetorical conduct remain to be spelled out. As a prelude to this pivotal step in our argument, I now introduce several explanatory hypotheses relating the resources of rhetoric to the recurring coherence problems of conversation.

The fundamental paradox to be explained concerns the notoriously suspect qualities of rhetoric when these become conspicuous in conversational practice. Recall that Habermas's program of universal pragmatics attempted to universalize certain felicity conditions as *validity claims* for grounding the meaning of particular speech act utterances. The movement (which Habermas identifies with argumentation) is from the most localized level of speech acts to the largest horizon of lifeworld, or form of life, then back again. There is nothing in between.[24] And since rhetorical practice, as a rule, does not gain its credibility through the singularity of symbolic acts themselves—that is, commands, warnings, and so forth,—but rather through symbolic acts in some more complex anticipatory sequence, or even *acts in sequence juxtaposed to each other*, it is not surprising that the entire domain of rhetoric is usually found impoverished from such an abstract perspective.

Through the middle-range horizons of interpretation—that is, episode, encounter, and frame—made available by the language-action paradigm,[25] a quite different picture begins to emerge. For one thing, we can appreciate rhetorical junctures of premeditation, disturbance, and disputation on their own emergent level of understanding. For another, from the examples within ordinary discourse that we have considered so far, it is apparent that these actual locations of rhetoric are not necessarily inferior to, but simply different from, the ongoing give-and-take of conversation.

Finally, we should be able to demystify qualities of rhetorical competence accompanying the presence of rhetoric in such cases. When rhetoric "happens" to a conversation, we witness a transition from the relatively open, unguarded stance of a fellow conversationalist (which

Gadamer idealized) to the more judicial stance of a collaborative, reflective audience. Accompanying this difference in initial stance is a difference in the way we are now expected to attend to messages. Quite unlike the traditional speech act view (which Habermas universalized), audiences are not off to one side, making only binary judgments about speaker sincerity, comprehensibility, and so forth. The mode of reflection called forth by rhetoric's emergence tends to clash with such binary limitations, primarily because it is much more complex than these admit. Since we are now *addressed*, we must affiliate with an unfolding message that we are expected to complete, reflect on, and be held accountable for. We must think about this message, as it were, from a distance, in that we must be prepared to invent our own message about what is being said. Critical to this new stance that we are called upon to take is the fact that we are being addressed as more than a unique individuated self. We are being addressed as a representative other, as a provisional exemplar of how others *ought* to think. Even when we are disputing or differing with an other in conversation, this rhetorical complexity is evident. Either our own choices are appraised in terms of some larger categorical tendency (of character, relationship, or lifeworld), or we are addressed in such a way as to remove us from immediacy, so that we can think reflectively about other problems or issues. Shortly, we will examine the formal prototype of this reflective discourse; but first we will turn to the issue of normative grounding for conversational rhetoric.

Given that the emergence of rhetoric within conversation calls for a more complicated (but by no means inferior) mode of address and engagement, how are we to account for the apparent derogation of rhetoric as somehow marginal to optimal communicative practice? On a theoretical level, we have observed that one reason may be the ethereal qualities of the models themselves: Habermas's idealized conception of argumentation or Gadamer's notion of spirited conversation. Next to these admittedly otherworldly conceptualizations, the practical devices of rhetoric seem out of place: a carnival barker at a music recital. But it must be countered that even in the unfolding world of discourse practice, the uncovering of rhetoric within conversation may pose serious, even lethal coherence problems to an ongoing discourse. Here is a representative example:

S: Hello, Mr. Farrell?
F: Yes, it is.
S: And how are you today, Mr. Farrell?

F: Oh, I'm fine . . . and who might you be?

S: Oh, I'm fine too, Mr. Farrell. (*Apparent misconstrual*) Listen, I have just a couple of informational questions to ask you on energy, and I wonder if you'd be kind enough to help me out.

F: Well, I'm trying to watch the Bulls game and this is the third call I've——

S: This won't take a minute, Mr. Farrell. Then I'll let you get back to your game. . . . Do you know very much about energy conservation?

F: Well, actually I know quite a bit. . . . What sort are you referring to?

S: In the home. . . . For instance, Mr. Farrell, what would you say is the cheapest and safest form of energy for home use right now?

F: Gas, which we already have. Listen, you said this——

S: Wrong, Mr. Farrell. It's oil, oil-generated heating lamps, to be specific. They're cheap, they're safe, they're con——

F: Alright, what firm is this, what do you want?

S: Kerosan home heating lamps, Mr. Farrell. We'd just like to send you some——

F: Look, I'm sorry but I do business at the office, and you have been wasting both our times——

(*click*)

The episode sketched here may seem to have been ill fated from the beginning. The parties are not acquainted, and interruptions abound. Yet it continues after a fashion until the salesperson's avowedly rhetorical aim is detected. Each of us could cite instances among more or less familiar interactants in which discourse itself is a pretext, and displaying one's etchings is not the real aim of the conversational encounter. Yet the abrupt, unfinished, or hostile dislocation of discourse (all of which obviously strain our expectations of coherence) is not the only fate of emergent rhetoric. In *My Dinner with André,* as Thomas Frentz memorably demonstrated,[26] a morally compelling moment of forced choice is made available through what can only be described as the agency of rhetoric. Why the difference?

Without attempting to exhaust the synchronic possibilities for rhetoric in conversation, I will now introduce several interrelated suggestions for explaining the shifting normative status of this controversial art.

First, *it is the concealment of rhetoric that undermines its conver-*

sational legitimacy. In this sense, Habermas was partially correct in marginalizing so-called strategic discourse for withholding its intentions (thereby violating his sincerity condition). Where he went wrong was in assuming that such discourse needed to hide its intentions because of some intrinsically unsavory quality. There are times when hiding our rhetorical aims or shading over conspicuous differences among inter-actants (as in negotiation or highly ritualized exchange) is not suspect at all, but merely diplomatic. But this is because we are playing by the rules. That is why the phone call reported above collapses, while the elo-quence of André and Wally's conversation illuminates. It is also why we tolerate shameless dissembling and manipulation from, say, a real estate broker, but are unlikely to tolerate it from, say, a paramour.

Even though the disclosure of persuasive intent is rarely sufficient to persuade, it is very important to the legitimation of rhetoric. It may even be, from time to time, its own best definition of meaningful success. Even if I am unable to console you, you may be touched by the *sincerity* of my attempt. But, one may well ask, what of the concealed rhetoric that actually works in conversation—the successful seduction, the slick con job? In such cases, success of a sort has been achieved, but at con-siderable cost. Since only one of the would-be interactants can be said to have accomplished his or her aims, it is difficult to see how the pleasure of a fulfilling conversation can be reciprocal in such cases. This may be one reason why would-be Lotharios frequently brag of their conquests. What is lost, in our less than courtly era, is what Burke called "pure per-suasion,"[27] the willful pleasure of complicity. For this reason, a second hypothesis must be considered.

It appears that *rhetoric cannot operate effectively in conversation un-less there is an implied consensus from at least one of the parties to attend to unfolding discourse as an interested, collaborating audience.* In other words, rhetoric cannot operate effectively in conversational set-tings unless we let it. Now a generation of research has established that all intelligible conversation requires the assumption of certain back-ground understandings that are available to interactants.[28] What I am sug-gesting, however, is that a different order of more purposeful consensus, a *practical consciousness*, must be invoked if the inferential movement and episodic force of rhetoric is to play a constructive role in ongoing communication.[29] By consenting to the interpretative horizon offered by an advocate, the audience for rhetoric is asked to suspend (for the time being) its individuated intent in favor of a more reflective attitude based on potentially generalizable norms and conventions. In ongoing conversational practice, of course, it is usually easier to recognize the retraction of social knowledge premises than to attend consciously to their effective convergence. Yet, difficult or not, it is precisely this sense of convergence that now demands our attention.

Hence our third hypothesis is that *the working of rhetoric within conversational discourse helps us to formalize expectations about rhetoric's characteristic modes of reflection on the materials of civic life.* Put another way, there is no contradiction between regarding rhetoric as an audience-centered mode of discourse that employs ordinary conventions and appearances as its proofs and regarding this same practice as a reflective, critical, and even *inventional* art. We have already pointed to rhetoric's reflective capacity for cases of ordinary conversation. It remains to be seen whether this same dynamis is available to rhetorical practice when we examine it in its more familiar settings.

When there is deep suspicion of all things public, the transition from conversation to civic rhetoric is not automatic. So I will proceed cautiously in explaining how the use of a neglected coherence convention might help to expand the creative agenda for rhetorical practice. Then I will show how the practical reason of rhetoric, or its phronēsis, might allow civic discourse to move in a direction that is critical and inventional at the same time.

What complicates the aesthetic dimension of both conversation and rhetoric is their appearance and completion within real, experienced time. Although this fact is critical to the varying principles of coherent understanding in conversation and rhetoric, it has been neglected by most studies of natural discourse. The classic formulations of Paul Grice, for instance, offer background postulates of quantity, quality, relation, and manner that are alleged to be constitutive of meaning for all conversational discourse. Yet, helpful as these formulations are, there is no postulate that grasps the sequential emergence of conversation (and other natural discourse) over time. The closest we come to an acknowledgment of the temporal dimension is the statement by Grice "that there is some sort of understanding (which may be explicit, but which is often tacit) that, other things being equal, the transaction should continue in appropriate style unless both parties are agreeable that it should terminate."[30] This norm seems sensible enough on the face of it, until we search for counter examples to test its power. Then we are left with the analytic equivalent of a Yogi Berra maxim for when the game is over (answer: when it's over). A more serious omission perhaps is the developmental character of utterances in conversation: that they may disclose a truth, develop a theme, lead us beyond our initial understanding, and add to the collective enrichment of conversation itself. This is the aspect of communicative action best captured by the notion of *narrative.*

Simply put, the notion of *narrative implicature* presupposes that utterances within communicative episodes acquire some aspect of their meaning from the fact that they follow one another in time. This means that form in communicative action is understood to be more complex than the incremental sequencing of utterances, each of which is appropriate in some fashion to what comes immediately before. In common practice, we frequently leave the immediacy of act and response (for example, "How are you?"—"Fine") for reminders, promises, and delayed reactions. More important, perhaps, we assume that prolonged encounters with one another will deepen our mutual understanding over time. The postulate of *narrative implicature* suggests this.

Three more specific clauses may now be spelled out as we attempt to differentiate narrativity in rhetoric and conversation; these are clauses of *continuity, cumulation,* and *culmination.*[31] In general, they may be said to guide what discourse is about (a *subject* dimension), how communication develops (a *process* dimension), and how utterances situate and constrain subsequent conduct among interactants (an *action* dimension). Although conversation and rhetoric each feature some variation of the continuity, cumulation, and culmination clauses, their specific uses and inflections of these clauses are typically quite different. To appreciate these differences, however, we must briefly allude to the sorts of expectations captured by our postulates.

Beginning with the norm of *continuity,* we postulate that participants will maintain the range of temporal reference established by preceding utterances. This could be things in general, the here and now, the future, the past, and relationships among them. We shift levels of signification only with due notice and tacit consent. Equally important is the informal expectation that communication is somehow additive in significance over time, that it *accumulates* meanings and nuances from prior utterances. Of course, this doesn't always happen. We have all participated in conversations that go nowhere and try to avoid topics where there is no learning curve. Such mutual evasion brings us to the metacommunicative ("Well, then, this has been very helpful") and recognizably *rhetorical* pole of our continuum. And finally, critical to natural discourse, is what I take to be the actional component of *culmination*. Unless the "house rules" dictate otherwise (the nonsense world of *Alice in Wonderland*,[32] for instance), we take seriously what is said during the real time of communicative episodes. Again, I refer not to some abstract, universalizable condition of truth, but to the more practical, even negotiable, matter of *plausibility*. More is at stake here than the truthfulness of communicators. When we make promises, issue warnings, offer polite commands, even ask and answer questions, we create fragile bonds of affiliation that form and reflect our interpersonal character. The way we do this must strike the casual onlooker as odd; for to one overhearing it, face-to-face talk must appear discontinuous and fragmentary, a sort of verbal chaos. This should not surprise us; for without some sense of narrative continuity, cumulation, and culmination, casual observation would probably have the last word on this subject. Although there are no doubt more exceptions than may be accommodated even in a project of this scope, I want now to illustrate some variations in the narrative postulate for a generic understanding of conversation and rhetoric.

Although both conversation and rhetoric occur within the natural unfolding of *encounter* time (the ongoing life history of communicators), one of these communicative forms is typically shaped through some mode of premeditation. We also concede rhetoric's popular understanding as disputational, positional, instrumental in its aims, presumptuous in its methods, and so forth. This concession is made because the variation in use of our narrative postulate is based entirely on this (somewhat caricatured) popular understanding.

In contrast to rhetoric, conversation tends to be focused on the immediacy of its utterances. Most of the time, we are simply saying to each other what we are thinking at the time. *In general, then, the narrative expectancy of conversation moves horizontally through encounter time, rather than hierarchically through levels of significance.* Despite numerous exceptions (such as Socratic dialogue and André's dinner) most of the time, in most encounters, the principle of continuity requires only that we attend continuously to the subject of an episode until the subject is exhausted and thus shifted (with implied consent). In any conversation, there will be peaks and valleys and a general growth of knowledge, disclosure, and even relationship through a discontinuous range of topics.

For rhetoric, the separation of the time of thought from the time of expression has critical implications for the use of narrative. This distance, or durational lapse, requires *first* that continuity be an explicit aesthetic responsibility of the advocate or speaker. In the prototype of public speech, there is usually direct reference to the shared context of audience and speaker, the social knowledge of lifeworld norms and values, and even the commitments inherited from previous speech acts publicly performed. The rhetorical qualities of style are thus narrative markers for the continuity of social experience. *Unlike conversation, rhetorical discourse is expected to deepen hierarchically as it moves through introduction, preview, body, and conclusion.*

This initial attribute of continuity allows us to mark off further critical differences between the conversational and rhetorical expectations of narrative—namely, in the clauses of cumulation and culmination. Where cumulation is concerned, informal conversation typically brackets worldly constraints in the interests of dialogue. It is transitory, indefinite, and usually—apologies to Mr. Berra—over when it's over; that is, it is no more lasting than the time it is helping to pass. *This means that the developmental quality of conversation is internal to the duration of the episodes themselves.* Unless otherwise specified, for informal conversation, cumulative development extends beyond the episode only for the relationship, not for the cognitive significance of utterances themselves. Now if I underscore a commitment, a promise, or a warning to you, there may well be implications for future encounters—a topic to be avoided, a proposal to be remembered, perhaps even a relationship to be ended. But these special occasions appear to be striking *rhetorical* exceptions—perhaps of the sort that help to prove the rule. To the extent that the conversation itself is a means to other, extrinsic ends (whether those of task, disclosure, seduction, or cure), it is not the informal type of discourse described earlier.

The contrast is instructive. Rhetoric is a discourse that develops processually in the direction of something beyond itself. The outcome is always outside the momentary utterance of discourse itself. This fact is critical for an understanding of the peculiar narrative development of rhetorical address. In our conversational guises (premeditation, disputation) the narrative movement takes us *outward*, toward some further end.[33] But this narrative trait is even more conspicuous in the case of public advocacy. The principle touchstones of rhetoric, discourses that have been, as it were, removed from history, are developmental sequences in a larger narrative. Lincoln's second inaugural address is more than a marker in his own biography of eloquence. It is a still unfinished call to bind up the nation's wounds. In fact, *every instance of public advocacy*

*cumulates in an external direction, beyond the initial historical mo-
ment of its occurrence.* This mysterious tendency of eloquence to deepen
its range of meaning with the passage of time will be discussed shortly.
For now it introduces the most important application of narrative to
ordinary discourse: the postulate of culmination.

The most obvious cases of accounting in ordinary informal conversation involve violations of rules. Usually these are acknowledged and re-
paired within the ongoing episode; for example, "Will you stop referring
to your Dad in the third person, like he's not here? He's here, y'know."
"I know. Sorry." Allowing for variations in temperament, it is still worth
asking why this is the case. One possible explanation is that the actional
dimension of conversational choice is always rooted in the present tense.
To go back over choices that have already been made (that cannot be un-
done) is irrelevant and may even be thought to be mean-spirited. Another
possibility is that conversation is an emergent by-product of multiple
interactants and creative choices. Barring pathologies, the precise mix is
unlikely to recur in exactly the same utterances.

My point becomes clearer when we reflect on the exceptional cases of
utterances whose episodic force transcends the immediate occasion of
their expression. Consider, for instance, the blurred rhetorical distance
between promise and threat: "Look, I'm not going to do anything now,
pal. Life's a long time. But some time, a long time from now, something horrible's going to happen to you. And when it does, that'll be me
smiling." Our Jimmy Cagney parody underscores an important point. By
undertaking obligations in the presence of others or forecasting an impending series of events, the conversational actor binds personal choice
to social facts that transcend the half-life of an episode. Promises, warnings, commands, and so forth are each unexceptional cases of *rhetorical*
conduct.

*In striking contrast to most instances of ordinary conversation, then,
rhetorical advocacy is held to a principle of narrative accounting across
episodes.* In return for this grant of premeditative authority (originally a
right of *author*ship), the audiences of public rhetoric impose the counterfactual expectation that advocates at least appear to keep public promises and heed their own commands and public warnings. In practice,
of course, there are few instances of public discourse that could withstand this narrative expectation. Social circumstances shift. In politics,
we quickly discover, appearances are reality. And rhetoric, above all, is
about chance and circumstance, about learning in public. The problem

is that, without some such counterfactual sense of cultural memory and an expectation of narrative accountability, it would be impossible to take any rhetorical utterances seriously. We may be near to such a cultural situation; but in my view, we have not actually arrived. We ask again: May rhetoric be liberating?

ENTHYMEMATIC REFLECTION AS RHETORICAL INVENTION

I have sought in these pages to reposition rhetorical practice so that it may be seen as more than the residue of some purer discursive form and as having promise for the future. My avenue for doing this has been the traditional association of rhetoric and conversation as forms of natural discourse. We have found that the complementary relationships between these practices suggest important contributions that each may make to the problem of coherence in discourse. We have also been able to elicit a certain normative expectation for the disclosure and legitimation of rhetoric within discourse practice through the warranted consensus of the interacting parties themselves. Most important, we have found within the coherence expectations for rhetoric a capacity for free variation over the range of interpretative horizons: act, episode, encounter, and form of life. Within this free variation—through the imposition of theme, frame, relation, duration, and act—we find a discourse of considerable normative moment and power. This rhetoric may become ritual (rich or hollow); or it may—and does—break all the ceremonial rules. Exceptional rhetoric marks its actual time in the duration of memory, even as its words anticipate and enhance the destiny of others.

What remains is to show how the formal technai of rhetoric may be able to generate new dimensions of practical consciousness while working within the received opinions, appearances, and conventions of everyday life. This inventional process, which may be glimpsed within our earlier conversational setting, typically involves an intersection between the rhetorical speaker's suggested interpretative horizon and the audience's received opinions, cultural norms, or encounter conventions and rules. Given the capacity of rhetoric to range over previous utterance episodes for its topics, themes, and proofs, it is possible for a kind of practical wisdom, or phronēsis, to emerge in this sudden joining of otherwise distinct perspectives and horizons. The movement, I need hardly add, is both topical and enthymematic. This follows directly from our intuition that rhetorical form is inherently composed of more than the singular speech act type. More than this, rhetorical utterances are only comprehensible *at all* when they extend elliptically to become part of unfinished episodes, thereby allowing the inferences of others to become constitutive of meaning.

I now wish to suggest that rhetoric, despite its traditional and quite justifiable association with the preservation of cultural truisms, may also perform an act of *critical interruption* where the taken-for-granted practices of a culture are concerned. Not unlike the reflective act of logos in Havelock's original conception, the phenomenon of rhetorical interruption juxtaposes the assumptions, norms, and practices of a people so as to prompt a reappraisal of where they are culturally, what they are doing, and where they are going. If we can succeed in this, then it follows that rhetoric has the potential and the promise of using these same ordinary conventions to forge a meaningful reflective consciousness in civic life. The following are some unlikely exemplars.

Jesse Jackson

In 1988, the Reverend Jesse Jackson became the first black American to have his name placed in nomination for the presidency of the United States. Moreover, Jackson finished the presidential primaries with more votes and more primary victories than anyone except the eventual Democratic party nominee. Many observers from the mainstream American press speculated about the source of Jackson's remarkable burst of rhetorical dynamis. Undeniably he was, and is, a powerful speaker. In an anti-rhetorical era in which audiences purportedly flee from advocacy, the television viewership increased continually the longer Jackson spoke. But if there were still doubts concerning his eloquence and its power, they were swept away by his historic "Common Ground" address to the Democratic convention in 1988.[34] There, before a mainstream audience of convention delegates and one of the largest viewing audiences in recent history, Jackson intoned this memorable passage:

> They work hard every day. I know. I live among them. I'm one of them. . . . They catch the early bus. They work every day. They raise other people's children. They work every day. They clean the streets.

They work every day. They drive vans and cabs. They work every day. They change the beds you slept in at these hotels last night and can't get a union contract. They work every day.

No more. They're not lazy. Someone must defend them because it's right, and they cannot speak for themselves. They work in hospitals. I know they do. They wipe the bodies of those who are sick with fever and pain. They empty their bedpans. They clean out their commodes. No job is beneath them, and yet when they get sick they cannot lie in the bed they made up every day.

America, that is not right.[35]

Inevitably, members of the audience increased their audible participation in this message, from murmurs of assent to an active voicing of the refrain. And what does this repetition and antithesis tell us? It is an unusually depictive figure of thought, a refutative enthymeme animating appearances from the margins of society. The invisible, voiceless people, those we scarcely nod to in the hall, are here "witnessed" (in Jackson's own words). We will return to this theme. But what is being refuted? The reprocessed Social Darwinist dream of late capitalist America. Recall Herbert Spencer's version of the enthymeme (see chap. 2). All premises stated, it scanned thus: Free enterprise encourages hard work. Hard work leads to success. Success=Justice. Usually all the premises are not stated, of course. As in most unexamined dogma, they do not need to be stated. This is the theme of the Protestant ethic, of every Horatio Alger novel, and of most Hollywood history. And lest we forget, it was the theme of Ronald Reagan's "Morning in America" mythology.[36] What made the myth powerful was that even the poor tended to believe it. For much of the twentieth century, for better or worse, this bit of folk wisdom was part of America's social knowledge. This is what Jackson set out to refute. How?

First, by presenting a rarely examined world of counter-appearances. Not only does the repetition counter the myth that the poor are lazy and don't want to work; it is punctuated by a recurring arrested temporal development—that still they are poor and, most memorably, that they are denied satisfaction of the minimal, menial needs they minister to in others. How is this validated? Through the audience's own verbalized assent, through its very presence, and second, by presenting these menial, usually invisible acts of servitude within a public forum and linking them to the agent as victim. Juxtaposed as they are—the menial service and the denial of need—the depiction of these appearances becomes deeply ironic: to change the sheets of a hospital bed one can't afford to sleep in. When the irony of acts is replayed as public policy, the weight of blame deepens accordingly. Now we have the most serious charge of all: hypocrisy. We are shown to have framed and inculcated a myth we had no intention of living by.

But now I am shifting voices, which brings me to the most powerful rhetorical feature of this discourse. Notice that the "they" of the audience *expressed* does not include the full audience that is *addressed*. It is *we*, Jackson included, who work every day. It is *you* we work for. This is the first political campaign discourse in many years that has spoken from outside the margins of the political culture without ever abandoning the voice and strategy of direct address.

Over a generation earlier, a right-wing nativist by the name of George Wallace mounted a protest campaign for the presidency in both 1968 and 1972. He spoke for some of the disempowered poor whites in rural America. *But*—and this difference is critical—even Wallace used the recurrent stump speech theme "Send *them* a message." For those who considered the Jackson message too volatile, even inflammatory, I have one cautionary note. No one who speaks to you directly has abandoned hope.

Jackson has a powerful message for poor whites as well: "When they take away your farm, and take away your land, they turn the lights out. And all of us look just alike in the dark when the lights go out." Now we are in the much more conventional, polar terms of "we" and "they." But note that Jackson and his largely black constituency have now joined "you," literally to become "we." "When a child screams, it does not cry in black or white. That child cries in pain."[37] None of these figurative inferences are possible without an acknowledgment of previous episodes: episodes of hard, pointless work, loss of treasured possessions, racial scapegoating and division. And in each case the insight that is generated is of an entirely practical order, based on a felicitous conjunction of truths and norms (social justice, fairness, the right of ownership, the universality of suffering) that we all can be said to accept.

It is the disturbance and displacement of continuity in the realization of these norms that creates a moment of *interruption*. With participatory figures like these, Jackson was able to recapture a power of identification outside the mainstream pieties of normal politics. This is rhetorical argument as invention, refiguring the channels and avenues of civic participation.

Betty Friedan

Despite the failure to pass the Equal Rights Amendment and the still volatile question of abortion rights, there has been no more successful movement in twentieth-century America than the feminist movement. The transition from the patronizing lip service of a cold war commercial culture to a visible presence in almost all major occupations and professions has been accomplished in less than three decades, in one of the most conservative political climates imaginable. The achievements of the women's movement would not have been possible, of course, without heroic struggle and sacrifices by a great many persons. But it was one singularly powerful rhetorical document that exposed the hypocrisy and contradictions within America's cultural landscape and invented a rhetorical language of sufficient power and normative resonance to generate a liberating alternative. I refer to Betty Friedan's brilliant work *The Feminine Mystique*.[38]

To appreciate the inventional power of this work, recall that the entire cumulative chorus of social science, education, commercial advertising, political leadership, and journalism was once unanimously opposed to a public participatory role for women.[39] No less a liberal icon than Adlai Stevenson, confidant of Eleanor Roosevelt, counseled graduating college seniors that their most noble and precious contribution to civic life was "in the living room with a baby in your lap or in the kitchen with a can opener in your hand."[40] To the extent that women's voices were allowed to be heard at all, they became (like that of Margaret Mead) part of the chorus. It seems unimaginable that any countervailing argument could be invented from received opinion in such a repressed, undifferentiated condition.

Therein lies the genius of Friedan's rhetorical invention. As a psychologist and mother of three children, Friedan realized, I suspect, that theory would be unconvincing, testimony from experts impossible to find, and academic argument easy to ignore. The only way to bring such a vast, silenced problem to light was through the voices and experiences of its victims. Her first compelling chapter openly acknowledges her lack of conventional rhetorical resources in its title, "The Problem that Has no Name."

The problem lay buried, unspoken, for many years in the minds of American women. It was a strange stirring, a sense of dissatisfaction, a yearning that women suffered in the middle of the twentieth century in the United States. Each suburban wife suffered with it alone. As she made the beds, shopped for groceries, matched slipcover material, ate peanut butter sandwiches with her children, chauffeured Cub Scouts and Brownies, lay beside her husband at night—she was afraid to ask even of herself the silent question—"Is this all?" For over fifteen years there was no word of this yearning in the millions of words written about women, for women, in all the columns, books, and articles by experts telling women their role was to seek fulfillment as wives and mothers. Over and over women heard in voices of tradition and of Freudian sophistication that they could desire no greater destiny than to glory in their own femininity.[41]

With this powerful opening, Friedan serves notice that this book will be a quest for the name that is missing, an attempt to put into words what all this endless stream of words has failed to express. But in the absence of supporting cultural resources, even the most sympathetic reader must wonder how such expression can be rendered in a convincing manner.

Friedan employs a remarkable combination of strategies to implicate the reader in her unfolding argument. Her primary mode of proof is a cumulation of first-person testimonials from women themselves. Continually framed in opposition to the gleaming billboards of popular culture ("If I have only one life, let me live it as a blonde"[42]), these personal narratives become cumulatively overpowering, *precisely because the narrator lacks the name, the words to explain her real condition.* Here is a typical instance:

I ask myself why I'm so dissatisfied. I've got my health, fine children, a lovely new home, enough money. My husband has a real future as an electronics engineer. He doesn't have any of these feelings. He says maybe I need a vacation, let's go to New York for a weekend. But that isn't it. I always had this idea we should do everything together. I can't sit down and read a book alone. If the children are napping and I have one hour to myself I just walk through the house waiting for them to wake up. I don't make a move until I know where the rest of the crowd is going. It's as if ever since you were a little girl, there's always been somebody or something that will take care of your life: your parents, or college, or falling in love, or having a child, or moving to a new house. Then you wake up one morning and there's nothing to look forward to.[43]

These stories are so affecting because they are disingenuous attempts to reflect on the lifeworld, but without a fully developed vocabulary with which to do so. It remains the nameless problem. Note that these stories also present us with a repetition of recognizable ordinary life episodes from past and present; yet the stories manage to interrupt even their own episodic progression by constantly expressing dissatisfaction with the absence of meaning. Thus we find ourselves identifying and participating in a most familiar way.

But for all this, something else remains nameless; and that is the secret of their normative power. Friedan's dissection of mass culture is still, almost thirty years later, something to behold. She discovers that the women's magazines of the fifties and beyond include a new genre as a staple: namely, confined victims (the handicapped, the deaf, the blind, and the physically maimed). She writes: "Does it say something about the new housewife readers that, as any editor can testify, they can identify completely with the victims?"[44] All this is illuminating, even if more than a little nauseating. But in the shadow of this deadening neglect, how was Friedan able to move us from pity to outrage, to gain the moral upper hand? After all, a lack of satisfaction with the cherished world of mom, apple pie, and the girl next door, the Barbie doll world of domesticity, is hardly the sort of thing that can be decided by a show of hands. Taboos remain powerful, and perhaps no infraction is more disturbing than the hint that Donna Reed was secretly unhappy.

For all its notoriety and reputed subversion of the sacrosanct, I believe that the secret to The Feminine Mystique's rhetorical power is the complete and utter ordinariness of its normative conventions. When a woman is reported to have had a nervous breakdown upon discovering that she can not breastfeed her baby, when terminal cancer patients refuse a drug that might have saved their lives because its side effects are said to be unfeminine, one does not have to be Abraham Maslow to realize that our priority of needs has become seriously and shamefully disturbed.[45] In more traditional terms, what is it that this culture of domestic compliance denies to women? Let us start with autonomy, the freedom to choose, an equal voice, a directed life, and the pursuit of happiness. One can open any page of this text and find them. These are the norms which are so subversive of contemporary culture: the same enlightenment norms which purport to be the foundation of contemporary culture.[46] This use of cultural conventions *against* prevailing practice also suggests a developmental view of reform. Friedan offers her critique not as a denial of this repressive culture, but as an unfinished promise for the redemption of its better impulses. She writes:

> Who knows what women can be when they are finally free to become themselves? Who knows what women's intelligence will contribute when it can be nourished without denying love? Who knows of the possibilities of love when men and women share not only children, home and garden, not only the fulfillment of their biological roles, but the responsibilities and passions of the work that creates the human future and the full human knowledge of who they are? It has barely begun, the search of women for themselves. But the time is at hand when the voices of the feminine mystique can no longer drown out the inner voice that is driving women on to become complete.[47]

Ironically enough, this revolutionary text is also one of the great works of modernity.

Why "ironically," one might ask. Because the legacy of this work is far from clear. On the one hand, *The Feminine Mystique* has been the occasion of persistent, forceful consciousness raising and a movement for liberation that has permanently altered the political landscape. Among those who were most moved and charged by the original discourse, the moment of first encounter is still memorable. An excellent description of how such consciousness raising expands a rhetorical awareness of previous episodes and encounters is offered by Vivian Gornick: "We saw our inner lives being permanently marked by the words we spoke. We were changing before each other's eyes, taking our own ideas seriously, becoming other than we had been. *We were, in fact, reincarnating as the feminists of previous generations, although what this actually meant was understood only slowly and perfectly. I remember reading Elizabeth Cady Stanton and feeling amazed that a hundred years ago she had said exactly what I was now saying. Amazed, and gratified.*"[48] On the other hand, this new feminist consciousness, of which Friedan could only dream, is also experienced as an insightful convergence of interpretative horizons. Only this time the horizons are removed from immediacy and are so vast as to dwarf the petty barriers of time and place. These horizons, which swallow up the details of particularity, also connect Stanton to Gornick, past to future.

But of this future? As I suggested, it is unclear. Some adherents of contemporary feminism have rejected much of the vocabulary and tradition of emancipatory discourse (the very discourse that supplies Friedan's background verities) as logocentric and a male-dominated charade. There is also a recognizably indulgent quality to at least some features of this new autonomy.[49] Yet there are other signs, so subtle as to be over-looked in many quarters, which seem to point in a different direction. On 9 March 1989 the Congress of the United States rejected President Bush's nominee for the post of Secretary of Defense, John Tower. This was the first time a presidential cabinet nomination had been rejected in thirty years. Only one Republican voted against the nomination: a woman from Kansas, Nancy Kassebaum. In Kassebaum's fine, heartfelt speech explaining her decision, she noted a number of reservations about Tower. But here is what I judge to be the strongest: "If we are going to have a strong defense force which consists of both men and women, we are going to have to insure fairness. I am not confident that Senator Tower would give these issues the priority they demand or would dem-onstrate the necessary sensitivity to their seriousness."[50] One example does not make for sweeping conclusions. But it is interesting that the commentators who even noticed her speech, applauded Senator Kasse-baum for her courage. Nowhere was she challenged about her motives. This instance of public rhetoric, which would have been utterly unin-telligible in the years prior to *The Feminine Mystique,* is one small bit of evidence that feminism is quietly entering the accepted conventions of social knowledge.

So far we have examined two extended excerpts of rhetorical discourse in an attempt to illustrate their reflective and inventional qualities. It is undeniable that each of our cases is also *critical* and is rooted in a dissonance within the ongoing practices of the culture. Even in their overt critique, however, there is an unmistakable convergence between the particularities under discussion (working every day, daily domestic routines) and the larger horizon of implied norms which inform a flour-ishing (or an unfulfilling) lifeworld. We should also note the instructive contrast between the sorts of inferences called forth in each example. Since the plight of women has not yet been named ("the personal has not yet become political"), this plight, like the women themselves, must be outside the participatory arenas of civic life. For this reason, all that may be cumulated are recurring instances of conduct from private life. It can be only in their cumulative weight and in their utter absence of an articulate political dimension that a genuine grievance is constituted in the first place.

One social grouping has the appearance of success, but without fulfillment. The other lacks even the preliminary promise. And the implied judgment that each must be restored to a more *proper* positioning within the human community literally and figuratively could not be made without our reliance on still vital social knowledge convictions.

We are left, however, with an interesting problem. These convictions are surely not constant or universal. In some ages and episodes of history they may be vibrant and effective, only to atrophy and disappear over time. Then, too, they may be suppressed or perverted. Granted that at least a normative *potential* for a sense of reason and civic virtue is embedded in rhetorical traditions, as well as rhetoric's ongoing reflective relationship with conversation, what do we do about the many cases in which our most cherished cultural norms are at odds with political life itself, where they are refused the simple prospect of civic expression? Put another way, is it possible—as Arendt once hoped[51]—for the very articulation of a culture's doxa, its general opinion, to become constitutive of an affirmative public moment?

Václav Havel

An honest answer to the preceding question would have to be: not very often. Rhetoric *alone* is rarely, if ever, sufficiently powerful to overturn obstinate hegemonic arrangements. And if, occasionally, a Mandela or a Sakharov emerges from custody to speak grave truths, it is usually through the fortuitous tactical arrangements of others. This is not to underestimate the power of the rhetoric which emerges or its importance for the rebirth of public life. Now and again the ineffable qualities of insight and the occasional demands for utterance are gathered together in one luminous moment.[52] What appears in retrospect to have been obvious all along presents and individuates itself at the time as something rather extraordinary. We call this phenomenon of presentation and individuation *eloquence*.

To explain the workings of eloquence is a somewhat portentous undertaking. Eloquence is less a specific genre of speech than a recognizable honorific quality—moreover, less an observed quality than a felt, received sense of being addressed in a certain way. Based on our preceding analysis, we might hazard the hypothesis that the inventional power of eloquent rhetoric derives from its ability to subsume particulars within themes and frames of larger generality.[53] The symmetries of our earlier genre contrast may be of some assistance here. Conversation is largely rooted in, and ruled by, the predictable conventions of a common life-world. To the extent that it admits of inventional departures, these are likely to emerge through highly individualistic, local differentiations. Rhetoric works in exactly the opposite direction: it begins in the realm of immediacy and local constraint and, albeit rarely, works its way into a more general sphere of thought, meaning, and reflection. Paradoxically, rhetoric which stays local, particularistic, and immediate in its range is likely to do little to inculcate the meanings of its time. It is the equivalent of conversation that never strays beyond the conventions of politeness. Great rhetoric, on the other hand, finds an imaginative way to individuate breadth of vision within the recognizable particularities of appearance. Of course, the difference between a spacious rhetoric of eloquence and an overblown rhetoric of bombast is never as transparent as one would like. I suspect that the moment of truth in the best rhetoric comes when *a larger vision is wedded clearly to both the critical judgment and the ordinary convictions of others, all at the same time.* In my view, Václav Havel's speech to the Czech people was such an address. As Lewis Lapham writes: "More than anything else, we have need of a believable story, because without a believable story we have no means of connecting the past to the present, the dead to the living, the citizen to the state."[54]

The story surrounding Václav Havel's emergence as president of his native Czechoslovakia is, even in retrospect, so remarkable as to strain credulity.[55] A self-effacing playwright, imprisoned dissident, and avant-garde intellectual (with a fondness for rock and roll), Havel was by most accounts reluctant to assume leadership of even the improvised oppositional group he helped found, the Civic Forum. Then, after years of political subjugation and enforced confinement, he was pushed into the public arena with the sudden, sweeping opposition to the Czech Communist party. Asked to be a candidate for the presidency on the Civic Forum platform, he reluctantly agreed and was unanimously elected. It is unlikely that any of his fictionalized characters ever played a more improbable role than the one he was about to perform.[56] Once a witness to this moment of transformational history, he was now to enact its central interpretative part. And Havel, something of a novice in the actual *making* of speeches, had to come up with something to say. What?

The most serious rhetorical problem facing the Czech populace was an absence of any participatory public *sense.* Following the brief flurry of amicable resistance in the extraordinary year 1968, there had been a brutal suppression and an attitude toward power that bordered on cynical resignation. Observers wrote that sausages and beer were all it took to control the Czech citizenry. Expatriate writers such as Kundera have documented, perhaps with an excess of enthusiasm, the tendency of all relationships and institutions to corrupt themselves by following the path of least resistance.[57] One speech, even that of a civic hero, would be unlikely to dispel such an unfortunate legacy. At its best, it might interrupt this tyranny of convenience. That is what Havel set out to do.

In his startling opening remarks, Havel distanced himself from the entire recent history of ritual utterances: "For forty years you have heard on this day from the mouths of my predecessors, in a number of variations, the same thing: how our country is flourishing, how many more millions of tons of steel we have produced, how we are all happy, how we believe in our Government and what beautiful prospects are opening ahead of us. I assume that you have not named me to this office so that I, too, should lie to you."

The reversal is aptly prefigured by Havel's own ironic recitation, and even this by the depersonalized mouths which (interchangeably, it seems) speak *at us:* the tons of steel buttressed by eudaimonia and happiness, a farcical escalation of hyperbole that is bound to be cut short. As we supply the premise to Havel's innuendo (that they have all lied), we link in our thoughts the democratic selection of Havel and the restoration of an occasion for speaking the truth. In such a moment of ēthos, some harsh truths follow immediately: "Our country is not flourishing. The great creative and spiritual potential of our nation is not being applied meaningfully. Entire branches of industry are producing things for which there is no demand while we are short of things we need." It is customary, even in a democracy, to blame the old regime for all manner of calamity. Havel reinvests this convention with meaning, by blaming the *hypocrisy* of the state for defects not only of policy, but of *character* as well. In simple but haunting language, he details a legacy of exploitation and neglect: "The state, which calls itself a state of workers, is humiliating and exploiting them instead. Our outmoded economy wastes energy, which we have in short supply. The country, which could once be proud of the education of its people, is spending so little on education that today, in that respect, we rank 72d in the world."

And it continues. Interestingly, it moves from "The country" to "We." "*We* have spoiled our land, rivers and forests, inherited from *our* ancestors, and *we* have, today, the worst environment in the whole of Europe.

Adults die here earlier. . ." This passage, to which I have added emphasis, offers a subtle foreshadowing of what is to be a central thematic movement in the discourse: from outside to inside, external world to inner resources, *it* to *us*. The object of the speech is to gather our inner resources, through the recognition and witnessing of others, to convert and disclose the self as political, as a public character once again. This speech, like the very best eloquence, speaks to the eyes and the heart simultaneously.

The body of the speech enacts a classic Burkean pattern of guilt, sacrifice, and purification, even as it resonates with enthymemes of recognition:

> The worst of it is that we live in a spoiled moral environment. We have become morally ill because we are used to saying one thing and thinking another. We have learned not to believe in anything, not to care about each other, to worry only about ourselves. The concepts of love, friendship, mercy, humility or forgiveness have lost their depths and dimension, and for many of us they represent only some sort of psychological curiosity or they appear as long-lost wanderers from faraway times, somewhat ludicrous in the era of computers and spaceships.

This is a remarkably blunt, confrontational statement. Spoken to a mass audience at such an auspicious moment, it seems almost to strain against the conditions for its best reception. If all its pronouncements are true in all their extremity, then even a well-intentioned address such as this is bound to fail. But this is where Havel's strategic acumen shows its force.

Note first of all his several references to Czechoslovakia's riches of heritage and tradition. There is more going on here than nostalgia. Havel wants to displace the myth of irreversibility that is often applied to a world after virtue. As he carefully portrays it, the past several generations are, in this larger scheme of Czech heritage and tradition, an aberration. The Czech people have had to learn not to believe in anything. Perhaps, given time, they, and we, might relearn what we have lost. But what of the overriding sense of *fate* and determinism, this still powerful legacy from the previous regime?

The clue is found in Havel's wonderfully bewildered juxtaposition of ludicrous virtue with computers and spaceships. He continues this opposition between the externality of things and the lost spirit by using the mechanism of fate against itself. Here are his words: "The previous regime, armed with a proud and intolerant ideology, reduced people into the means of production and nature into its tools. So it attacked their very essence, and their mutual relations. Out of talented and responsible people, ingeniously husbanding their land, it made cogs of some sort of great, monstrous, thudding, smelly machine, with an unclear purpose. All it can do is, slowly but irresistibly, wear itself out, with all its cogs." Purists will have reason to object to this characterization of Marxist thought; surely the original dream was precisely the opposite of this reduction. But what Havel has captured indelibly is its mechanistic metaphor of determinism: originally a view of history, only to become a scenario of reproduction robbed of all human agency. Here is the human truth buried in the second law of cybernetics: that no machine can run forever. This "great, monstrous, thudding, smelly machine" can only wear itself out with all its cogs. Thus there is a double basis for hope. Our tradition of virtue and character may be more resilient than we know; and the externalized, technological vision of human nature must, by definition, be a finite one. The question to be asked, even if it cannot be answered, is what phantom of inner nature might have survived this moment of passage? Is the machine to be succeeded by ghosts? And what evidence is there, finally, that we will find it within ourselves to rise to this extraordinary occasion?

To answer these questions, Havel must provoke a moment of confession wherein the character of his audience is exposed as capable of an accounting. Paradoxically, we must acknowledge our complicity in our ruined legacy if we are ever to rise above it. And so, Havel's perilous charge: "If I speak about a spoiled moral atmosphere I don't refer only to our masters. . . . I'm speaking about all of us. For all of us have grown used to the totalitarian system and accepted it as an immutable fact, and thereby actually helped keep it going. None of us are only its victims. We are all also responsible for it."

These are not comforting words; and probably only someone who had spent five years in confinement and exile could speak them. But the words are absolutely necessary as a public existential moment; for if it is the case that our cynical quiescence made our "masters" (not an idle choice of terms, I am sure) possible, then it is just as surely the case that our willful complicity may redefine our future as well. Havel is adamant on this connection: "It would be very unwise to think of the sad heritage of the last forty years only as something foreign, something inherited from a distant relative. On the contrary, we must accept this heritage as something we have inflicted on ourselves. *If we accept it in such a way, we shall come to understand that it is up to all of us to do something about it"* (emphasis added). Havel has embarked on a political variation of Pascal's wager. Let us act as if we have always existed in some fashion, if only to have made such tyranny possible. But let us also act *as if* we have existed so that there may be hope, some redemption for damaged lives.

There follows an explicit exhortation to civic responsibility, an invitation which, on a less auspicious occasion, might seem to border on the platitudinous: "Freedom and democracy, after all, mean joint participation and shared responsibility. If we realize this, then all the horrors that the new Czechoslovak democracy inherited cease to be so horrific. If we realize this, then hope will return to our hearts." Apropos as these sentiments are, the occasion demands something more concrete and more particular, the sort of proof which might make this optimism plausible. Without some such moment of individuation, the discourse would remain what it has been to this point: a well-intentioned expression of harsh, necessary truths, but nothing more.

The something more which follows is the sort of proof, the moment of truth, which only rhetoric can provide: the luminous moment of political transformation itself, unanticipated and still mysterious, which only this present public audience may fully recognize. From such fragile and daring questions as these are publics constructed:

> Everywhere in the world, people were surprised how these malleable, humiliated, cynical citizens of Czechoslovakia, who seemingly believed in nothing, found the tremendous strength within a few weeks to cast off the totalitarian system, in an entirely peaceful and dignified manner. We ourselves are surprised at it. And we ask: Where did young people who had never known another system get their longing for truth, their love of freedom, their political imagination, their civic courage and civic responsibility? How did their parents, precisely the generation thought to have been lost, join them? *How is it possible that so many people immediately understood what to do and that none of them needed any advice or instructions!* (emphasis added)

In the context of the speech's own masterful sense of duration—the betrayal of a legacy of character, the deterministic reduction of spirit to machine, our own complicity in this cynical lie of hopelessness—

Havel's bold appeal to the unknown infuses the present moment with an extraordinary power to heal and recover. The power, of course, is due in large part to the elegant resolution offered to the problem of guilt and complicity. The real proof that we may yet be responsible for our fate is that we have overturned the fatalists. Yet this power would be unfathomable without the spontaneous, collective participation of a newly empowered audience within the speech as a civic text. As if in response to each mysterious rhetorical question, the audience roared back, "That is it!" and "There it is," with one voice. The passage is itself more complicated than the univocal response allows. The absence of "advice" and "instructions" in a refutative enthymeme is a doubly ironic rejoinder to the party, as well as a tribute to Havel's favorite political tactic of improvisation. Yet the very craft of the discourse is called into question; and we are left to ponder the strange novelty which this rhetoric has left behind, a founding moment of civic life: "Now it depends only on us whether this hope will be fulfilled, whether our civic, national and political self-respect will be revived. Only a man or a nation with self-respect, in the best sense of the word, is capable of listening to the voices of others, while accepting them as equals, of forgiving enemies and of expiating sins."

A strange creation, this new citizen. There is for this modern consciousness a sense of respect that is *not* egoistic, that is aware of the price already paid for its realization, willing to listen to others and to forgive. Such newfound humility is possible only because some of the sins to be forgiven are one's own. This remarkable speech brought together the absent civic culture of silenced generations and the prerogatives of a political ceremony. The result was a luminous moment which all assembled could treasure through their own collective authorship. As Havel concluded his remarks, the metonymy he borrowed from the Prague Spring seems almost understated in its fait accompli acknowledgment: "My most important predecessor started his first speech by quoting from Comenius. Permit me to end my own first speech by my own paraphrase. *Your government, my people, has returned to you*" (emphasis added).

CONCLUSIONS AND IMPLICATIONS

In this phase of our project, we have been concerned with relationships between the legacy of rhetorical tradition and promising developments in language pragmatics. It should be clear that the neglected middle-range horizons of contextuality (encounter and episode) provide the decisive cognitive resources for rhetoric as a figurative language of conversational and public coherence. Our path to this conclusion has required a circuitous series of steps. We have had to show that coherence in natural discourse is an emergent phenomenon that requires rhetorical intervention on a case by case basis. The interconnections of rhetoric and conversation have also proved fruitful. If conversation provides an ongoing reflective background condition for rhetoric, a cure for its monological proclivities, rhetoric often intervenes to salvage discursive form.

Most important, perhaps, we may now appreciate the way in which rhetorical practice may itself be inventional. Although it always relies on what *appears*, as inflected by received opinions and convention, it may also recombine and individuate these so as to *interrupt* the quotidian of ordinary policy and practice. It may, and does, suggest alternative construals of perspective (Jesse Jackson), issues for controversy (Betty Friedan), and even constituencies of accountable others (Friedan and Havel). In every case, the movement of rhetoric, despite and because of its urgency, is that of a situated, partialist discourse. It is from part to unrealized larger picture. But this is not to lessen or demean the value of such discourse. Neither the normal nor the exceptional operation of rhetoric, in other words, is an impure distortion, but rather an ethically significant instance of a developing communicative art.

There are critical implications of this repositioning of rhetoric, particularly for the normative appreciation of its practice. For one thing, the very capacity of rhetoric to range so widely over temporal horizons of act, episode, encounter, and lifeworld suggests a kind of symmetrical counsel of conscientiousness: to keep the public faith, to guard well the resources of authority, integrity, and responsibility, and to be accountable for and to one's word. Secondly, and despite much lamentation to the contrary, it is simply not the case that we are living in dark times where civic discourse is concerned. It was Hannah Arendt who pronounced this verdict on the contemporary era, a generation or so ago. Speaking only of the capacity of discourse to be rebuffed and reversed by action, she believed "the semblance of rationality" to be what finally provokes rage.[58] The reversal of speech and action by subsequent events is not unique to our era, of course. And Havel's own dream of unity must seem distant too in the indirect light of subsequent events. For all this, Arendt herself could never have foreseen that this same "dark era" which gave us Havel's brilliant discourse would also give us Sakharov's dissent, Mandela's overtures toward liberation, the Palestinian Declaration of Independence, even Gorbachev at the United Nations, all within less than a decade. There is also a thriving community of performance art, rap, and public talk that obstinately thwarts and challenges the forces of censorship at every turn.[59] It is no refutation of Arendt's pronouncement to realize that the very aversion and rage which respond to hypocrisy in real discourse are definitive evidence that a sense of accountability and practical judgment may show some flickering signs of life. In a compromise between dark times and a thousand points of light, we might allow that our times are, like most times, partly cloudy, with a slight chance of precipitation.

If an aesthetic of rhetoric prompts us to attend to the various modes of interpreting, reappropriating, and even revising the meanings of past experience, an ethic of rhetoric must attend to the moral of the story: such issues as what public character is implied by the course we have taken, what forms of social learning are yet available to us, what legacy of experience we wish our story to yield to future generations, which episodes in our unfinished and unbounded narrative of collective action are irretrievable or lost, which need to be ended altogether, which prolonged, which begun anew, and which audiences, so far neglected, need to have their own stories articulated. There are, of course, many more such issues. I have mentioned these because they offer a way of sharpening current means of articulating practical judgment.

But one final point: Jackson, Friedan, and Havel are all rhetorical exceptions. In their ethereal accomplishments, their extraordinary moments, they hardly reaffirm the availability of this productive art for the rest of us. Yet, if there is to be a rhetorical culture, presumably its egalitarian tradition must make room for the ordinary. Can it? What of the rest of us? May a practical art still allow for a meaningful pedagogy for all, for prodigies and couch potatoes equally? In the concluding chapter, I will explore the strong claim that even rhetoric's distortions, failures, and deformations are inventional, constructive, and amenable to the cultivation of phronēsis.

To possess an art of real life has long been the rhetorician's dream. Yet it is a dream that can be seriously entertained only so long as it does not become too entertaining. The question, bluntly put, is whether we can be actors in, and authors of, the same unfinished story without doing damage to the one indispensable outcome of successful rhetoric: character. Hannah Arendt thought not. She writes: "What the story-teller narrates must necessarily be hidden from the actor himself, at least so long as he is in the act or caught in its consequences, because to him, the meaningfulness of his act is not in the story that follows. Even though stories are the inevitable results of action, it is not the actor but the story-teller who perceives and 'makes' the story."[60] Rhetoric and conversation remain the primary art forms of everyday life. They work best, I believe, when left to this limited, but most important canvas. They work most truthfully when they remember the truth there is to tell: its unmistakable past and its unfinished possibility.

7

Criticism, Disturbance, and Rhetorical Community: Reanimating the Occasions for Rhetoric

We were immemorially people of the countryside, far from the courts of princes, living according to rituals we didn't always understand and yet were unwilling to dishonor because that would cut us off from the past, the sacred earth, the gods. Those earth rites went back far. They would always have been partly mysterious. But we couldn't surrender to them now. We had become self-aware. Forty years before, we would not have been so self-aware. We would have accepted. We had made ourselves anew. The world we found ourselves in—the suburban houses, with gardens . . . we couldn't go back. There was no ship of antique shape now to take us back. We had come out of the nightmare; and there was nowhere else to go.

—V. S. Naipaul, *The Enigma of Arrival*

We shall die with every stone we love so much. We do not know where the conscience of the world has been staying recently. Therefore, here is our last report to it: When our souls reach the seventh sky, we hope we shall see you from above.

—Miso Mihocevic, Letter from Dubrovnik, 1991

The word is what gets people riled and sparked. The coup showed the power of the word when it's going to so many people's ears, and how you really have to be careful how you use it. You can spark people up, but if you spark them up and don't give them no directions on how it can help them, people will lose it. They'll lose it and blame you for getting them sparked and not directing them.

—Chuck D, "Public Enemy"

Eloquence deepens and distinguishes the contours of a practice, as do all noble exceptions, the few showing the many what might be accomplished. But for the pedestrian art of rhetoric, these "many" are more than also-rans in the parade; they are also the constitutive stuff of the art. Ours has been the century of Mahler and Shostakovich and of Elvis, Janis, and Chuck Berry as well. Rhetoric works its magic inconspicuously, in small successes as well as noble failures. Above all, it works *both* sides of the street. In this chapter, I address a problem which haunts contemporary practice: namely, that if rhetoric is such a practical art, why is it that only exceptional cases of eloquent oratory are invoked as evidence of its craft? What about the less than distinguished rest of us? Since civic rhetoric is a practice admitting to certain relational goods, its ethical and aesthetic significance should be found not only at the Guggenheim, but among the hoi polloi, dirty fingernails and all.

REREADING RHETORICAL CULTURE

For the vocabulary of Aristotle's *Rhetoric* to have anything to say to modern cultural occasions, three concepts emerge as pivotal: the impetus for rhetorical *meaning*, which we find in Aristotle's seminal understanding of phronēsis, typified by deliberative prudence; a concept of rhetorical *form*, which we have found in the prototype for public inference and judgment—the enthymeme; and a modern rhetorical *forum*, a space of engagement where in the modern constraints of rhetorical culture might assert themselves. This last notion particularly needs to be given additional weight through demonstration. But first we must refresh our understanding of a rhetorical culture.

Borrowing liberally from social anthropology, I define culture as the *common definition of places for the invention and perpetuation of meaning*. A culture offers to those who live in it symbols and families of practices that permit ongoing performances of meaning and value. As Zygmunt Bauman has observed:

> Culture is the only facet of the human condition and of life in which knowledge of the human reality and the human interest in self-perfection and fulfilment merge into one. The cultural is the only knowledge . . . for that matter, which is bold enough to offer the world its meaning instead of gullibly believing (or pretending to believe) that the meaning lies over there ready-made and complete, waiting to be discovered and learned. Culture is, therefore, the natural enemy of alienation. It constantly questions the self-appointed wisdom, serenity, and authority of the real.[1]

I have tried to move beyond the implicit *mechanism* of some contemporary anthropologies where the meaning and processing of cultures are concerned. One of the most problematic conceptual developments for the study of culture has been the sharp separation of *nature* and *culture* into two divergent, largely disembodied realms. The reader who has survived our earlier historical skirmishes will recognize this split as the unique contribution of the Enlightenment to the tension between nomos and physis. Beginning with Francis Bacon and the first discourses of modernism, a pantheon of Western philosophers began to posit that the "orders" of nature and of human nature were based on different, but analogous principles.[2] As the natural order became increasingly secular and depersonalized, the reflection and animism of human nature became increasingly suspect. The interim result, in studies as outwardly disparate as semiotics, neo-Marxism, cybernetics, structuralism, and deconstruction, has been to mark off a view of human nature that sees it as analogous, in varying degrees, to a mechanical, largely calculative vision of the natural world.

Without belaboring the specifics of each program, it has been the conspicuous failure of these anti-human sciences to recognize the reflective participatory stake we humans have in the *appearances* of our lives. By "appearances" I mean an ensemble of objects, habitats, paths, tools, tasks, icons, and more or less recognizable characters that engage and reassure inhabitants of a locale through their emergent familiarity.[3] My argument throughout has assumed that we constitute these appearances in ways that are, ultimately, not specifiable. But, more than this, it is that this participatory stake is literally part of our human logos; it cannot be banished. And once we begin to reconsider its cultural possibilities, the possibility of rhetoric must reemerge.

Rhetoric happens in unfinished historical episodes, wherein urgent circumstances require that we act, even though we lack complete, reliable grounds for determining what the best action might be. For a culture to be rhetorical, we must freely acknowledge the responsibility of civic discourse to unite the appearances of cultural affiliation with the plans and projects of public life. This is the classical heritage of Aristotle, reinterpreted liberally to suit our broader purposes.

There is, then, an intrinsic and an extrinsic justification for assigning importance to rhetoric in modern culture. Intrinsically, rhetoric is rooted in our natural, individual insufficiency.[4] We are not fixed biologically to a single environment. In fact, by the age of three, each of us has had to refigure the environment *symbolically*, well enough to move through multiple cultural horizons. But, paradoxically, there is a further element of partiality in our attempt to be inclusive. There is, to be sure, the irony of local origins (where philosopher-kingdoms and proletarian dictatorships betray the brush strokes of their authors). Grand systems, with every outward extension, tend to level, ignore, or repress inner differences. This may be why new world orders reappear as entropic microcosms of the old, with each ancient ultimate evil now localized as some parochial other. The all-too-human costs of this partiality are tragic. But it was Aristotle who found the one rhetorical universal in this same human trait: our partisanship for the familiar and, from within the world of the local and particular, our movement *toward* the other.

A key to understanding modern rhetorical occasions is that they often pit against one another cultures that occupy radically discrepant positions along dimensions such as identity, cohesion, and development.[5] Cultural lifeworlds that are closed to alternatives exert considerable power of definition over so-called regimes of pure tolerance.[6] A modern sense of the rhetorical, therefore, looks to a broader horizon, where reflection on our figurative use of language both *reminds us of* and *removes us from* our unconscious participation in the appearances of culture. Eugene Rochberg-Halton helps to explain this broader horizon in his important work *Meaning and Modernity*: "Just as all humans are living symbols, all real symbols are living beings, animated by, and in turn animating, individual and collective human existence. . . . The third level is the cultivation of symbols, the reciprocal giving of life through intelligible conduct to symbolic forms and the giving to human life of the larger meanings that the symbols in turn convey."[7] This is a mellifluous way of saying something that is really quite simple. Since it revolves around a practice that admits to radically variant degrees of performed quality, a rhetorical culture is something that must be cultivated. However, to continue in the same prescriptive mode, it is important to inquire just *how* this might be done.

There has never been a cultural system, however mechanized its outward conception, that has been able to energize and activate its own membership without some practical rhetorical correlate. When one is immersed in a cultural form of life, whether it be that of an urban East coast American or that of a Javanese peasant, one is unlikely to notice the rhetorical characteristics of ongoing cultural activities. This does not mean that they are absent or—worse yet—unimportant; only that our practices are taken for granted in a way that forecloses our sense of their uniqueness. However, rhetoric, in its venerable sense of art *form*, emerges when we recognize our activities as involving choices among an array of options. In pluralistic cultures, such recognition is possible whenever choices are made about optional courses of action. In highly fragmented cultures—that is, cultures with numerous strains among subcultures—such recognition comes microcosmically with every effort to achieve coordinated activity. In each case, rhetoric affords a measure of accessibility, at least to the extent that the other must be acknowledged as a witness to what we, as a collective membership group, do. In all the above senses, we note the ongoing cultivation of normal rhetoric.

Yet there is a broader range of encounter, where the ensemble of convictions, affiliations, and traditions we know as culture is introduced to a widening circle of acquaintance. The social theorist Anthony Giddens anticipates this type of encounter by arguing that power under late capitalism depends less on the overt expression of monopolistic tendencies than on the long-distance control of information.[8] In other words, contemporary so-called advanced societies exert their influence over more traditional societies through authoritative, rather than allocative resources. But even with the Western dominance of information systems generally,[9] there is an ongoing need for legitimation for those within the global forum defined by discourse. For Giddens, this means that we must be prepared to study "the global nature of social interaction in the modern era," particularly in episodes in which normative systems converge.[10]

Where I part company with Giddens is over his insistence that there are determinate structures for the formation, and even the expression, of this uniquely modern kind of power. The split between structural and ecological approaches to anthropology has been with us for more than a generation.[11] However, the cultural fragments of reason that we are able to decipher are themselves creations of constrained, but by no means fixed and finalized, beings. This is why it is essential to append to Giddens's important structuration project an ongoing interest in culture as a way of life, fraught with the fact of human agency, the messy concrete particularity of performed *action*.

The sort of encounter contexts that Giddens and company have in mind have many of the attributes of what once were regarded as "occasions."[12] Yet their principles of decorum are, understandably, far from coherent. When we consider contemporary examples such as the 1985 "Live-Aid" intercontinental music festival for African famine relief, the strange encounter of Ronald Reagan with mythology and memory at Bitburg, the student demonstrations and massacre at Tiananmen Square, the 1991 failed Soviet coup, the remarkable crumbling and "selling off" of the Berlin Wall that same year, it becomes apparent that something very different has begun to assert itself as a possible manner of presenting grievances and adjudicating collisions among our cultural norms. For want of a better phrase, I will characterize this as the *mediated rhetorical occasion*.

This new type of encounter brings together advocates, messages, and audiences—the traditional rhetorical triad—in a way that tends to resist the development of a consensus. Rather than beginning with broad-based social agreements, the new rhetorical occasion often begins only with public awareness of a brute actuality. To this extent what I am calling an occasion may remind readers of Victor Turner's very provocative notion of the *social drama* with its episodic sequencing of breach, division, crisis, redress, and resolution or irresolution.[13] In my terms, these expanded occasions inscribe a mediated moment or historical opening wherein all manner of rhetorical episodes (collaborative, controversial, even confrontational) are possible. But beyond this surface congruence, there are, in any recognizably modern sense of *occasion*, an asymmetrical distribution of interested membership groups, uneven access to channels of communication, conflicting informational sources, and overlapping episodes of interpretation. The question arises as to how, if at all, any form of discursive engagement can contribute to the advancement of human understanding in such settings. An appreciation of the *institutional* and the *cognitive* features of the rhetorical occasion can help us to answer this question.

An occasion may allow, as Aristotle recognized, for the expression of public difference (as in the rhetorical controversy or the conflict of interpretations); or it may be a moment or opening in an unfolding episode that is of special significance, that deserves to be marked, underscored, or celebrated. But whatever type of configuration an occasion presents us with (and there are obviously hybrid combinations of the above), it requires some extrinsic constraint for engaged rhetorical conduct to occur. In the discussion that follows, I take my cue from Hans Blumenberg's view that the "Darwinism of words" is given shape and modest normative constraint by what he terms "institutions."[14] The institutional modality most serviceable to rhetorical occasions is engendered by the local, civic, or global *forum*.

The notion of a rhetorical forum is a difficult one to grasp. The danger is either to define it in such a rarefied way that it can be found almost nowhere or to define it so loosely and flexibly that it is found everywhere we look. Here I seek a moderate middle way. However, a certain amount of messiness may help us to appreciate that rhetorical practice may help to engender, animate, and even subvert the workings of forums, as well as the other way around. Chaos may work in an inventional way.[15]

In the study of rhetoric, the most detailed attention to the notion of a forum has been offered by Stephen Toulmin and his associates. From their discussion in *An Introduction to Reasoning*, we learn that forums are formal and informal locations where argument is practiced; that the forum exerts an influence on the invention, as well as the judgment, of arguments; that different types of forum usually admit to corresponding types of discussion; and that the more formal a forum is (with the singular instance of a court of law serving as the prototype), the more developed and distinct is the idea of the rational standpoint for the introduction and adjudication of arguments themselves.[16] Consistent with my aims here, Toulmin and his colleagues stress the institutional constraints, positive and negative, which the forum exerts over the practice and direction of argumentative controversy. But although the term is broad enough to begin with, the sorts of examples focused on—law courts, professional scientific meetings, university seminars, congressional committees—have the effect of minimizing the broader, informal, ad hoc character of some forums, such as emerge through intercultural public episodes. Some intercultural public forums are highly formal and rule-governed, such as the United Nations General Assembly; and even some of the more festive events are still closely choreographed and staged, such as the Winter and Summer Olympics.[17] But there are also less structured, more or less extemporaneous settings where issues are raised, points challenged, and discourse engendered, literally within the temporal constraints imposed by interested others. Something of a forum takes shape here as well, I argue, at least to the extent that *a symbolic environment is created within which issues, interests, positions, constituencies, and messages are advanced, shaped, and provisionally judged.*

More broadly defined, a rhetorical forum is any encounter setting which serves as a gathering place for discourse. As such, it provides a space for multiple positions to encounter one another. And, in its most developed condition, it may also provide precedents and modalities for granting a hearing to positions, as well as sorting through their agendas and constituencies. This is a way of saying that a rhetorical forum provides a provisionally constrained context and an avenue of mediation among discourses that might otherwise be self-confirming, incommensurable, or perhaps not even heard at all.

The clearest historical antecedent of the rhetorical forum is probably the public space that emerges in some idealist renderings of the Athenian polis. Here, for instance, is that idealist Aristotelian Hannah Arendt:

> The polis, properly speaking, is not the city-state in its physical location; it is the organization of the people as it arises out of acting and speaking together, and its true space lies between people living together no matter where they happen to be. "Wherever you go, you will be a polis": these famous words became not merely the watchword of Greek colonization; they expressed the conviction that action and speech can create a space between the participants which can find its proper location almost any time and anywhere. It is the space of appearance in the widest sense of the word, namely the space where I appear to others as others appear to me, where men exist not merely like other living or inanimate things but make their appearance explicitly.[18]

These words provide a helpful, albeit somewhat misleading, basis for our own understanding. Arendt reminds us that the fact of interpersonal affiliation and individuation is prior to any of its institutional embodiments. This is another way of saying that a sense of forum emerges whenever there is the potential for resistance, for a third-party standpoint, which may emerge at any time in any ongoing conversation. This potential is critical, because it helps to explain why the idea of a forum (along with the *vox populi*, the court of last resort) has had such persistence and durability. A second implication of Arendt's words is the emergence of appearances, in all their plurality, within the web of interrelationships established through the presence of others. As I will try to show later on, it is the rhetorical forum which allows this plurality of appearances to be presented, witnessed, regarded, qualified, and subverted by the perspectives of others.

Yet, for all of this, Arendt's treatment tends to mystify and idealize the genuine presence of real live others in her original, rather wistful conception of classical political life. In an unintentionally aristocratic way, she thereby lends undue weight to the thesis that long-distance democracy and liberationist social movements are merely the further conformism of mass society in disguise. My own view is that the actual physical presence of persons in each other's public space is less important than the *conscious awareness* of each other's placement in the symbolic landscape of prospective thought and decision—the fact that other persons and constituencies make a difference and must therefore be taken into account in our deliberations.

We are beginning to approach the question of how a forum interacts with rhetorical practice. In the most general terms, we might say that a forum helps to stabilize rhetorical practice. By allowing topics to be classified as open for discussion and by encouraging advocates and their constituencies to exert some public influence, rhetorical forums lend a weight to rhetorical occasions. Appearances known to all may now be thematized and captioned; as these become ongoing features of our civic life, rhetorical occasions are animated and underscored. They become documented public events. Beyond these very general terms, the particular yield of a forum depends on how developed and historically stabilized it is,[19] the breadth of its compass or scope of coverage (which I will call "venue"), the genres or types of rhetorical practice involved, and the nature of the rhetorical occasion. That is why the answer is difficult to generalize.

A live rhetorical controversy—for instance, among opposition leaders to apartheid—will admit to very different frames and thematic constraints on rhetorical practice than will, let us say, a state funeral for a fallen leader or for that matter a peace conference among previously hostile groups. What is critical to the power and constraint of the forum is that two very different features of occasion may always intersect there: first, the custom and convention of normal practice,[20] and second, the reflective sense of uncertainty made available by the interests of others who are also involved, even if they are unrepresented directly by advocacy. Taken together, they provide the tension between strict adaptation and genuine invention. This may be only another way of saying that propriety always possesses both an ethical and an aesthetic dimension.

A working typology of rhetorical forums can only be suggested here. But it too would need to include several marks of differentiation. One might range from the formal, traditionally stabilized forum to the extra-institutional, socially emergent forum. A second dimension relates to scope, which can range from the technical, field-specific, and issue-defined to the more common, cosmopolitan, and civic-minded forum of greater generality. Then, of course, there is the whole matter of boundary conditions, from the local to the regional to the global. In the twentieth century, we have witnessed the development of highly formal institutions—for instance, the United Nations—designed to deal with common human and technical issues in global settings. So there is no *necessary* connection between degree of forum stability as formal stratification and degree of narrowness in either subject or venue. The matter of ritual and forum, the intersection of the sacred and the secular, is also important to the forum; for the very fact of affiliating consciously with any recurring rhetorical forum will require some meta-communicative acknowledgements. And this surely implies the figurative, participatory domain of ritual.

Rhetorical occasions, as we have seen, derive an institutional constraint from the forum. They may also elicit a reflective quality. When they do this, I believe it is because they expose highly divergent customs, conventions, rules, and sensibilities (what the Greeks called doxa) to each other. Although Aristotle insisted that rhetoric, like dialectic, had no subject matter exclusively its own, I have read his aesthetics of rhetoric somewhat against the grain as suggesting strong linkages to the mysteries of public thought. In at least a cursory way, I will now overview a way of conceptualizing this reflective domain in public thought. While I hesitate to claim universality for these analytic categories, they do exhibit a range of heuristic power when applied to the background conventions which are confronted and risked in mediated rhetorical occasions. Figure 2 illustrates the concepts I have in mind.

Even in the nonlinear relationships sketched here, the cognitive constructions of a culture become open to reflective understanding *when* they are acknowledged as requisites for decision; that is to say, when they are challenged in an accessible public forum. Following Geertz, it makes most sense to look for ways in which cultural thought expresses sentiment and belief, but with respect to an aspect of the social world that is open to alternative construals.[21] This aspect is what I am calling, for want of a better term, a "subject" domain. The subject may be rain, war, sex, a scandal, a crime, a good deed, a big event—any of those things about which we must make timely decisions. Whatever we are concerned enough about to judge worth telling to others may enter into the purview of a rhetorical culture. Subjects also possess a range, in specificity, generality, and urgency. They are, as we noted in chapter 1, thematized by the narratives and definitions of rhetoric.

By "grounds" I mean the fundamental presuppositions of a culture as these are available to critical reflection. Some such presuppositions are foreclosed to reflective analysis, of course. But, in general, there seems to be a finite number of presupposition types that might anchor those practices that are operative within a given form of life. These might include

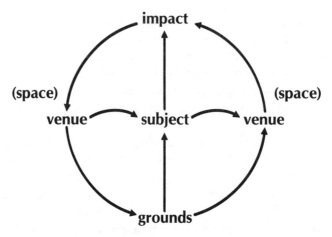

Figure 2. Normative horizon for topoi of social knowledge within the rhetorical forum.

faith, authority, tradition, myth, experience, and intuition. This list is neither exclusive nor exhaustive. We must allow for the fact that any epoch may inherit questions which the culture cannot answer within the presuppositions of its form of life.[22] At some stage either the presuppositions or the agenda of questions give way. The so-called modernization of cultures provides a sweeping illustration of this process, at least as it has been assimilated by modern ethnography. But something equally striking seems to happen to these same cultures whenever their reliance on instrumental reasoning is exposed as insufficient to deal with larger questions of purpose and meaning.[23] The so-called revolutions in Eastern Europe in 1990 seem to have been motivated equally by the madonna on the compact disc and the one on the church wall. Viewed this way, the exposure of, and reflection on, lifeworld presuppositions is not a process that moves in only a single direction.

On the horizontal plane of the diagram, I have included a membership "space," so as to leave room for gradations of inclusiveness and exclusion where admissible membership groups are concerned.[24] As is well known, cultures need exiles and scapegoats as a dialectical counterpoint to their own claims of affiliation. Every culture has its margins. Over and above the brute question of exile and privilege, however, this space indicates a scope of attribution for normative agreement. A culture that regards itself as the last hope of freedom in the hemisphere is situated somewhat differently from a culture that sees itself as an equal partner among a community of peoples.

Finally, I have located a category of force, or *impact*, to show what happens when subjects, membership audience, and cultural norms of agreement all work together collaboratively, even if controversially. Optimally, a cultural practice emerges. Collective projects involving liberation, human rights, incipient nationalism, job safety, or, for that matter, projects moving toward the repression of deviant groups, the assertion of privilege, the avenging of grievance, or the mitigation of disturbance are all examples of the normative impact which can result when cultural presuppositions are given a push in focus and direction. Despite the much-discussed hegemony of the American century, the rich heterogeneity of multicultural norms still presents a liberating capacity to stir reflection, through an acquaintance with the traditions, the interests, and the *lived experience* of others.

Taken together, this grid is less a form-of-life analytic than an overall framework marking off what Alfred Schutz once called zones of relevance for cultural lifeworlds.[25] Put another way, when the diagram is filled in, as it were, we would have the promise of a rhetorical *horizon* for addressing contemporary cultural contingencies. Our sense of rhetorical occasion is enriched heuristically with an appreciation of its institutional and cognitive features. What is missing from the framework as it stands is the sense of cultural performance that is supplied by real durational experience. This can come only from the arena of actual rhetorical practice.

The core of a rhetorical occasion may be a disturbance, an issue, or a contested perspective. Rhetorically, a forum then works as a pocket of disturbance, an eye of the storm, or core of tension around which other disparate positions and arguments may hover. The term "pocket" is a rough analogy to modern jazz, where wide-ranging, seemingly chaotic dissonance may, and usually does, begin to collect and gather itself around a central rhythmic core, recognizable by the emergent familiarity of departure and return. In the light of this analogy—if light it be— it is interesting that the Czech playwright Václav Havel has taken to referring to his own paradoxical political choices and fortunes as "improvisation."[26] Occasions may also take the form of unfolding events or emerging public affiliations that demand a name, a language, an agenda, or a form of address. In either case, the reflective affiliations of multiple parties need to be brought together in the ongoing episodes of civic life.

A single example may suggest the power of a rhetorical forum. When, after nearly ten years, the Sandinistas were not overthrown, but peacefully voted out of office, it proved to be the vindication of something called the Contadora process, rather than America's covert foreign policy. How that happened is interesting. A number of Central American states, led by President Arias of Costa Rica, initiated the Contadora process in an attempt to find a peaceful Central American solution to the war in Nicaragua. From the beginning, the United States covertly opposed the process, even attempting to subvert and overturn it,[27] at the same time as the American regime officially recognized the Sandinista government and Congress declared itself in favor of the Contadora process.[28] Despite increasingly devious American subterfuge, the process went forward, with Arias himself receiving the Nobel Peace Prize in 1988. Although almost no American newspapers mentioned the matter, I would argue that the integrity of this *public* process accomplished something a twenty-four-billion-dollar covert war was unable to accomplish: namely, a peaceful transfer of power.

The forums of rhetorical practice, once invented and used, begin to develop a life of their own. Sometimes they set in motion certain contraints of precedent, place, ritual expectation, and genre as to what may be presented and heard. And every now and then, they may even provoke a founding moment for the formation and stability of other institutions. Once founded and formed, these institutions cannot be arrested. Change in the world of public events marches to a logic that defies the closure of analytic rule.

REFIGURING RHETORICAL PRACTICE

In what we understand as its normalized condition, the rhetorical forum provides loose but recognizable admission criteria as to who may speak, what may be spoken about, and how they are to be held accountable for what they say and do. In a very general sense, each of these sets of contraints may be subsumed under the larger category of the *appropriate*, which is perhaps the closest we can come to a congruence between emancipatory reason and phronēsis. However, a rhetorical sense of the appropriate would identify norms that are more specific than universal validity claims. In the world of phainomena in which rhetoric must dwell, norms for speakers, messages, and constituencies are evoked which are provisional and situation-specific. We might think of them in the way shown in table 1.[29] Each of the three domains typically in-

Table 1. Relationships among cultural norms and rhetorical practice.

TYPE	LOCUS	VALUE
speaker-centered norm	*ēthos* or perspective	norm of authority
message-centered norm	*stasis* or issue	norm of integrity
constituency-centered norm	*krisis* or judgment	norm of conscience

Table © 1990 by The Pennsylvania State University. Reproduced by permission of The Pennsylvania State University Press.

cludes a host of more specific issues, topics, and concerns. *Authority,* for instance, is itself a highly complex matter, involving issues of accreditation, legitimacy of procedure, role definition, boundaries for expertise, and even constituencies of application. What I have done here is simply group together larger category types, where disturbance and controversy may help to perform important inventional tasks.

As stated above, a normalized forum—say, an awards ceremony or a court of law—will admit to fairly specific constraints along all three dimensions. Yet even in these cases, there is a further characteristic worth noting about a rhetorical sense of the appropriate. Instead of presupposing the appropriate as an a priori validity claim in advance of speech, *rhetorical practice enacts the norms of propriety collaboratively with interested collective others.* [30] In the rhetorical occasion, rhetoric is both the animated and the animator, because the very conditions of propriety are continually being reindividuated and renewed with every specific case and because particularly challenging disputes about what constitutes proper authority, integrity, and responsibility can have the effect of enriching, reframing, and perhaps reinventing the boundaries of rhetorical community itself. As White has suggested of cultural languages generally, this process of change and renewal is not always conspicuous, but it is surely ongoing.[31] The forum gives to an understanding of human agency the additional obligation to contribute discourse in such a way that conditions are in place for other discourse to continue as well. In this sense, rhetoric—even in its moments of excess and hyperbole—is always building through and beyond the brutish relationships between the strong and the weak.[32] Those who envision rhetorical justification as no more than an apology for force would do well to reflect on this additional compensatory dimension.

Before turning to several specific, extended episodes of rhetorical disputation, we must reconsider the problem of qualitative variation in rhetorical practice. Where the eloquence of completed textual exemplars is concerned, the critic's task is not controversial. The primary purpose of close, careful reading is to enhance what all finely crafted artifacts invite—appreciation. But mediated rhetorical occasions, like most real events, do not usually allow the leisure for such refinement. Fragmentary themselves, they tend to call forth other fragments: unfinished texts, one-sided accentuations of episodes, partial depictions of interest crudely stated. How can this add up to any sort of reflection?

We must concede that (*ceteris paribus*, of course) it helps greatly if social formations allow some space for critical reflection of audiences to emerge. In our discussion of rhetoric's path to recovery, I insisted that some such space might always be available in *principle*, to the extent that rhetoric is the counterpart of conversation. But I now grant that discursive pathologies are best avoided by envisioning partisan utterances not as the indefinite replication of culture industry in the product domain, but rather as partial increments in an unfinished, nonfinalizable process. Granted, there are real political limits to the powers of interpretation where the conditions of social life are concerned. I would only suggest that a more open consideration of the contemporary rhetorical scene might allow us to appreciate the difference between "last words" which (like Lincoln's second inaugural) make further utterances superfluous and "last words" which simply terminate discussion.

In the examples that follow, we are looking at not-so-eloquent rhetoric, discourse which, in the language of appearances, offers us only part of the picture. Taken entirely on its own, in the product domain, such discourse is distorted and malformed, a one-sided presentation of things that must crave correction. But that is where the other voices of rhetoric, the further venues of controversy and disputation enter the picture. The movement of rhetorical practice, even in episodes such as these, is always partial—that is to say, from part to whole. And this qualitative variation of rhetoric becomes most open to scrutiny when viewed within the larger arena of public possibilities implied by an open rhetorical forum.

Authority may be considered as a variation of ēthos, a grounded entitlement to offer a perspective on appearances based on some claim to a constituency.[33] The characteristic mode of address in the language of authority is, of course, the command. And, given this imperative mood, it is not unusual to find authority treated as an antithesis of argument. Hannah Arendt, for instance, writes: "Authority, on the other hand, is incompatible with persuasion, which presupposes equality and works through a process of argumentation. Where arguments are used, authority is left in abeyance."[34] This time, I think, Arendt's Platonic version of classicism has pressed her received understanding of authority in an incongruous direction. For my project of reintroducing a sense of reflection into the world of political action, however, it is essential to regard authority as itself a form of argument. It must derive grounds for its pronouncements. It must stipulate conditions for the sphere of activity proper to its use. And, most important, it may always be challenged, disputed, and even disobeyed.

Even in well-structured forums, the inscription of authority may be opened to propriety dispute. When newly anointed rhetorical hero Václav Havel visited Kurt Waldheim in Austria, he was quickly denounced for having thereby lent legitimacy to Waldheim's questionable past.[35] Havel's supporters replied by observing that Havel had visited Austria to attend the Salzburg festival, not to see Waldheim. His conduct, in other words, could be redeemed by a different understanding of its context. But once the issue had been raised, this was not the end of the matter. Here, for instance, is Havel at Salzburg after Waldheim had introduced him: "A person who is afraid of what is yet to come is generally also reluctant to look in the face of what has been. And a person afraid to look at his own past must fear what is to come. . . . Those who falsify history do not protect the freedom of the nation but rather constitute a threat to it. The idea that a person can rewrite his autobiography is one of the traditional self-deceptions of Central Europe. Trying to do that means hurting oneself and one's fellow countrymen. When a truth is not given complete freedom, freedom is not complete."[36] Perhaps that is why even this issue of perspective is unlikely to be resolved easily, for it is difficult to imagine eloquent and confrontational lines such as these delivered at a purely *aesthetic* occasion.

While some concerns about authority lend themselves to provisional resolution through a more proper positioning within a forum, others are not nearly so tidy. In a manner which nicely corroborates modernity's valorizing of the private, former president Ronald Reagan developed the reputation not of a *good man speaking well*, or even a good rhetorician, but rather of a "great Communicator." Interestingly, in light of our earlier felicity conditions for public responsibility, Reagan also became known as the "Teflon President," the person to whom (in modern parlance) no crisis or failure would ever stick. However, later generations may well look back to two examples of disputation regarding authority from the

Reagan regime as illustrating how the rhetorical forum can exert a corrective or moderating tendency within the ongoing process of historical episodes.

Consider first the revealing series of episodes surrounding President Reagan's decision to pay a commemorative visit to Bitburg.[37] For all practical purposes, the visit was not intended to be a major event. Yet, in the symbolic terms which allow us to grapple with cultural memory, the visit became such. To pay even indirect tribute to SS troops and to those who took part in what was arguably the twentieth century's most barbaric episode seemed to many in the United States, Israel, and Europe to strain (and *stain*) the meaning of reconciliation.

The Bitburg situation, whose complexity can only be hinted at here, presents us with a stark reminder that even the politics of privatism has its limits. Within days of his scheduled visit, Reagan's proposed itinerary had become a deeply troubling public issue.[38] Ostensive norms of alliance and reconciliation, trumpeted forth by presidential advance men, were forced to make room for the mute insistence that some cultural and historical wounds could not be made to vanish on command. Still the public relations apparatus whirred away, shortening the ceremony itself to eight minutes—as if to suggest that the real-life duration of a symbolic act might dictate the attention span of history.[39] Further, the ceremony, was surrounded on all sides by a choreography of what American commentators have come to call "great communication": moving soliloquys from the president on behalf of the Jewish war dead at Bergen-Belsen.[40]

But the same historical and cultural narrative that gave the president's eloquence memorial power also served to sharpen the performative outrage of the Bitburg gesture. If there is a lesson here, it is that not all historical episodes may be flattened out by speaking well or even by "great communication." Yet, paradoxical as it may seem, the failures of this discourse may have performed a kind of civilizing function, giving revisionist political theater an unexpected reflective turn.

Before his visit, Reagan stated in a press conference: "And I felt that, since the German people have very few alive that remember even the war, and certainly none of them who were adults and participating in any way, and the [sic], they do, they have a feeling and a guilt feeling that's been imposed upon them. And I just think it's unnecessary."[41] Even disregarding the factual errors, this is a remarkable sentiment from any political leader, suggesting that cultural memory need extend no further than the actuarial charts for a single generation—a memory whose useful service is over once senility begins.

Yet as we have envisioned the process, the rhetorical cognition made possible by a multitextured occasion may sometimes place the individual advocate in a morally charged encounter.[42] In terms of symbolic, as well as spatiotemporal, horizons, visits to another country can be broadening. The Bitburg "flap" (as the public relations apparatus described it at the time) raised the quite serious question of whether even the president of the United States possessed the breadth of perspective to authorize a redefinition of a twentieth-century marker event. It could even be claimed that the debate about this issue was a positive development, rekindling an encounter with a dark memory as our turbulent century draws to a close.

AUTHORITY AND PERSPECTIVE:
REAGAN AND GORBACHEV

A second example of disputation over perspective also involves former president Reagan, as well as his remarkable Soviet counterpart, Mikhail Gorbachev. It concerns the report that each made to his respective constituency after their somewhat anticlimactic summit meeting in Reykjavik in 1986. By almost any measure of summitry success, material or symbolic, the failure of the leaders at Reykjavik to arrive at even a modicum of agreement placed pronounced constraints on their post-summit rhetoric. The issues were highly complex, involving everything from definitions of defensive and offensive weapon capabilities to procedures for reliable verification to the Reagan administration's largely hypothetical strategic defense initiative "Star Wars." But it can be safely said, I think, that the Soviet Union was more eager for a substantial, long-term nuclear disarmament treaty than were the officials representing the United States. To this we might add that the American representatives seemed genuinely surprised by the radical nature of the Soviet proposals.

The subsequent failure to achieve even a modest agreement presented each leader with the general feature of what we earlier described as a mediated rhetorical occasion. The leaders had encountered a class of problems which defied (for them, at any rate) technical solution. They obviously represented different cultural constituencies. They were eventually compelled to address an extrinsic—even global—audience, and their positions did appear to shift in light of each other's rhetoric. This entire setting forced at least a modicum of disclosure and human agency. Thus, despite obvious shortcomings, there is reason to believe that their exchange of discourses occurred within and helped to animate an enlarged rhetorical forum. The ideal citizen of the world who digests both speeches may even detect a modicum of provisional truth in each address.[43]

Reagan's speech.   Reagan framed his nationally televised address as a report to the American people on "what took place in these discussions." Maintaining that the implications of the talks "are enormous and only just beginning to be understood," the American president gave initial emphasis to an American offer for general and complete disarmament, an offer which—it is implied—the Soviet negotiators rejected. But—and this mood is implicit throughout the speech—there is reason for great optimism: "While we parted company with this American offer still on the table, we are closer than ever before to agreements that could lead to a safer world without nuclear weapons" (p. 4). The tone of the speech is affirmative; and this upbeat sense of progress in the face of adversity frames much of the selective chronology we find in the speech itself.

As a preface to his narrative, Reagan began with two devices that were almost generic features of his rhetorical style. The first of these is a characteristically informal use of direct address. He speaks to his audience, "You, the American people," and tells them that he regards them as "full participants." He even says: "Believe me, without your support, none of these talks could have been held" (p. 4). Such unadorned, plain-spoken language performed a number of symbolic functions for the president. First, and most obviously, it bound together an honorific version of the American ēthos with that of Reagan himself, so as to offer a noble purpose for the nation's part in the talks. Second, it provided a subtle mark of contrast between the more open democratic traditions of the United States and the Western vision of the Soviet Union as a closed, authoritarian system. Third, in the wake of major confusions and contradictions about the actual negotiating position taken by America's representatives, it promised that candor and disclosure would clarify any lingering doubts and misperceptions. For the remainder of the speech, the contrast between Reagan's first-person direct address to the American people and his less direct, scarcely perceptible acknowledgment of other audiences provides one of the more striking paradoxes of his advocacy.

The second figurative device for which the President was renowned was the homespun allegory invoked to condense and simplify complex issues. In introducing his discussion of what transpired during the negotiations, Reagan began with a kind of primer on the deterrence policy of *Mutual Assured Destruction*, and his own dreams for his Strategic Defense Initiative: "So here we sit with thousands of nuclear warheads targeted on each other and capable of wiping out both our countries" (p. 4). Following this blocking of the scene, Reagan introduced a more sweeping, global rationale for the controversial initiative: "Believing that a policy of mutual destruction and slaughter of their citizens and ours was uncivilized, I asked our military a few years ago to study and see if there was a practical way to destroy nuclear missiles after their launch but before they can reach their targets rather than just destroy people. This is the goal for what we call SDI" (p. 4).

The body of Reagan's speech was widely viewed as an attempt to counter criticism that his commitment to Star Wars had been the chief obstacle to a successful treaty. In this light, it is interesting that, of the nine remaining passages dealing specifically with the negotiations themselves, all but one were concerned with the Strategic Defense Initiative. In the first few, Reagan presented himself as taking the iniative with respect to the troublesome question of SDI. To use his own language, "I offered a proposal that we continue our present research. . . . I explained that even though we would have done away with our offensive ballistic missiles, having the defense would protect against cheating." The president, in one of his homespun figurative analogies, "likened it to our keeping our gas masks even though the nations of the world had outlawed poison gas after World War I." According to Reagan's narrative, "we seemed to be making progress on reducing weaponry" (p. 5), despite Gorbachev's opposition to SDI; and the first day ended on a note of optimism.

The second day began on that note as well, in Reagan's version of events. The respective negotiation teams, who had worked through the previous night, returned with considerable areas of agreement and possible compromise. But then, Reagan acknowledges, substantial differences arose. On his telling, the Americans sought to mollify Soviet concerns about SDI by proposing a ten-year moratorium on the deployment of Star Wars defenses, during which time "all offensive ballistic missiles, of all ranges, would be eliminated." However, the Soviets demanded wording in the final treaty that "would have kept us from developing the SDI for the entire ten years." In Reagan's colloquial rendering of events, "he was killing SDI and unless I agreed, all that work toward eliminating nuclear weapons would go down the drain—cancelled." For all this, the president's conclusion is characteristically buoyant: "So I think then you can see that we did make progress in Iceland on a broad range of topics" (p. 5). By and large, this concludes his recitation of events.

On the matter of constituency, it is apparent that the president was not only speaking to an American audience, but was appealing to a national set of social knowledge convictions to interpret events, explain motivations, and express policy objectives. In speaking of his own suspicions of Soviet objectives, as well as repeated Soviet violations of previous treaties, he betrays a residue of cold war cynicism. In one particularly homespun commonplace, the president noted: "When it comes to human rights and judging Soviet intentions, we are all from Missouri: you have got to show us" (p. 5). And if the key issue of this speech is the positioning of SDI, it is worth noting that the president's recalcitrance on Star Wars is justified by a solemn pledge to the American people that he will not trade it away. Beyond this ground of conviction, when the president returned in the conclusion of his speech to the Star Wars issue, he did so in light of *American* reservations: "I realize some Americans may be asking tonight: Why not accept Mr. Gorbachev's demand?" (p. 5). His answer is that SDI is "America's insurance policy," and further on that "SDI is America's security guarantee." He concludes by suggesting that "the American people should reflect on these critical questions. How does a defense of the United States threaten the Soviet Union or anyone else?" (p. 5). The *New York Times* suggested that, at this point, Reagan was almost pleading with Gorbachev to give up his opposition to SDI. But this seems naive. In light of the ease with which a successful missile defense could unsettle a shrinking deterrence balance (thus allowing a first-strike capability), it is unlikely that Reagan expected this rhetorical question to be persuasive to the General Secretary. The question is posed to the same constituency for whom the speech was intended and addressed, those most likely to rally behind a popular president in difficulty—the American people.

Finally, we come to the most interesting characteristic of the Reagan speech—its form of inference. Outwardly, it is presented as a straightforward narrative of events, with clear deliberative intent. The idea is to explain the happenings clearly from an American perspective and then to leave room for future compromise and agreement. However, this outward deliberative framework is complicated by two factors: first, the president's generic use of discourse as a language game designed to frustrate policy formation, and second, the unprecedented opposition within his own language between technological and utopian terminologies. As my colleagues G. Thomas Goodnight and Janice Rushing have demonstrated, the Reagan argument is usually comprised of noble objectives (his own), but then qualified by scenic constraints and attributions of motive so sinister as to make it impossible to implement the objectives in question.[44] His speeches on "zero option" and SDI both provide dramatic evidence of this textual double bind. In the post-Reykjavik report, he attempts something of this same strategy, but with an important difference.

In this speech, the President not only had to explain deterrence theory and SDI, two highly complex, technical subjects; he also had to juxtapose both these with the more rarefied utopian dream of a world without nuclear weaponry, a vision which had often been a key feature of his previous language games. This time, in other words, he was not rejecting arms control or limited cutbacks as too little; he had come up against an actual Soviet agreement to reduce and eliminate nuclear weaponry from the earth altogether—hence the ambiguities of proposal and motive. Why, after all, would the Soviets want this? Reagan alludes to unnamed, sinister motives. Yet it is our strength that has brought them to the conference table. He says as much. Then why not accede to the condition on Star Wars? If we are that strong, we don't need it. Here Reagan, within a short paragraph, reverts to an earlier, but now less plausible, strategy: "Why are the Soviets so adamant that America remain forever vulnerable to Soviet rocket attack? As of today, all free nations are utterly defenseless against Soviet missiles" (p. 4). This must come as a forbidding thought to those who had earlier placed confidence in the strength of the American deterrent. The entire speech seems to fold in on itself this way. In trumpeting America's strength as the secret of summit success, Reagan pronounced that this summit was thus very different from previous ones—as if to suggest that at all previous summits, America had been weak. The president's reversion to symbolic form thus presents a strange new twist to an old, previously reliable strategy. This deliberative form of language did indeed collapse on itself, but with a significant difference. The reiteration of old pieties to trusted audiences now seems to construe a developing world-historical situation from the margins of provinciality.

Gorbachev's speech.   As was the custom for his addresses, the General Secretary's speech was longer and considerably more comprehensive than the American president's. It also took the form of a report, designed to highlight the Soviet position on key events and issues of the negotiations. However, two aspects of it reflect key departures both from custom and from Reagan's speech. First, Gorbachev had the benefit of the president's version of events and could be understood as replying to the president. Second, this speech was, in design and execution, consistent with his own glasnost policy. For instance, after the summit stalemate, Gorbachev gave a lengthy press conference, whereas Reagan did not. Throughout his formal speech, there is an obvious consistency of doctrine; yet Gorbachev showed little interest in adopting a doctrinaire, party position. His tone is one of insistent disclosure and, I would judge, exasperation.

Gorbachev began his speech by acknowledging that the recently concluded talks represented "an important political event, an event the consequences of which, as we are sure, will be felt for a long time to come in international affairs" (p. 6). Proclaiming that "stopping the arms race" was the primary item on the Soviet agenda at the Reykjavik talks, he attempted to put this theme in perspective. To do this, he must first set aside certain Western misconceptions about Soviet motives and conditions: "What then are the motives why we're so insistent on making this the most important issue? Very often from abroad we hear that the reason is that we have internal difficulties in our country. The West thinks or hopes that perhaps the Soviet Union will, in the final analysis, be unable to bear the arms race, economically will break and will therefore come and bow to the West. . . . *And this, by the way, was also something that we noted in the speech by President Reagan after the meeting"* (p. 6; emphasis added).

This remarkably blunt reference allowed him to assert that such hopes as these are "built upon sand" and "dangerous as well." He continued, as one might expect, to assert the unity, vision, economic power, and strength of the Soviet Union and its people. "But," he added abruptly, "to play a power *game,* we do not want this. This is an extremely dangerous activity, in our rocket nuclear age. We are firmly convinced that this feverish state—long-term feverish state—of international affairs carries with it a threat of the nuclear challenge and therefore we must take steps away from the nuclear abyss" (p. 6). Sincere or not, this interruption of cold war convention provided a motivational exigence that helped to sustain his narrative. It also recaptured a sense of Soviet initiative for the talks.

The body of Gorbachev's address is a remarkably detailed accounting of the talks themselves, containing some striking contrasts and surprises in relation to the Reagan version. According to Gorbachev, it was the Soviet Union that proposed the initial, five-year, 50 percent reduction in nuclear weaponry. Gorbachev describes the overall proposals this way: "These measures, had they been accepted, would make a new beginning—open a new era in the life of mankind, a nonnuclear era. This would make a real breakthrough in the international situation which would be absolutely real. It was not just a matter of reducing nuclear arms as was the case in SALT I, SALT II, and other treaties. But here we were speaking about the actual elimination of nuclear weapons in a relatively short time" (p. 6). However, it was the last, pivotal feature of the Soviet proposal that interfered with an effective outcome of the discussions. This final item was that both sides abide by the strict interpretation of the ABM treaty *and* the treaty banning nuclear weapons testing. As Gorbachev explained, "We're entering into a completely new situation," and "we have to protect ourselves from all kinds of eventualities." Specifically, the concern was that a radically new weapon or nuclear defense initiative might "undermine the equality of the two sides in disarming" (p. 6). On the matter of SDI or, in Gorbachev's words, "this problem that the Administration has created for itself when the President himself has gotten involved in space weapons," the General Secretary conceded that the American side should be permitted to engage in laboratory research under the terms of the ABM treaty but insisted that both sides affirm that they will not withdraw from the treaty for ten years, by which time nuclear weaponry would be eliminated.

After allowing that the American side posed questions, asked for clarifications, and raised objections, Gorbachev claimed that he would accept complete verification for compliance, including on-site inspection. But at this point of Gorbachev's version, there was an impasse of major proportions, largely due to American intransigence. To hear his view of the difficulties, "The President and his Secretary of State started right away, one might say, to talk about certain objections and disagreements. In these words, we could immediately hear the kind of tone that we were already familiar with, which we had heard time and again for months at the Geneva talks" (p. 6). In this more heated rendering of the difficulties, Gorbachev openly attacked the ēthos of the American president. He began by presenting himself as incredulous at the president's resistance to accepting his proposals: "We are proposing to engage in talks on missiles in Asia, we are proposing to accept your position in Europe—and now you're going back on your own proposals, Mr. President? How can you do that?" At this point, Gorbachev reported, he gave the president a copy of a draft agreement which "we could then sign during my visit to the United States." But after lunch the president replied with "a mothball type of tract which is now stifling and suffocating the Geneva talks. All sorts of intermediate interim proposals and levels and so on and so forth. Not one single new thought. Not a single fresh approach, not a single new idea that would contain at least a hint of some kind of solution, some kind of movement forward" (p. 6). Gorbachev described the situation that was developing as "really rather dramatic," and in language proper to such an occasion, stated: "It was becoming clear, comrades, that the Americans came to Reykjavik without having anything behind their souls. The impression that we got was that they came here simply to gather the fruits into their own basket, that they came empty-handed."[45]

This revealing accusatory tone suggests that the General Secretary interpreted the American resistance to his proposals in a highly personalized manner. Beyond this, and imprinting itself on the form of this speech, is an intensity of character indictment so extreme as to border on vilification. Gorbachev tells his audience that repeatedly he had to ask the president to listen more attentively, to take his proposals seriously. The ten-year full elimination agreement is reached *only* because the President "found it difficult to fight against his own zero-option proposal." But when the "last straw" of SDI was raised anew and Reagan offered to share the technological results and the system itself with the Soviets, Gorbachev shares his reply to the president: "Mr. President, I cannot take this idea of yours seriously, the idea that you will share results on SDI with us. You don't want to share with us even equipment for dairy plants at this point, and now you're promising us that you're going to share results on SDI development? This would be a second American revolution if something like this happened, but revolutions don't happen

that often" (p. 6). With the refusal of the United States to compromise on
SDI or anything else, Gorbachev concludes, with apparent anger: "I said
quite clearly that I now have doubts as to the sincerity, to the honesty of
the U.S. position, that you are intending to do something that might be
detrimental to the U.S.S.R. side" (p. 6).

And so "we were at a standstill." Gorbachev acknowledges that, in exasperation, he made of the Soviet proposals a package and said that without United States compliance to the ABM and test treaties, all else was
invalid. In his words, "the President and the Secretary of State reacted
to this firmness on our part very painfully." So, inevitably, the question
of how to end the meeting was discussed. As for how to conclude this
speech, Gorbachev's unprecedented step, all the better to dramatize the
poignancy of regret, was to read aloud to his worldwide audience the text
which he and President Reagan did *not* sign at Reykjavik:

> The U.S.S.R. and the United States would undertake for a period
> of 10 years not to take advantage of the right of withdrawing from
> the ABM treaty and during this period to adhere strictly to all its
> provisions. Testing of all space elements of anti-ballistic defense in
> space will be eliminated except research and testing in laborato-
> ries. Within the first five years through 1991, strategic offensive
> weapons will be reduced fifty percent. During the second five years
> of this 10-year period, the remaining fifty percent of strategic offen-
> sive weapons of the two sides will be eliminated. Thus, by the end
> of 1996, the strategic weapons of the U.S. and the U.S.S.R. will be
> totally eliminated." (p. 7)

One might well debate whether such a proposal was realistic or politically prudent. But there is little doubt that, within the forum of global
possibilities, it was rhetorically powerful. There also seems little doubt
that Gorbachev himself was moved by the appeal of this vision. In his
peroration, he states: "Being literally within one, two, or three steps
from reaching a decision or decisions, that could have become historic
for our entire nuclear missile era, these steps we were unable to take. So
there was no turning point in world history. Although—I will say that
once again—although it was possible" (p. 7). As if sensing the weight
of this failed possibility, this road not taken, Gorbachev professes: "Our
conscience is clear. One cannot reproach us for anything. We did all we
could." The failure, put in the most stinging language imaginable, was
a failure of nerve, vision, and character, a failure of American leader-

ship: "Our partners did not have enough breadth of approach, broad-mindedness, understanding of the historic moment, the courage and de-termination." In conclusion, Gorbachev reminds the United States and his larger audience that these proposals are still on the table, that the United States may need time to clear its thinking, to resist the pressures of its highly technical military industries, and to broaden its understand-ing of the new forces at work in the world. He pledges to work tirelessly to develop a "constructive, realistic approach to the political situation" (p. 7).

I have been suggesting that disputation over perspectives on authority might perform a reflective inventional function. In light of this claim, it is worth continuing our parallelism across constituency, or "venue," and form of inference—as we did with Reagan—to see where it may lead. Like Reagan, Gorbachev addressed his remarks to the immediate audi-ence and to his constituency, the Soviet people. Yet, there is considerable textual and performative evidence that Gorbachev is also addressing a wider constituency, wider than the Soviet bloc and surely wider than that addressed by Reagan. In his attempts to disclose the tactical think-ing of the West and his evaluation of the Reagan team's performance at the summit, Gorbachev is clearly introducing considerations and inter-ests that transcend the locale of his own cultural base. In fact, he speaks frequently of the interests of Europe, of "freeing its peoples from the fear of nuclear catastrophe," the people of other continents, even of mankind, and the "world-historical situation." There is no conclusive evidence that Gorbachev succeeded in reaching such a constituency. Nor can I prove that the Soviet leader sought to do anything more profound than isolate Reagan within the intercultural forum through the broader ap-peals of this visionary discourse. But the broader aim seems difficult to deny.

There are also important departures in the pattern of inference em-ployed by Gorbachev. He introduces certain doctrinaire assumptions in-ternal both to the Soviet Union ("We are strong") and to the ritual of power politics ("We will match you move for move"). But he introduces these only to pay brief respect to realpolitik and then sets the language game aside. This is a noteworthy development, largely because the real-politik vision of strength and moves is closely related to Reagan's own political language. This is why Gorbachev is able to speak with such disdain of Reagan's "levels and interim and intermediate balances." The remainder of Gorbachev's inferential style, his "way of thinking" in public, is also based on a kind of policy narrative. But this narrative, despite overlaps in events and episodes, is very different in tone from that of Reagan.

Gorbachev presents us with a deliberative framework, but one with an unmistakable tragic motif. In Wittgenstein's later notes, he writes: "All tragedies could begin with the lines, 'Everything would have worked out alright were it not for the fact that . . . .' "[46] This is the predominant tone of Gorbachev's address. This may help to explain why it takes an abrupt turn toward the forensic mood of accusation. The tone of tragedy is characteristic of the well-intentioned participant who has realized (peripeteia) the fateful turn of events. But since in this case "our conscience is clear" and "we did all we could," it is only our partners in historical failure, now our antagonists, who are blamed and indicted. This may be one reason why the attack is so harsh; the magnitude of missed opportunity only serves to intensify the crime. So this rather unusual address lingers over the narrative juncture of "what might have been," only to add, as if as an afterthought, that both the proposals and the door remain open for future progress (p. 7). Whether Gorbachev's sorrow was genuine is a matter of conjecture for his biographers.[47] But there is little question that this appeal to vision and possibility, this open acknowledgment of missed opportunity, helped to solidify his initiative within a developing rhetorical forum.

The disputation over authority at Reykjavik helps to engender a sense of "event," as well as a horizon of appreciation that literally would not have been possible within the singular perspective of either man.[48] For instance, despite the discrepancies I have emphasized here, it is interesting that the two key participants were able to generate a remarkable degree of congruence about what happened and what possibilities remained. Since much of the publicity surrounding the talks stressed their conflict, rather than their common ground,[49] it is particularly interesting that the dispute over stated and unstated occurrences should have disclosed a reliable account of the episode. The clearer picture of Reykjavik is afforded not by one of the speeches, but rather by both taken together.

Once this core domain of convergence is granted, however, the more critical issue has to do with some startling discrepancies in perspective on authority. Reagan, speaking to a national constituency, was forced to subordinate *peace* to *strength* as a term of value and neither to make nor to acknowledge any compromise or concessions. Gorbachev, projecting his discourse toward an international constituency, listed the concessions of his nation proudly, as a signal act of good faith and vision. Reagan's national constituency turned him toward a solid cultural consensus of pledges and commitments. Gorbachev's projected international constituency seemed to loosen his ties to doctrine, allowing for speculation on historical moments and possibilities. Earlier, I remarked that Gorbachev's was a tragic view, preoccupied with the opportunities that had been missed. Reagan's was the more avowedly optimistic. This fits his less engaged stance as one who presides, who rationalizes mistakes and failings and awaits a better day and another chance. But Gorbachev played a most unusual tragedian, one not ruled by fate but alive to the fresh possibility of a unique historical moment. His was the more aggressive public stance of seizing the exigence and passing lethal public judgment should we fail. His was, in other words, a rhetoric of *jamais vu:* the fresh, unprecedented character of the moment. And, as a Marxist of a new generation, he was a tragedian of grand design. Reagan, on the other hand, was a most unusual optimist. His tendency was to see these exchanges in repetitive patterns, just as his mythologies of both Soviet doctrine and deterrence policy repeated along familiar lines. His was a rhetoric of déjà vu: the representative anecdote being "There we go again!" He was a comedian of necessity.

In light of this curious inversion of world views, it is worth asking whether the global forum served to remove *and* remind the advocates of their own doctrinal participations. Within the elliptical transitions of ongoing history, no one can answer with any certainty. But it may be that a genuine agreement, in this time and age, required both the bedrock of mythic strength ("no concessions") in the West and the framework of visionary possibility ("although it was possible") from the Soviet Union.[50] The figurative language of both stability and transformation have been seen to work together before.

INTEGRITY AS ISSUE:
ELIZABETH LINDER AND CONNIE MACK

As I am using the term, "integrity" deals with the way issues and positions fall out and hold up over the course of an ongoing episode.[51] In a rhetorical sense, integrity is less an attribute specifically applicable to persons and their character than an emergent, acquired trait of messages that are presented and upheld in public life. It is the openness of a rhetorical forum that brings our positions from a stance of foreclosure to one of exposure. The normalized rhetorical forum's persistence in time, its durability, provides a place stable enough for the normative expectation of integrity to emerge. Within such a forum, positions hold still long enough to elicit some sense of their answerability.[52] If one's positions and messages have integrity, they will either withstand public scrutiny or react, respond, and correct themselves in light of opposed positions and messages. If they lack integrity, as a great many political messages do, they will run and hide, grin and spin. There is a sense in which all serious political disputation is about integrity; for this is what allows the *fact* of dispute to acquire meaning. For this reason, integrity may be seen as the opposite of *hypocrisy*.[53] Note, for instance, that in our last example the clash of perspectives at Reykjavik led Gorbachev to attack the American team's *integrity*. Even here, the attack was less on private character than on the inability of the president to abide by his own public proposals.

While not every personality or character easily admits to the possibility of integrity, the *norm* of integrity becomes available to us only through the unfolding of an episodic *sequence*. As we saw in chapter 6, we must be able to follow through on the claims of utterances over time, to see if action matches intent, if promise yields fulfillment. Such a process takes *time*.

I would now like to shift the setting a bit and deal not with a long-term ritual process, but with a more condensed episode, one of the pivotal episodes in the Reagan administration's notorious Iran–contra scandal. It occurred in mid-April 1987, long after the most notable revelations of illegal weapons sales and equally illegal state sponsorship of the contras in Nicaragua. Around this time a young man by the name of Benjamin Linder, an American civilian working on domestic support projects in Nicaragua, was killed by contra forces there. Linder was engaged in building dams and with irrigation projects, the sorts of engineering projects that Peace Corps volunteers still engage in. He died in a country which still had, and *has*, diplomatic relations with the United States. He was unarmed when he was shot in the head at close range.[54]

The episode involves the parents of Benjamin Linder and a young Congressman, Connie Mack of Florida. The exchange occurred before a crowded hearing of the House Western Hemisphere Subcommittee, which had been called into session to investigate the conduct of the contras *and* the circumstances of Linder's death. Testimony and eyewitness accounts had already established that he was ambushed, unarmed, and shot at close range. Here is an excerpt from the exchange:

Mack: I guess what really has me upset is that I just cannot understand how you can use grief that I know you feel, use it to politicize this situation. Or to allow yourself to be used to politicize
this situation. You are caught, as your son was, in a cross fire, a
struggle between two ideas.

Elizabeth Linder (interrupting): My son was *not* caught in a cross
fire!

Mack: You are caught in a cross fire here today between two different
beliefs. There is a group that feels their goal and their objective in Nicaragua is to bring about peace at any price. There are
those who, on their own soil, are fighting for freedom. I guess
the reason I find this so difficult is that I don't want to be tough
on you, but I really feel that you have asked for it.

(*cries of "Oh no!" and commotion in the audience*)

Elizabeth Linder: That was about the most cruel thing you could
have said.

Mack: I don't consider it cruel. I consider it to be the point. We're
not here today listening to all the details of your son's death.
We're here publicizing a particular point of view, and I think
you'll have to take the questions.[55]

Here, too, albeit in much more condensed form, is a dispute about
the propriety of discourse. The unmistakable evidence for this comes
from the constant indexical references to occasion and setting ("what
the Linders are here today doing," "what we're here today doing," and so
forth). There is also an entire sequence of meta-communicative claims,
referring to each other's discourse—using grief to politicize, saying
something cruel, whether the discourse is to the point, whether one is
being tough on the Linders, whether they have to take the questions,
and so forth. Notice that Mack does not question the sincerity of the
Linders; he concedes it is grief that they genuinely feel. What he questions is the political uses of these emotions, in this forum, at this time.
Although Mack nowhere says so, his concerns about propriety focus on
the domain of integrity: what their discourse is actually doing over the
course of the episode.

But critics should notice that Mack is not content simply to raise questions. He too wants to turn this exchange in a figurative direction; and
so we get the observation that the Linders, like their son, are caught in a
political and ideological cross fire. This is where Elizabeth Linder draws
the line. In a voice of ice, she interrupts: "My son did not die in a cross

fire." It is an abrupt denial of Mack's figurative gambit, a return to the literal plane. It has the added virtue of being true. Her son was shot in the head, literally executed by contras. Optimally, such a rhetorical interruption would force some kind of reflection on the part of the actors— but not this time.

Mack goes right back to his disputed analogue, placing the Linders in the same false position that he has placed their son, and then implies that both have gotten what they deserved, that they have in effect asked for it. One could give Congressman Mack something he wouldn't grant Benjamin Linder—the benefit of the doubt—and assume that he wasn't trying to say that the Linders deserved their son's death. Even so, the false association—corrected once by Elizabeth Linder—is never qualified by Mack, and one is left with the distinct impression that, just as Linder deserved his death, so his parents deserve their grief.

This is what makes Elizabeth Linder's interjection, "That was about the most cruel thing you could have said," so powerful. It is totally consistent with her original point, spontaneously sincere, and it says—by way of implicature—"How dare you!!!"[56] While I doubt that it was her intent, Elizabeth Linder has granted the issue of integrity and totally reversed the accusation. As the exchange trails off, Mack (a bit like Joe McCarthy, for those with long memories) seems not to grasp what has gone wrong.

There are several grounds for questioning the integrity of Mack's discourse. Most obviously, he contradicts his own point in lecturing the Linders about politicizing their grief. He can't resist jockeying for position in politicizing his own figurative understanding of how and why the Linders are here. They, like their son, are in a cross fire. So he abandons the aesthetic distance he claims to have. Second, Mack's figure is based on a literally false claim—that Linder died in a cross fire—and, supposing it were true, the even less plausible notion that someone who dies in a cross fire somehow deserves his fate for having been there in the first place. Finally, as the figure seems to gallop away from him, he abandons any pretext of qualification—for audience, mood, or setting. Only then does a sort of cruelty by accretion surface.

But now the qualifier. While I have little respect for the merits of Mack's position, he does in fact have a defensible response, a response he attempts to make. It is that grief is a private emotion, inappropriate to this public forum. If you want to politicize your grief, then fine, let's talk politics. That is what he means by "I think you'll have to take the questions." By now, of course, it is too late.

It is difficult to know when an audience will sense that a boundary has been violated, a norm stretched to the breaking point. But this particular exchange was condensed further and then repeated, on both the network evening news and CNN news over some 48 hours. A majority of Americans always opposed the contra support system, whether it was regarded as legal or not. And in the context of the surrounding scandal, an episode like this may have functioned as a metonymy of policy choice. Even without the figurative drama of children running from American bombers or civil rights demonstrators splashed against walls by the hoses and dogs of Bull Connor, there are some condensed associations that simply derail the reduplicative capacities of our political discourse. Thus it was that the moral equivalent of the Founding Fathers belatedly began to lose its license to kill.

This example also involved a dispute about propriety. But here it was not about the authority to define a forum for proper conduct. Rather, the forum is presupposed. No one questions the propriety of the House Subcommittee. Rather, what was at issue was the integrity of what was said within the forum. How well did the discourse stand up to reflection over the course of the episode and maintain coherence within its own assumptions and responsiveness to the interjected thoughts of others? I think it can be shown that Mack's discourse was severely deficient where such integrity is concerned. But what is more important, as in our examples of disputation over authority, is that in the disturbance of this dispute lay a domain of invention. Granted, it has taken a singular horror to make the inventional dispute possible; an American civilian has shown us what countless Nicaraguan civilians have already experienced. The other has become oneself. But in openly disputing the integrity of discourse in an acknowledged public place, we are also beginning to reopen a place for the domain of conscience as it pertains to policy formation. While this inventional task is hardly complete, it is already no small accomplishment.

RESPONSIBILITY AS CONSCIENCE: JENNINGER AT KRISTALLNACHT

Responsibility, as conceptualized here, involves the internalization of the voice of others as an encounter with conscience. Here "conscience" may be thought of rhetorically as the state of acting as an audience and

a witness for what one is and does.[57] Now the propriety of such an encounter may itself be challenged. The paths and implications of action
are continuous, irreversible, and never completely foreordained. It is a
curiosity of the moral claim's generality that almost any decision or act
can be charged with ramifications in this area. At the same time, only
Hegel's "beautiful soul" would find all choices and concerns to have
moral weight. For those courses of conduct which raise moral issues,
there is no easy way to designate a proper tribune of judgment.

So this third range of concerns for the practice, forms, and forums of
rhetoric is a complex, and even treacherous, territory to chart. Sometimes such concerns require that our intuitions direct us beyond our
arguments. Accordingly, I want to borrow liberally from the work of
James Boyd White to suggest that the clash of moral stances need not
terminate discussion but can function as an inventional challenge to
continue discourse.[58] While it is true that audiences are usually more
comfortable judging their adversaries than themselves, this does not
mean that reflection and rhetoric are always at odds with one another.
At times, as in Lincoln's second inaugural address, words are found to
uncover themes larger than any partisan position. Even in more recent
episodes, we may, and do, agonize over the propriety of our positions,
their distance from our deeds, and the boundaries for judgment and responsibility in our life and time. Occasionally even flawed and failed
rhetoric finds itself addressing conscience.

My final example is not easy to discuss. Moreover, it is on a different
level from what has gone before. It entails the question of propriety on
the broadest scale imaginable. If our first case examined appearance and
propriety in terms of the authority to define and the second examined
private versus public propriety from the point of view of the integrity of
discourse practice itself, the third considers culture and the historical
practice of propriety from the stance of generational and historical distance—historical accountability for itself. My suspicion is that when the
crimes are unfathomable and the stain indelible, no conventional forum
can contain the discourse.

On 10 November 1988, the Speaker of the West German parliament,
Philipp Jenninger, gave a remarkable commemorative address on the
fiftieth anniversary of the terrible events known as "Kristallnacht," the
night when the Nazi regime more or less officially inaugurated its
policy of exterminating the Jews by burning the synagogues, rounding up
random ghetto Jews, forcing evictions, and so forth—the whole policy

known as the pogroms. The circumstances surrounding the entire commemorative affair were volatile. Kristallnacht had never been officially
commemorated before (although everyone knew what it meant). Three
years earlier, the aforementioned Bitburg affair had sparked a passionate debate about guilt and responsibility, who the real victims of the
war were, the uniqueness of this genocidal policy, whether the German
people could ever atone for these events, and so on.[59] There had also been
debate about historical revisionism in Germany concerning the war, a
debate in which Habermas himself played a leading role.[60]

In the midst of all this we find a solemn ceremony, to which hun-
dreds of dignitaries, Jewish leaders, state representatives from Israel,
survivors, and German politicos have been invited, and in the midst of
the ceremony, a remarkable keynote address by the Speaker of the West
German parliament. The speech so shocked those assembled—diplo-
mats, Greens, Social Democrats, Free Democrats—that many walked
out. Others tried to shout down passages of the speech. Reaction was
so uniformly negative in Germany that Jenninger was forced to resign
early the next morning.[61] In the Western press, which printed only small
excerpts from the speech, the initial impression was that Jenninger somehow endorsed the taboo National Socialist sentiments and had given
expression to anti-Semitism. Later interpretations corrected this false
impression but nonetheless concluded that Jenninger had been guilty of
monumental impropriety.

Indeed, anyone who wonders about the generalizability of rhetoric's
compositional requirements would do well to consult the editorial commentary on this conspicuous failed effort. As the New York Times
summed things up, "The consensus among politicians, newspapers and
many Germans today was that Mr. Jenninger had seriously erred in
the style and timing of his presentation."[62] Prominent scholar Sebastian Haffner said: "He had no sense of occasion. He said true things
at the wrong moment." He went on to observe: "The 10th of November is not the right moment to think of fascination with Hitler, which
certainly existed. If a man has been murdered, one doesn't speak at
his funeral about the interesting personality of the murderer."[63] Willy
Brandt, former chancellor, said he was especially saddened, "because Jenninger didn't intend anything bad; he simply didn't rise to the occasion."
Jenninger himself was shaken but took the critique to heart. His resignation letter acknowledged: "My speech was not understood in the way
I meant it by many of those who heard it."[64]

A professor of German history, David Schoenbaum, provided the cue that sparked my own active interest when he observed: "When you read the whole text, it's really a decent enough speech. But it sounded to them like he identified with the things he quoted and discussed."[65] How, we might wonder, was such a thing possible? Here is one reading.

The speech attempts to document and chronicle the unfathomable historical crimes of this period in German history in painstaking detail. But Jenninger does this from what he probably thought was the only place that they could be made comprehensible—a sometimes ironic, sometimes diagnostic, imposed distance, a place outside his own chosen occasion and forum. Although I began my reading with genuine regard for Jenninger's moral courage, I soon came to understand why many people left. Even in translation, the text was eerily claustrophobic. Just as the speech could not contain its event, so the forum could not contain the speech. First the audience left, then the speaker. A day later, only the message remained—and the mystery of an event for which there were no words.

This is a very lengthy speech, a speech motivated by epic ambition. Not the least of its problems was its attempt to combine a heroic style with a gesture of atonement. After acknowledging the many luminaries in attendance and ominously implicating both Germanies in the events being commemorated, the first jarring indicator of disturbance emerges when Jenninger announces the purpose of his address: "It is not the victims rather but us who have to remember and give an account, for the crimes happened in our neighborhood, because we Germans want to get a clear comprehension of our history and from this, doctrines for the development of our present, our future."[66] At this point, I found myself thinking of the extraordinary Syberburg film *Our Hitler*, and apparently so did others. There was shouting from the audience, to which Jenninger responded: "Please, let this dignified event proceed in the prepared form!" The shouting continued, followed by: "Please understand if I must ask for your silence."

Jenninger then proceeded to offer a very detailed, chronological account of what happened on Kristallnacht: the destruction of over 200 synagogues, the death of 100 Jews, and the displacement of 30,000 more to concentration camps. Jenninger also made public the largely unspoken truth of Kristallnacht. As he put it, "It was chosen to mark a turning point in the political experience of the Jewish people. The time for a legal pretext for moral offenses was at an end. Now began the path toward the systematic destruction of Jews in Germany and in large parts of Europe." At this point, the speaker invoked the deeper, more problematic question of support and complicity. Most commemorative speakers, at related events, limit themselves to, as the *New York Times* put it, "expressions of remorse and shame." Jenninger appears to take direct issue with the sufficiency of such sentiments. As he said, "We speak of dismay and shame, about pity, even about disgust and horror. But only very sporadically was there compassion and practical solidarity, support and help. We saw the ending, and what would come. But most of us looked away and were silent. Even the churches said nothing." These are impassioned words, but in their passion, they are openly confrontational as well. They literally implicate everyone.

Now follows the lengthy section of history and quotation that many found problematic. Jenninger quotes a minister of the German judiciary under Hitler who claimed that Hitler derived the legitimacy of his rule from a form of consensus building. He recalls bits and pieces of the Third Reich as spectacle, the uniforms, the Summer Olympic games in Berlin. The tone shifts, almost imperceptibly, to the deepest irony: "Rather than being driven to a state of despair and hopelessness, the people were optimistic and self-confident. Did not Hitler help enact what Wilhelm the Second could only promise, namely to lead Germany toward the time of its greatness? Was he not really chosen by Providence, a Führer who is given to our people only once in a thousand years?" And then, "Certainly, ladies and gentlemen, no one other than Hitler had such a margin of support for leading Germany back from its defeats."

One can only imagine what the actual audience thought of these sentiments. To some extent they were true. But the endorsement of Hitler as savior in the early months and years is here equated ironically with the endorsement of pogroms and the abomination of official genocide. My own feeling is that at least some Germans might have been entitled to a right of denial or a plea of temporary disorientation—a disorientation that many in the West (including Joseph Kennedy, Charles Lindbergh, and the Pope) must share. I cannot prove that historical abomination and endorsement are linked ironically. But there seems to be no other way to explain the chiasma of discomfort. One of the developing curiosities of this speech is that it implies no identifiable external stance from which the point of the irony may be grasped, no immunized place for author and audience to grasp its terrible secret. This may be another way of saying that these events, in their very enormity, are too close to their audience to permit space for reflection and eventual renewal.

This is particularly true of one notorious passage in the speech which refers to the Jews in an ironic mode. Here is Jenninger: "And as for the Jews, hadn't they in the past, after all, impudently sought a position that they did not deserve? Must they now not accept a bit of disciplining? Hadn't they, in fact, deserved to be put in their proper place? And above all, apart from the wild exaggerations which were not to be taken seriously, did not basic parts of this propaganda accord with one's own speculations and convictions?" The pain here is almost palpable. There is no way one can internally concede this view in light of the audience and the ineradicable historical consequences. There is no way to deny their thematic truth. In the absence of a clear normative place from which to concede and move beyond their meaning, the irony beckons to its audience as a bleak, epochal taunt, origin and destiny unknown.

It is here that the most confounding sections of the speech appear. For reasons that are not clear to me, Jenninger is determined to show that there is a tragic determinism to all that has happened to the Jews, based on the philosophy and folklore of German culture. For instance, he goes back a hundred years to show that it was common to link the vagaries and excesses of industrial capitalism to the Jews. He links a flood of publications by respected scholars and historians to this tendency, among them figures both within and outside Germany. What Jenninger is suggesting—and it had been suggested by many before him—is that Hitler did not invent his ideas, but rather borrowed and melded them into a peculiarly volatile concoction, and that with the particularly apropos theft of Darwinism, he was able to cloak his world view with a claim to scientific respectability. While *Mein Kampf* is still difficult to appreciate as anything but a crude, demented tract, Jenninger sees its themes as having been legitimated in other, unlikely places. Abruptly, Jenninger interrupts his own narrative of influences with a sudden accumulation of irreversible events: "In this sequence originated the factories of death. From the gas stoves, to extermination ovens, and crematoriums, while the shooting continued. Those innocent victims were not even allowed to have an executioner. Those culprits compensated for the hangman through the monstrous industrialized methods, true to their terminology, for exterminating 'vermin.' And today, in light of this last terrible event, we do not want to close our eyes." There is no Greek chorus to distract us from this descent into the maelstrom.

Irony, Burke wrote, presumes a loss of faith. But the loss of faith can never be total, or the compensation of meaning will never be regained. I found myself wondering about this as Jenninger takes us further and further beneath and beyond the conventions of recovery. In what I regard as his last irretrievable figure, he intones:

> It was Dostoevsky who put forth the proposition: "If God does not exist, everything is permissible." If there is no God, then all is relative and imaginary. It is *there*, only through the deeds of men. Then, there are no ordinances of value, no binding moral precepts, no criminal offenses, no guilt, no remorse of conscience. And then remember, for those who know this secret,—that "everything is permissible"—that all is suspended about our deeds, excepting our own will. We are free to completely disregard and set aside all codes of moral worth.

In light of all the earlier irony, this meta-maxim is almost dizzying in its implications. As a more nihilistic vision of nomos and physis is disjoined, one senses that it is designed to show what happens when modernity is fully endorsed. In fact, Jenninger later pronounces this same maxim, now filtered through the postmodern consciousness of Nietzsche as well, as "a prophetic anticipation of the political offenses of the twentieth century." My question is how we can retrieve our moral sensibilities once we have reified and recast them as emblems of a devolving history of ideas.

Jenninger wants to make the whole matter turn on questions of fact—hence his odd amalgam of ceremonial and forensic discourse. But he assumes that the fact, once disclosed, will be so horrific as to force confession and then retribution. The Dostoevsky–Nietzsche section is followed by an indescribable, poignant eyewitness account of a family of eight waiting to be executed by the SS. Here is an excerpt:

> After an order of an SS man who was holding a riding or dog whip in his hand, the people that were leaving the truck—men, women and children of every age—had to get rid of their clothes and put them, divided by shoes, underwear and outerwear, away. . . . Without screaming or crying the people got undressed, stood together with their families, kissed and said goodbye and waited for a sign of another SS-man, who stood by the grave and had a whip in his hand as well. . . . I watched a family of about eight persons, a man and a woman both aged about fifty years, with their children, who were about one, eight, and ten years old, as well as two grown-up daughters of about twenty and twenty-four years. An old woman

with snow-white hair held the one-year-old child in her arms, was singing him a song and tickling him. The child squealed with joy. The couple watched this with tears in their eyes. The father had a boy of about ten years and talked to him quietly. The boy fought back his tears. The father pointed to the sky with his finger, fondled him over his head and seemed to explain something to him. The SS-man at the grave shouted something to his comrade. This man separated about twenty persons from the rest of the group and gave the order to go behind the hill of soil. I went around this hill and stood on top of the huge grave. The people lay packed closely on top of the other in a way that only their heads were visible. From almost all the heads blood ran down over them. A couple of the shot people still moved. Some raised their arms and turned their heads so as to show that they were still alive.

I have felt a sense of violation even transcribing these twice-borrowed words. Imagine direct witness of their public expression. Here the tension between Jenninger's ironic moral arbitrariness and his exhaustive righteousness is eviscerating.

This passage is followed by the revelation that the eyewitness is himself an SS agent. After this comes an amazingly clinical acknowledgment by Hitler as to why the extermination program was a bureaucratic necessity. The speech by Hitler concludes: "Altogether we can say that we have fulfilled this most difficult task in love to our people. And we have not lost on our inside, in our hearts, souls, or character." I do not know how many remained in the audience to be moved, or appalled, by this candid tribute to German stoicism.

Jenninger then returns to his central thesis, as if in a litany of case law: "Many Germans allowed themselves to be blinded and seduced by National Socialism. Many more made these offenses possible through their willful ignorance. Many others committed the offenses themselves. The question of our guilt and evasion of responsibility must be answered by each person for himself. But which ever way we turn, we will come full circle, to face our public and ourselves." This is the key figurative anecdote of the speech. There is no refuge in the privacy of conscience. Even on this commemorative occasion, personal guilt is a public matter. This may be why the speech gives the distinct impression of having invaded cultural privacy in a public space.

Despite one's predilection for sympathy, this is a very difficult speech with which to affiliate. It has moments of grave, even heroic, eloquence; and I can only hope that history will treat it more favorably than its immediate, fleeing audience. But we are in the last years of a millennium; and although it is a time for perorations, there is much to explain that will never, that cannot, be explained. We are likely to see many addresses, perhaps not so distinguished, but as ambitious, as that of Philipp Jenninger. So some thoughts are in order.

In some senses, Jenninger's speech is the answer to the old introductory philosophy question of whether you can really address a rational forum, even in Nazi Germany. A typical answer is that you cannot, and that this implies a form of radical relativism. My feeling is that Jenninger has already granted the impossibility of reasoned address and so has resorted to indirection as confrontation—hence his self-consciously ironic style. I have no objection to the style on its own terms. My concern is that it may have abandoned more direct, reflective address prematurely, without ever having given it a fair chance. In Jenninger's discourse, and probably without his intent, the members of his German audience have been made characters in a performative symbolic act, rather than witnesses to, and judges of, their own role in history. Of course, it is not up to the audience to decide whether it is guilty. But neither is it entirely up to Jenninger, who, in a lengthy speech of atonement, says little to implicate himself, other than employing the editorial "we" a great deal. He seems to aspire to the role of the great German neo-expressionist Anselm Kiefer. But here we have an enlarged rhetorical canvas, but no coherent vision.

What causes people to displace themselves from the very presence of a discourse? to remove themselves from the forum in which discourse is addressed? I think that if we were to unpack it fully, we might find something like a figurative oppression, a violation of *distance* where some discourse is concerned. In other words, we are afraid to become a full partner in such discourse for fear of having to entertain sympathies that oppose our identity. I also feel this way about the PLO Declaration of Independence. But then there is the temporal imposition of discourse and the weight it carries. This is most obvious with Jenninger's and Germany's burdens from the ages. When these intersect, in the immediacy of address (as they do here), presence becomes intolerable. Absence and rhetorical exile are the only resort.

But is absence really possible? Jenninger did the unthinkable in his

November address when he condensed and disclosed this burden within a duly anointed, conventional political forum. Even in attempting to flee from the address, the audience becomes part of its larger enacted performance. That was surely not Jenninger's intent; but it is exactly what happened.

So there is a problem of invention here as well—the problem, if you will, of inventing an audience for a speech that cannot be heard; of moving beyond the authority to define a forum, through the integrity of discourse within a forum, to the responsibility of discourse which must defy or displace the conventions of a forum of judgment. Putting aside the general unevenness of the speech, its failure to create a consistently powerful *mood*, we are left with its principle figurative device of confrontation and judgment—irony. My question is whether irony can be used as a technique of reaffirmation. We know that irony can turn tables and displace pretense—perhaps most memorably in Mark Antony's funeral oration. But there, I would argue, the position to be redressed is not really marginal, and the audience is made witness to betrayal by others. Remember too that we are dealing with Mark Antony by way of Shakespeare by way of Kenneth Burke. Philipp Jenninger, by way of Farrell, is surely a bit more of a reach.

Like Shakespeare's Mark Antony, Jenninger employed irony so as to shift ceremonial rhetoric to forensic indictment. But unlike Antony, he wanted to indict the audience for betraying itself. He wanted to say: so are *we* all honorable men? I am not suggesting that Jenninger's task was impossible, but it was—to say the least—very, very difficult. The task was made virtually unmanageable by his attempt to launch irony without any larger reflective space to pass judgment. There can be no true irony for the nihilist, because there can be no transcending secret to be shared. Put another way, the secret behind the dark revelations of this speech is that there *is* no secret. By the time he has endorsed Dostoevsky's death of God, hence everything is permissible equation and Nietzsche's transvaluation of values, there can be no normative ground sufficiently compelling to license Jenninger's outrageous quest for atonement.

From Jenninger's own position, there can be no moment of true guilt or true redemption. In the postwar world, the theater of the absurd tried to find at least a temporary solution to this problem. But as every dramatic absurdist worth noting has noted, the absurd cannot offer this confrontation with responsibility and conscience in real time. Jenninger performed as a serious, conscientious German attempting to deal with forces and phenomena literally beyond his control. He was reduced—sadly, I feel—to the stance of an unwitting and ineffectual absurdist.

There is, incidentally, one unmistakable indicator of this failed atonement toward the conclusion of the address. Jenninger has just taken what seems an extemporaneous jab at revisionist historians in Germany. He appears to catch himself in mid-sentence: "That is why the demand to 'finally close off—end' our past is so senseless," he says. "Our past will not be stilled. It cannot be made to go away. This is, of course, with the exception of the very young—who could not be held to be guilty." What is wrong with these words? I think of another great German ironist, Hannah Arendt, and what she might have done with this allusion, this afterthought qualifier. The very young, natality, the renewal of the world, the redemption of the past through rebirth. Perhaps we can never forget this horrible past. But as we replenish the earth, maybe something will rise from the pond of ashes. Maybe we will learn to forgive.[67] But these words are never spoken. The whole speech could have been directed toward the child, not those we have killed, but those who survive, the new possibility, the world unborn. But the discourse is responsible only for, and to, the past, and it refuses to turn toward the future.

Very rarely in the examples I have discussed is there a moment in which the advocate of a contested position abides by judgment in its more traditional form, as if to concede error and conform to an authoritative verdict. But by any conventional measure, Jenninger's speech is such a case. As we have seen, it was judged immediately and harshly. But it now raises some challenging issues for rhetorical culture.

So let us rejoin our hypothesis on propriety disputes. It can be claimed that the Bitburg and the Iran–contra cases showed a certain degree of variation and reflection where authority and integrity were concerned. In each case, there was an inventional space of liminality. In the Reykjavik episode, dispute over something as apparently simple as what actually happened revealed the limitations of perspective, grounds, and even chosen constituency in the validation of a single speaker's authority. In the Linder case there was the initial battle about whether it was appropriate to express certain forms of emotion in an already legitimated forum. But that is only the surface of what was involved. We were then, as in all occasions of disturbance, reminded of our own participatory stake in what has been done. Subsequently we were removed from the immediacy of this setting—if only by the jarring dispute and mutual interruptions of proper procedure. This encouraged us to reflect. Finally, it invited us to choose. In saying that the Linder case presented us with an ethical inventional occasion, I mean that we are thrown back on our own convictions and forced to ask what is wrong with this picture. The result, if the picture is jarring and discrepant enough, is an occasion to test our integrity and eventually an opening for the emergence of something like conscience.

My last example might appear to be the most problematic. After all, the vehicle of moral confrontation was forced to relinquish his post. The Frankfurt paper and most commentators treated the Jenninger discourse as an unmitigated disaster. One editorial caption read "The End of the Dialectic," as if there were literally nothing more that could be said productively about Germany's "responsibility for its past."[68] The speech was, of course, monumentally inappropriate. So how can we see this same self-destructive phenomenon as inventional?

To answer this question, we need to remind ourselves that rhetoric transpires on more than a product-centered, instrumentalist domain. Most of the time, we tend to think of rhetoric as a form of instrumentality, a linear technē for hammering our wills into shape. This deprives rhetorical practice of much of its creativity, since it can only hit—or miss—what it is aiming at. The occasional exceptions (a Cooper Union, Gettysburg, or "I have a dream") are usually accorded special touchstone status—the work, after all, of exceptional persons. The rest of rhetoric is dismissed as distorted, perishable discourse, "old news." But if we think of rhetorical texts episodically, as I have been urging throughout this book, then certain expanded inventional options become available. Rhetoric can sometimes (in its very lack of full compass and closure) invert or blur the conventional way in which things have taken shape for us. It can throw us back on ourselves, to ask what we have become through all that we have simply taken for granted. Most important, in occasions of disturbance—like the congressional hearing on Linder, like Bitburg, and like the Kristallnacht commemoration—the text of rhetoric may be glimpsed as but one performative passage in a larger sequence.

So, with all due respect to the *Frankfurter Zeitung,* it was not the end of the dialectic. In holding his admittedly confused, out-of-focus mirror up to a clouded, taboo subject, Jenninger threw a harsh public light on painful memories. Of tens of thousands of letters that Jenninger received from all over the world, all but forty or fifty were supportive of his intent. So, true to his awkward spirit of atonement, he now feels that "my sacrifice in resigning from office was very much worthwhile." But that is not the point either.[69]

The point is that even this dispute seems to have worked inventionally, moving us beyond pragmatics and even personal ethics, prompting us to rethink the generational bounds of moral responsibility, and placing us in the uncertain horizon of a community of conscience. And so, as our examples have moved from authority through integrity to moral responsibility, the inventional responsibilities of rhetorical practice have widened. I hope to have shown that it is one responsibility of engaged rhetorical criticism to help this process along.

As in the world of aesthetics generally, we are reminded frequently of the inadequacy of "mere" words to capture the beauty, or perhaps the radical ugliness, in a human work. Works such as Alan Resnais's *Night and Fog*, Picasso's *Guernica*, and the "No Trespassing" sign in *Citizen Kane* all come to mind. It is not paradoxical—or at least it *should* not be—that these eloquent silences have the effect of rejuvenating discourse. Far from devaluing words and works, such willfully failed approximations may enrich and deepen our language of mood, sentiment, and expression. A language of value which is employed only technically will surely reify values. But a language of value which is *never* employed in practical settings will just as surely atrophy.

Rhetoric, as I have tried to show here, is more than the product, more even than the practice; it is the entire process of forming, expressing, and judging public thought in real life. The moods of this practice and process are dependent on the durational capacities of the art. We may *regret* the past that cannot be changed. We may *suspect* the proposals of those who inhabit our present day. But the very continuity of the human project requires something more. It requires, Hannah Arendt reminds us, the mood and the emotional capacity for forgiveness. It also requires, as Walter Benjamin notes, the rejuvenating capacity to *wish*. Here are his words: "A wish . . . is a kind of experience. The earlier in life one makes a wish, the greater one's chances that it will be fulfilled. The further a wish reaches out in time, the greater the hopes for its fulfillment. But it is experience that accompanies one to the far reaches of time, that fills and divides time. Thus a wish fulfilled is the crowning of experience."[70]

My aim, in attempting to articulate and recover the value heritage of classical rhetorical tradition has been nothing more than to restore the power and resilience of the *wish* in the thought and expression of our civic life. If theory, rooted ideally in the tradition, helps us to pose interesting questions for criticism and retrieve the heuristic value of its results, criticism presents us with methods for studying performance and competence in the whole domain of practice. And, where rhetorical study is concerned, engaged critical practice revives one of our deepest human cravings: to reengage the rich, elliptical adventure of civic life.

Notes

INTRODUCTION

1. James Boyd White, *When Words Lose their Meaning: Constitutions and Reconstitutions of Language, Character, and Community* (Chicago: University of Chicago Press, 1984), p. 66.
2. Charles S. Maier, *The Unmasterable Past: History, Holocaust, and German National Identity* (Cambridge, Mass.: Harvard University Press, 1988), p. 16.

1 RHETORIC AND DIALECTIC AS MODES OF INQUIRY

1. Edwin Black's provocative new work *Rhetorical Questions* (Chicago: University of Chicago Press, 1992) explores the relatively uncharted convergence of questions and "appearances" from a perspective I find quite compatible with my own.
2. Joseph Welch, quoted in *Point of Order*, documentary film of the Army–McCarthy hearings, edited and directed by Emile d'Antonio, 1968.
3. Hans-Georg Gadamer, *Hegel's Dialectic: Five Hermeneutical Studies* (New Haven: Yale University Press, 1976), p. 105.
4. Unless otherwise indicated, all citations from Aristotle are taken from *The Works of Aristotle; Translated into English*, ed. W. D. Ross (London: Oxford University Press, 1968) and references are given in parentheses in the text. The volumes cited are the *Analytica Posteriora*, trans. G. R. G. Mure; the *Topica*, trans. W. A. Pickard-Cambridge; the *Rhetoric*, trans. W. Rhys Roberts; and the *De Interpretatione*, trans. E. M. Edghill.
5. Richard McKeon, "Dialogue and Controversy in Philosophy," *Philosophy and Phenomenological Research* 17, no. 2 (Dec. 1956): 151–57.
6. For a fascinating study of the complex problems of agency and change in Aristotle, see Sarah Waterlow, *Nature, Change, and Agency in Aristotle's* Physics (Oxford: Clarendon Press, 1988).
7. See, e.g., the highly speculative alternative account of Ernesto Grassi, *Rhetoric as Philosophy: The Humanist Tradition* (University Park: Pennsylvania State University Press, 1980), esp. chap. 2.

8. Eugene Rochberg-Halton, *Meaning and Modernity: Social Theory in the Pragmatic Attitude* (Chicago: University of Chicago Press, 1986), p. 97.

9. On my reading of this passage, it would not be possible to defend the definable form proper to a syllogism without recourse to dialectic.

10. The shift of positions on question is accompanied by a further transformation of *pistis* from first principle to opinion to persuasion or proof. Some guarded support for the position can be found in William Grimaldi's comprehensive commentary on the highly diverse *rhetorical* meanings of *pistis*. In the *Rhetoric*, the term encompasses inferences about the character, subject matter, and even the emotional importance of a proposition. This variation of usage is consistent with a variation of origin, such as that suggested above; thus it may refer to an aspect of truth, a belief about generalities, or an adherence to, or concern about, something. See William M. A. Grimaldi, *Aristotle, Rhetoric I: A Commentary* (New York: Fordham University Press, 1980), pp. 350–54. See also J. D. G. Evans, *Aristotle's Concept of Dialectic* (Cambridge: Cambridge University Press, 1977), pp. 28–42.

11. Maurice Merleau-Ponty, *Sense and Non-Sense*, trans. H. I. Dreyfus and P. A. Dreyfus (Evanston, Ill.: Northwestern University Press, 1964), p. 13.

12. Martha Nussbaum, *The Fragility of Goodness: Luck and Ethics in Greek Tragedy and Philosophy* (Cambridge: Cambridge University Press, 1986), p. 246. The whole line of thought on phainomena pursued in this essay has been inspired by Owen Barfield's remarkable work *Saving the Appearances: A Study in Idolatry* (London: Faber and Faber, 1957).

13. The equation of contemporary purveyors of appearance with modern news media might seem somewhat precious were it not for the fact that every attempt to impose repression through martial law has been accompanied by a ban on "outside" news coverage. Where authoritarian regimes are concerned, even the disclosure of appearances is considered a serious crime, a form of subversive activity. See Jacobo Timerman, *Chile: Death in the South*, trans. R. Cox (New York: Random House, 1988), pp. 62–67.

14. John Berger and Jean Mohr, *Another Way of Telling* (New York: Pantheon Books, 1982), p. 113.

15. U.S.S.R. Moscow Cinema Group, dist., *War and Peace*, 1971.

16. See Walter Benjamin, "The Work of Art in the Age of Mechanical Reproduction," in *Illuminations*, trans. H. Zohn, ed. H. Arendt (New York: Schocken Books, 1976), pp. 220–21.

17. See Mikhail Bakhtin, *Speech Genres and Other Late Essays*, trans. V. W. McGee, ed. C. Emerson and M. Holquist (Austin: University of Texas Press, 1986), pp. 134–35.

18. Berger and Mohr, *Another Way*, pp. 118–19.

19. John Lennon, "Imagine," produced by John Lennon, Yoko Ono, and Phil Spector, from EMI Records album *Imagine* (EMI Blackwood Music, Inc., 1971).

20. Cornelius Castoriadis, "Reflections on 'Rationality' and 'Development'," *Thesis Eleven* 10–11 (1984/85): 23–26.

21. Grimaldi, *Aristotle, Rhetoric*, p. 349.

22. Castoriadis, "Reflections"; also Jürgen Habermas, *Communication and the*

Evolution of Society, trans. T. McCarthy (Boston: Beacon Press, 1979), pp. 95–130.

23. Richard McKeon, "Dialectic and Political Thought and Action," *Ethics* 65, no. 1 (Oct. 1954): 17–19; there is a sense in which this chapter is a very detailed postscript to McKeon's extraordinarily condensed and definitive article.

24. Or, for a more enjoyable time, consider Henri Lefebvre, *The Sociology of Marx* (New York: Pantheon Books, 1968), chaps. 2 and 3. Lefebvre reviews the problem of Marxist dialecticians interpreting other Marxist dialecticians in an interesting way.

25. Here I am thinking especially of Jürgen Habermas, *Knowledge and Human Interests,* trans. J. J. Shapiro (Boston: Beacon Press, 1971). In this work, Habermas devotes himself specifically to voices that tended to get left out of late Enlightenment German dialectics. It is a brilliant work, and perhaps the exception that proves the rule.

26. Aristotle specifically addresses this problem in both dialectic and rhetoric, and concludes that each universal method may be used for good or ill purpose, meaning that each takes its individuated character from that of the persons employing the method. He might have added, but did not, that how dialectic is used does not typically implicate a person's moral character. Put another way, dialectic is only a morally consequential method when it would stand in for and replace rhetoric.

27. For overviews of this fascinating character, see Fred R. Dallmayr, *Twilight of Subjectivity: Contributions to a Post-Individualist Theory* (Amherst: University of Massachusetts Press, 1981), pp. 115–28. More recently, a fine edited collection includes essential biographical work. It is Judith Marcus and Zoltan Tarr, eds, *Georg Lukács: Theory, Culture, and Politics* (New Brunswick, N.J.: Transaction Publishers, 1989). See esp. pp. 1–15 and Marshall Berman, "Georg Lukács's Cosmic Chutzpah," ibid., pp. 137–53.

28. Georg Lukács, "What is Orthodox Marxism?," in *History and Class Consciousness: Studies in Marxist Dialectics,* trans. R. Livingstone (Cambridge, Mass.: MIT Press, 1971), p. 10.

29. This is Dallmayr's reading, *Twilight of Subjectivity,* pp. 121–23. It also seems to be supported by Lukác's own self-criticisms.

30. Berman, "Cosmic Chutzpah," pp. 154–55; also Georgy Markus, "The Soul and Life: The Young Lukács and the Problem of Culture," *Telos* 32 (Summer 1977): 104–07.

31. Marcus and Tarr, eds., *Georg Lukács,* pp. 3–5.

32. Lukács, "Orthodox Marxism," p. 23.

33. All the quotations in this paragraph are taken from Lukács, "Reification and the Consciousness of the Proletariat," in *History,* pp. 197–99.

34. Hannah Arendt, *The Human Condition* (Chicago: University of Chicago Press, 1958), esp. pp. 188–92.

35. "A Conversation with Georg Lukács," transcribed by Franco Ferrarotti, in Markus and Tarr, eds, *Georg Lukács,* pp. 207–18. See also Theo Pinkus, ed., *Conversations with Lukács* (Cambridge, Mass.: MIT Press, 1975).

36. Lukács, "Reification," pp. 203–04.

37. Ibid., p. 204.

38. Pinkus, ed., *Conversations with Lukács,* pp. 16–18.

39. Perspicuity is discussed by Aristotle in *Analytica* 97b30–37. It appears to be the affirmative counterpart to "quick wit," discussed at 1.89b10–19. Both qualities appear to be morally neutral. Phronēsis, by contrast, locates this same sense of prudential reason in the world of public affairs, where it is not neutral at all. Rhetoric may be envisioned as a practical art enacting phronesis through the timely choice (kairos) of collaborative agents.

40. The Welch–McCarthy exchange not only figures prominently in histories of the period—e.g., William Manchester, *The Glory and the Dream: A Narrative History of America 1932–1972* (Boston: Little, Brown, and Co., 1974)—and memoirs of the times—e.g., Emmet John Hughes, *The Ordeal of Power: A Political Memoir of the Eisenhower Years* (New York: Atheneum, 1963) and I. F. Stone, *The Haunted Fifties* (New York: Vintage Books, 1969)—but is considered one of the marker events in the political history of television (see Edward W. Chester, *Radio, Television, and American Politics* [New York: Sheed and Ward, 1969], pp. 93–98). For the text of the exchange itself, I have relied on a transcription of the documentary footage in Emile d'Antonio's award-winning film of the hearings, *Point of Order.* This has been supplemented by occasional background information from the books listed above.

41. Stone, *Haunted Fifties,* pp. 72–79.

42. Manchester, *Glory,* pp. 702–04.

43. Chester, *Radio,* pp. 95–96.

44. See as one example Christopher Lasch, "The Life of Kennedy's Death," *Harper's,* Oct. 1983, pp. 32–40.

45. Irving Louis Horowitz, *Ideology and Utopia in the United States, 1956–1976* (London: Oxford University Press, 1977), pp. 124–30.

46. Kenneth Burke, *Dramatism and Development* (Barre, Mass.: Clark University Press with Barre Publishers, 1972), pp. 44–48.

47. Chester, *Radio,* p. 94.

48. Cited in Manchester, *Glory,* p. 714.

49. Ibid., p. 715.

50. Ibid., p. 714.

51. Manchester, *Glory,* pp. 715–16.

52. Chester, *Radio,* pp. 97–98.

53. Manchester, *Glory,* pp. 715–16. The allusions and accompanying embarrassment related to the fact that Schine and Cohn were more than just "good friends," which, in the United States in the 1950s, was even worse than being a Communist.

54. An interesting reading of this intersection may be found in Max Horkheimer and Theodor W. Adorno, *Dialectic of Enlightenment,* trans. J. Cumming (New York: Seabury Press, 1972).

55. I am alluding to a controversial position that is sometimes attributed to Habermas, although it is also characteristic of other German philosophers influenced by Kant. Later, we will address the universal pragmatics and dis-

course ethics projects directly, in an attempt to show the necessity of rhetoric for any serious attempt to enact the idealities of language.

2 RHETORICAL REFLECTION:
TOWARD AN ETHIC OF PRACTICAL REASON

1. W. K. C. Guthrie, *A History of Greek Philosophy*, Vol. 3: *The Fifth-Century Enlightenment* (Cambridge: Cambridge University Press, 1969), pp. 55–134.
2. Ibid., pp. 106–08; see also Eric Voegelin, *Order and History*, Vol. 2: *The World of the Polis*, pp. 305–11.
3. The ideological dimensions of this battle are addressed memorably by Habermas in his swipe at Gadamer: namely, that he does not wish to retreat to a pre-Kantian philosophical position, on the grounds that it would require that he privilege an antiquarian form of life (Jürgen Habermas, "Morality and *Sittlichkeit*: The Hegelian Critique of Kantian Ethics," *Northwestern University Philosophy and Comparative Literature Colloquium*, 15 Oct. 1986). Others who have taken this position include Karl-Otto Apel, *Transformation der Philosophie* (Frankfurt-am-Main: Suhrkamp, 1973). In a rather different sphere, there is the formidable project envisioned by J. Rawls, *A Theory of Justice* (Cambridge, Mass.: Harvard University Press, 1971).
4. Nor does this stark position lack adherents. See J. M. Cooper, *Reason and Human Good in Aristotle* (Cambridge, Mass.: Harvard University Press, 1977). See also Stephen Holmes, "The Community Trap," *New Republic*, 28 Nov. 1988, pp. 24–28.
5. Thomas Nagel, *Mortal Questions* (Cambridge: Cambridge University Press, 1979), pp. 24–39; Bernard Williams, *Moral Luck: Philosophical Papers, 1973–1980* (Cambridge: Cambridge University Press, 1981), esp. chap. 2.
6. Nussbaum, *Fragility of Goodness*. I might add that the conversion of such moral problems into typifications has a great deal to do with their appearance of incommensurability; for instance, "punishing the guilty" versus "abiding by procedural rules of evidence." Given certain legal procedural conceptions of guilt for the case in question, there may be no contradiction at all, because the individual in question will *not* be guilty on procedural grounds. Attention to circumstance and occasion might do much to dissolve supposedly irresolvable moral dilemmas. See Albert R. Jonsen and Stephen Toulmin, *The Abuse of Casuistry: A History of Moral Reasoning* (Berkeley: University of California Press, 1988), pp. 23–47.
7. Peter Winch, *Trying to Make Sense* (Oxford: Basil Blackwell, 1987), p. 173.
8. This refers to a point originally made by Richard McKeon, who argued that Aristotle provided a method of inquiry, an organon that worked without a priori postulates. There is, I believe, ample evidence for McKeon's claims about the predominance of a Platonic rendering of Aristotle—literally too much to be cited here. See, for a sampling, Amélie Oksenberg Rorty, ed., *Essays on Aristotle's Ethics* (Berkeley: University of California Press, 1980). For a necessary corrective, see Nussbaum, *Fragility of Goodness*.
9. Martha Nussbaum, "An Aristotelian Conception of Rationality," in idem,

Love's Knowledge: Essays on Philosophy and Literature (New York: Oxford University Press, 1990), p. 95.

10. George Kennedy, *The Art of Persuasion in Greece* (Princeton: Princeton University Press, 1963), pp. 82–85.

11. Guthrie, *History of Greek Philosophy,* 3: 63–64.

12. I have relied on two principle translations of *Protagoras,* the standard Jowett translation, extensively revised by M. Ostwald (New York: Library of Liberal Arts, 1958), and the more recent translation with commentary by B. A. F. Hubbard and E. S. Karnofsky, *Plato's Protagoras: A Socratic Commentary* (Chicago: University of Chicago Press, 1982). Citations are given in parentheses in the text.

13. H. I. Marrou, *A History of Education in Antiquity,* trans. G. Lamb (New York: Sheed and Ward, 1956), p. 79.

14. Isocrates, *Antidosis,* trans. G. Norlin, Loeb Classical Library, (Cambridge, Mass.: Harvard University Press, 1982), 253–56. Citations are given in parentheses in the text.

15. Alasdair MacIntyre, *After Virtue: A Study in Moral Theory* (Notre Dame, Ind.: University of Notre Dame Press, 1981), pp. 52–58.

16. By any standard except a literal one, of course. Aristotle's *Rhetoric* is a fragmentary work, not actually written by Aristotle, but probably dictated by him to one of his more gifted students, teaching assistants, or slaves.

17. MacIntyre, *After Virtue,* pp. 293–301. It is of interest to find MacIntyre allowing that some practices are capable of evil outcomes. I expect that torturing suspected witches in Salem is the sort of thing he has in mind. However, there may also be practices that have the effect of producing evil *on occasion.* Here I think of the indictments of rhetoric. The underlying premise of my argument speaks to the interpenetration of theory and practice when it comes to the good and evil outcomes of any technē.

18. There is a growing body of interesting research in this area. So far, the only essay which assigns rhetoric an important role in the cultivation of *philia,* where civic life is concerned, is Nancy Sherman, "Aristotle on Friendship and the Shared Life," *Philosophy and Phenomenological Research* 47, no. 4 (June 1987): 589–613.

19. On this important methodological placement of rhetoric as the counterpart of dialectic, see Lawrence D. Green, "Aristotelian Rhetoric, Dialectic, and the Traditions of Ἀντίστροφος," *Rhetorica* 8, no. 1 (1990): 5–27.

20. For the most part, I am relying on the standard translation by W. Rhys Roberts. I have checked this translation against others, most notably the new translation by George A. Kennedy, *On Rhetoric: A Theory of Civic Discourse* (New York: Oxford University Press, 1991). While the Kennedy translation is enormously helpful in bringing diverse interpretations together in a readable fashion, I do not see it as breaking any new interpretive ground. Throughout my openly revisionist reading, I will be relying also on the two great commentaries on Aristotle's *Rhetoric,* those of Edward Cope, *The Rhetoric of Aristotle. With a Commentary,* vols. 1, 2, and 3, ed. J. E. Sandys (Salem, N.H.: Ayen Co. Publishers, 1987), and Grimaldi, *Aristotle, Rhetoric.* On the matter

of interpretation and revision, Kennedy is not quite as speculative as I am. Yet he believes my rendering of emotion and community to be consistent with the view of Aristotle and concedes the need in other places for "the reader to write upon the text, a very modern thing to do" (George Kennedy, Response regarding his translation of Aristotle's *Rhetoric* presented at a meeting of the Rhetoric Society of America, Minneapolis, 22 May 1992, pp. 2–3).

21. Aristotle, *Eudemian Ethics: Books I, II, and VIII,* trans. M. Woods (Oxford: Clarendon Press, 1982).
22. Nussbaum, *Fragility of Goodness,* chap. 10. In an earlier chapter on Plato's *Protagoras,* Nussbaum draws attention to several other characteristics of technē that are frequently overlooked by current commentators: its universality, teachability, precision, and concern with explanation (p. 95).
23. Paul Ricoeur, *The Rule of Metaphor: Multidisciplinary Studies of the Creation of Meaning in Language,* trans. R. Czerny (Toronto: University of Toronto Press, 1979), p. 28.
24. Grimaldi, *Aristotle,* Rhetoric, p. 5.
25. Ibid.
26. This becomes very important for the possibility of reason in theories of rhetoric. If it is the case that logos, once presenting itself as reason in everyday culture, provides us with a form of power, then it is difficult, not to mention pointless, to marginalize reason vis-à-vis the theoretical mission of rhetoric; for how else are we to discover and unmask these sly, slippery guises of logos?
27. Trans. Grimaldi, *Aristotle,* Rhetoric, pp. 3–4.
28. Ibid., p. 9.
29. Ricoeur, *Rule of Metaphor,* p. 30.
30. Silvia Gastaldi, "*Pathē* and *Polis:* Aristotle's Theory of Passions in the *Rhetoric* and the *Ethics,*" *Topoi* 6 (1987): 105–10.
31. Henry W. Johnstone, Jr., "Response," *Philosophy and Rhetoric* 20, no. 2 (1987): 130. See also Robert L. Scott, "The Tacit Dimension and Rhetoric: What it Means to be Persuading and Persuaded," *Pre-Text* 2, nos 1 and 2 (1981): 115–24.
32. Ricoeur, *Rule of Metaphor,* p. 30.
33. This is a major theme in Nussbaum, *Fragility of Goodness,* esp. chaps. 2–4.
34. Howard Gold, "Praxis: Its Conceptual Development in Aristotle's *Nicomachean Ethics,*" *Graduate Faculty Philosophy Journal* 6, no. 1 (1977): 111-12.
35. MacIntyre, *After Virtue,* p. 161.
36. Grimaldi, *Aristotle,* Rhetoric, pp. 194–95.
37. Ibid., p. 195.
38. A more striking and even stronger connection is established in the following critical passage: "If virtue is a *faculty* of beneficence, the highest kinds of it must be those which are most useful to others, and for this reason men honor most the just and the courageous" (1366b5).
39. Consider, e.g., the remarkable discussions of honor, the noble, kindness, courage, even philia, throughout the *Rhetoric.* This is the sort of thing that has caused some of Aristotle's commentators to regard this document as Sophistical. It is only when we sense the way in which occasion, audience,

circumstance, and proof frame each shading of virtue and its meaning that we can see its inventional possibilities.

40. Lloyd F. Bitzer, "Aristotle's Enthymeme Revisited," *Quarterly Journal of Speech* 45, no. 4 (1959): 399–408.

41. Thomas B. Farrell, "Knowledge, Consensus, and Rhetorical Theory," *Quarterly Journal of Speech* 62, no. 1 (1976): 1–15. See also Barbara Warnick, "Judgment, Probability, and Aristotle's *Rhetoric*," *Quarterly Journal of Speech* 73 (1989): 299–311.

42. Bitzer, "Aristotle's Enthymeme," p. 403. The argument can be pressed in the exterior direction sought by Bitzer in "The Rhetorical Situation," *Philosophy and Rhetoric* 1, no. 1 (1968): 1–17, by suggesting that enthymematic conclusions become concrete not only through being instantiated in the assent of specific audiences, but also through being rooted in the indexical capacity of any historical setting to admit or constrain variation.

43. Perhaps the clearest, albeit ambiguous, passage is *Rhetoric* 1357a23–1357b. The phrasing of my own text here was suggested to me by the mellifluous Gerard Hauser.

44. Although the literature on this subject is voluminous, a fascinating introduction is offered by S. M. Cahn, *Fate, Logic, and Time* (New Haven: Yale University Press, 1967).

45. Sarah Waterlow, *Passage and Possibility: A Study of Aristotle's Modal Concepts* (Oxford: Clarendon Press, 1982), pp. 32–33.

46. See Nagel, *Mortal Questions*; Williams, *Moral Luck*; Nussbaum, *Fragility of Goodness*.

47. See Associated Press reports from cover stories in the *New York Times*, 4–9 July 1988. The source was listed throughout as "Pentagon spokesman." Now, as an additional bit of coloration, suppose that the American ship the *Vincennes* was actually in Iranian waters as the airliner was shot down; cf. Michael R. Gordon, "Cover-up Denied in Downing of Iranian Passenger Jet in '88," *New York Times*, 22 July 1992, A5.

48. I am not speculating about the legal ramifications of this unfinished episode. The point is that we do not know which circumstances will prove crucial to the determination of any case, or even whether there will be a case to be determined, in advance of the case itself.

49. Charles Taylor, *Human Agency and Language: Philosophical Papers*, vol. 1 (Cambridge: Cambridge University Press, 1985), pp. 18–42.

50. This discussion is about the four points of *stasis* in forensic and deliberate controversy. Even though the adjudication of questions regarding the character of past and present action may benefit from a retrospective sense of the better argument, the character of action itself remains contingent insofar as it depends on the believable *characterization* of an action. Put another way, the judgment in any forensic controversy is not about facts but about what they mean.

51. Edwin Black, *Rhetorical Questions*, chap. 4.

52. Grimaldi, *Aristotle, Rhetoric*, p. 350.

53. This point is clearer in Lane Cooper's translation of 1356a, which runs: "As

a rule we trust men of probity more, and more quickly, about things in general, while on points outside the realm of exact knowledge, where opinion is divided, we trust them absolutely." He then cautions: "This trust, however, should be created by the speech itself, and not left to depend upon an antecedent impression that the speaker is this or that kind of man" (*The Rhetoric of Aristotle*, trans. L. Cooper [New York: Appleton-Century-Crofts, 1932]).

54. MacIntyre, *After Virtue*, p. 153.

55. There are several quite good texts of Roosevelt's first inaugural, among them: George W. Hibbitt, ed., *The Dolphin Book of Speeches* (Garden City, N.Y.: Dolphin Books, 1965), pp. 274–80; and Richard Hofstadter, ed., *Great Issues in American History: From Reconstruction to the Present Day, 1864–1969* (New York: Vintage Books, 1969), pp. 351–57. These have been checked against a reconstructed videotext of the speech which includes the inaugural ceremony, "Presidential Inaugurals: A Look Back," C-Span video, 21 Jan. 1988.

56. Manchester, *Glory and the Dream*, pp. 74–81.

57. Samuel Eliot Morrison, *The Oxford History of the American People*, Vol. 3: *1869 to the Death of John F. Kennedy, 1963* (New York: New American Library, 1972), p. 298. See also Frederick Lewis Allen, *Since Yesterday: The 1930s in America, September 3, 1929–September 3, 1939* (New York: Harper and Row, 1940), esp. chap. 5. These studies are far from data-rich historiographies. But our intent is to try to understand the powerful subjectivity created by Roosevelt's famous speech.

58. Halford Ryan Ross, "Roosevelt's First Inaugural: A Study of Technique," *Quarterly Journal of Speech* 65 (1979): 137–39. See also idem, "Roosevelt's Fourth Inaugural Address: A Study of its Composition," *Quarterly Journal of Speech* 67 (1981): 157–66.

59. The burden of these rather sweeping reflections is entirely my own; but I am citing some well-known background material. On the recurrent theme of Social Darwinism, e.g., see Richard Hofstadter, *Social Darwinism in American Thought* (Boston: Beacon Press, 1944).

60. Richard Edwards, *Contested Terrain: The Transformation of the Workplace in the Twentieth Century* (New York: Basic Books, 1979). See also John Patrick Diggins, *The Lost Soul of American Politics: Virtue, Self-Interest, and the Foundations of Liberalism* (New York: Basic Books, 1984).

61. Stuart Ewen, *Captains of Consciousness: Advertising and the Social Roots of the Consumer Culture* (New York: McGraw-Hill, 1976). See also Elizabeth Stevenson, *Babbitts and Bohemians: The American Twenties* (New York: Macmillan, 1967). For some indication of the effects of consumer consciousness on the working poor, see the classic study of Robert S. and Helen Merrell Lynd, *Middleton: A Study in Modern American Culture* (New York: Harcourt, Brace and World, 1929), pp. 250–90.

62. Morrison, *Oxford History*, 3: 296.

63. David S. Shannon, ed., *The Great Depression* (Englewood Cliffs, N.J.: Prentice-Hall, 1960), pp. 91–121.

64. Frank Freidel, *Franklin D. Roosevelt: A Rendezvous with Destiny* (Boston: Little, Brown and Co., 1990), pp. 34–87. See also Jordan A. Schwarz, *Lib-*

eral: Adolf A. Berle and the Vision of an American Era (New York: Free Press, 1987).

65. Citations from the speech are from the sources listed in note 55. I want to thank Terence Morrow for bringing the pun on FDR's first name to my attention.

66. Ross, "Roosevelt's First Inaugural."

67. Manchester, *Glory and the Dream*, p. 77.

68. White, *When Words Lose their Meaning*, pp. 10–60.

69. George Kennedy, *Classical Rhetoric and its Christian and Secular Tradition, from Ancient to Modern Times* (Chapel Hill: University of North Carolina Press, 1980), p. 63.

70. MacIntyre, *After Virtue*, pp. 52–58.

71. Ibid., pp. 175–76.

72. White, *When Words Lose their Meaning*, pp. 69–71. White's phrase is "culture of argument"; but perhaps "culture of justification" better captures the sort of practice he envisions.

73. D. S. Hutchinson, *The Virtue of Aristotle* (London: Routledge and Kegan Paul, 1986), pp. 108–22. For an analogous approach to the plight of contemporary education, see Mortimer J. Adler (on behalf of the members of the Paidea Group), *The Paidea Proposal: An Educational Manifesto* (New York: Macmillan, 1982): idem, *Paidea Problems and Possibilities: A Consideration of Questions Raised by the Paidea Proposal* (New York: Macmillan, 1983).

74. MacIntyre, *After Virtue*, pp. 144–45; Ronald Beiner, *Political Judgment* (Chicago: University of Chicago Press, 1983).

75. Arthur Schopenhauer, *Essays of Schopenhauer*, 1st ed. (New York: Wiley, n.d.) pp. 24–28.

76. H-G. Gadamer, "Rhetoric, Hermeneutics, and the Critique of Ideology: META-CRITICAL Comments on *Truth and Method*," in *The Hermeneutics Reader*, ed. Kurt Mueller-Vollmer (New York: Continuum, 1985). Thanks to Walt Fisher for bringing this to my attention.

3   IN THE HORIZON OF NECESSITY:
TRAGIC RHETORIC AND PUBLIC CHARACTER

1. Richard Rorty, *Consequences of Pragmatism: Essays 1972–1980* (Minneapolis: University of Minnesota Press, 1982).

2. Herbert Marcuse, *The Aesthetic Dimension: Toward a Critique of Marxist Aesthetics* (Boston: Beacon Press, 1978).

3. Gadamer's position on rhetoric is more subtle and complex than I have represented it here. However, I believe his to be a Platonized Aristotle. For a position friendlier to that articulated here, see Gadamer, "Rhetoric, Hermeneutics," pp. 274–92.

4. Robert Sokolowski, *Presence and Absence: A Philosophical Investigation of Language and Being* (Bloomington: Indiana University Press, 1978).

5. Continental philosophers such as Grassi, *Rhetoric as Philosophy*, pp. 42–45, employ the mature Cicero's esteem for civic culture as a ground for their

own restorational projects. The point of this choice of illustrations is that our own interpretative revisions of classical theory depend on unexamined assumptions about the mimetic qualities available to the language of rhetorical practice.

6. For the rather disconcerting "brutality of being" hypothesis, see Ernesto Grassi, "Italian Humanism and Heidegger's Thesis of the End of Philosophy," *Philosophy and Rhetoric* 13 (1980): 92.

7. T. S. Dorsch, e.g., considers the overall burden of Plato's many treaments of poetry to be far from negative; see his *Classical Literary Criticism* (Harmondsworth, Middlesex: Penguin, 1965). See also G. M. A. Grube, "Plato's Theory of Beauty," *Monist* 11 (1927): 203. The alternative view derives from Edgar Wind, *Art and Anarchy* (Evanston, Ill.: Northwestern University Press, 1963), pp. 17–56; see also Eric Havelock's argument that mythos is the nonreflective poetic monologue that precedes (at least historically) the interactive testing of claims that logos implies (*Preface to Plato* [New York: Grosset and Dunlap, 1967], pp. 70–90).

8. E. H. Gombrich, *Art and Illusion: A Study in the Psychology of Pictorial Representation* (Princeton: Princeton University Press, 1960), p. 117.

9. "In a narrative illustration, any distinction between the 'what' and the 'how' is impossible to maintain" (ibid., p. 129). In this chapter, I attempt to dislodge rhetorical study from its epistemic obsession with prior philosophical assumptions, as well as its anxiety with other more privileged discursive forms. My thinking here owes much to a continuing dialogue with Robert Harriman's "Status, Marginality, and Rhetorical Theory," *Quarterly Journal of Speech* 72 (1986): 38–54, and elaborates on the theme of Thomas S. Frentz's fine essay "Rhetoric, Time, and Moral Action," *Quarterly Journal of Speech* 71 (1985): 1–18.

10. Havelock, *Preface to Plato*, pp. 29–67.

11. Plato, *The Republic of Plato*, trans. F. M. Cornford (London: Oxford University Press, 1941), pp. xv–xxix. For a rather different view, see Alvin W. Gouldner, *Enter Plato: Classical Greece and the Origins of Social Theory*, vol. 2 (New York: Harper and Row, 1971), chap. 7.

12. E.g., Michael Holquist, *Dostoevsky and the Novel* (Evanston, Ill.: Northwestern University Press, 1986), pp. 56–67; Leo Tolstoy, *What is Art?* (Indianapolis: Bobbs-Merrill, 1960).

13. Gombrich, *Art and Illusion*, p. 90.

14. Plato, *Republic*, pp. 80–92.

15. Plato, *Republic*, 10. 598, trans. Paul Shorey; cited in Gombrich, *Art and Illusion*, p. 126.

16. Recall that in the *Gorgias* Plato had Socrates demonstrate that it was better to endure injustice at the hands of others than to be the instrument of an injustice (trans. W. C. Helmbold [Indianapolis: Bobbs-Merrill, 1962], pp. 31–39). In an almost imperceptible way, Aristotle has woven this demonstration into his theory of katharsis.

17. Most recently, see Calvin O. Schrag, "Rhetoric Situated at the End of Philosophy," *Quarterly Journal of Speech* 71 (1985): 164–75. See also the concluding

arguments of Allen Megill, *Prophets of Extremity: Nietzsche, Heidegger, Foucault, Derrida* (Berkeley: University of California Press, 1985), pp. 339–53.

18. Here I have in mind the collective overturning of representational conventions by twentieth-century art movements. I have always found it intriguing that while there could be no inter-art translation across traditional conventions, there would soon be surrealist poetry, painting, music, and cinema. See Suzi Gablick, *Has Modernism Failed?* (New York: Thames and Hudson, 1985), pp. 73–88.

19. Richard McKeon, *Thought, Action, and Passion* (Chicago: University of Chicago Press, 1954), p. 108.

20. Ibid., p. 12. See also Richard McKeon, "Rhetoric and Poetic in the Philosophy of Aristotle," in *Aristotle's Poetics and English Literature*, ed. E. Olson (Chicago: University of Chicago Press, 1965), pp. 201–36.

21. I want to thank a former student and colleague, Michael Bowman, for bringing this point to my attention. See also John J. Cleary, *Aristotle on the Many Senses of Priority* (Carbondale: Southern Illinois University Press, 1988).

22. Although Dorsch is the primary translation employed in this reading, several additional translations have been consulted: Ingram Bywater, *Aristotle's Rhetoric and Poetic* (New York: Modern Library, 1954); S. H. Butcher, (New York: Library of the Liberal Arts, 1956); Gerald F. Else (Ann Arbor: University of Michigan Press, 1967). Where nuances of style are essential to my argument, I have relied on D. W. Lucas, *Aristotle's Poetics: Introduction, Commentary and Appendixes* (Oxford: Clarendon Press, 1968).

23. For the phrase in parentheses, I have included S. H. Butcher's alternative translation.

24. See, e.g., William Schweiker, *Mimetic Reflections: A Study in Hermeneutics, Theology, and Ethics* (New York: Fordham University Press, 1990); also Kendall L. Walton, *Mimesis as Make-Believe: On the Foundations of the Representational Arts* (Cambridge, Mass.: Harvard University Press, 1990).

25. The entire analysis, from this point on, is indebted to McKeon, "Rhetoric and Poetic." McKeon's comprehensive speculative essay is essential reading for anyone interested in the investigative capacities of these arts. My related interest is in the mimetic status of the discourse these arts create.

26. The concept of "moral luck" claims that character and other attributions of value often depend on chance outcomes, contingencies over which universals have little control. See Nagel, *Mortal Questions*, pp. 24–39. In this essay, I am particularly interested in expanding on the ethic of contingency in the rendering of practical choice.

27. S. H. Butcher, *Aristotle's Theory of Poetry and Fine Art* (London: Macmillan, 1920), pp. 165–66.

28. Ludwig Wittgenstein, *Culture and Value*, trans. P. Winch (Chicago: University of Chicago Press, 1981), p. 12e.

29. Nussbaum, *Fragility of Goodness*, p. 382.

30. Ibid.

31. My analysis of catharsis as "communicative" is indebted to Charles Kauffman's insightful essay "Poetic as Argument," *Quarterly Journal of Speech* 67 (1981): 407–15.

32. Butcher, *Aristotle's Theory*, pp. 253–54.

33. Wittgenstein, *Culture and Value*, p. 50e.

34. Nicole Loraux, *The Invention of Athens: The Funeral Oration in the Classical City*, trans. A. Sheridan (Cambridge, Mass.: Harvard University Press, 1986), p. 337.

35. Loraux argues that the city as "social imaginary" is the real hero of the Athenian funeral oration. Should katharsis prove to be a rhetorical process with inescapably public overtones, the realm of the political and its origins would need to be reexamined.

36. Garry Wills, *Kennedy Imprisonment: A Meditation on Power* (Boston: Little, Brown, and Co., 1982).

37. To the best of my knowledge, this speech has not been reprinted. For this analysis, I have checked a transcript against a videotape of the speech, CBS News, 22 Nov. 1983. As regards authorship, the speech-writer was probably Robert Shrum, the principal author of the barn-burner at the 1980 Democratic Convention and Kennedy's press secretary at the time the 1983 speech was delivered. However, there is more than a trace of New Frontier cadence and figuration in it. Readers with long memories may wish to check similarities in Theodore C. Sorensen, "RFK: A Personal Memoir," *Saturday Review*, 22 June 1968.

38. The citations given here are taken directly from E. M. Kennedy, "Speech from Trinity Church," 22 Nov. 1983.

39. In Peggy Noonan's entertaining memoir *What I Saw at the Revolution: A Political Life in the Reagan Era* (New York: Ivy Books, 1990), the author takes a gratuitous shot at New Frontier rhetoric for gripping the nation in a "stoicism mania" (p. 271). She modestly credits Reagan and her own Challenger speech for effectively ending this prohibition on public mourning. Ms. Noonan is a marvelous speech-writer, but a lousy rhetorical historian. Granted, twenty years is a long time to keep a stiff upper lip; but I do refer her to this speech.

40. See Ronald Schliefer, *Rhetoric and Death: The Language of Modern and Postmodern Discourse Theory* (Urbana: University of Illinois Press, 1990), pp. 88–103.

41. Butcher, *Aristotle's Theory*, p. 234.

42. Action, of course, is its own end, whereas poiēsis is always for the sake of something beyond itself. See J. L. Ackrill, "Aristotle on Action," in *Essays on Aristotle's Ethics*, ed. A. O. Rorty (Berkeley: University of California Press, 1980), pp. 93–103. I am not suggesting that such a qualitative distinction would hold up today.

43. Hans Robert Jauss, *Aesthetic Experience and Literary Hermeneutics*, trans. M. Shaw (Minneapolis: University of Minnesota Press, 1982), p. 35.

44. Not to bite the text which binds me; but see Robert Con Davis and Ronald Schliefer, eds., *Rhetoric and Form: Deconstruction at Yale* (Norman: University of Oklahoma Press, 1985).

45. Barnett Newman, "The New Sense of Fate," unpublished essay cited in Thomas Hess, *William DeKooning*, catalogue of the exhibition organized by the Museum of Modern Art and shown at the Tate Gallery, London, 1968. In

his paper of 1951, "What Abstract Art Means to Me," DeKooning also mentioned the bomb: "Today, some people think that the light of the atom bomb will change the concept of painting once and for all. The eyes that actually saw the light melted out of sheer ecstasy. For one instant, everybody was the same color. It made angels out of everybody. A truly Christian light, painful but forgiving."

46. Fredric Jameson, *The Political Unconscious: Narrative as a Socially Symbolic Act* (Ithaca: Cornell University Press, 1981), p. 102.

4   AFTER RHETORICAL CULTURE: THE SPECTACLE OF MODERNITY

1. This is not to suggest that radical criticism of the sort that implies and anticipates a revolutionary program is always inappropriate or self-negating. From the perspective sketched here, however, revolution requires a program; for this reason, it is as much a return to basic principles as an exercise in novelty. It is not so much a deconstruction of the ordinary as a transformation. However fashionable it has become, the total rejection of the given in the interest of some renegade self can *only* manifest itself as a form of introspection, a rather diminished political regime. See, as one critical example, William E. Connolly, *Politics and Ambiguity* (Madison: University of Wisconsin Press, 1987), esp. chap. 7: "Discipline, Politics, Ambiguity."

2. For a state-of-the-art appraisal of the role of tradition in our discipline, see Michael McGee's "Reflections on the Proper Uses of Dead Greeks" (Paper read at the summer conference on argumentation, Alta, Utah, Aug. 1983). The critique of Aristotelian reason as technique ranges from Horkheimer and Adorno's *Dialectic of Enlightenment* to Ricoeur's numerous treatises on a phenomenology of aesthetics, esp. *Rule of Metaphor*. See also Paul Ricoeur, *Time and Narrative*, vols. 1–3, trans. K. Blarney and D. Pellauer (Chicago: University of Chicago Press, 1984–88).

3. This is most conspicuously the case in *After Virtue*. The problem is restated somewhat in his more recent work *Whose Justice/Which Rationality?* (Notre Dame, Ind.: University of Notre Dame Press, 1988), pp. 124–45.

4. Donald C. Bryant, "Rhetoric: Its Function and Scope," *Quarterly Journal of Speech* 39 (1953); reprinted in *The Province of Rhetoric*, ed. J. Schwartz and J. Rycenga (New York: Ronald Press Co., 1965), pp. 3–36.

5. There is no question but that the meaning of technē undergoes certain shifts and refinements as we move from the Sophists through Plato and Aristotle. Aristotle's sense of the term is probably closest to the sorts of meanings claimed by Plato in the *Protagoras*. See Nussbaum, *Fragility of Goodness*, pp. 94–97.

6. On this matter, see Kathleen Jamieson, *Eloquence in an Electronic Age* (New York: Oxford University Press, 1988). I find that many of my own students agree with her pessimistic findings.

7. See chaps 1–3 above. None of these readings is particularly controversial. What is unusual in my approach is that I am reading *Rhetoric* through these other sources *at one and the same time*.

8. Witness the case of the Sophists themselves. Today one thinks of the martyr complex indulged in by our underpaid professors, along with their elaborate rationales for the new sophistry of consulting and grant-sponsored research.

9. Not to be coy, I intend a broad map of associations, figurative and literal. See also Miso Mihoćevic, "A Cry of the Heart from Dubrovnik," 22 Nov. 1991, printed in *Wall Street Journal*, 3 Dec. 1991.

10. See Stephen Holmes, "The Polis State," *New Republic* 198 (6 June 1988): 32–39.

11. Beiner, *Political Judgment*, p. 3.

12. The phrase is Hannah Arendt's.

13. Ronald Beiner, "Do We Need a Philosophical Ethics? Theory, Prudence, and the Primacy of *Ethos*," *Philosophical Forum* 20 (1989): 230–43.

14. Ibid., pp. 233 and 235.

15. Beiner, paraphrasing Gadamer, ibid., p. 240.

16. Ibid., p. 235.

17. Ibid., p. 236.

18. Gadamer believes in some sort of association between logos and habituation too. But he would make the latter inductively prior to the former. He also strenuously resists the possibility of any neutral, third-party standpoint that might redeem the idea of reason in the first place. Put another way, he offers little resistance to the historicized reduction of reason. This is an important point of contention for what follows.

19. Victor Turner, "Liminality and the Performative Genres," in *Rite, Drama, Festival, Spectacle*, ed. J. J. MacAloon (Philadelphia: Institute for the Study of Human Issues, 1984), p. 40.

20. Quoted by G. E. M. Anscombe, "Human Essence" (Keynote lecture to the World Congress of Philosophy, 1988); by permission of the author.

21. Ibid.

22. Nussbaum, *Fragility of Goodness*, p. 286.

23. This invention of the negative is seen by Burke to be integral to the very notion of humanity. See, e.g., "Definition of Man," *Hudson Review* 16, no. 4 (Winter 1963–64); reprinted in Kenneth Burke, *Language as Symbolic Action: Essays on Life, Literature, and Method* (Berkeley: University of California Press, 1968), pp. 3–24.

24. See esp. Hans Blumenberg, *The Legitimacy of the Modern Age*, trans. R. M. Wallace (Cambridge, Mass.: MIT Press, 1983); idom, *Work on Myth*, trans. R. M. Wallace (Cambridge, Mass.: MIT Press, 1985). Finally, see Blumenberg's recently translated essay "An Anthropological Approach to the Contemporary Significance of Rhetoric," trans. R. M. Wallace, in *After Philosophy: End or Transformation*, ed. K. Baynes, J. Bohman, and T. McCarthy (Cambridge, Mass.: MIT Press, 1987), pp. 429–59.

25. Castoriadis, "Reflections on 'Rationality' and 'Development'."

26. H. B. Acton, *The Illusion of the Epoch: Marxism-Leninism as a Philosophical Creed* (London: Routledge and Kegan Paul, 1955), pp. 107–72.

27. See Blumenberg, *Legitimation of the Modern Age* and "Anthropological Approach," pp. 446–48.

28. The baselines are different, of course, in keeping with the agendas of the vari-

ous projects. One interesting difference between MacIntyre and Horkheimer and Adorno is the role that logos is allowed to play in the world prior to decline. MacIntyre is willing to grant practical reason a complicity in premodern understandings of virtue that it could never have in Horkheimer and Adorno's *Dialectic of Enlightenment*. For them, Odysseus has already given the lie to "the cunning of reason."

29. This is a bit ironic, given the critical importance that Gadamer attaches to the concept of habituation. See H. G. Gadamer, "Letter to Richard J. Bernstein," trans. J. Bohman, published in Bernstein, *Beyond Objectivism and Relativism: Science, Hermeneutics, and Praxis* (Philadelphia: University of Pennsylvania Press, 1983), p. 265.

30. See any of Foucault's works prior to 1983. See too Michel Foucault, *Power, Truth, Strategy*, ed. M. Morris and P. Patton (Sydney: Feral Publications, 1979). Throughout the interviews recorded there, the discourse alludes to a subject-centered humanism that is never quite spelled out.

31. Michael Camille, *The Gothic Idol: Ideology and Image-Making in Medieval Art* (Cambridge: Cambridge University Press, 1989), esp. chaps 1–4.

32. Frank M. Clover and R. Stephen Humphreys, "Toward a Definition of Late Antiquity," in *Tradition and Innovation in Late Antiquity*, ed. F. M. Clover and R. S. Humphreys (Madison: University of Wisconsin Press, 1989), pp. 3–21.

33. G. W. F. Hegel, *The Phenomenology of Mind*, trans. J. B. Baillie (Evanston: Harper and Row, 1967), pp. 757–58.

34. Herschel Baker, *The Image of Man* (Evanston: Harper and Row, 1961), p. 132.

35. Reported by Rudolph Arbesmann in Introduction to *Tertullian: Apologetical Works and Minius Felix Octavius* (New York: Fathers of the Church, Inc., 1950), p. xviii. The most detailed historical background, on this and other biographical issues, is found in Timothy David Barnes, *Tertullian: A Historical and Literary Study* (Oxford: Clarendon Press, 1971). Several works anticipate the transition from Roman Republic to Roman Empire, as characterized in this essay. See Jerome Carcopino, *Daily Life in Ancient Rome* (New Haven: Yale University Press, 1964); and M. Rostovtzeff, *Rome* (New York: Oxford University Press, 1960). In addition to these standard reference works, a valuable introduction to Roman consciousness during this period is offered by Edith Hamilton, *The Roman Way* (New York: W. W. Norton, 1932).

36. Dennis Groh, "Tertullian's Polemic against Social Cooptation," *Church History* 40 (1971): 10.

37. Tertullian, *Apology* in *Apologetical Works*, 50. 12f.

38. The text under examination, *De Spectaculis*, is found in *The Writings of Septimus Florens Tertullianus*, vol. 1, trans. S. Thelwall (Edinburgh: T & T Clark, 1869). Thelwall's translation is reprinted in *Dramatic Theory and Criticism*, ed. B. F. Dukore (New York: Holt, Rinehart, and Winston, 1974), pp. 85–94. The Thelwall translation has been checked with Tertullian, *Apology and De Spectaculis*, trans. T. R. Glover (New York: Loeb Classical Library, 1931). Citations from the Thelwall translation are provided in parentheses in the text. Robert Sider, *Ancient Rhetoric and the Art of Tertullian*,

(London: Oxford University Press, 1971) remains the single definitive study of the rhetorical influences on Tertullian. However, as noted earlier, no attempt has yet been made to probe the cognitive dilemma that Tertullian's theological stance created for his rhetorical practice.

39. Barfield, *Saving the Appearances*, p. 82.

40. It is interesting that, in the present era of genetic engineering and increased technologizing of the body, the heart continues to defy our well-intentioned efforts to harness its meaning and operation. See Charles Siebert, "Rehumanization of the Heart: What Doctors have Forgotten, Poets have always Known," *Harper's*, Feb. 1990, pp. 53–60.

41. See Gerald Lewis Bray, *Holiness and the Will of God: Perspectives on the Theology of Tertullian* (Atlanta: John Knox Press, 1979), pp. 3–13, and Rudolph Arbesmann, Introduction, pp. xv–xvii. See also F. Forrester Church, "Sex and Salvation in Tertullian," *Harvard Theological Review* 68 (Apr. 1975): 83–101; E. Evans, "Tertullian's Theological Terminology," *Church Quarterly Review* 139 (Oct.–Dec. 1944); Christian T. Lievestro, "Tertullian and the *Sensus* Argument," *Journal of the History of Ideas* 17 (Apr. 1956): 264–68; and Justo L. Gonzalez, "Athens and Jerusalem Revisited: Reason and Authority in Tertullian," *Church History* 43 (Mar. 1974).

42. Indeed, Baudrillard seems to invite such comparisons when he writes: "This is precisely what was feared by the iconoclasts, whose millennial quarrel is still with us today. Their rage to destroy images arose precisely because they sensed this omnipotence of simulacra, this facility they have of effacing God from the consciousness of men, and the overwhelming destructive truth which they suggest: that ultimately there has never been any God, that only the simulacrum exists, indeed that God himself has only ever been his own simulacrum" ("The Precession of Simulacra," *Art and Text* 11 [Sept. 1983]: 5). To which we may well reply: "Never? Only? Ever? Any?" In his very French reverie, Baudrillard has forgotten that a simulation without a mimetic other is no simulacrum at all, but only some manner of truth. Unlike the ontological anxiety of Tertullian, Baudrillard's is a rage of confusion.

43. Paul Connerton, *The Tragedy of Enlightenment: An Essay on the Frankfurt School* (Cambridge: Cambridge University Press, 1980). Also, Isaiah Berlin, *Against the Current: Essays in the History of Ideas* (New York: Viking Press, 1980).

44. Carl Becker, *The Heavenly City of the Eighteenth-Century Philosophers* (New Haven: Yale University Press, 1959).

45. Berlin, *Against the Current*, p. 1.

46. G. E. M. Anscombe, "Human Essence."

47. Richard Bernstein, "The Rage against Reason," in *Construction and Constraint: The Shaping of Scientific Rationality*, ed. E. McMullin (Notre Dame, Ind.: University of Notre Dame Press, 1988), pp. 189–221.

48. Admittedly, I am gathering up and shading over some pronounced individual differences here. It is best to think of Enlightenment reasoning as admitting to one or more of these tendencies, rather than instantiating all of them.

49. W. H. Auden, "Hymn to St. Cecilia," Opus 27 (1942). I have excerpted a section

from the complete choral work scored by Benjamin Britten; Virgin Classics LTD (London, 1988). Thanks to Meg Zulick.

50. Max Horkheimer, "The End of Reason," originally published in *Philosophy and Social Sciences* 9 (1941); written and circulated as a polemic on the eve of Horkheimer's own exile and reprinted in *The Essential Frankfurt School Reader*, ed. A. Arato and E. Gebhardt (New York: Urizen, 1978), pp. 26–47. Citations from the latter are given in parentheses in the text.

51. William James, "The Present Dilemma in Philosophy," in *Pragmatism, The Will to Believe, and Other Essays* (New York: Washington Square Press, 1963), pp. 7–10.

52. Brian Shaw argues convincingly that the period of "The End of Reason" marked a decisive turning point in Horkheimer's thought, from a radical Marxism to a "pessimistic Jewish transcendentalism." See Brian Shaw, "Reason, Nostalgia, and Eschatology in the Critical Theory of Max Horkheimer," *Journal of Politics* 47 (1985): 160–81.

53. For an illuminating discussion of Arendt's problematic distinction between meaning and truth, see Mark Pollock, "A Reconsideration of the Prospects for Rhetoric in Hannah Arendt's Political Philosophy" (Ph.D. diss. Northwestern University, 1989), pp. 20–37. For a provocative attempt to synthesize practical reason with some intuitions of critical theory, see Shawn W. Rosenberg, *Reason, Ideology, and Politics* (Princeton: Princeton University Press, 1988), pp. 85–158. Subsequent sections in the present book spell out some implications of such a synthesis.

54. See esp. Ernst Cassirer, *Symbol, Myth, and Culture: Essays and Lectures of Ernst Cassirer*, ed. D. P. Verene (New Haven: Yale University Press, 1979).

55. See Ernst Bloch's monumental 3-vol. work *The Principle of Hope*, trans. N. Plaice, S. Plaice, and P. Knight (Cambridge, Mass.: MIT Press, 1986), esp. pp. 33–95.

56. Blumenberg, "Anthropological Approach."

57. Emmanuel Levinas, *Ethics and Infinity*, trans. R. A. Cohen (Pittsburgh: Duquesne University Press, 1985), pp. 71–72. The lines in question are: "Paternity is a relationship with a stranger who, entirely while being Other, is me. It is the relationship of the ego with a selfsame ego who is nonetheless a stranger to the ego. The son in fact is not simply my work, like a poem or manufactured object, neither is he my property. Neither the categories of power nor those of having can indicate the relationship with a child. Neither the notion of cause nor the notion of ownership permit grasping the fact of fecundity. I do not have my child, I *am* in some way my child. . . . Paternity is not simply a renewal of the father in the son and his confusion with him. It is also the exteriority of the father in relation to the son. It is a pluralist existing." See also Tamar Katriel and Pearla Nesher, "Childhood as Rhetoric," *Language Arts* 84, no. 8 (1987): 875–85.

58. Bakhtin, *Speech Genres*, p. 150.

5 UNIVERSAL PRAGMATICS AND PRACTICAL REASON: FROM DEFORMATION TO REFORMATION

1. G. Thomas Goodnight, "Generational Argument" (keynote address presented at the First International Conference on Argumentation in Amsterdam, 3–6 June 1986). See also idem, "The Personal, Technical, and Public Spheres of Argument: A Speculative Inquiry into the Art of Public Deliberation," *Journal of the American Forensic Association* 18 (1982): 214–27.

2. Ernst Bloch, *A Philosophy of the Future*, trans. J. Cumming (New York: Herder and Herder, 1970), pp. 91–92.

3. This sense of insufficiency derives from Blumenberg, "Anthropological Approach," pp. 446–49.

4. Theodor Adorno, *Negative Dialectics*, trans. E. B. Ashton (New York: Seabury Press, 1973). Today Adorno's project is receiving renewed attention. See Albrecht Wellmer, *The Persistence of Modernity: Essays on Aesthetics, Ethics, and Postmodernism*, trans. D. Midgley (Cambridge, Mass.: MIT Press, 1991); also Fredric Jameson, *Late Marxism: Adorno, or, the Persistence of the Dialectic* (New York: Verso, 1990).

5. A condensed version of Cuomo's remarks was published in the *New York Review of Books*, 25 Oct. 1984, pp. 31–37. Here, I am relying on a full videotape of Cuomo's speech entitled "Religious Belief and Public Morality: A Catholic Governor's Perspective," delivered 13 Sept. 1984 and reproduced by permission of the archives of the University of Notre Dame.

6. Jürgen Habermas, "What is Universal Pragmatics?," in *Communication and the Evolution of Society*, trans. T. McCarthy (Boston: Beacon Press, 1979), p. 28.

7. Ibid., p. 58. See also the early essay of Jürgen Habermas, "Wahrheitstheorien," in *Wirklichkeit und Reflexion*, ed. H. Fahrenbach (Pfullingen: Neske, 1973), pp. 211–65.

8. The Habermas categories and prototypes, rigorous in formulation, tend to blur with the stress of performance; cf. Habermas, "Wahrheitstheorien," pp. 250–61; also idem, *The Theory of Communicative Action*, Vol. 2: *Lifeworld and System: A Critique of Functionalist Reason*, trans. T. McCarthy (Boston: Beacon Press, 1987), pp. 62–71.

9. Bitzer, "Rhetorical Situation."

10. We find this claim as early as Jürgen Habermas, *Knowledge and Human Interests*, trans. J. Shapiro (Boston: Beacon Press, 1971), p. 54. It is elaborated later in this work, pp. 301–317, and becomes a key to the program of communicative reason.

11. Habermas makes this fact clear in his important discussion of methodology in Jürgen Habermas, *On the Logic of the Social Sciences*, trans. S. W. Nicholsen and J. A. Stark (Cambridge, Mass.: MIT Press, 1988), pp. 89–143. He explores the matter further in his treatment of "reconstructive linguistics" in "What is Universal Pragmatics?," pp. 15–21.

12. Habermas, "What is Universal Pragmatics?," pp. 64–68.

13. Thomas McCarthy, *The Critical Theory of Jürgen Habermas* (Cambridge,

Mass.: MIT Press, 1978), p. 308. Habermas's first extensive discussion of this important construction may be found in "Wahrheitstheorien," pp. 258–62.

14. One school of thought believes that such departures and inflections are constitutive of *meaning* in conversational practice. See H. P. Grice, "Logic and Conversation," in *Syntax and Semantics: Speech Acts*, ed. P. Cole and J. L. Morgan (New York: Academic Press, 1975).

15. Bitzer, "Rhetorical Situation," pp. 3–12.

16. Grice, "Logic and Conversation," p. 17; see also H. P. Grice, "Meaning," in *Philosophical Logic*, ed. P. F. Strawson (Oxford: Oxford University Press, 1967), pp. 39–49.

17. Habermas, "What is Universal Pragmatics?" p. 41.

18. Ibid. This aside makes quite clear what the difficulty is. Habermas wants to draw analogies between aspects of speech and types of socially significant conduct.

19. Allen W. Wood, "Habermas's Defense of Rationalism," *New German Critique* 35 (1985): 158.

20. Jürgen Habermas, *The Theory of Communicative Action*, Vol. 1: *Reason and the Rationalization of Society*, trans. T. McCarthy (Boston: Beacon Press, 1984), pp. 26–31.

21. Jürgen Habermas, *The Philosophical Discourse of Modernity: Twelve Lectures*, trans. F. Lawrence (Cambridge, Mass.: MIT Press, 1987), pp. 185–210.

22. See Hubert L. Dreyfus and Paul Rabinow, "What is Maturity? Habermas and Foucault on 'What is Enlightenment?,'" in *Foucault: A Critical Reader*, ed. D. C. Hoy (Oxford: Basil Blackwell, 1986), pp. 110–11. Correct or not, this attribution seems to derive from Habermas's analogizing of psychological and social development. Cf. *Communication and the Evolution of Society*.

23. Wood, "Habermas's Defense," pp. 160–62. David Ingram attempts to soften the force of Wood's critique in *Habermas and the Dialectic of Reason* (New Haven: Yale University Press, 1987). He reinterprets Habermas as conceding the embeddedness of perlocutionary features in some aspects of speech. However, Ingram does not engage Wood's denial of separate utterance types; and he concedes that perlocutionary speech need not conceal its aims. This seems to be the overall thrust of Wood's indictment.

24. Habermas, *Theory of Communicative Action*, 1: 288–95.

25. Wood, "Habermas' Defense," pp. 158–59.

26. Ibid., p. 158. Habermas finally addresses Wood's argument in "Toward a Critique of the Theory of Meaning," in *Postmetaphysical Thinking: Philosophical Essays*, trans. W. M. Hohengarten (Cambridge, Mass.: MIT Press, 1992), pp. 82–83. He offers that some perlocutionary effects may be openly aimed at, but maintains that these could be accomplished through direct intervention *alone*. This, of course, is incorrect for the countless rhetorical situations in which the engagement of concerted action by *audiences* must counter the insufficiency of solitude. He reinterprets Wood's complimentary teacher example as not really strategic speech at all, but indirect communication *ultimately* subordinated to goals of communicative action. This is slippery indeed. One could claim, without unduly pressing matters, that almost all

strategic speech—even lying—might defend itself as subordinated *ultimately* to communicative action ("I'll tell her eventually, when she's ready; but I just don't want to hurt her feelings"). Once wishful thinking and self-deception enter the picture, the categories seem less than serviceable.

27. Blumenberg, "Anthropological Approach," p. 447.
28. Jürgen Habermas, *The Structural Transformation of the Public Sphere: An Inquiry into a Category of Bourgeois Society*, trans. T. Berger and F. Lawrence (Cambridge, Mass.: MIT Press, 1989; first pub. 1962). A wealth of useful commentaries on this long-standing project has begun to appear, among them Craig Calhoun, ed., *Habermas and the Public Sphere* (Cambridge, Mass.: MIT Press, 1992); and Axel Honneth, *The Critique of Power: Reflective Stages in a Critical Social Theory*, trans. K. Baynes (Cambridge, Mass.: MIT Press, 1991). Although not exclusively concerned with Habermas, the following works also address the public sphere project: Jean I. Cohen and Andrew Arato, *Civil Society and Political Theory* (Cambridge, Mass.: MIT Press, 1992); Fred R. Dallmayr, *Polis and Praxis: Exercises in Contemporary Political Theory* (Cambridge, Mass.: MIT Press, 1984); Helmut Dubiel, *Theory and Politics: Studies in the Development of Critical Theory*, trans. B. Gregg (Cambridge, Mass.: MIT Press, 1985); Nancy Fraser, *Unruly Practices: Power, Discourse and Gender in Contemporary Social Theory* (Minneapolis: University of Minnesota Press, 1989), esp. pt. 3. Two essays that have influenced my own approach to the public sphere concept are Gerard A. Hauser, "Administrative Rhetoric and Public Opinion: Discussing the Iranian Hostages in the Public Sphere," in *American Rhetoric: Context and Criticism*, ed. T. W. Benson (Carbondale: Southern Illinois University Press, 1989), pp. 323–85; and Goodnight, "Personal, Technical, and Public Spheres."
29. Habermas, *Structural Transformation*, p. 160.
30. Ibid., pp. 214–44. See also Joel Whitebrook, "The Problem of Nature in Habermas," *Telos* 40 (1979): 41–70.
31. Jürgen Habermas, *Moral Consciousness and Communicative Action*, trans. C. Lenhardt and S. W. Nicholsen (Cambridge, Mass.: MIT Press, 1990), esp. pp. 195–217: "Moral Consciousness and Ethical Life: Does Hegel's Critique of Kant Apply to Discourse Ethics?"
32. Ibid., p. 202.
33. See Carroll C. Arnold, "Johnstone's 'Wedge' and Theory of Rhetoric," *Philosophy and Rhetoric* 20, no. 2 (1987): 18–28; also Johnstone Jr., "Response," pp. 129–34.
34. Habermas, *Moral Consciousness*, pp. 202–03.
35. Ibid., p. 207.
36. Jürgen Habermas, "Law and Morality," in *The Tanner Lectures on Human Values*, vol. 8, ed. S. M. McMurrin (Cambridge: Cambridge University Press, 1988), pp. 240–41.
37. A similar intuition is articulated by one of Habermas's students, Albrecht Wellmer, in "What is a Pragmatic Theory of Meaning? Variations on the Proposition, 'We Understand a Speech Act when we Know what makes it Acceptable,'" in *Philosophical Interventions in the Unfinished Enlighten-*

ment Project, ed. A. Honneth, T. McCarthy, C. Offe, and A. Wellmer, trans. W. Rehg (Cambridge, Mass.: MIT Press, 1992), p. 211. He states: "Certain validity claims become, or come to the aid of, special illocutionary acts by being inserted into pragmatically characteristic situation relations. For example, the claim that doing *p* is the best course of action for *a* becomes a *piece of advice* or a recommendation when I say it to *a* in a situation where a decision still has to be made. The claim that the government or the parliament has no right to restrict basic democratic liberties becomes a *protest* if I address this validity claim to the government or parliament (as in a public demonstration). The claim that it is best to go home or to postpone a meeting becomes a *proposal* when I raise this validity claim opposite an affected person." Wellmer seems to ambiguate his well-founded intuition by blurring claims with *types* of utterance. What need to be spelled out are the ways in which utterance acts change in different settings, *thereby* differentiating the manner in which validity claims are fulfilled.

38. C. Perelman and L. Olbrechts-Tyteca, *The New Rhetoric: A Treatise on Argumentation*, trans. J. Wilkinson and P. Weaver (Notre Dame, Ind.: University of Notre Dame Press, 1969), pp. 14–15. Here rhetorical argumentation is concerned with securing "the adherence of minds."

39. Kenneth Burke, "A Dramatistic View of the Origins of Language," in *Language as Symbolic Action*, pp. 419–43.

40. C. Perelman, *The Idea of Justice and the Problem of Argument*, trans. J. Petrie (London: Routledge and Kegan Paul, 1963); idem, *The New Rhetoric and the Humanities: Essays on Rhetoric and its Applications* (Dordrecht: Reidel, 1979).

41. Perelman, *Idea of Justice*, p. 6.

42. Habermas, "Wahrheitstheorien," pp. 250–61.

43. Perelman, *Idea of Justice*, pp. 6–7.

44. Ibid., p. 28.

45. See my chap. 2 and discussion of Black, *Rhetorical Questions*, chap. 3.

46. Perelman, *Idea of Justice*, p. 40.

47. Ibid.

48. Ibid.

49. Ibid.; emphasis added.

50. C. Perelman, "Act and Person in Argument," in *Idea of Justice*, 176–77.

51. Habermas, "Morality and Ethical Life," in *Moral Consciousness*, pp. 210–11. An interesting series of alternative amendments to universal pragmatics can be found in Raymie E. McKerrow, "Critical Rhetoric: Theory and Practice," *Communication Monographs* 56 (June 1989): 91–111.

52. Kenneth Burke, *Counter-Statement* (Berkeley: University of California Press, 1971), p. 31.

53. Kenneth Burke, *A Rhetoric of Motives* (Berkeley: University of California Press, 1969), p. 267.

54. Burke, *Dramatism and Development*, last lecture: "Order, Secret, and the Kill," p. 44.

55. Kenneth Burke, *The Rhetoric of Religion* (Berkeley: University of California Press, 1961), p. 16.

56. There is evidence that, in the strictest of terms, Habermas would concede the point. Debate then revolves around the implications of conceding that all "views from nowhere" are really views from "somewhere." Later we note Thomas McCarthy's suggestion that the idealized context surrounding practical discourse is best construed as a regulative ideal. See Thomas McCarthy, "Philosophy and Social Practice," in *Philosophical Interventions*, p. 258.

57. Kenneth Burke, *A Grammar of Motives* (Berkeley: University of California Press, 1969), p. 197.

58. Habermas, *Theory of Communicative Action*, 2: 260–96.

59. Ibid., pp. 274–75.

60. Farrell, "Knowledge, Consensus," pp. 12–15.

61. Abraham Lincoln, "Second Inaugural Address," in *Dolphin Book of Speeches*, pp. 272–73.

62. For political background on the controversy, see Wayne Barrett, "Holier than Thou: The Backroom Politics of Archbishop O'Connor," *Village Voice* 29 (1984): 11–24; also Charles Krauthammer, "The Church–State Debate: The Governor and the Bishops Appeal to Heaven," *New Republic*, 17 and 24 Sept., pp. 15–18.

63. MacIntyre, *After Virtue*, pp. 6–7.

64. The governor was invited to address a conference at Notre Dame on the theme "Religion and Government." His audience therefore included the scholarly audience of Notre Dame conferees, Notre Dame's own faculty, and a very large contingent of students. My text is taken from a videotape of the 13 Sept. 1984 speech supplied by the Notre Dame archives and used by permission.

65. Jürgen Habermas, "Individual Will-Formation in Terms of What is Expedient, What is Good, and What is Just" (Paper read at Northwestern University, Fall 1988).

66. Ibid., question and answer session following presentation.

67. Fred Barnes, "Who is Mario Cuomo?" *New Republic* (8 Apr. 1985): 19.

68. The citations that follow from Cuomo's speech of 13 Sept. 1984 are taken from the source given in note 64.

69. Lincoln, "Second Inaugural Address," p. 273.

70. Jürgen Habermas, "The Unity of Reason in the Diversity of its Voices," in *Postmetaphysical Thinking*, p. 144.

71. Bitzer, "Rhetorical Situation."

72. Cornelius Castoriadis, *The Imaginary Institution of Society*, trans. K. Blamey (Cambridge, Mass.: MIT Press, 1987). See also Stephen L. Leonard, *Critical Theory in Political Practice* (Princeton: Princeton University Press, 1990).

73. The lifeworld, of course, is that of liberal modernity. See MacIntyre, *After Virtue*, chaps. 1–3.

74. John F. Kennedy, "Religion and Government," in *Dolphin Book of Speeches*, p. 182.

6   RHETORICAL COHERENCE:
REFIGURING THE EPISODES OF PUBLIC LIFE

1. Habermas, *Theory of Communicative Action*, 1. 328–30.
2. See ibid., p. 331.
3. White, *When Words Lose their Meaning*.
4. See Bakhtin's seminal essay "The Problem of Speech Genres," in *Speech Genres*, pp. 68–73.
5. This presupposition of modernity is essential to Habermas's entire orientation to communicative action. While a cooperative principle seems necessary for full reflection on validity claims, the fact remains that such reflection is in order *because* Habermas envisages communication as having to overcome a problematized distance *between subjectivities.* See Ingram, *Habermas and the Dialectic of Reason*, pp. 1–42.
6. Havelock, *Preface to Plato*, p. 91.
7. Ibid., p. 84.
8. Ibid.
9. Ibid., p. 87.
10. Ibid., p. 91.
11. Ibid.
12. H-G. Gadamer, *Truth and Method* (New York: Seabury Press, 1975), p. 345.
13. Ronald Wardhaugh, *How Conversation Works* (Oxford: Basil Blackwell in association with André Deutsch, 1985). See also R. Harré, ed., *Life Sentences: Aspects of the Social Role of Language* (London: Wiley, 1976); and Malcolm Coulthard and Martin Montgomery, eds., *Studies in Discourse Analysis* (London: Routledge and Kegan Paul, 1981).
14. "My Dinner with André," produced by W. Shawn and A. Gregory (New York: Grove Press, 1981).
15. Michael Walzer, "Interpretation and Social Criticism," in *Tanner Lectures on Human Values*, 8. 26–27.
16. See Alfred Schutz, *Reflections on the Problem of Relevance*, ed. R. M. Zaner (New Haven: Yale University Press, 1970), pp. 66–92.
17. See Farrell, "Knowledge, Consensus." Most recently, see idem, "From the Parthenon to the Bassinet: Death and Rebirth along the Epistemic Trail," *Quarterly Journal of Speech* (1990).
18. T. Farrell and T. Frentz, "Communication and Meaning: A Language–Action Synthesis," *Philosophy and Rhetoric* 12, no. 4 (1979): 253.
19. André Breton, *Manifestoes of Surrealism* (Ann Arbor: University of Michigan Press, 1972), p. 23.
20. Quoted in T. Frentz and T. Farrell, "Language-Action, a Paradigm for Communication," *Quarterly Journal of Speech* 62 (1976): 345–47.
21. Ibid., pp. 346–47.
22. See Wendy Steiner, *The Colors of Rhetoric: Problems in the Relation between Literature and Painting* (Chicago: University of Chicago Press, 1982), pp. 29–49. In the late twentieth century, a multitude of lethal questions have come to occasion *disturbance* in the most private forms of talk. The interested

reader should consult Mara Adelman, "Play and Incongruity: Framing Safe-Sex Talk," *Health Communication* 3 (1991): 139–55. See also idem, "Sustaining Passion: Eroticism and Safe-Sex Talk," *Archives of Sexual Behavior* (in press).

23. See, e.g., Charlotte Ford, *Etiquette: Charlotte Ford's Guide to Modern Manners* (New York: Clarkson N. Potter, 1988), pp. 6–13. For a lively treatment of this subject's history, see John F. Kasson, *Rudeness and Civility: Manners in Nineteenth-Century Urban America* (New York: Hill and Wang, 1990).

24. Habermas, "What is Universal Pragmatics?," pp. 15–21.

25. See Frentz and Farrell, "Language-Action."

26. Thomas S. Frentz, "Rhetoric, Time, and Moral Action," *Quarterly Journal of Speech* 71, no. 1 (1985): 1–18.

27. Kenneth Burke, *The Philosophy of Literary Form* (New York: Vintage Books, 1957), p. 276.

28. Thomas P. Wilson, "Conceptions of Interaction and Forms of Sociological Explanation," *American Sociological Review* 35 (1970): 697–709.

29. See Farrell, "Knowledge, Consensus," pp. 4–6.

30. Grice, "Logic and Conversation," pp. 11–19.

31. See T. Farrell, "Narrative in Natural Discourse: On Conversation and Rhetoric," *Journal of Communication* 4 (1985): 109–27.

32. See Douglas R. Hofstadter, "Stuff and Nonsense," in *Metamagical Themas: Questing for the Essence of Mind and Pattern* (New York: Basic Books, 1985), pp. 213–32.

33. The narrativity of conversation and rhetoric has been a theme of long standing in speech-communication research. See, e.g., J. T. Marshman, "The Use of Narrative in Speaking," *Southern Speech Bulletin* 4, no. 1 (1938): 1–6; also Floyd K. Riley, "The Conversational Basis of Public Address," *Quarterly Journal of Speech* 2 (1928): 232–42. A detailed review of speech textbooks, while not for the fainthearted, would probably disclose a sound intuitive awareness of episodic time in everything from motivated sequences to models of *dispositio.*

34. Jackson's 1988 speech has been printed under several different titles, including "Common Ground and Common Sense" and "Keep Hope Alive." The version I am using here is a transcript from a videotape of the speech, delivered 19 July 1988 in Atlanta. For an illuminating discussion of Jackson's rhetorical career, see Cathy Fallon Ayers, "The Rhetorical Expression of Authority through Religious, Civil Rights and Political Terministic Screens: Strategic Choices of Jesse Jackson's 1984 and 1988 Presidential Campaigns" (Ph.D. diss., Northwestern University, 1990).

35. Ibid. This excerpt formed a popular part of Jackson's campaign "stump" speech. As many candidates do, he employed the most tried and practiced parts of his regular speech for what might have been his nomination acceptance speech. This only added to the poignance.

36. I refer to the full text of Reagan's 1984 "Morning in America" reelection campaign commercial; thanks to Julian Kanter of the University of Oklahoma for this copy.

37. Jesse Jackson, set speech, quoted in *Nation*, Apr. 1988. See also Maureen Barry, John Powechek, and Don Rose, "What Happened to the Jackson Campaign?," *New Patriot* 1, nos. 2, 3–6.

38. Betty Friedan, *The Feminine Mystique* (New York: Doubleday, 1963).

39. Ibid., preface. To this, it might be added that women in America had, by the nineteen-fifties, experienced an almost classic case of frustrated expectations. As Friedan documents, 'Rosie the Riviter' and her colleagues had worked side by side with men during the war years for a global liberationist cause. After this heady period, however, she was expected to go home with the returning GIs and produce children. See next note.

40. Adlai Stevenson, quoted in ibid., p. 61.

41. Ibid., p. 15. For evidence of a renewed appreciation of this important text, see Rachel Bowlby, "'The Problem with No Name': Rereading Friedan's *The Feminine Mystique*," *Feminist Review* 27 (Autumn 1987): 61–75. See also Elizabeth A. Powell, "Friedan's Theory of Identity and the Confinement Metaphors in *The Feminine Mystique*" (unpublished essay, Northwestern University).

42. Friedan, *Feminine Mystique*, p. 17.

43. Ibid., pp. 21–22.

44. Ibid., p. 52.

45. Ibid., p. 17.

46. As a simple test of this proposition, I refer readers to a document adopted by the General Assembly of the United Nations, 10 Dec. 1948, entitled, ironically enough, "The Universal Declaration of the Rights of Man," in *The Modern World: 1848 to the Present*, ed. H. Kohn (New York: Macmillan, 1963), pp. 291–96.

47. Friedan, *Feminine Mystique*, p. 378.

48. Vivian Gornick, "Who Says We haven't Made a Revolution?: A Feminist takes Stock," *New York Times Magazine*, 16 Apr. 1990, p. 24; emphasis added.

49. Here I refer to Andrea Dworkin and Kate Linker among others. In one of the more ludicrous confusions of the personal and the political, extramarital affairs of women have been valorized as a form of political liberation. See the recent, savage review by Barbara Probst Solomon, "Our Sisters, Our Lovers," *New York Times*, 9 July 1992, p. A11. Some compensatory wisdom may be found in Ursula K. LeGuin, "She Unnames Them," *New Yorker*, 21 Jan. 1988; idem, "The Hand that Rocks the Cradle Writes the Book," *New York Times Book Review*, 22 Jan. 1989; also Julia Kristeva, *Powers of Horror: An Essay on Abjection*, trans. L. S. Roudiez (New York: Columbia University Press, 1980). See most recently Ellyn Kaschak, *Engendered Lives: A New Psychology of Women's Experience* (New York: Basic Books, 1992).

50. Sen. Nancy Kassebaum, *Congressional Record—Senate*, 9 Mar. 1989, S2460–61. See also "Kassebaum Told Bush of Decision," *Washington Post*, 10 Mar. 1989, p. A18.

51. Arendt, *Human Condition*, pp. 80–130.

52. See Garry Wills, "The Words that Remade America: Lincoln at Gettysburg," *Atlantic Monthly*, June 1992, pp. 57–79. Thanks to Michael McFarland. See

also David Zarefsky, *Lincoln Douglas and Slavery: In the Crucible of Public Debate* (Chicago: University of Chicago Press, 1990).

53. This construal of eloquence is one I believe to be generally consistent with the implications of Bitzer, "Rhetorical Situation." See also R. Hart, *The Sound of Leadership: Presidential Communication in the Modern Age* (Chicago: University of Chicago Press, 1987); and Jamieson, *Eloquence in an Electronic Age.*

54. Lewis H. Lapham, "Notebook: Play on Words," *Harper's,* May 1990, p. 16.

55. For recent background, see Thomas Omestad, "Ten-Day Wonder," *New Republic,* 25 Dec. 1989, pp. 19–22. A fine journalistic treatment of the events in Eastern Europe, including the Prague Fall, is now available in Timothy Garton Ash, *The Magic Lantern: The Revolution of '89 Witnessed in Warsaw, Budapest, Berlin, and Prague* (New York: Random House, 1990), esp. pp. 78–156.

56. Václav Havel, "New Year's Day Address," 1 Jan. 1990, *New York Times* translation. This edited version, from which the following citations have been taken, has been checked and corrected against the version reprinted from the Federal Broadcast Information Service, East Europe, 90-001 (Washington: U.S. Government Printing Office, 2 Jan. 1990). The complete text of this speech is available in *Vestnik* 401 (Feb. 1990): 3–5. Special appreciation to the former Czech Embassy in Chicago.

57. Milan Kundera, *The Unbearable Lightness of Being,* trans. M. H. Heim (New York: Harper and Row, 1984), pp. 250–95.

58. Hannah Arendt, *Crises of the Republic* (New York: Harvest-Harcourt, 1972), pp. 160–61. See also the discussion of hypocrisy, rage, and forgiveness in chap. 7.

59. See Stephen Holden, "The Stark Oratory of a Wild Karen Finley," *New York Times,* 23 July 1992, p. B3.

60. Arendt, *Human Condition,* p. 192.

7   CRITICISM, DISTURBANCE, AND RHETORICAL
COMMUNITY: REANIMATING THE OCCASIONS FOR RHETORIC

1. Zygmunt Bauman, *Culture as Praxis* (London: Routledge and Kegan Paul, 1973), p. 176.

2. This is essentially the argument of Rochberg-Halton, *Meaning and Modernity,* chaps. 3–6. See also Peter Winch, "Understanding a Primitive Society," in *Rationality,* ed. B. Wilson (Oxford: Oxford University Press, 1970), pp. 78–111; R. Horton, "Professor Winch on Safari," *European Journal of Sociology* 17 (1976): 157–80.

3. This conception of appearances is derived from Nussbaum, *Fragility of Goodness,* chap. 8; also Berger and Mohr, *Another Way of Telling,* pp. 81–131. There is also the utterly unique work by Barfield, *Saving the Appearances,* esp. pp. 15–28.

4. Blumenberg, "Anthropological Approach," pp. 446–49.

5. On the quandary of development, see Castoriadis, "Reflections on 'Ratio-

nality' and 'Development'," pp. 23–26; and more recently idem, "The Retreat from Autonomy: Post-Modernism as Generalized Conformism," *Thesis Eleven* 31 (1992): 14–23; also Clifford Geertz, *The Interpretation of Cultures* (New York: Basic Books, 1973), esp. "The Growth of Culture and the Evolution of Mind," pp. 80–83. This plight of modern societies and perhaps of modernism generally is given focus and insight in Blumenberg, *Legitimacy of the Modern Age.* See also A. Giddens, *A Contemporary Critique of Historical Materialism*, Vol. 1: *Power, Property, and the State* (Berkeley: University of California Press, 1983).

6. Habermas, *Philosophical Discourse of Modernity;* idem, *Structural Transformation of the Public Sphere.*

7. Rochberg-Halton, *Meaning and Modernity*, p. 143. See also Richard McKeon, "Symbols, Myths, and Arguments," in *Symbols and Values: An Initial Study Conference on Science, Philosophy, and Religion in their Relation to the Democratic Way of Life*, 13th symposium (New York: Harper, 1954), p. 20. Another author who challenges the linear theory of cultural development is Victor Turner, *Dramas, Fields, and Metaphors: Symbolic Action in Human Society* (Ithaca: Cornell University Press, 1974). See also idem, *On the Edge of the Bush: Anthropology as Experience* (Tucson: University of Arizona Press, 1985); V. Turner and E. M. Bruner, eds., *The Anthropology of Experience* (Urbana: University of Illinois Press, 1986).

8. Giddens, *Contemporary Critique;* also idem, *The Constitution of Society: Outline of the Theory of Structuration* (Berkeley: University of California Press, 1986), pp. 101–19.

9. See Jeremy Turnstall, *The Media Are American* (New York: Columbia University Press, 1977); also Anthony Smith, *The Geopolitics of Information: How Western Culture Dominates the World* (New York: Oxford University Press, 1980).

10. Giddens, *Contemporary Critique*, pp. 40–41.

11. See Marshall Sahlins, *Culture and Practical Reason* (Chicago: University of Chicago Press, 1976); also Giddens, *Contemporary Critique*, pp. 100–09.

12. See Robert Harriman, "Prudence/Performance," *Rhetoric Society Quarterly* 21, no. 2 (1991): 26–36; also Thomas Rosteck and Michael Leff, "Piety, Propriety, and Perspective: An Interpretation and Application of Key Terms in Kenneth Burke's *Permanence and Change*," *Western Journal of Speech Communication* 53 (Fall 1989): 327–41.

13. Turner and Bruner, eds., *Anthropology of Experience*, p. 39. See also James W. Fernandez, *Persuasions and Performances: The Play of Tropes in Culture* (Bloomington: Indiana University Press, 1986).

14. Blumenberg, *Work on Myth.* See also idem, "On a Lineage of the Idea of Progress," *Social Research* 41 (1974): 5–27; and idem, *Legitimacy of the Modern Age.*

15. See James Gleick, *Chaos: Making a New Science* (New York: Viking Penguin, 1987). To my less than hardened scientific imagination, "chaos" seems to be the rediscovery of an Aristotelian *modality* in a world once thought reducible to analytic discipline, a new world disorder that bears a startling resemblance to Barfield's rainbow.

16. Stephen Toulmin, Richard Rieke, and Allan Janik, *An Introduction to Reasoning* (New York: Macmillan, 1979), pp. 14–16.
17. See Thomas B. Farrell, "Media Rhetoric as Social Drama: The Winter Olympics of 1984," *Critical Studies in Mass Communication* 6 (1989): 158–82.
18. Arendt, *Human Condition*, pp. 198–99.
19. Michael Herzfeld, *The Social Production of Indifference: Exploring the Symbolic Roots of Western Bureaucracy* (New York: Berg, 1992), pp. 71–98.
20. Obviously there is a vast range here, from the bureaucratic to the tribal. But there may be considerably less variation among the *ways* in which custom constrains rhetorical choice in different cultures than our ethnocentric models of development suggest. Consider, e.g., William P. Murphy, "Creating the Appearance of Consensus in Mende Political Discourse," *American Anthropologist* 92, no. 1 (Mar. 1990): 24–41; and Maurice Charland, "Postmodern Rhetorics of Technology: The Montreal Fluoridation Controversy," *Canadian Journal of Communication* 17 (1992): 177–90. We clearly need more work in the vein of Robert Paine, ed., *Politically Speaking: Cross-Cultural Studies of Rhetoric* (Philadelphia: Institute for the Study of Human Issues, 1981).
21. Geertz, *Interpretation of Cultures*, pp. 80–83.
22. See Blumenberg, *Work on Myth*. Blumenberg's brilliantly ironic argument is that each time so-called modernity has moved further into secular history, triumphantly leaving mythology behind, it has mythologized its triumphs. Thus it has inherited, and now occupies, a vast domain of enigmatic questions for which it has no answer.
23. The ubiquitous Václav Havel, "The End of the Modern Era," *New York Times*, 1 Mar. 1992, Op-Ed.
24. The idea for this membership space comes from Joseph Tussman, *Obligations and the Body Politic* (New York: Oxford University Press, 1974), chap. 2: "The Member," pp. 23–58.
25. Schutz, *Reflections on the Problem of Relevance*, esp. chap. 3: "The Interdependence of the Systems of Relevance," pp. 53–75.
26. See J. Weisberg, "Crushed Velvet," Washington Diarist, *New Republic*, 5 Mar. 1990, p. 42.
27. Amazingly, a fairly detailed outline of this long-term subversive campaign surfaced in the mainstream press. See "U.S. Said to Sabotage Peace Talks for Contras," *Chicago Tribune*, 10 May 1987, sec. 1, p. 27. Much more detailed investigative reporting by Alfonso Chardy can be found in *Miami Herald*, 10 May 1987; special appreciation to *Tribune* international editor Judy Peres.
28. The U.S. Senate voted 97 to 1 on 12 May 1987 to endorse the Contadora peace process (*Congressional Record*, 12 May 1987, no. 39, S3807).
29. What I have attempted to do here is to take speaker-centered, message-centered, and constituency-centered approaches to the value assumptions underlying contentious practical questions. All three, loosely grouped under the umbrella of prudential reason, would be bracketed as validity claims according to the universal pragmatics position and would be presupposed as an array of received opinions, or doxa, according to the more conservative Aristotelian position. Treating them as matters of dispute admitting multiple

conceptions at cross-purposes allows for the possibility of disputation about the nature of our assumptions and ends in view, while at the same time admitting the possibility that practical reason may explore and reinvent criteria applicable to reflective thought and action. Obviously, even a sound intuition leaves tough procedural questions for future work.

30. Here my reference is to the overall thrust of Habermas's critical theory. For a more detailed treatment of the issues involved, see Thomas B. Farrell, "The Ideality of Meaning of Argument: A Revision of Habermas," in *Dimensions of Argument: Proceedings of the Second Summer Conference on Argumentation*, ed. G. Ziegelmueller and J. Rhodes (Annandale, Va.: Speech Communication Association, 1981), pp. 905–26. A more elaborate version of this argument is spelled out in chap. 5.

31. White, *When Words Lose their Meaning*, pp. 290–91.

32. See Richard McKeon's incisive treatment of corollary obligations within the constitutions of language, in "Power and the Language of Power," *Ethics* 69 (Jan. 1958): 98–115.

33. Thomas B. Farrell, "Knowledge in Time: Toward an Extension of Argumentative Form," in *Advances in Argumentation Theory and Research*, ed. J. R. Cox and C. A. Willard (Carbondale: Southern Illinois University Press, 1982), pp. 134–35.

34. Hannah Arendt, *Between Past and Future: Six Exercises in Political Thought* (New York: Viking Press, 1961), p. 93.

35. Following an initial editorial criticism of Havel's Salzburg visit in the *New York Times*, 29 July 1990, Paul Hartman wrote to the *Times* defending Havel (1 Aug. 1990). For a partial text of Havel's actual remarks, I have relied on Václav Havel, "The Velvet Hangover," trans. Kaca Polackova Henley, *Harper's* 281 (1990): 18–21.

36. Havel, "Velvet Hangover," p. 20.

37. For a fascinating account of the Bitburg controversy, including many of the primary documents, see Geoffrey Hartman, ed., *Bitburg in Moral and Political Perspective* (Bloomington: Indiana University Press, 1986).

38. Ronald Reagan, news conference, 11 Feb. 1986, quoted in *New York Times*, 23 Feb. 1986, p. 11.

39. White House statement, Washington, 22 Feb. 1986, printed in *New York Times*, 23 Feb. 1986, p. 11.

40. Ronald Reagan, "Remarks of President Reagan at Bergen-Belsen Concentration Camp," 5 May 1985, quoted in *Bitburg*, ed. Hartman, pp. 253–55.

41. Ronald Reagan, presidential news conference, 21 Mar. 1985, quoted in ibid., p. 92.

42. Karen Wright, "The Road to the Global Village," *Scientific American* 262, no. 3 (Mar. 1990): 83–94.

43. For transcripts of both speeches I am relying on the published *New York Times* accounts. Reagan's speech has been checked against an audio tape, but I have been unable to obtain the full taped version of the Gorbachev address. Interestingly, Gorbachev's memoir of his summit conferences with the U.S. conspicuously omits his remarks following the failed Reykjavik summit;

yet there are numerous references to the episode throughout Gorbachev's collected speeches and remarks. See Mikhail Gorbachev, *At the Summit: How the Two Superpowers Set the World on a Course for Peace* (New York: Richardson, Steirman and Black, 1988). The citations in the text specify the page number in the transcript in parentheses.

44. See G. Thomas Goodnight, "Ronald Reagan's Re-Formulation of the Rhetoric of War: Analysis of the 'Zero-Option,' 'Evil Empire' and 'Star Wars' Addresses," *Quarterly Journal of Speech* 72, no. 4 (1986): 390–415; also Janice Rushing, "Ronald Reagan's 'Star Wars' Address: Mythic Containment of Technical Reasoning," *Quarterly Journal of Speech,* 72, no. 4 (1986): 415–34.

45. At one point in the ensuing controversy, the Soviet delegation offered, in the spirit of glasnost, to make public its own transcript of the Reykjavik discussions. It had requested that a stenographer be allowed to transcribe the conversation. See also Len Ackland, "The Administration's Disarray," *Bulletin of the Atomic Scientists* 43, no. 1 (Jan.–Feb., 1987): 2.

46. Wittgenstein, *Culture and Value,* p. 12e. He adds that this is a one-sided view of tragedy.

47. When the definitive biography is written, it should allow that his intuitions about the U.S. believing that the Soviet Union would be unable to bear the arms race proved to be accurate in the most ironic ways for Gorbachev himself—yet another reason for excluding this particular speech from his summitry collection. See Gorbachev, *At the Summit.*

48. Throughout this study, I have been suggesting that it is rhetoric which makes public events possible, by giving voice to utterances that caption and thematize their meaning. This intuition is developed further throughout the remainder of this chapter.

49. See, e.g., Hodding Carter III, "Be Grateful They Didn't Agree," *Wall Street Journal,* 16 Oct. 1986, p. 31; also Stephen J. Solarz, "Arms Control—Art of the Possible," *New York Times,* 22 Dec. 1986, p. 19; Maureen Dowd, "Reporter's Notebook," *New York Times,* 13 Oct. 1986, p. 8; Ackland, "Administration's Disarray."

50. Ackland, "Administration's Disarray."

51. While my use of the word *integrity* will strike some as eccentric, it seems loosely consistent with what Habermas has come to call a third level of argumentative presupposition, "the rhetorical level of processes"; see Jürgen Habermas, *Moral Consciousness,* p. 87.

52. "The individual must become answerable through and through: all of his constituent moments must not only fit next to each other in the temporal sequence of his life, but must also interpenetrate each other in the unity of guilt and answerability" trans. V. Liapunov, Mikhail Bakhtin, *Art and Answerability: Early Philosophical Essays by M. M. Bakhtin,* ed. M. Holquist and V. Liapunov (Austin: University of Texas Press, 1990), p. 2. In our own time, we are more likely to recognize answerability through its widely praised bureaucratic opposite, deniability.

53. Arendt, *Human Condition,* pp. 236–46.

54. Although there was an almost willful silence in the American press about

this sorry episode, several eulogies were delivered in Congress. Aside from the testimonial exchange with Congressman Mack, there was no real dispute over the circumstances of Linder's death. See James Ridgeway, "Point Blank," *Village Voice*, 26 May 1987, pp. 40–41.

55. Ibid. The excerpt has been checked for accuracy with the *Congressional Record* and a C-Span videotape.

56. Those who have traced my argument about rhetorical *appearance* from chap. 1 may consider this interjection to be a post-cold war equivalent of Joseph Welch's rhetorical question "Have you, at long last, no sense of decency?" The effect is quite similar.

57. On this elusive question of conscience, which most people recognize but few are able to explain, I am particularly indebted to Michael Hyde. See M. Hyde, "The Conscience of Rhetoric: Heidegger's Poetic Mistake" (paper read to Speech Communication Association, Chicago, 3 Nov. 1990).

58. "The paradoxical combination of certainty and uncertainty, of clarity and silence, makes the world at once intelligible and alive with tension, both for us as readers and for the actors within it. No simple print-out of a cultural pattern, this is a world of contention and struggle in which everything can be put into question, a moral and rhetorical universe in which the actors constantly claim meanings for what is said and done and do so in competition with each other. It lives by a politics of persuasion, upon a premise of instability. In this it may be a model of all politics." The world of which James Boyd White speaks is that of Homer's *Iliad*. See White, *When Words Lose their Meaning*, pp. 55–56.

59. See Theodor W. Adorno, "What Does Coming to Terms with the Past Mean?" in *Bitburg*, ed. Hartman, pp. 114–29. The best recent work placing this controversy in perspective is Maier, *Unmasterable Past*.

60. Jürgen Habermas, "Von Offentlichen der Historie," *Die Zeit*, 7 Nov. 1986. See, earlier, Habermas, "Neoconservative Culture Criticism in the United States and West Germany," trans. R. A. Berman, *Telos* 56 (1983): 75–89. An initial account of the furor can be found in Serge Schmemann, "Blunt Bonn Speech on the Hitler Years Prompts a Walkout," special to the *New York Times*, 11 Nov. 1988, p. 1.

61. For further discussion and response, see Judea B. Miller, "Jewish Victims and German Indifference," *Christian Century*, 14 Dec. 1988, pp. 1144–45; also Victoria Barnett, "Jewish Victims and German Sensitivity," *Christian Century*, 15 Mar. 1989, 287–88. For a remarkable misconstrual of the speech and the reasons for its failings, see Jeffrey Herf, "Philipp Jenninger and the Dangers of Speaking Clearly," *Partisan Review* (1989): 225–36.

62. Serge Schmemann, "Bonn Speaker Out after Nazi Speech," *New York Times*, 12 Nov. 1988, p. 1.

63. Sebastian Haffner, quoted in ibid.

64. Philipp Jenninger, quoted in ibid.

65. David Schoenbaum, quoted in ibid., p. 4.

66. Philipp Jenninger, "Speech of Commemoration," 10 Nov. 1988. Full German

text available in *Die Zeit,* 10 Nov. 1988, pp. 4–6. Translation by T. Farrell and J. Stoeckler-Sihvonen. Citations in the text are all from this translation.

67. See Adorno, "Coming to Terms," p. 123.

68. Arendt, *Human Condition,* p. 240.

69. Philipp Jenninger, quoted in Serge Schmemann, "A Very German Storm," *New York Times,* 14 Dec. 1988, p. A4.

70. Benjamin, *Illuminations,* p. 257. See also J. Robert Cox, "Against Resignation: Memory and Rhetorical Practice" (paper read at International Communications Association, Chicago, 1986).

Bibliography

Adelman, Mara. "Play and Incongruity: Framing Safe-Sex Talk." *Health Communication* 3 (1991): 139–55.

——. "Sustaining Passion: Eroticism and Safe-Sex Talk." *Archives of Sexual Behavior* 21 (1992): 281–94.

Adler, Mortimer J. (on behalf of the members of the Paidea Group). *The Paidea Proposal: An Educational Manifesto.* New York: Macmillan, 1982.

——. *Paidea Problems and Possibilities: A Consideration of Questions Raised by the Paidea Proposal.* New York: Macmillan, 1983.

Adorno, Theodor. *Negative Dialectics.* Translated by E. B. Ashton. New York: Seabury Press, 1973.

Arendt, Hannah. *Between Past and Future: Six Exercises in Political Thought.* New York: Viking Press, 1961.

——. *Crises of the Republic.* New York: Harvest-Harcourt, 1972.

——. *The Human Condition.* Chicago: University of Chicago Press, 1958.

Aristotle. *Eudemian Ethics: Books I, II, and VIII.* Translated with a Commentary by Michael Woods. Oxford: Clarendon Press, 1982.

——. *Nicomachean Ethics.* Translated by W. D. Ross. In *The Basic Works of Aristotle,* edited by Richard McKeon. New York: Random House, 1941.

——. *On Rhetoric: A Theory of Civic Discourse.* Translated by George A. Kennedy. New York: Oxford University Press, 1991.

——. *Poetics.* Translated by Ingram Bywater. New York: Modern Library, 1954.

——. *The Politics of Aristotle.* Edited and translated by Ernest Barker. New York: Oxford University Press, 1968.

——. *Rhetoric.* Translated by W. Rhys Roberts. New York: Modern Library, 1954.

——. *The Works of Aristotle.* Edited by W. D. Ross. London: Oxford University Press, 1968.

Ash, Timothy Garton. *The Magic Lantern: The Revolution of '89 Witnessed in Warsaw, Budapest, Berlin, and Prague.* New York: Random House, 1990.

Austin, J. L. *How to Do Things With Words.* Edited by J. O. Urmson. New York: Oxford University Press, 1962.

Badcock, C. R. *The Psychoanalysis of Culture.* Oxford: Basil Blackwell, 1980.

Baker, Herschel. *The Image of Man.* New York: Harper and Row, 1961.

Bakhtin, Mikhail. *Art and Answerability: Early Philosophical Essays by M. M. Bakhtin.* Translated by V. Liapunov. Edited by M. Holquist and V. Liapunov. Austin: University of Texas Press, 1990.

——. *The Dialogic Imagination: Four Essays.* Translated by Caryl Emerson and Michael Holquist. Edited by Michael Holquist. Austin: University of Texas Press, 1981.

——. *Speech Genres and Other Late Essays.* Translated by Vern W. McGee. Edited by Caryl Emerson and Michael Holquist. Austin: University of Texas Press, 1986.

Barfield, O. *Saving the Appearances: A Study in Idolatry.* London: Faber and Faber, 1957.

——. *Speaker's Meaning.* Middletown, Conn.: Wesleyan University Press, 1967.

Barwise, J., and Perry, J. *Situations and Attitudes.* Cambridge, Mass.: MIT Press, 1983.

Baudrillard, G. *For a Critique of the Political Economy of the Sign.* Translated by Charles Levin. St. Louis, Mo.: Telos Press, 1981.

——. *The Mirror of Production.* Translated by Mark Poster. St. Louis, Mo.: Telos Press, 1985.

Bauman, Zygmunt. *Culture as Praxis.* London: Routledge and Kegan Paul, 1973.

Baynes, K.; Bohman, J.; and McCarthy, T. *After Philosophy: End of Transformation.* Cambridge, Mass.: MIT Press, 1987.

Becker, Carl. *The Heavenly City of the Eighteenth-Century Philosophers.* New Haven: Yale University Press, 1959.

Becker, L. *Reciprocity.* London: Routledge and Kegan Paul, 1986.

Beiner, Ronald. "Do We Need a Philosophical Ethics? Theory, Prudence, and the Primacy of *Ethos.*" *Philosophical Forum* 20, no. 3 (Spring 1989): 230–43.

——. *Political Judgment.* Chicago: University of Chicago Press, 1983.

Bell, B. I. *Crowd Culture: An Examination of the American Way of Life.* New York: Harper and Brothers, 1952.

Benjamin, Walter. *Illuminations.* Translated by Harry Zohn. Edited with an Introduction by Hannah Arendt. New York: Schocken Books, 1969.

Bentley, E. *Rallying Cries.* Evanston, Ill.: Northwestern University Press, 1977.

Berger, John, and Mohr, Jean. *Another Way of Telling.* New York: Pantheon Books, 1982.

Berlin, Isaiah. *Against the Current: Essays in the History of Ideas.* New York: Viking Press, 1980.

Bernstein, R. *Beyond Objectivism and Relativism: Science, Hermeneutics, and Praxis.* Philadelphia: University of Pennsylvania Press, 1983.

Bernstein, R. J., ed. *Habermas and Modernity.* Cambridge, Mass.: MIT Press, 1985.

Bitzer, Lloyd F. "Aristotle's Enthymeme Revisited." *Quarterly Journal of Speech.* 45, no. 4 (1959): 399–408.

——. "The Rhetorical Situation." *Philosophy and Rhetoric* 1, no. 1 (1968): 1–17.

Black, Edwin. *Rhetorical Criticism: A Study in Method.* Madison: University of Wisconsin Press, 1968.

——. *Rhetorical Questions.* Chicago: University of Chicago Press, 1992.

Bloch, Ernst. *A Philosophy of the Future.* Translated by J. Cumming. New York: Herder and Herder, 1970.

———. *The Principle of Hope.* Translated by Neville Plaice, Stephen Plaice, and Paul Knight. Cambridge, Mass.: MIT Press, 1986.

Blumenberg, Hans. "An Anthropological Approach to the Contemporary Significance of Rhetoric." Translated by R. M. Wallace. In *After Philosophy: End or Transformation,* edited by Kenneth Baynes, James Bohman, and Thomas McCarthy, pp. 429–59. Cambridge, Mass.: MIT Press, 1987.

———. *The Legitimacy of the Modern Age.* Translated by Robert M. Wallace. Cambridge, Mass.: MIT Press, 1983.

———. "On a Lineage of the Idea of Progress." *Social Research* 41 (1974): 5–27.

———. *Work on Myth.* Translated by R. M. Wallace. Cambridge, Mass.: MIT Press, 1985.

Breton, André. *Manifestoes of Surrealism.* Ann Arbor: University of Michigan Press, 1972.

Brockriede, Wayne. "Toward a Contemporary Aristotelian Theory of Rhetoric." *Quarterly Journal of Speech* 52, no. 1 (1966): 33–40.

Bruner, E. *Text, Play, and Story: The Construction and Reconstruction of Self and Society.* Washington, D.C.: American Ethnological Society, 1984.

Bryant, Donald C. "Rhetoric: Its Function and Scope." In *The Province of Rhetoric,* edited by Joseph Schwartz and John Rycenga, pp. 3–36. New York: Ronald Press Co., 1985.

Bunn, J. H. *The Dimensionality of Signs, Tools, and Models.* Bloomington: Indiana University Press, 1981.

Burke, K. *Attitudes toward History.* Los Altos, Calif.: Hermes, 1959.

———. *Counter-Statement.* Berkeley: University of California Press, 1971.

———. *Dramatism and Development.* Barre, Mass.: Clark University Press with Barre Publishers, 1972.

———. *A Grammar of Motives.* Berkeley: University of California Press, 1969.

———. *Language as Symbolic Action: Essays on Life, Literature, and Method.* Berkeley: University of California Press, 1968.

———. *Permanence and Change: An Anatomy of Purpose.* Berkeley: University of California Press, 1954.

———. *The Philosophy of Literary Form.* New York: Vintage Books, 1957.

———. *A Rhetoric of Motives.* Berkeley: University of California Press, 1969.

———. *The Rhetoric of Religion.* Berkeley: University of California Press, 1961.

Butcher, S. H. *Aristotle's Theory of Poetry and Fine Art.* London: Macmillan, 1920.

Cahn, S. M. *Fate, Logic, and Time.* New Haven: Yale University Press, 1967.

Calhoun, Craig, ed. *Habermas and the Public Sphere.* Cambridge, Mass.: MIT Press, 1992.

Camille, Michael. *The Gothic Idol: Ideology and Image-Making in Medieval Art.* Cambridge: Cambridge University Press, 1989.

Castoriadis, Cornelius. *The Imaginary Institution of Society.* Translated by Kathleen Blamey. Cambridge, Mass.: MIT Press, 1987.

———. "Power, Politics, Autonomy." In *Cultural-Political Interventions in the Un-*

finished Project of the Enlightenment, translated by Barbara Fultner, edited by Axel Honneth, Thomas McCarthy, Claus Offe, and Albrecht Wellmer, pp. 269–97. Cambridge, Mass.: MIT Press, 1992.

———. "Reflections on 'Rationality' and 'Development'." *Thesis Eleven* 10–11 (1984/85): 18–35.

———. "The Retreat from Autonomy: Post-Modernism as Generalized Conformism." *Thesis Eleven* 31 (1992): 14–23.

Charland, Maurice. "Postmodern Rhetorics of Technology: The Montreal Fluoridation Controversy." *Canadian Journal of Communication* 17 (1992): 177–90.

Cleary, John J. *Aristotle on the Many Senses of Priority.* Carbondale: Southern Illinois University Press, 1988.

Cohen, Jean L., and Arato, Andrew. *Civil Society and Political Theory.* Cambridge, Mass.: MIT Press, 1992.

Conley, Thomas M. "The Enthymeme in Perspective." *Quarterly Journal of Speech* 70 (1984): 168–87.

Connerton, Paul. *The Tragedy of Enlightenment: An Essay on the Frankfurt School.* Cambridge: Cambridge University Press, 1980.

Connolly, William E. *Politics and Ambiguity.* Madison: University of Wisconsin Press, 1987.

Cooper, J. M. *Reason and Human Good in Aristotle.* Cambridge, Mass.: Harvard University Press, 1977.

Cope, Edward Meredith. *The Rhetoric of Aristotle, with a Commentary, Vols. I, II, and III.* Edited by John Edwin Sandys. Salem, N.H.: Ayer Co., Publishers, 1877.

Coulter, J. *The Social Construction of Mind: Studies in Ethnomethodology and Linguistic Philosophy.* Totowa, N.J.: Rowman and Littlefield, 1979.

Coulthard, Malcolm, and Montgomery, Martin, eds. *Studies in Discourse Analysis.* London: Routledge and Kegan Paul, 1981.

Cox, J. Robert. "Against Resignation: Memory and Rhetorical Practice." Paper read at a meeting of the International Communication Association, Chicago, 1986.

——— and Willard, Charles Arthur, eds. *Advances in Argumentation Theory and Research.* Carbondale: Southern Illinois University Press, 1982.

Craig, Robert T. "What would a Practical Theory of Language and Communication be like?" Paper presented at Speech Communication Association Annual Convention in Boston, Mass., 6 Nov. 1987.

Crocker, David A. "Markovic's Concept of *Praxis* as Norm." *Inquiry* 20 (1977): 1–43.

Dallmayr, Fred R. *Polis and Praxis: Exercises in Contemporary Political Theory.* Cambridge, Mass.: MIT Press, 1984.

Davidson, D. *Essays on Action and Events.* Oxford: Clarendon Press, 1980.

Davis, Robert Con, and Schliefer, Ronald, eds. *Rhetoric and Form: Deconstruction at Yale.* Norman: University of Oklahoma Press, 1985.

Diggins, John Patrick. *The Lost Soul of American Politics: Virtue, Self-Interest, and the Foundations of Liberalism.* New York: Basic Books, 1984.

Doxtader, Erik. "A Preliminary Inquiry into the Status of Public Argument in the post-Soviet World." Paper presented at Speech Communication Association Convention, Chicago, Ill., 3 Nov. 1992.

Dreyfus, Hubert L., and Rabinow, Paul. "What is Maturity? Habermas and Foucault on 'What is Enlightenment?'" In *Foucault: A Critical Reader*, edited by D. C. Hoy, pp. 109–23. Oxford: Basil Blackwell, 1986.

Dubiel, Helmut. *Theory and Politics: Studies in the Development of Critical Theory*. Translated by B. Gregg. Cambridge, Mass.: MIT Press, 1985.

Dukore, Bernard F. ed. *Dramatic Theory and Criticism*. New York: Holt, Rinehart and Winston, 1974.

Edwards, Richard. *Contested Terrain: The Transformation of the Workplace in the Twentieth Century*. New York: Basic Books, 1979.

Evans, J. D. C. *Aristotle's Concept of Dialectic*. Cambridge: Cambridge University Press, 1977.

Ewen, Stuart. *Captains of Consciousness: Advertising and the Social Roots of the Consumer Culture*. New York: McGraw-Hill, 1976.

Farrell, T. "Aspects of Coherence in Conversation and Rhetoric." In *Conversational Coherence: Studies in Strategy and Form*, ed. R. Craig and K. Tracy, pp. 259–85. Beverly Hills, Calif.: Sage, 1983.

———. "Knowledge, Consensus, and Rhetorical Theory." *Quarterly Journal of Speech* 62, (1976): 1–5.

———. "Narrative in Natural Discourse: On Conversation and Rhetoric." *Journal of Communication* 4 (1985): 109–27.

———. "Practicing the Arts of Rhetoric: Tradition and Invention." *Philosophy and Rhetoric* 24 (1991): 183–213.

———. "Reason and Rhetorical Practice: The Inventional Agenda of Chaim Perelman." In *Practical Reason in Human Affairs*, ed. J. L. Golden and J. J. Pilotta, pp. 259–86. Dordrecht: Reidel, 1986.

———. "Rhetorical Resemblances: Paradoxes of a Practical Art." *Quarterly Journal of Speech* 72 (1986): 1–19.

———. "The Tradition of Rhetoric and the Philosophy of Communication." *Communication* 7 (1983): 151–80.

——— and Frentz, T. "Communication and Meaning: A Language–Action Synthesis." *Philosophy and Rhetoric* 12, no. 4 (1979): 215–56.

——— and Goodnight, G. T. "Accidental Rhetoric: The Root Metaphors of Three Mile Island." In *Communication Monographs*, vol. 48, pp. 271–300.

Fernandez, James W. *Persuasions and Performances: The Play of Tropes in Culture*. Bloomington: Indiana University Press, 1986.

Fisher, Walter. *Human Communication as Narration: Toward a Philosophy of Reason, Value, and Action*. Columbia: University of South Carolina Press, 1987.

Forrester, James W. *Why You Should: The Pragmatics of Deontic Speech*. Hanover, N.H.: University Press of New England, 1989.

Foucault, Michel. *Power, Truth, Strategy*. Edited by Meaghan Morris and Paul Patton. Sydney: Feral Publications, 1979.

Fraser, Nancy. *Unruly Practices: Power, Discourse and Gender in Contemporary*

Social Theory. Minneapolis: University of Minnesota Press, 1989.

Freidel, Frank. *Franklin D. Roosevelt: A Rendezvous with Destiny.* Boston: Little, Brown and Co., 1990.

Frentz, T. "Rhetoric, Time, and Moral Action." *Quarterly Journal of Speech* 71, no. 1 (1985): 1–18.

—— and Farrell, T. "Language-Action, a Paradigm for Communication." *Quarterly Journal of Speech* 62 (1976): 333–49.

Friedan, Betty. *The Feminine Mystique.* New York: Doubleday, 1963.

Gablick, Suzi. *Has Modernism Failed?* New York: Thames and Hudson, 1985.

Gadamer, H-G. "Appendix, a Letter by Professor Hans-Georg Gadamer." In *Beyond Objectivism and Relativism: Science, Hermeneutics, and Praxis,* p. 265. Philadelphia: University of Pennsylvania Press, 1983.

——. *Hegel's Dialectic: Five Hermeneutical Studies.* New Haven: Yale University Press, 1976.

——. *Truth and Method.* New York: Seabury Press, 1975.

Gastaldi, Silvia. "*Pathe* and *Polis:* Aristotle's Theory of Passions in the *Rhetoric* and the *Ethics.*" *Topoi* 6 (1987): 105–10.

Gauthier, D. *Morals by Agreement.* Oxford: Clarendon Press, 1986.

Geertz, Clifford. *The Interpretation of Cultures.* New York: Basic Books, 1973.

——. *Local Knowledge: Further Essays in Interpretive Anthropology.* New York: Basic Books, 1983.

Giddens, Anthony. *A Contemporary Critique of Historical Materialism,* Vol. 1: *Power, Property, and the State.* Berkeley: University of California Press, 1981.

——. *The Constitution of Society: Outline of the Theory of Structuration.* Berkeley: University of California Press, 1984.

Gleick, James. *Chaos: Making a New Science.* New York: Viking Penguin, 1987.

Goffman, Erving. *Frame Analysis.* New York: Harper Colophon Books, 1974.

Gombrich, E. H. *Art and Illusion: A Study in the Psychology of Pictorial Representation.* Princeton: Princeton University Press, 1960.

Goode, W. J. *The Celebration of Heroes: Prestige as a Control System.* Berkeley: University of California Press, 1978.

Goodnight, G. Thomas. "Generational Argument." Keynote address presented at the First International Conference on Argumentation in Amsterdam, 3–6 June 1986.

——. "The Personal, Technical, and Public Spheres of Argument: A Speculative Inquiry into the Art of Public Deliberation." *Journal of the American Forensic Association* 18 (1982): 214–27.

——. "Ronald Reagan's Re-Formulation of the Rhetoric of War: Analysis of the 'Zero-Option,' 'Evil Empire' and 'Star Wars' Addresses." *Quarterly Journal of Speech* 72, no. 4 (1986): 390–415.

Gorbachev, Mikhail. *At the Summit: How the Two Superpowers Set the World on a Course for Peace.* New York: Richardson, Steirman and Black, 1988.

Gouldner, Alvin W. *Enter Plato: Classical Greece and the Origins of Social Theory,* vol. 2. New York: Harper and Row, 1971.

Grassi, Ernesto. "Italian Humanism and Heidegger's Thesis of the End of Phi-
losophy." *Philosophy and Rhetoric* 13, no. 2 (1980): 79–97.
——. *Rhetoric as Philosophy: The Humanist Tradition.* University Park: Penn-
sylvania State University Press, 1980.
Grimaldi, William M. A. *Aristotle, Rhetoric I: A Commentary.* New York: Ford-
ham University Press, 1980.
——. *Aristotle, Rhetoric II: A Commentary.* New York: Fordham University
Press, 1988.
Guthrie, W. K. C. *A History of Greek Philosophy,* vol. 3: *The Fifth-Century
Enlightenment.* Cambridge: Cambridge University Press, 1969.
Habermas, J. *Autonomy and Solidarity.* Edited by Peter Dews. London: Thetford
Press, 1986.
——. *Communication and the Evolution of Society.* Translated by Thomas
McCarthy. Boston: Beacon Press, 1979.
——. *Knowledge and Human Interests.* Translated by Jeremy J. Shapiro. Boston:
Beacon Press, 1971.
——. "Law and Morality." In *The Tanner Lectures on Human Values, VIII,*
edited by S. M. McMurrin, pp. 217–81. Cambridge: Cambridge University
Press, 1988.
——. *Legitimation Crisis.* Translated by Thomas McCarthy. Boston: Beacon
Press, 1975.
——. *Moral Consciousness and Communicative Action.* Translated by Christian
Lenhardt and Shierry Weber Nicholsen. Cambridge, Mass.: MIT Press, 1990.
——. *On the Logic of the Social Sciences.* Translated by S. W. Nicholsen and J. A.
Stark. Cambridge, Mass.: MIT Press, 1988.
——. *The Philosophical Discourse of Modernity: Twelve Lectures.* Translated by
Frederick J. Lawrence. Cambridge, Mass.: MIT Press, 1987.
——. *Philosophical-Political Profiles.* Translated by Frederick J. Lawrence. Cam-
bridge, Mass.: MIT Press, 1983.
——. *Postmetaphysical Thinking: Philosophical Essays.* Translated by William
Mark Hohengarten. Cambridge, Mass.: MIT Press, 1992.
——. *The Structural Transformation of the Public Sphere: An Inquiry into a
Category of Bourgeois Society.* Translated by Thomas Burker and Frederick
Lawrence. Cambridge, Mass.: MIT Press, 1989. First pub. 1962.
——. *The Theory of Communication Action,* vols. 1 and 2. Translated by Thomas
McCarthy. Boston: Beacon Press, 1984 and 1987.
Harré, R., ed. *Life Sentences: Aspects of the Social Role of Language.* London:
Wiley, 1976.
Harriman, Robert. "Prudence/Performance." *Rhetoric Society Quarterly* 21, no. 2
(1991): 26–36.
Hart, Rod. *The Sound of Leadership: Presidential Communication in the Modern
Age.* Chicago: University of Chicago Press, 1987.
Hauser, Gerard A. "Administrative Rhetoric and Public Opinion: Discussing the
Iranian Hostages in the Public Sphere." In *American Rhetoric: Context and
Criticism,* edited by Thomas W. Benson, pp. 323–83. Carbondale: Southern
Illinois University Press, 1989.

——and Cushman, Donald P. "McKeon's Philosophy of Communication: The Architectonic and Interdisciplinary Arts." *Philosophy and Rhetoric* 6 (1973): 211–35.

Havelock, Eric A. *Preface to Plato.* New York: Grosset and Dunlap, 1967.

Hegel, G. W. F. *The Phenomenology of Mind.* Translated by J. B. Baillie. New York: Harper and Row, 1967.

Herzfeld, Michael. *The Social Production of Indifference: Exploring the Symbolic Roots of Western Bureaucracy.* New York: Berg, 1992.

Hofstadter, Douglas R. *Metamagical Themas: Questing for the Essence of Mind and Pattern.* New York: Basic Books, 1985.

Hofstadter, Richard. *Social Darwinism in American Thought.* Boston: Beacon Press, 1944.

Honneth, Axel. *The Critique of Power: Reflective Stages in a Critical Social Theory.* Translated by K. Baynes. Cambridge, Mass.: MIT Press, 1991.

Horkheimer, Max. "The End of Reason." *Studies in Philosophy and Social Sciences,* 9 (1941): 366–88. Reprinted in *The Essential Frankfurt School Reader,* edited by Andrew Arato and Eike Gebhardt, pp. 26–47. New York: Urizen Books, 1978.

——and Adorno, Theodor W. *Dialectic of Enlightenment.* Translated by John Cumming. New York: Seabury Press, 1972.

Horowitz, Irving Louis. *Ideology and Utopia in the United States, 1956–1976.* London: Oxford University Press, 1977.

Hoy, David Couzens, ed. *Foucault: A Critical Reader.* Oxford: Basil Blackwell, 1986.

Hutchinson, D. S. *The Virtues of Aristotle.* London: Routledge and Kegan Paul, 1986.

Hyde, Michael. "The Conscience of Rhetoric: Heidegger's Poetic Mistake." Paper read to Speech Communication Association, Chicago, 3 Nov. 1990.

Ignatieff, M. *The Needs of Strangers: An Essay on Privacy, Solidarity, and the Politics of Being Human.* New York: Viking Penguin, 1986.

Ingram, David. *Habermas and the Dialectic of Reason.* New Haven: Yale University Press, 1987.

Jakobson, R. *Verbal Art, Verbal Sign, Verbal Time.* Minneapolis: University of Minnesota Press, 1985.

James, William. *Pragmatism and Other Essays.* New York: Washington Square Press, Inc., 1963.

Jameson, Fredric. *Late Marxism: Adorno, or, the Persistence of the Dialectic.* New York: Verso, 1990.

——. *The Political Unconscious: Narrative as a Socially Symbolic Act.* Ithaca: Cornell University Press, 1981.

Jamieson, Kathleen. *Eloquence in an Electronic Age.* New York: Oxford University Press, 1988.

Jauss, Hans Robert. *Aesthetic Experience and Literary Hermeneutics.* Translated by M. Shaw. Minneapolis: University of Minnesota Press, 1982.

Johnstone, Henry W. *The Problem of the Self.* University Park: Pennsylvania State University Press, 1970.

Jonsen, Albert R., and Toulmin, Stephen. *The Abuse of Casuistry: A History of Moral Reasoning.* Berkeley: University of California Press, 1988.

Kaschak, Ellyn. *Engendered Lives: A New Psychology of Women's Experience.* New York: Basic Books, 1992.

Katriel, Tamar. *Talking Straight: Dugri Speech in Israeli Sabra Culture.* Cambridge: Cambridge University Press, 1986.

Kauffman, Charles. "Poetic as Argument." *Quarterly Journal of Speech* 67 (1981): 407–15.

Keane, John. *Democracy and Civil Society.* London: Verso, 1988.

Kennedy, George. *The Art of Persuasion in Greece.* Princeton: Princeton University Press, 1963.

——. *Classical Rhetoric and its Christian and Secular Tradition, from Ancient to Modern Times.* Chapel Hill: University of North Carolina Press, 1980.

Kristeva, Julia. *Powers of Horror: An Essay on Abjection.* Translated by Léon S. Roudiez. New York: Columbia University Press, 1980.

Leonard, Stephen L. *Critical Theory in Political Practice.* Princeton: Princeton University Press, 1990.

Levinas, Emmanuel. *Ethics and Infinity.* Translated by Richard A. Cohen. Pittsburgh: Duquesne University Press, 1985.

Loraux, Nicole. *The Invention of Athens: The Funeral Oration in the Classical City.* Translated by Alan Sheridan. Cambridge, Mass.: Harvard University Press, 1986.

Lucas, D. W. *Aristotle's Poetics: Introduction, Commentary and Appendixes.* Oxford: Clarendon Press, 1968.

Lukács, Georg. *Conversations with Lukács.* With Hans Heinz Holz, Leo Kofler, and Wolfgang Abendroth. Edited by Theo Pinkus. Cambridge, Mass.: MIT Press, 1975.

——. *History and Class Consciousness: Studies in Marxist Dialectics.* Translated by Rodney Livingstone. Cambridge, Mass.: MIT Press, 1971.

Lynd, Robert S., and Lynd, Helen Merell. *Middleton: A Study in Modern American Culture.* New York: Harcourt, Brace & World, 1929.

McCarthy, Thomas. *The Critical Theory of Jürgen Habermas.* Cambridge, Mass.: MIT Press, 1978.

——. *Ideals and Illusions: On Reconstruction and Deconstruction in Contemporary Critical Theory.* Cambridge, Mass.: MIT Press, 1991.

McFarland, Thomas. *Originality and Imagination.* Baltimore: Johns Hopkins University Press, 1985.

MacIntyre, Alasdair. *After Virtue: A Study in Moral Theory.* Notre Dame, Ind.: University of Notre Dame Press, 1981.

——. *Whose Justice? Which Rationality?* Notre Dame, Ind.: University of Notre Dame Press, 1988.

McKeon, Richard. "Dialectic and Political Thought and Action." *Ethics* 65, no. 1 (1954): 1–33.

——. "Dialogue and Controversy in Philosophy." *Philosophy and Phenomenological Research* 17, no. 2 (Dec. 1956): 151–57.

——. "Power and the Language of Power." *Ethics* 69 (1958): 98–115.

——. "Rhetoric and Poetic in the Philosophy of Aristotle." In *Aristotle's Poetics and English Literature*, edited by Elder Olson, pp. 201–36. Chicago: University of Chicago Press, 1965.

——. "Symbols, Myths, and Arguments." In *Symbols and Values: An Initial Study Conference on Science, Philosophy, and Religion in their Relation to the Democratic Way of Life*, 13th symposium. New York: Harper, 1954.

——. *Thought, Action, and Passion.* Chicago: University of Chicago Press, 1954.

McKerrow, Raymie, E. "Critical Rhetoric: Theory and Practice." *Communication Monographs* 56 (June 1989): 91–111.

Maier, Charles S. *The Unmasterable Past: History, Holocaust, and German National Identity.* Cambridge, Mass.: Harvard University Press, 1988.

Manchester, William. *The Glory and the Dream: A Narrative History of America, 1932–1972.* Boston: Little, Brown, and Co., 1974.

Marcus, J., and Zoltán, Tarr, eds. *Georg Lukács: Theory, Culture, and Politics.* New Brunswick, N.J.: Transaction Publishers, 1989.

Marcuse, Herbert. *The Aesthetic Dimension: Toward a Critique of Marxist Aesthetics.* Boston: Beacon Press, 1978.

Marrou, H. I. *A History of Education in Antiquity.* Translated by George Lamb. London: Sheed and Ward, 1956.

Megill, Allen. *Prophets of Extremity: Nietzsche, Heidegger, Foucault, Derrida.* Berkeley: University of California Press, 1985.

Merleau-Ponty, Maurice. *Sense and Non-Sense.* Translated by H. I. Dreyfus and P. A. Dreyfus. Evanston, Ill.: Northwestern University Press, 1964.

Morrison, Samuel Eliot. *The Oxford History of the American People*, Vol. 3: *1869–the Death of John Kennedy, 1963.* New York: New American Library, 1972.

Murphy, William P. "Creating the Appearance of Consensus in Mende Political Discourse." *American Anthropologist* 92, no. 1 (Mar. 1990): 24–41.

Nagel, Thomas. *Mortal Questions.* Cambridge: Cambridge University Press, 1979.

Noonan, Peggy. *What I Saw at the Revolution: A Political Life in the Reagan Era.* New York: Ivy Books, 1990.

Northrop, F. S. C. *Philosophical Anthropology and Practical Politics: A Prelude to War or Just Law.* New York: Macmillan, 1960.

Nussbaum, Martha. *The Fragility of Goodness: Luck and Ethics in Greek Tragedy and Philosophy.* Cambridge: Cambridge University Press, 1986.

——. *Love's Knowledge: Essays on Philosophy and Literature.* New York: Oxford University Press, 1990.

——, ed. *Politically Speaking: Cross-Cultural Studies of Rhetoric.* Philadelphia: Institute for the Study of Human Issues, 1981.

Perelman, C. *The Idea of Justice and the Problem of Argument.* Translated by J. Petrie. London: Routledge and Kegan Paul, 1963.

——. *The New Rhetoric and the Humanities: Essays on Rhetoric and its Applications.* Dordrecht: Reidel, 1979.

——, and Olbrechts-Tyteca, L. *The New Rhetoric: A Treatise on Argumentation.* Translated by J. Wilkinson and P. Weaver. Notre Dame, Ind.: University of Notre Dame Press, 1969.

Waterlow, Sarah. *Nature, Change, and Agency in Aristotle's* Physics. Oxford: Clarendon Press, 1988.

——. *Passage and Possibility: A Study of Aristotle's Modal Concepts.* Oxford: Clarendon Press, 1982.

Wellmer, Albrecht. *The Persistence of Modernity: Essays on Aesthetics, Ethics, and Postmodernism.* Translated by D. Midgely. Cambridge, Mass.: MIT Press, 1991.

White, H. *Tropics of Discourse.* Baltimore: Johns Hopkins University Press, 1978.

White, James Boyd. *When Words Lose their Meaning: Constitutions and Reconstitutions of Language, Character, and Community.* Chicago: University of Chicago Press, 1984.

Whitebrook, Joel. "The Problem of Nature in Habermas." *Telos* 40 (1979): 41–70.

Williams, Bernard. *Moral Luck: Philosophical Papers, 1973–1980.* Cambridge: Cambridge University Press, 1981.

Williams, R. *Culture and Society: 1780–1950.* New York: Columbia University Press, 1983.

Wills, Garry. *Kennedy Imprisonment: A Meditation on Power.* Boston: Little, Brown, and Co., 1982.

Winch, Peter. *Trying to Make Sense.* Oxford: Basil Blackwell, 1987.

——. "Understanding a Primitive Society." In *Rationality,* edited by Bryan Wilson, pp. 78–111. Oxford: Oxford University Press, 1970.

Wind, Edgar. *Art and Anarchy.* Evanston: Northwestern University Press, 1963.

Wittgenstein, Ludwig. *Culture and Value.* Translated by Peter Winch. Chicago: University of Chicago Press, 1980.

Wolff, J. *The Social Production of Art.* New York: New York University Press, 1984.

Wood, Allen. "Habermas's Defense of Rationalism." *New German Critique* 35 (1985): 144–64.

Zarefsky, David. *Lincoln, Douglas, and Slavery: In the Crucible of Public Debate.* Chicago: University of Chicago Press, 1990.

Index